Jackie as Editor

Also by Greg Lawrence

Time Steps (with Donna McKechnie)
Colored Lights (with Broadway composers John Kander and Fred Ebb)
Dance with Demons: The Life of Jerome Robbins
The Little Ballerina and Her Dancing Horse (with Gelsey Kirkland)
The Shape of Love (with Gelsey Kirkland)
Dancing on My Grave (with Gelsey Kirkland)

Jackie as Editor

The Literary Life of
Jacqueline Kennedy Onassis

Greg Lawrence

Thomas Dunne Books
St. Martin's Press
New York

THOMAS DUNNE BOOKS.
An imprint of St. Martin's Press.

JACKIE AS EDITOR: THE LITERARY LIFE OF JACQUELINE KENNEDY ONASSIS.
Copyright © 2011 by Greg Lawrence. All rights reserved.
Printed in the United States of America. For information, address
St. Martin's Press, 175 Fifth Avenue, New York, N.Y. 10010.

www.thomasdunnebooks.com
www.stmartins.com

Book design by Rich Arnold

Library of Congress Cataloging-in-Publication Data

Lawrence, Greg.
   Jackie as editor : the literary life of Jacqueline Kennedy Onassis / Greg
Lawrence.—1st ed.
            p. cm.
   Includes bibliographical references and index.
   ISBN 978-0-312-59193-9 (alk. paper)
   1. Onassis, Jacqueline Kennedy, 1929–1994.   2. Book editors—United
States—Biography.   3. Editors—United States—Biography.   4. Presidents'
spouses—United States—Biography.   I. Title.
   PN149.9.O53L39 2011
   070.4'1092—dc22
   [B]

                                                     2010037256

First Edition: January 2011

10 9 8 7 6 5 4 3 2 1

For Karen Chase, my anchor in the sky

Contents

Jackie as Editor

Introduction

⌒〰⌒

Jackie's Secret Garden

If you produce one book, you will have done something wonderful
in your life.   —JKO

Norman Mailer once called her "the Prisoner of Celebrity," aptly
characterizing Jacqueline Kennedy Onassis as the ultimate object
of media mythmaking; but Mailer was unaware that by the time
he wrote those words, in 1983, the world's most famous woman had already masterminded what was to be her escape from the constraints of
fame. After two chapters of Jackie's life had been defined by two extraordinary men, after she had been venerated by the world as the widowed
First Lady and then vilified for marrying the unworthy Greek, after being
portrayed as an extravagant, gold-digging spendthrift in thrall to jewelry and
couture fashion, she was going to find fulfillment on her own terms, and she
would do so, for the most part, comfortably outside the media glare and
public awareness.

Whatever else she may have been during her lifetime—tragic heroine,
elusive sphinx, reluctant icon—Jackie also distinguished herself as an intensely dedicated career woman who left behind an impressive legacy of
books. While Mailer described her as "a princess lighted by a million

flashbulbs," he underestimated how artfully Jackie had arranged her private and public lives, an instinctual survival strategy she perfected over time that would ultimately enable her to accomplish her own liberation. Jackie found a professional sanctuary in the world of publishing that was virtually unassailable, even for the paparazzi who staked out her office and boorishly delighted in stalking her.

Her literary bequest has been all but hidden in plain sight since her death, even with a sensational Sotheby's auction that included much of her enormous personal library, because Jackie rarely allowed herself to be credited for her work as an editor. Her name appears on the covers of a scant few of the titles that she published, only occasionally turning up buried in her grateful authors' acknowledgments. Yet Jackie's books, along with her personal writings, are perhaps the best window we will ever have into her heart and endlessly inquiring mind.

In the aftermath of Aristotle Onassis's death, despite the obstacles and intrusive indignities of celebrity, Jackie managed to transform her public image—what she once dismissed as "a little cartoon that runs along the bottom of your life . . . one that doesn't have much to do with your life." By devoting herself to her career and role as mother, while carrying on with her commitments to the arts, the preservation of historic landmarks, and JFK's memory, she reinvented herself, adopting a more reserved style, while at times displaying the panache of a postmodern saloniste.

Contrary to the Greta Garbo mystique with which she was identified, Jackie was never reclusive. She possessed a grand spirit of adventure and harbored a sense of irony about life that served as a kind of armor, whether she was jogging in her beloved Central Park, mingling in society, or pursuing quixotic book projects that would take her all over the world. Determined to define herself by her actions, she was well aware that her every move would be scrutinized. During the last two decades of her life, photographs of her on horseback at shows in Virginia and New Jersey began to replace reports of indulgent shopping sprees and lunches at Orsini's and La Côte Basque. The public sightings eventually included her entrances and exits at the publishing houses where she worked. She was more likely to be seen visiting the New York Public Library than attending glitzy parties or traditional society events. There were many nights when she dined at home with her kids, whom she often described as the most important responsibility in her life, and then spent the rest of the evening diligently at work in her library.

A savvy witness to the last century's golden age of publishing as it gave way during her career to megaconglomerates and rampant commercialism, Jackie managed to create an impressive body of work, shepherding more than one hundred titles, despite the undermining corporate culture of at least one of the two publishing houses that employed her. As the bottom-line exigencies of marketing triumphed over the traditional domain of editorial discretion and power, she championed books that were dear to heart and fought fiercely for them. She recruited her own private army, enlisting her authors and collaborators as guardians of Camelot, as it were—that lofty Arthurian conceit, which she suggested to historian Theodore H. White for his JFK eulogy that appeared in *Life* magazine after the tragedy in Dallas. Although Jackie was exercising poetic license with her reading of history, she quietly continued to nurture the concept of Camelot through the books she helped create, with many of them hearkening back to themes from her White House years.

By design, Jackie's editorial efforts were to be anonymous. Regardless of how much work she did on a manuscript, she was old-school and adhered faithfully to the self-effacing credo espoused by the legendary editor Maxwell Perkins: "The book belongs to the author." She was part of that tradition of editors who established relationships with their authors that went beyond the formalities of collaboration and commerce. In a publishing world that no longer exists, these editorial stewards of an earlier generation took an interest in the lives of their writers and established lifelong friendships with them, which meant more than simply breaking bread with them or lending them money when they were in need. Like Perkins, Jackie held fast to the belief that there could be nothing more important than books, and she revered their creators.

A former publisher of *Rolling Stone, New York,* and *New West* magazines, Joe Armstrong was a trusted friend of Jackie's during her later years and recounted a telling moment with her. "I remember being with her at the Vineyard the last summer she was there. She had just had turned sixty-four. I remember in her living room she had all these books, and she said, 'These are my other best friends.'"

Extreme modesty as much as natural shyness contributed to her much-publicized penchant for privacy. As an editor, Jackie displayed a playful mastery of the publishing arena, while acting as advocate for her authors. Her writers and books were the means through which she would express by proxy her ideals in the world of belles lettres, ideals she forged in the personal and historical realities of her own past, even as it was transformed into myth before her eyes.

Jackie, like most of us, had her share of idiosyncrasies, foibles, and character flaws, and there was to be contention along the way with some of her authors and colleagues. But after committing a personal affront or gaffe, she was humble enough to offer apologies, often with flowers and

handwritten notes. It should come as no surprise that, as she was an immensely coveted figure in the social marketplace, people would attempt to
take advantage of her, and at times she felt compelled to banish some erst-
while friends and collaborators from her world. Anyone who betrayed her
confidence to the press was to be "thrown out of the palace," as she put it
to one of her colleagues. It wasn't so much ego that led her to cut ties as the
insecurities and emotional burdens she carried. Having to inure herself to
a past that had been devoured by the first television generation was no easy
feat. Jackie's stepcousin, the esteemed author Louis Auchincloss, put it
simply: "It's very hard to be the most famous woman in the world."

Referring to Jackie's early career as an editor, Gloria Steinem asked,
on the cover of *Ms.* magazine in March 1979, "Why Does This Woman
Work?" Jackie provided clues in what was to be, aside from a few cryptic
public utterances, her last interview for nearly fifteen years. She recalled,
"I remember a taxi driver who said, 'Lady, you work and you don't have
to?' I said, 'Yes.' He turned around and said, 'I think that's great!' " With
touching eloquence, she went on to describe the reasoning that led her to
resume a career in midlife, at the age of forty-six. "What has been sad for
many women of my generation is that they weren't supposed to work if they
had families. There they were, with the highest education, and what were
they to do when the children were grown—watch the raindrops coming
down the window pane? Leave their fine minds unexercised? Of course
women should work if they want to. You have to do something you enjoy.
That is the definition of happiness: 'complete use of one's faculties along
the lines leading to excellence in a life affording them scope.' It applies to
women as well as to men."

The quotation Jackie cited was one that JFK also cited on occasion,
with various translated formulations attributed to Aristotle and Epictetus
(without pinning it down, Edith Hamilton identified the passage simply as
"an old Greek definition of happiness"). Steinem applauded Jackie's break
with her past and with the domineering men she had endured. "Given
the options of using Kennedy power or living the international lifestyle
of an Onassis, how many of us would have chosen to return to our own
talents, and less spectacular careers?" Jackie herself confided to a friend at
the time, "I have always lived through men. Now I realize I can't do that
anymore."

Jackie's books and visionary scope would afford her the perfect venue
to achieve a discreet, understated measure of excellence in her chosen field.
Steinem told me, "As for why she chose to be an editor as opposed to some
other profession, I think it's quite simple: She loved books. They were
windows into hearts, minds, ideas, and the world. Books were powerful. If

my memory is right, her son, John, commented to the media that she died surrounded by the books and people she loved."

The views expressed in this book, let it be clear from the outset, will necessarily reflect the affection of those who shared their reminiscences about a part of Jackie's life that has been overlooked. A number of her friends decided to speak about her for the first time because they felt her professional endeavors had not been adequately chronicled or appreciated, while a few others felt bound to silence, as they weighed confidentiality and issues of privacy even in the workplaces they once shared with her. With her steadfast commitment to secrecy, Jackie would surely never have allowed these pages to be written during her lifetime. But, hoping to pay tribute to her memory 15 years after her death, more than 125 of her former collaborators in the publishing world have come forward with their tales of Jackie, yielding a *Rashomon* that could only have been inspired by a unique and enigmatic principal player.

One of her sympathetic allies in the press, celebrity columnist Liz Smith, reported on Jackie's Manhattan life for many years and suggested to me, "I never underestimated her. I quietly, simply admired the hell out of her. She was struggling in New York always against great odds, the great odds of her own fame and notoriety. Onassis had been the blot on her escutcheon."

A longtime curator at the Metropolitan Museum's Costume Institute, Katell Le Bourhis, recalled a day when Jackie visited her at the museum and revealed some of those qualities that by nature and pedigree she sought to cultivate in her life and in her books: "One day I remember very correctly, I was like sad, mad, too much work, not much help; I was in a bad mood, the world seemed to me very hostile. She said that day, 'But Katell, you are very privileged, you have your books. You are here at the Metropolitan Museum; you have your beautiful objects.' And then I realized that probably for her, that world of literature, history, French culture, humanist culture, as probably being a secret garden in her life, but also something that helped her go through life as something very private to her. But through remarks like that, you could feel that she was talking about herself. I was very touched when she said that."

Of course, Jackie touched many lives, her fate having led her onto the pages of history, her public persona magnified almost to the point of grotesque caricature in the Andy Warhol era, only to be further distorted by our collective imagination. The third act of Jackie's saga, which began after her two marriages played out on the world stage, has for the most part been minimized by her biographers, even though it spanned more than nineteen years—almost a third of her life devoted to a calling that became a fervent mission. Jackie regarded books as pathways to enlightenment, each a journey of intellectual enchantment, each affording her the opportunity to interact with people who shared her love of literature and passion for knowledge.

A Renaissance woman grounded by her professional endeavors and sustained by the bonds of family—that was the Jackie whom I came to know. As one of her authors, I was fortunate to have worked with her over the last decade of her life. I have my own lasting impressions, one in particular shared by most of the authors, friends, and colleagues who graciously offered up their memories for this book. While Jackie always carried with her the burden of her history, she was not one to flaunt or finger the scars of her life. When working, she conducted herself simply as a professional. The inescapable phantoms of her past were there when we began our exchanges, but they quickly receded, overshadowed by her goodwill and charm, which were displayed with every gesture and, as many observers have noted, delivered with seemingly effortless grace. She could conquer all with just a parting wave and that beguiling, luminous smile, even with her eyes concealed behind the signature dark glasses.

As Senator Ted Kennedy noted in his eulogy, delivered on May 23, 1994, "Jackie would have preferred to be just herself, but the world insisted that she be a legend, too."

In Jackie's secret garden, guided by her heart's compass over a lifetime and by her love affair with books, the legacy lives up to the legend.

I

A Special Destiny

During the summer of 1975, after entering her second widowhood, Jackie resumed her life in Manhattan with her children, hoping somehow to establish some normalcy in their lives. At the time, some of Jackie's friends noticed that she seemed to have fallen into a malaise, with fitful bouts of boredom and restlessness. Society chronicler Stephen Birmingham had dated Jackie briefly when she was a Vassar undergraduate and kept in touch with her in later years. Of this dismal interlude while Jackie was cast adrift, Birmingham said, "When she telephoned friends to chat, she seemed to have little to chat about." More than just an episode of midlife ennui, it was to be a prolonged period of mourning that sometimes found Jackie listless and lingering for hours over breakfast and the morning newspapers in her apartment at 1040 Fifth Avenue. Jackie once admitted, "I have a tendency to go into a downward spiral of depression or isolation when I'm sad."

The world was not about to leave her in peace. On a visit she made in August to the amphitheater at Epidaurus, a hostile Greek crowd taunted

Jackie with jeers and cries of "You left your dead husband." Her tormen-
tors were apparently unaware of how sudden and unexpected Ari's death
had been, and blamed Jackie for not being with him when he died. On
March 15, 1975, in Neuilly-sur-Seine, France, Onassis had succumbed to
bronchial pneumonia, a complication of the myasthenia gravis with which
he was afflicted in his last years. Jackie was in Manhattan at the time.
Though the marriage was failing, Jackie had stayed in Paris dutifully to
support Ari through his surgery earlier that month, until being assured by
his doctors that he was stable. She then returned to New York to be with
Caroline for the airing of an NBC documentary that her daughter had
worked on as a member of the production crew, under the tutelage of film
producer Karen Lerner. Karen was the ex-wife of Alan Jay Lerner, lyricist
for the musical *Camelot,* and a friend of JFK's going back to their school-
days at Choate.

Karen was staying as a guest in Jackie's opulent apartment, sleeping in
Onassis's bed in a bedroom next to Jackie's. "On the morning of March
15," Lerner remembered, "she came in and said, 'Ari's dead.' You know,
she got a lot of criticism for being in New York because she was giving a
party on the day this little documentary aired for Caroline." With her dinner party scheduled to take place the following evening, Jackie told Karen,
"I am going to Paris, so you stay here and you be the hostess. . . . I don't
want anything to disturb this—it's for Caroline and I just want it to go
ahead."

Lerner, who had known Jackie during the Kennedy era and through
her marriage to Onassis, later observed, "Jackie changed more during the
year after Ari died than at any other time I knew her." At least in part,
Jackie was simply reacting that year to events beyond her control, but that
gut-wrenching interval would lead her into another world. After enduring
the public ordeal of Ari's funeral in Greece, Jackie's conflicts with Ari's
daughter, Christina, and her efforts to reach a financial settlement with the
Onassis estate became the subject of much tabloid speculation. In April
The New York Times reported that Ari had been planning to divorce Jackie
in the months before he died and that Christina felt great bitterness toward
her former stepmother, a story that circulated widely but was later denied by
Christina in the *Times* at Jackie's request.

The supposed conflict between Christina and Jackie was apparently
exaggerated, though there was surely no great affection between them while
their lawyers negotiated a settlement of the Onassis inheritance. The photographer Marc Riboud, a friend of Jackie's, later described one occasion
during which he saw no sign of hostility between them. "Once I was visiting Jackie in her New York apartment, after Ari Onassis died, when all the

papers were full of stories about a fight between Jackie and Christina Onassis. Christina unexpectedly dropped in, and I tried to excuse myself, but Jackie said, 'Oh, no, stay and we'll have a good time.' She and Christina sat there telling stories about Ari and laughing together. They certainly were not fighting."

Jackie remained publicly mum on the subject. A close friend of Jackie's at the time, Cheray Duchin (now known as Cheray Zauderer Duchin Hodyes), the first wife of society bandleader Peter Duchin, blamed the Onassis camp for Jackie's travails, saying, "Nobody gave her a chance to grieve because the nastiness kept pouring out."

While picking up the pieces and avoiding the media as much as possible, Jackie soon fell back into her familiar Manhattan routines. Caroline, then seventeen years old, was planning to go to London to take art courses at Sotheby's, while fourteen-year-old John, the last member of the Kennedy family to have Secret Service protection, was attending Collegiate, a school on the city's Upper West Side. With her children requiring fewer hours of attention, Jackie had time on her hands.

One morning, as she jogged through Central Park, wearing her customary blue jogging suit and white running shoes, she was accosted by a reporter and asked for an interview. She stopped only long enough to put him off, explaining, "My life is very dull right now. I'm doing just very ordinary everyday things. Really, my life at the moment would make very uninteresting reading. Do you think it would be of much interest for anyone to know that I go shopping at the local A&P?" Jackie added, "I'm sure I'm going to be watched closely for the next year or so. Maybe people will find out what Jackie is really like and write something different for a change."

Jackie had her share of detractors who added gratuitous insult to injury, including Truman Capote, with whom she had had a falling-out after he published his "Ladies Who Lunch" short story installments in *Esquire*, excerpts from his book *Answered Prayers: The Unfinished Novel* (published posthumously in 1987). Capote heaped ridicule on Jackie: "And, in life, that is how she struck me—not as a bona fide woman, but as an artful female impersonator impersonating Mrs. Kennedy." Capote also disparaged Jackie for treating her friends "like red rubber balls—playing with them, rolling them into obscurity, and then exclaiming six months later, 'Oh, I've missed you.'"

The distinguished author and attorney Louis Auchincloss, with the advantage of having known his stepcousin since he was young, explained, "I have some reason to suspect that Jackie was a person of peculiarly visual memory. I believe with her it was a case of out of sight being literally out of mind. If she had chanced on me in Washington, she might well have exclaimed, 'Where have you been? . . . Why don't you come around?' I have heard other people complain of being forgotten or dropped by Jackie, and I think this may well have been the reason."

During this down period, as she tried to come to terms with her losses, grieving for Jack again as well as for Ari, she was visiting a shiatsu-acupuncturist, Lillian Biko, and a psychoanalyst, Nadine Eisman. Biko later told *Cosmopolitan* magazine, "Jackie's tension is the result of her anxiety. She has problems because she's so secretive. Which is why she sees me." While secrecy and enforced discretion were no doubt part of her defensive armature, Jackie was reexamining herself as never before and assessing her options with an eye to her future.

Two years earlier, while married to Onassis, she had considered taking on a TV project for NBC, when the network offered her a half million dollars to anchor a show about the endangered art treasures of Venice and Angkor Wat. Jackie was tempted, but Onassis reportedly dissuaded her with the imperious dictum, "No Greek wife works." After some heated discussion, sensitive to Onassis's failing health and not wishing to provoke more acrimony than already existed between them, she gave up on the idea. Still, the desire to find creative outlets would stay with her, though it was mostly stifled until Ari was gone.

Aware that Jackie was floundering that summer, Letitia (Tish) Baldrige, who had served as social secretary for the former First Lady, suggested the idea of pursuing a career as a way for her to lift her spirits and challenge herself. Baldrige, then running a public relations firm in Manhattan, told *The New York Times,* "I really felt she needed something to get out in the world and meet people doing interesting things, use that energy and that good brain of hers. I suggested publishing. Viking was my publisher, and I said to her, 'Look, you know Tommy Guinzburg—why don't you talk to him?' "

At an afternoon tea with Baldrige, Jackie initially responded to the idea of entering the workforce with lighthearted skepticism, "Who, me—work?" But by the fall of 1975, she was seriously contemplating the prospect of embarking on a career. Baldrige later said, "Jackie reached that moment every woman reaches when she needs to get involved, to put her mind to work." Hardboiled journalist Jimmy Breslin offered his outspoken advice to her: "You should work as an editor. What do you think you're going to do, attend openings for the rest of your life?"

Jackie had known publisher Thomas Guinzburg for at least twenty years. At Yale, he roomed in the same hall as Jackie's stepbrother, Hugh D. Auchincloss. Guinzburg had been part of the original *Paris Review* circle in the 1950s, a group that included George Plimpton and Peter Matthiessen, and he later inherited Viking Press from his father, Harold K. Guinzburg. While Tom Guinzburg was initially "thunderstruck" by the prospect of having Jackie join his house, he discussed the idea of her becoming an editor over lunch one afternoon at Manhattan's Le Périgord. By the end of their meeting, they agreed the discussions would continue.

Viking was not the only publishing house that Jackie approached. A former editorial director at Random House, Jason Epstein, wrote in his memoir, *Eating*, "One day Jackie Onassis called me to ask if she could take me to lunch at Lutèce. We met a week or so later. . . . My friend Pete Hamill, who had once taken Jackie out, said it was like 'taking King Kong to the beach.' . . . We took a table upstairs, in one of the small rooms, and ordered shad roe, the first of the season. She asked if there was a job for her at Random House. She wanted to be an editor. . . . However, there was a problem. Entry-level editorial jobs were scarce and much in demand. . . . I told Jackie that I believed she would take the job seriously, be a good colleague, and learn the ropes easily. But I also told her that we would have to create an opening for her, and this might not be fair to the assistants. Before I could ask her to let me talk it over with my colleagues, she said that she understood my problem and didn't want to impose."

Reminiscing wistfully, Tom Guinzburg told me, "I have a favorite anecdote. During that summer before she came to work, I was sitting with Jackie at her apartment on Fifth Avenue. Caroline was coming in from one school or another, and Jackie went to answer the phone. And Caroline said to me . . . 'It's not true, is it, that my mother's gonna come and work with you in the publishing thing?' I said, 'I think it is true, I hope it's true. You ought to talk about it with her yourself.' She just looked at me with contempt, the disdain of a teenager, and said, 'But what's she going to *do*?'"

It was a fair question, and an ambivalent Jackie mulled it over at length. Guinzburg told her, "You're not really equipped to be an editor. It's not that you don't have the talent for it, the ability for it, but you don't have the background and the training and you, I think, would suffer in a publishing house because that would set up some kind of competitive atmosphere with the other editors. But what you can do is to be a consulting editor . . . somebody who doesn't have what we call line responsibilities, they're not assigned books, they don't even have necessarily to work out of the office. Their primary job is to acquire books." Guinzburg said, "I then explained to her that as she became more familiar with publishing procedures, she could work on the books and with the writers to whatever extent appealed to her. She could create books and so on."

Characterizing Jackie's naïveté about the then male-dominated business world, Tish Baldrige told *People* magazine, "Jackie was not a feminist. Now, she might have had feminist leanings without really knowing it. . . . She never had to fight for anything in a man's world. It would never have occurred to her to question why there wasn't a woman on a board of directors."

Betty Friedan characterized Jackie as "a closet feminist." Gloria Steinem likewise felt that Jackie's sympathies were on the side of the emerging women's movement, if only privately. "One doesn't have to act in public to be a feminist. Wherever Jackie was, she definitely spoke in her own voice. She was warm, funny, loyal and a great girlfriend in the best sense. I think she just found public life too shallow, simpleminded, intrusive, too likely to make her—and others—into symbols rather than real and nuanced people.

"I don't think she used men as beards or worked through them, but rather found them amusing companions—in somewhat the way worldly men find women to be. One key is probably her father, 'Black Jack' Bouvier. By most accounts, she adored him, and he adored her, [and] confid[ed] in her which mothers of her classmates he had affairs with. Perhaps this gave her a view of sexuality that wasn't so dependent on loyalty or singularity in the way that, say, friendship was loyal. I've always hoped and assumed—based on no evidence—that she had affairs before and after her marriage, too, and possibly during (though certainly not on Jack's scale). In any case, I don't believe she saw Jack's affairs as threatening to her or to their permanency in each other's lives.

"I doubt this was her mother's attitude about her father's affairs—but then, her mother was a much more conventional woman. This was symbolized to me by the fact that she once said, according to Jackie, 'The trouble with you, Jackie, is you never play bridge with your bridesmaids.'"

Steinem added, "As a very small and utterly unsexual example of Jackie's attitude, she once seated me next to Onassis at a small dinner in New York, because, as she said, 'You will disagree with him, and that will keep him interested and amused.'"

One of Jackie's former editorial colleagues, author Harriet Rubin, offered another interpretive spin, suggesting that she "found, I think, a better strategy than feminism's defiance and insistence on a woman's voice being heard. Jackie didn't practice defiance but rather besting the existing order. She didn't confront men and injustice. She was a student of the eighteenth-century Frenchwomen salonistes who advanced revolutionary principles through conversation and wit. She didn't stand alone but allied herself with powerful men and had her say through them, sort of like a master puppeteer. In the eighties, we feminists considered Gloria Steinem brilliant for speaking in her own voice. Jackie did not speak in her own voice, not in public, anyway. She seemed always to be speaking through a Kennedy, an Onassis, or a Tempelsman. Feminism didn't understand that, given the way the world is structured, a too-smart woman needs a man as a cover, a beard."

In the publishing world, Jackie would act on her own and rely on her own resources, and often had to win over both male and female colleagues to get her way. Hired by Guinzburg at the end of the summer of 1975 as a consulting editor at Viking, she was to be paid $200 a week, working part-time four days a week. Of course, Jackie didn't need the money—she had inherited a substantial trust from JFK and eventually settled with Christina Onassis for $26 million. Financial considerations aside, Jackie's decision to become a working woman had not been undertaken lightly. She became enamored with the idea of finding a calling, and she would soon be able to achieve a different kind of independence than she had ever known before.

Jackie told a writer for *Newsweek* what she anticipated her new job would entail: "I expect to be learning the ropes at first. You sit in at editorial conferences, you discuss general things, maybe you're assigned to a special project of your own." Even before the press and public had accepted this sudden change of employment status, Jackie felt compelled to defend her career move, and the fact that she, of all people, had been hired. She explained, "It's not as if I've never done anything interesting. I've been a reporter myself and I've lived through important parts of American history. I'm not the worst choice for this position."

Jackie had not had a paying job since 1953, when she was a $42.50-a-week inquiring camera girl for the *Washington Times-Herald*. But she did have previous experience editing and consulting on several biographies of JFK that came out not long after his death. The first of these, *John F. Kennedy, President*, by veteran *Time* magazine journalist Hugh Sidey, was published in 1964. Sidey's editor at Atheneum, Simon Michael Bessie, later recalled that Jackie read the galleys and submitted copious detailed notes on them, although Sidey himself did not acknowledge Jackie's contribution in the book.

A year later, Jackie performed the same service for JFK's former presidential aide and speechwriter Theodore (Ted) Sorensen for his book *Kennedy*. Sorensen told me, "After I finished the first draft of my first big book, I gave Jackie the manuscript and asked her to take a look, because I thought she could be helpful, and she was *enormously* helpful. In her handwriting on long yellow-lined notepads, she gave me comment after comment."

In his memoir, *Counselor,* Sorensen lauded Jackie's assistance: "Jackie proved to be a superb editor, correcting typographical errors, challenging mistaken assumptions, defending some of her husband's personnel decisions, suggesting useful clarifications, and repeatedly setting the record straight on matters not known to me, specifically noting whom JFK privately admired and whom he did not. . . . In addition to asking me to tone down my references to JFK's praise of LBJ, she made a number of specific suggestions."

Sorensen offered a number of examples of Jackie's editorial critiques. He quoted her notes verbatim in his book with regard to JFK's sensitivity to press criticisms, with Jackie suggesting that Jack "had learned how to roll with the punches and they bemused rather than upset him. He became so tolerant—like a horse you see in the field in summer—the flies have annoyed him at first—but there are long months before they will go away—so he does his work—which is eating grass—and just flicks his tail—Whenever I was upset by something in the papers—he always soothed me and told me to be more tolerant—if you want examples of this—I have many to give you. They even extend into international relations. . . ."

Voicing her maternal concerns, Jackie also tried to set the record straight with reference to her children, writing, "His father never called him John-John—only John. That nickname now plagues the little boy—who may be stuck with it all his life. I know your book deals with more important things—but it would be great if you could put that nickname to bed."

Sorensen had included in his manuscript a reference to young Caroline's "firmly ordering a cameraman at an airport 'No Pictures.' " Jackie wrote, "Please delete—not fair to her—She is such a tender little girl and she got that horror of the press from me." Referring to both Caroline and John, she explained, "I had to teach them all over again—that cameramen were all right—a part of their father's life and they must behave in front of them in a way that would show they had the same good manners their father had."

Jackie's involvement with the authors of two subsequent books about JFK was more problematic and disheartening for her and for Robert Kennedy as well. The two of them were consulted first by William Manchester, for his book about JFK's assassination, *The Death of a President,* and later by Paul B. Fay Jr., known as Red, for his memoir, *The Pleasure of His Company.* With regard to Manchester and his book, Ted Sorensen remembered,

"Bill had interviewed me at length for his book, while I was writing mine on Cape Cod. I found it difficult to talk about the assassination, and from time to time broke off the interview simply to recompose my thoughts and emotional balance. When it was finally published, his book stirred enormous hostility to the point of litigation from the Kennedy family."

Jackie had granted interviews to Manchester, and later had reservations about his rendition of the assassination and what she had shared with the author. When the book was about to be serialized by *Look* magazine, which paid Manchester $665,000 for the rights (a record at the time), Jackie voiced her disapproval and became mired in unsuccessful legal efforts to block publication. She felt after the fact that she had provided too many intimate details and private recollections to Manchester. Her requests for deletions in the book mostly went unheeded by Manchester. RFK's aide John Seigenthaler suggested, "Bill was an excellent journalist, but I had the feeling that in some ways he had taken advantage of her vulnerability."

Even after winning concessions and agreeing to an eleventh-hour court settlement, Jackie came to regret having attempted to micromanage JFK's memory and uphold the Kennedy family agenda. Ironically, in just the first few years after the book's publication, in 1967, the John F. Kennedy Library received a generous financial reward of more than a million dollars in royalties, but the library didn't allow public access to the book or to the author's papers. Despite the fact that the book's profits helped build the library, it was effectively written out of history.

Jackie and Robert Kennedy were also invited to review the manuscript for Fay's book about his relationship with JFK, which dated back to when both men served as PT boat commanders during World War II. Fay, nicknamed "Red" for his striking mane, had served as an usher at the Kennedys' wedding. Sorensen described him as "one of the president's two or three best friends." But Jackie and Bobby were not pleased with his book, deeming it overly candid and, according to Jackie, rife with vulgarities. With one critical note, she couldn't resist putting a needle into Fay, suggesting with regard to a questionable passage, "Leave it. Don't you see it makes Red look awful." For his part, Fay rejected most of the proposed changes from the Kennedy camp, but this time they decided to avoid the discord and pitfalls of trying to take legal action to prevent the book from being published.

While these early editing experiences involved Jackie in dealing with books about the fallen president, she might also have had a hand even earlier in JFK's Pulitzer Prize–winning *Profiles in Courage*. Ted Sorensen's role in the writing of that book was for a time a source of controversy for Kennedy, besmirching his reputation as sole author, but the matter was later put to rest with Sorensen testifying that he had played only a supportive part, in much the same way that he had worked with JFK on speechwriting. In his preface to *Profiles in Courage,* JFK acknowledged, "This book would not have been possible without the encouragement, assistance and criticisms offered from the very beginning by my wife, Jacqueline . . ."

During a recent conversation, Sorensen said of Jackie, "I don't think she had anything to do with *Profiles in Courage.*" Yet at the same time, he allowed for the possibility that Jackie may have offered her husband the benefit of her editorial feedback during the writing process. "It was being written under nose, so to speak, both in Florida and in Washington. I haven't the slightest doubt, knowing JFK's proclivities, that he would have read the chapters to her. And since she was a natural-born editor, it's very possible that she made suggestions here and there; but if so, that was never related to me, so I don't really know. As I say, that is my assumption, but I really have no hard information. I wasn't there."

In addition to those books for which she gave editorial advice, Jackie also organized the publication of two books while she was First Lady, which afforded her experience in other aspects of the book trade. The first evolved from her campaign to renovate the White House. Realizing that she would need large sums of money in order to purchase the historical furnishings and artwork that would have to be acquired, she instigated the publication of an official White House guidebook to help fund the project. *The White House: An Historic Guide* was entirely her idea, undertaken with assistance from the National Geographic Society. Jackie also took the initiative to establish the White House Historical Association to oversee a variety of publications, including a book entitled *The Presidents of the United States,* which was ultimately completed only after the JFK assassination.

Assigned to oversee Jackie's White House guide, Robert Breeden was then a staff member of *National Geographic.* He remembered that she chose all of the art and furnishings to be pictured in the book, and even selected the typeface. According to Breeden's assistant, Don Crump, "She was very outspoken and very precise in what she liked and what she didn't like. And her ideas were really quite good. She carefully went through the final version page by page." Even during her years as First Lady, Jackie was already displaying the incisive literary sensibility and wielding the clout that she would one day use to great advantage in the publishing world.

As a prospective editor, Jackie brought a great many assets to the table, with her activism on behalf of the arts and the exclusive social circles to which she had access. She also possessed a world of experience to draw on, along with her own modest writing accomplishments, which went back to boarding school and college days. At the beginning of 1974, Jackie and her sister, Lee, published a journal they coauthored under the title *One Special Summer,* about their trip to Europe in 1951, with illustrations by Jackie that showed off what critics praised as a deliciously naughty wit.

Jackie had immersed herself in literature and the arts her entire life. Indeed, her mother found her reading Chekhov plays at the age of six. As a precocious child, in addition to studying ballet and competing in equestrian shows, she wrote poetry and filled sketchbooks with drawings and artwork. Interviewed for a PBS documentary in 1999, her cousin, author John Davis, said, "I used to remember how her personality would change from this rather delicate dreamy young girl of let's say seven or eight years old to a fearless equestrian in total command of the horse, always winning the blue ribbon. But then she would retire to read poetry, history, Shakespeare—as a little girl—so she mixed sensitivity with a certain toughness."

While in college, she took an interest in both journalism and fiction. She later admitted, "Like a lot of people, I dreamed of writing the Great American Novel." Before graduating in 1951 from George Washington University (where she had transferred for her senior year, after spending her junior year at the Sorbonne), Jackie had decided to pursue some form of writing professionally and wrote a series of essays that won *Vogue* magazine's Prix de Paris contest. The prize was the opportunity to work as a staff writer in the magazine's Paris and New York offices, but Jackie's mother pressured her into turning it down, wanting to keep her close to home. Looking back, Jackie admitted her angst about accepting the prize and moving to France. "I guess I was too scared to go. I felt then that if I went back I'd live there forever, I loved Paris so much."

In one of Jackie's *Vogue* essays, she was already thinking like an editor, as she described how the magazine might present perfume to its readers. "Perfume was just as effective in piquing the male olfactory glands before our era of adjective-laden advertisements. Why not quote some of the poetry it has inspired? It is also analogous to wine. Both are liquids that act upon the closely related senses of taste and smell to produce an intoxicating effect. Wine has had an even stronger appeal in literature, from Omar Khayam to Colonel Cantwell and Renata. Why not pilfer some of its drawing power and incorporate it into an article on perfume?"

Late in 1974, with Ari's tacit approval, Jackie approached the formidable *New Yorker* magazine editor William Shawn and persuaded him, over lunch at La Caravelle, to allow her to write an anonymous piece for the Talk of the Town pages. Jackie's article was a savvy interview essay entitled "Being Present," celebrating the opening of the International Center of Photography (ICP). She described how this new museum was dedicated to photojournalism and documentary photography in the tradition of three fallen leaders of the field "who were killed in the nineteen-fifties while on picture assignments: David Seymour (Chim), Werner Bischof, and Robert Capa." ICP was destined to become one of the world's leading centers for the preservation and teaching of photography, and Jackie played a key role at its inception.

Jackie had been encouraged to lend her support by Karl Katz, the head of the Metropolitan Museum's special projects division. She and Katz became founding board members of ICP, supporting the renowned photographer Cornell Capa (Robert's younger brother) and his quest to establish a photography museum at the old Audubon house on Fifth Avenue. A frequent escort of Jackie's, Katz was dubbed by the press as "Jackie's intellectual boyfriend." In the years ahead, thanks to his connections and position at the Met, he would promote a number of authors and book projects, faithfully steering them to her.

The work of French photographer Marc Riboud was featured in one of the early ICP exhibitions in 1975, and Jackie would later champion his work in America. Riboud related his memory of meeting her for the first time. "I was invited for dinner with her at Maxim's in Paris. There was Jackie, Aristotle Onassis, and a couple of friends of Jackie I didn't know then, and me. My wife [artist, author, and poet Barbara Chase-Riboud] was invited, but happened not to be in town. Jackie was traveling back from a Greek island, with Onassis, and she was in Paris for two days.

"I was at that time covering the war in Cyprus between the Greeks and Turks. . . . I missed them in Athens, where I was just back from the war. But they found me later in Paris. Jackie called my home . . . and I was out . . . but my *femme de ménage,* the lady taking care of the house, heard that it was a message from Madame Onassis. She told me, 'Madame Onassis called and told you that you must go to dinner.'

"At this dinner I found that I was sitting opposite the most important woman in the world, and we talked. And Aristotle Onassis was not in the very best mood, and talking not too elegantly. Whenever there would be a pretty girl passing by in the restaurant he would speak about pretty girls, and Jackie was a little bit embarrassed. We talked about photography. . . . Cornell Capa was about to start the International Center for Photography, and we spoke about that. And we spoke about politics, and we laughed. She loved laughing, and loved making jokes and gossiping nicely.

"I remember walking out of Maxim's that night and the throng of photographers waiting for her. She asked me if I wanted to drive home with them by car. I don't know why I said, 'No, It's all right. Thank you very much.' Then we decided to meet again in New York." Without yet knowing that she would soon become an editor, Jackie had struck up a friendship with one of her future authors.

Another photographer friend who was involved with Jackie and the International Center of Photography was Peter Beard, famous not only for his photographs of endangered African wildlife but also for portraits of supermodels and rock stars such as Mick Jagger, David Bowie, Iman, and Veruschka. On the rise at the age of thirty-seven, Beard was charismatic and iconoclastic, with movie-star looks. His retinue included Jackie's sister, Lee Radziwill (with whom he had a romantic affair), Andy Warhol, Truman Capote, Andrew Wyeth, Terry Southern, and Francis Bacon. Jackie wrote an afterword for Beard's lavishly illustrated work *Longing for Darkness: Kamante's Tales from Out of Africa,* which was published in November 1975. This wondrously evocative tome was inspired by the African adventures of the Danish aristocrat Baroness Karen von Blixen (better known as Isak Dinesen, her nom de plume) and her classic memoir, *Out of Africa.* That book chronicled many of Blixen's personal experiences in Kenya, where she owned and maintained a coffee plantation from 1914 to 1931.

Beard recalled, "Jackie loved *Longing for Darkness* and wrote an essay for Kamante Gatura, Blixen's Kikuyu cook and manservant, who was a central figure in *Out of Africa.*" Beard told me that Jackie's participation allowed for the book to be published. "She was very irritated. Holt, Rinehart and Winston turned it down, and I think Doubleday . . . and she had some quite amusing suggestions of what we might do, like having some native dances up in Newport [Rhode Island]. . . . Basically, she wrote the afterword, and it was only on that ground that the book was accepted."

In her afterword, which was printed in her elegant longhand, Jackie wrote, "What an extraordinary surprise and gift it was when Peter Beard first showed me the fables and drawings of Isak Dinesen's beloved Kamante. I had not known he was still alive. To hold his drawings was like touching a talisman that took you back to a world you thought had disappeared forever. Maybe I was so affected because *Out of Africa* has always meant more to me than any other book. . . . It seems to me that so many of the movements of today, ecology, anti-materialism, communal living— were all in *Out of Africa.*"

Jackie quoted one of her favorite Dinesen passages, which read, in part, "If I know a song of Africa, of the Giraffe, and the African new moon lying on her back, of the ploughs in the fields, and the sweaty faces of the coffee-pickers, does Africa know a song of me?" Jackie concluded, "Yes, it does have a song for her. It is Peter Beard and Kamante who made it for her. Kamante's drawings and Peter Beard's photographs share a purity—of a wild animal looking at the camera with free and vulnerable eyes."

The tales in the book were recorded by Beard, and hand-lettered in their English translation by Kamante's sons, accompanied by line drawings and by photos showing the Kenyan landscape and lifestyle that surrounded Dinesen during her years there. Jackie accurately portrayed Dinesen as one of the first white people to realize that "black is beautiful," and she related with approval Dinesen's redefinition of "true aristocracy" as nobility of spirit. That nobility shines through in the Kikuyu, Maasai, and Ngong stories. Jackie also recognized that the way of life this book and Dinesen's story depict was imperiled by the forces of development.

No wonder Beard's book captured Jackie's imagination. The tales themselves are not like conventional animal fables, where the anthropomorphized animals learn lessons from their deeds and eventually come to a moral à la Aesop. Instead, they are autobiographical accounts of instances in Kamante's life—how he worked as a cook, how he related to the Kikuyu chiefs, and the mixture of Africans and Europeans who always populated Dinesen's farmstead. In some ways, these tales are a supplement to the extraordinary life of the Baroness von Blixen herself, recounting how she advised Kamante not to fear death, how she could shift from the everyday world to the world of fabulist imagination by sighting a single bird in the woods. This book is one of those rare objects, like Peter Beard's earlier masterpiece *Eyelids of Morning*, that combine visual splendor and discerning commentary in an irresistible volume.

While the book clearly held a special appeal for Jackie, before it came out she had second thoughts about her contribution, according to the publisher William Jovanovich. In his memoir, *The Temper of the West,* Jovanovich revealed that one of Jackie's lawyers called him and asserted that she wanted to withdraw her essay after the book was "already printed, in proofs." Jackie may have balked due to her literary insecurities, or perhaps she was giving in to her sister's spite after her romantic fling with Beard soured that summer. While preparing for her entrance at Viking, Jackie acquiesced to the publication of the book with her afterword included, and she would maintain her friendship with Beard in the years ahead. He represented the kind of cutting-edge artistic resource that Jackie had at her disposal and would bring with her to the job.

Early in 1975, Jackie again entered the public arena, joining the Municipal Art Society and embracing the cause of saving New York's venerable Grand Central Terminal, fighting to prevent the building from being torn down and replaced by a skyscraper. Then-congressman Ed Koch said, "She was very gutsy and determined—a real fighter. Even though it was Grand Central Station, Jackie gave the battle a visibility and a legitimacy it might not have had otherwise."

A trustee of the Municipal Art Society, Fred Papert, described Jackie's involvement with the group as hands-on activism rather than merely symbolic posturing, telling Dominick Dunne for *Vanity Fair,* "It's easy to get the impression that what she brought to the cause was just her celebrity. But before that she was in on strategy meetings. Showing up at rallies, concerts, and train trips was the least of it."

Jackie's work with the group would lead to several books, and some years later, she contributed a foreword to the commemorative book *Grand Central Terminal,* published by the Municipal Art Society. The book's author and editor, Deborah Nevins, said that Jackie played no direct role in the book's publication: "Jackie wasn't involved in that project, even though, of course, it was close to her heart." Jackie's commitment to the cause traced back to her efforts with Jack in the 1960s to save Lafayette Park and preserve historic Washington. In her introductory essay, Jackie offered heartfelt praise for the landmark preservation movement: "New York City is the center of civilization in our day as Athens, Rome, Persepolis were in theirs. Her citizens have recognized that by banding together they can save its loved buildings from destruction."

With her citizen-of-the-world mentality, Jackie was cautiously selective with respect to the causes to which she chose to lend her support, and she would bring that same discriminating judgment into the editorial domain from her first day on the job. Once she embraced a project, she proceeded with boundless zeal. The quixotic ideal of preserving works of literature and enriching cultural discourse would be a touchstone she would use to acquire and develop literary properties and to line her own cherished bookshelves.

On Monday, September 22, 1975, after rising from bed promptly at 8:00 A.M. in her fifteen-room apartment overlooking Central Park and the Metropolitan Museum of Art, Jackie boiled herself an egg, donned a conservative gray shirt-dress, and eventually hailed a taxi in front of her building that would take her to the offices of Viking Press, at 625 Madison Avenue. That cab ride was destined to lead her to a monumental turning point, a fact that no one, not even Jackie, realized at the time. She was stepping into a rich chapter of publishing history, as Viking was a house with a prestigious heritage and a stable of brilliant editors, whose authors included, over the years, James Joyce, D. H. Lawrence, John Steinbeck, Sherwood Anderson, Dorothy Parker, Arthur Miller, Saul Bellow, and Thomas Pynchon. At the time employees of the house referred to it as "The Viking Press."

Jackie's new job had been announced the week before in *The New York Times,* and a mob gathered on the sidewalk along Madison Avenue at Fifty-eighth street, awaiting her arrival, which had been postponed several days. The gawk-stalkers caught barely a glimpse, as she kept a low profile exiting the cab, evading the crowd through an entrance at the side of the building. The scene outside resembled a Hollywood opening, and the serene grace she projected under the circumstances was itself an accomplishment. Any public appearance by Jackie during these years was heralded as an *"event."* Tom Guinzburg described the scene: "It was a circus, of course, because of who she was, how she would accommodate herself to normal life. There were bomb threats, security people, and press people dressed up as messengers."

That morning Guinzburg introduced Jackie to her fellow employees, took her out to a lunch of chicken salad in the Edwardian Room at the Plaza Hotel, and then led her to a photographic shoot with the renowned *Life* magazine photographer Alfred Eisenstaedt. He had taken JFK's official presidential portrait and had photographed Jackie on previous occasions. Eisenstaedt photographed her in the spartan office she had been assigned, with its small, workmanlike desk, swivel chair, filing cabinets, and one window overlooking Madison Avenue. The photographer later said, "In that little office at Viking, with all her books and papers piled up around her, she looked like a kid straight out of college, all excited about her first job."

When Jackie arrived at Viking, Gael Towey was a mechanical artist who worked on many of the illustrated books published by Viking's Studio Books division. Now chief creative officer at Martha Stewart Living Omnimedia, Towey observed Jackie's routine when having to face the ever-present paparazzi: "She liked to have hamburgers across the street, and there was a side door to the building that led out to Fifty-eighth Street, and there was a hamburger joint directly across the street—I mean the simplest kind of deli with a counter. And we always knew that there were photographers lurking everywhere, and she would stand on the inside of the door and hold herself upright, put her shoulders back, look up, and say, 'Smile!' And then she'd walk out smiling. As soon as the door opened, you knew that there would be all these flashbulbs."

Jackie was endlessly photographed outside the office despite her efforts at disguise and the many available freight entrances she dashed through in Manhattan. In the office, Guinzburg encouraged his employees to help Jackie get her bearings. One of her fellow editors, Barbara Burn, said, "Tom Guinzburg came to me and said, 'Would you take her to lunch and explain what a consulting editor does? You two have so much in common.' Her daughter had gone to Concord Academy, which is where I went, we both were horse people, and we had a special interest in art and art history.

"So I asked her to lunch, and she said, 'Oh, absolutely, that would be great.' I made a reservation up at the Carlyle hotel, which I figured would be convenient to her apartment. When we went into the restaurant, I said, 'Burn, two,' but they paid no attention to *me* and immediately cleared a table for eight and sat us down.

"We had a terrific lunch. She said, 'Look, the only other consulting editor at Viking is Malcolm Cowley. I couldn't begin to do what he does.' He was a very important writer, we had published a number of his books, and at the time his job at Viking was editing the Portable Library and a series of critical texts for students. And Jackie said, 'So I don't know exactly what it is I'm supposed to do.' We talked about what she would be interested in doing, and we discussed the possibilities. Then she paid for lunch, and I said, 'Be sure to keep the receipt.' She said, 'Oh, never mind, I paid in cash.' I said, 'No, no, you're supposed to charge it and keep the receipt.'

"Then we went back to the office. Walking down the street with her was like being on the prow of a ship. People just parted in front of us, staring at her. She was never impolite. She never looked anybody in the eye, but she never complained about it. She was completely comfortable with herself. She was determined to become an editor at that point, so she did what we all do—she apprenticed. In those days you learned at the feet of the people who knew what they were doing, and then you could do it yourself. Eager young people go to Radcliffe and NYU publishing programs, but they don't learn much about editing there. You can memorize the Chicago style manual, but that doesn't make you an editor. You learn by doing, and Jackie was willing to start at the beginning, reading manuscripts and writing reports and so on."

Rich Barber, who had worked in publishing for a number of years and was Viking's public relations director, remembers being deputized by Tom Guinzburg to familiarize Jackie with the basics of book publishing and its seasonal production demands. "Tom said, 'I want you to teach Jackie what publishing is about, what the time frame is.' That was my assignment. He knew that editors like Alan Williams and Cork Smith would take care of the editorial side. There's nothing in publishing that's really hard to learn; it tends to come with repetition and being around the business, and knowing why things are done this way and not some other way.

"We had a very elaborate production schedule for all books that basically went into effect the minute a book was bought. Normally from the time a book was transmitted to its publication ran anywhere from nine months to a year. All the little stages along the way were marked off and dated—all of the different steps that went on with each book. I spent a number of session hours with Jackie using that as the template for each of the kinds of books we did, and telling her about the kind of problems we were going to have. She was a really quick study . . . and she took notes . . . she asked very intelligent questions, and it gave her a leg up on at least knowing the mechanics of what was going on."

The office next door to Jackie's was occupied by another one of Viking's gifted editors, Elisabeth Sifton, who is now senior vice president of Farrar, Straus and Giroux and editor at large of Hill & Wang. The daughter of noted theologian Reinhold Niebuhr, Sifton suggested, "Jackie never became completely integrated into the editorial department. The rest of us were in and out of each other's offices all the time, arguing and squabbling about how much money to pay for what kind of project, or discussing procedural issues of getting books ready, manuscripts ready for composition and so on. And she was not much involved in all of that, as we'd expected. After all, she hadn't been a book editor before, and she was obviously a very special kind of book editor. Jackie was cordial, pleasant, I liked her, but given the nature of her history and her fame, she was of course not like the rest of us."

Jackie made every effort to fit in, bringing to the job an attitude of unassuming professionalism, making her own coffee, placing most of her own phone calls, and making her own copies at the Xerox machine. Working part-time, she would phone in conscientiously on her days off. Viking office memos were addressed by initials, and Jackie preferred "JBO," perhaps an act of independent self-assertion, with the "B" for her maiden name, Bouvier, rather than "JKO."

Another up-and-coming Viking editor, Daniel Okrent, who later served as the first ombudsman of *The New York Times,* said his exchanges with Jackie were positive and collegial. "I remember in the very beginning, I was involved with a project—I can't remember what it was about—but I was soliciting her support for it. And she really didn't understand the politics of the publishing house. I think that she was a little bit appalled and kind of taken aback by my probably overly coarse representation of why her support for this project, whatever it was, was necessary. I remember her eyes kind of popping. 'Really? I'm supposed to do that?' "

According to Okrent, for her projects, Jackie operated to some extent outside the company's editorial meetings, having direct access to Tom Guinzburg, as they were old friends and traveled in the same social circles. "If she wanted to do something," Okrent explained, "she went to Tom, and Tom said yes, whereas at most publishing houses you go through a much more attenuated process." Okrent also remembered his colleagues' initial skepticism about Jackie and her position as a consulting editor: "We were all excited when we heard that she was coming, a little bit nonplussed. This was the biggest celebrity in the world, and she's going to work with us. Tom knew a lot of well-known people—I remember when Princess Grace came to the office, and that created a lot of buzz. . . . When Jackie came we were happy to have her. But there were some—I wouldn't say it rose to the level of resentment, but there was some rolling of the eyes: What the hell does she know about book publishing or about editing? She's never done this before; she's here because of her name, because of her social connections with Tom, yaddee-yaddee-yadda. But when she came in she did not have any airs that reflected any of that, so I think that even those who might have been skeptical . . . were convinced."

Guinzburg remembered discussions with Jackie about potential books they might pursue. "Jackie and I used to go out and talk and she had marvelous ideas. And we would sometimes double-team a prospect. I remember we were going to do a book on the interiors of yachts, we were going to do that before anybody got around to doing it. It was an obvious idea, but she had access to those yachts. We almost had Frank Sinatra, and he was a friend of mine, too, and he worshipped Jackie, and he wanted to do a book. We all had an evening together, and then his lawyer pulled the plug on that."

Guinzburg also described one of Jackie's first mentors, Bryan Holme, who ran Studio Books. "Jackie loved illustrated books, and she was training under the most benevolent eyes of Bryan Holme, who specialized in them. He was one of nature's noblemen, and a genius, and nobody could ever figure out how he did it. I know in principle he worked backwards. He went from a retail price and then just put in numbers for every single thing in the budget, and then when he got to the end, the agent would say, 'Well, that only leaves twelve cents for my author.' And Bryan would say, 'Hmm, we don't have to use that glue. We could use another glue and save money. And we don't really have to take the paper from the bowels of interior Japan.' He would tinker with it to the point where everybody was happy, and Jackie worked with him on several projects.

"I think Jackie got along with the ones who were acolytes. I mean, the first couple of weeks were tough because all the kids put on their best clothes and Jackie put on her black pants and T-shirt. That was her way of meeting them halfway. Jackie wasn't going to put on any airs. She was really willing to learn and to be collegial. . . . The atmosphere was pretty intense at the beginning because there was this assumption that this was . . . a public relations stunt, and that I was just pulling a fast one— that I was able to do based on the fact that I had known her a long time and her kids—and people assumed there was nothing substantive."

Barbara Burn described the unique atmosphere at the house just before Jackie arrived. "One of the nice things about Viking in those days, before Penguin bought us, is that we were a gentlemen's publisher and had been since the twenties. When I got there—I started there in 1965—and Ben Huebsch had just died, so had Pascal Covici, and they were two great editors. Tom Guinzburg's father, who had founded Viking with Ben Huebsch, had also died, and Tom was sort of a playboy in those days. He had helped found *The Paris Review* with George Plimpton, and he was not an unserious guy; but he suddenly found himself in charge, and it was quite a change. It was a great pleasure to work for him, because he got better and better and better. He was not always incredibly serious, but that added a light touch to the place. He served aquavit to us one morning when one of our authors won the Nobel Prize, and bells were rung whenever we made the best-seller list. People were really devoted to him and to the company."

Burn continued, "Jackie had a good innate sense of what made a fine illustrated book, and I know she learned a tremendous amount from Bryan Holme, who had run Studio Books since the thirties; his father before him had run *Studio* magazine in London and Studio Books in England. And she learned a great deal from him about layout and the way in which text and pictures should work together. And of course Bryan was one of these people that you just had to watch in order to understand how he worked; he didn't explain much, so you had to stand there and see what he did. Jackie kind of apprenticed herself to him and learned how he put books together. It was a pleasure to watch them."

Bryan Holme's son, Christopher, worked with his father and described the special relationship Bryan established with Jackie. "I know Jackie and my father often met and talked about this and that . . . and worked on their own projects as well. . . . He would take her down in the elevator and see her out sometimes in the evening, and she mentioned how the worst moment of her day was going from the lobby of the building into a cab while having to avoid all the people. She was there at Viking as an ordinary employee, and no one was supposed to pay special attention or bother her. My father was a very kind person, and everybody loved him. He got along well with everybody; but he wouldn't have put up with her if he thought she was just a dilettante and wasn't relatively serious about the work. They had similar taste, and it was more than a working relationship. I think there was more of a friendship there."

Gael Towey described an exchange between Jackie and Bryan Holme regarding a book of Alfred Eisenstaedt's photographs that brought up one of JFK's infamous infidelities. "Bryan was mocking up the cover, making a collage of photographs, so there was a composite of this cover sitting on a table. And Jackie walked in and looked at it, and then kind of discreetly asked Bryan if she could speak to him. She noticed that on the cover there was a picture of President Kennedy right next to a picture of Marilyn Monroe. Bryan was just thinking he was going to put all the famous pictures on the front because that will sell the book, never really putting the two and two together. After they came out of the office together, Bryan asked me to move the pictures around and put the Marilyn Monroe picture on the back. I think she just didn't want President Kennedy next to Marilyn Monroe. It was as simple as that."

Jackie's first assistant, Becky Singleton, recalled in a series of e-mails, "I joined Viking in 1973 shortly after college graduation. Since then, I had roamed through every department and can tell you firsthand, Viking's informality and the talent level in every department made it a learner's paradise. The news that Jackie had decided to start a career in publishing, that she would do so at Viking, and that Tom Guinzburg wanted me to work for her was delivered to me by Tom himself—all within the space of one very interesting minute. Although I wasn't particularly fascinated by the Kennedy mystique, and had never aspired to work for a celebrity, I immediately agreed to take on the job, simply because Tom asked me to do it. . . .

"I expected to like Jackie. I tend to like people unless they hit me on the head with a hammer or something. But I had no preexisting infatuation. In that sense, when she arrived, we would both be working with a blank slate. On Jackie's first day at the firm, I went down to the lobby to greet her. It was filled with photographers and flashing cameras. That didn't surprise me. Upstairs in my cubicle, dozens of manuscripts—many from reputable agents—awaited in towering stacks, along with several large canvas sacks of assorted types of 'Jackie mail.' For the past several days the phones had been ringing constantly, and as Jackie's assistant, I had already received the first of several offers of generous financial compensation from supermarket tabloids if I would agree to tell their readers 'the real story.'

"What surprised me in the lobby that morning was Jackie herself. I had expected her to be rather elegant and reserved. Instead, she was immediately gregarious. Ignoring the presence of photographers, she chatted in a lively way as we entered the elevator and by the time we got to the sixteenth floor, she had covered a remarkable range of topics—her passion for books, her career hopes, how each of her children had reacted to her decision to take a full-time job, what her friends thought, her concerns . . . etcetera. (No, the elevator wasn't slow that day and I'm not exaggerating.) By the time we emerged from the elevator, her sense of humor and apparent candor had totally charmed me. . . .

"I showed Jackie into her office, which was smallish but of workable size and it definitely had a window. Then I took her to my cubicle, which was located about thirty feet away from her door. When Jackie got her first glimpse of the stacks of manuscripts and mail that awaited her, she looked at me and started to laugh. By the time I had finished explaining my improvised call screening system—our phones weren't connected by intercom, so I intended to transfer legitimate calls to her, then rush down the hall to her office to let her know who was calling before she picked up the phone—we were both laughing. I remember feeling this incredible sense of relief. I thought, *She knows things are going to be crazy around here and she's okay with that.*

"Then Tom came in to whisk her away. I saw very little of her for the rest of the day. Jackie's crash course in publishing started on her first day. Tom took her on a tour of every department. On her second day, she attended a lengthy editorial meeting with other editors in senior trade. Immediately afterwards, she drafted a few query letters and began to make calls, as she put it, 'beating the bushes' for books. By the end of the week, she had drafted a long memo that contained more than twenty potential book projects she thought might be feasible, which was circulated to the other editors for their comments.

"Jackie caught on to the importance of query letters and she sent out quite a few. The one she sent to John Kenneth Galbraith immediately comes to mind. I can't recall what the letter said, but his response greatly amused her. She came into my cubicle, threw herself down on the chair, and said, laughing, 'He says that he wants to be wooed!' Actually I think she was delighted by his reply. She really didn't want special treatment. While he'd made it clear that she wasn't going to get any, at least not from him, he also managed to convey that he relished the idea of being wooed by her and felt that she would be marvelous at this particular aspect of her job. I think his response meant a lot to her. It was just what she needed to hear at that time."

Singleton also remembered photographer Peter Beard visiting the office on occasion to schmooze and discuss projects with Jackie. His book *The End of the Game* had been published by Viking's Studio Books in 1965. Singleton said of Beard, "He relished his own outlandishness, which meant that she could laugh with him, rather than at him. She was quite amused by the material he'd submitted for a book that detailed the plight of African elephants. She always referred to the project as '101 Dead Elephants,' which aptly described the subject matter of his photographs. . . ."

Singleton went on to describe Jackie's office routine. "To jump-start her apprenticeship, Jackie's plan was to be at her desk most mornings by 9:30, to read the circulating file of editors' correspondence and make some calls while she sipped coffee, then spend the rest of the day immersed in 'learning the ropes.' Putting this schedule into effect should have been easy. Unfortunately, to many people, both rabid fans and many others whose motives seemed less sentient, Jackie's entry into publishing had made her tantalizingly available. In order to clear a path for Jackie to get to her desk, Rich Barber usually had to go down to the lobby in the morning to dissuade people who were waiting there, because for one reason or another, they were determined to intercept her as she entered the building. Upstairs, Rich, myself, and Patti Rizzo, our stellar receptionist, combined forces to deal with those who actually made it to the sixteenth floor, where they camped out in the visitor's lounge and waited for her to emerge from the elevator.

"To give you some idea of the frenzied level of public interest that Jackie had to navigate through in order to begin her career in publishing, I will describe a portion of the events that occurred on a fairly typical morning: At about 10:00 A.M. Patti Rizzo called to summon me to the visitors' waiting area, where a person who wanted to see Jackie was causing a bit of a commotion. I went out to the lounge area and found there a very large gentleman who had managed to capture the attention of everyone else in the visitors' lounge by announcing that he had sticks of dynamite strapped to his chest. After an interesting discussion, I managed to persuade him to leave the manuscript he'd brought for Jackie with me, then made sure he wasn't actually wired with explosives before I began steering him towards one of the elevators.

"As I loaded him into one car, a familiar figure emerged from the other elevator. This gentleman, who always dressed in clerical garb, was mild-mannered but distinctly eerie. He had arrived several times before, always with the same request, which was to see Jackie before he died. After another very interesting discussion, I was able to turn him around and send him home for the day, and then quickly returned to my cubicle, where all of the phone lines were ringing.

"In rapid succession, I took calls from (1) Mike Wallace, who was determined to get Jackie to do a *60 Minutes* interview and professed to be amazed I wasn't interested in helping him out; (2) a woman who called daily to ask to speak to Jackie and, when told that this wasn't possible, would ask instead for a detailed description of what she was wearing that day (no to that as well); (3) another woman who called regularly but was much easier to deal with, as she simply wanted Jackie to know that Clive Barnes, a noted theater critic at that time, had parked a van in front of her apartment building and was engaged in the process of stealing her furniture, one piece at a time."

Singleton continued, "Throughout the early weeks, a mild form of pandemonium attended Jackie's comings and goings. Most of it was created by the media and by fanatic but harmless eccentrics. Sometimes it was far more serious. One day, at Jackie's request, I cleared the pile of manuscripts from the chair in my cubicle to make room for an FBI agent, who spent the day with me. He was there to record the conversation if a second call had come from a man whose previous call had delivered an alarming, seemingly genuine threat. Fortunately, that second call never came and the first call was eventually seen as a hoax. Jackie wasn't a detached person, particularly when threats to her family were involved. Yet her demeanor during this period suggested that the only thing on her mind was to listen admiringly as Bryan Holme explained the preparation process for sending photographs and artwork to the printer.

"She had been well aware that her attempt to assume a full-time position as a book editor would incite a fresh wave of public interest and that many in the media would be eager to print juicy tidbits that suggested she was falling flat on her face. The persistence she showed during those initial turbulent months convinced me that her passion for books, which she spoke of so eloquently, was completely genuine. She wasn't simply looking for something to do, as some had speculated. She had sensed a vocation."

Barbara Burn was also impressed with how serious Jackie was during her apprenticeship. "She absolutely dug right in. She came to editorial meetings. Sometimes she laid out her books by lining up the pictures along the corridor and got down on her hands and knees to sort and organize them. Everybody got used to her pretty quickly, I must say. I think we were all a little shocked that she smoked. There was a little bit of resentment, not a lot, at the beginning because she was going to make two hundred dollars a week, which in those days was not insignificant. In fact, it was what several full-time employees were getting, so they felt this wasn't quite fair. After all, she had only had experience as a roving photographer/reporter. In any case, everybody got over that pretty quickly. . . .

"I remember one time the Irish writer J. P. Donleavey called and said he wanted to talk to Jackie about a book project: he wanted to interview her on the subject of fox hunting. She was very gracious, and as he left she escorted him back out to the elevators; then she turned to me and said, 'You know, he really just wanted to meet me.'

"I gave her manuscripts to read, and other editors did, too. She would write reports in her handwriting. . . . The first report she wrote for me was on a book on Baudelaire, which was in French and had been sent by Gallimard or another French publisher. She read it promptly and wrote a perfectly straightforward report, describing what was in it and why it wouldn't be suitable for an American audience—just what the doctor ordered. And she was always willing to be edited herself, with her forewords and stuff. She was fine."

As far as the avalanche of publicity and requests for interviews at the time she joined the company, Guinzburg told me, "Rather than do interviews, we decided we would just have one get-together, so we invited a few folks up to the Carlyle hotel and sat around a table. There was a woman reporter from *The Washington Post* and she more or less implied that hiring Jackie was just a public relations stunt. She said, 'She's got no previous experience as an editor,' and I said, 'No, she doesn't. But I wonder who you had lunch with today or who you're going to have dinner with tomorrow. I can promise you on any given week Mrs. Onassis will be having dinner with somebody or with people out of which will come some of the most interesting books of the next decade. How can you think otherwise?'"

In January 1976, Jackie threw a dinner party at her apartment, arranged with three round tables, each seating six guests, who included Peter and Cheray Duchin, Arthur and Alexandra Emmet Schlesinger, Roger and Emma Jeanne Mudd, Barbara Walters, and Candice Bergen. Jackie beamed that evening when her guests stood and toasted her for rejoining the workforce.

Jackie's first book, *Remember the Ladies: Women in America, 1750–1815*, confirmed Guinzburg's faith that she could deliver, at least with respect to acquisitions. The project combined her passions for art and history, and reflected her awareness of an emerging women's market. Jackie soon proved that she was able to seize upon opportunities that would never have materialized for other editors who lacked her social entrée. Referring to

Remember the Ladies, Guinzburg suggested the project "wouldn't have come to Viking if she hadn't been involved."

For the nation's bicentennial, a landmark preservation committee in Plymouth, Massachusetts, was mounting an exhibition about the role of women in the eighteenth century. The committee included Mabel H. "Muffie" Brandon, who spearheaded the effort, and would later serve as social secretary in the Reagan White House. She was then the wife of Henry Brandon, Washington bureau chief of the Sunday *Times* of London (now Muffie Brandon Cabot, mother-in-law of George Stephanopoulos). Among the other members of the committee were society figures such as Joan Kennedy, Nancy Kissinger, Susan Mary Alsop, Barbara Howar, and Constance Mellon.

Brandon's idea was to publish a companion book for the exhibition. She told *The New York Times,* "My appointment at Viking was with Tom Guinzburg, and when I walked into the meeting, I was quite surprised to see Jackie there—she'd only been with Viking for a few days. As I explained the idea, I saw her eyes begin to light up. . . . She caught the idea immediately, and for the next two hours, she asked the most penetrating questions. She wanted to know what proportion of the text would be devoted to black women—to working women, to Indian women. . . . Finally, Tom Guinzburg turned to her and said, 'What do you think?' She said, 'Oh, let's do it.' Later, she took me on a tour of Viking—showed me the art department, the marketing department, the paperback division. She was so proud, so professional. It's obvious she's made her peace, that she was born for this. As for what she's been through in the past—well, life is a river and one searches one's way. Now she's made the quantum leap."

Describing Jackie as "a blend of iron and silk," Brandon remembered reviewing various items with her for inclusion in the book from historical sources. "We discovered that there was a root that women chewed to induce abortions. Jackie said, 'Put that in the book—we want it to be factual, and also earthy.'" According to Brandon, when they came across a letter from Martha Washington describing Georgetown, where Jackie had lived, as 'a dirty hole,' the former First Lady broke into laughter. They discovered that Martha Washington had written, "I lead a dull life—a state prisoner." Jackie was again thoroughly amused.

The discoveries of the abortion-inducing root and the Martha Washington letter were actually made by the two credited authors of the book, originally entitled *A Special Destiny.* The author-researchers, Linda Grant De Pauw and Conover Hunt, were academic authorities on this period of American history. Looking back, they offered points of view that contrast with the account given by Brandon at the time.

De Pauw, of George Washington University, who was given the title "consultant," recalled how she first became involved. "It was the eighteenth of April in nineteen seventy-five. I was giving a paper at an historical conference in Boston—I think it was the Organization of American Historians. And it was on Revolutionary War women, which was the field that I had been researching. After the presentation, a woman approached me and said her name was Muffie Brandon. I had never known anybody named Muffie before, and I wasn't going to hold it against her. She was very keen on having something done at the Mercy Otis Warren house for the bicentennial. This is an historical site in Plymouth, Massachusetts, and Mercy Otis Warren certainly was a significant woman of the American Revolutionary War period.

"At that point I was aware that what was known about women in the American Revolution was basically Betsy Ross and Molly Pitcher. So I said to Muffie, 'Mercy Otis Warren was an important person, and her house is important; but I really have a larger vision that I would like to pursue. . . .' I told Muffie that if she'd like to do something that had a little more breadth to it, I would be delighted to do it. And that is how the whole thing started. I was very young; I was thirty-five. I knew nothing about the 'fancy ladies'— that was how Conover Hunt and I referred to them—Muffie and the Kennedys and so on; they were totally off my radar."

Conover Hunt is now deputy director of the Fort Monroe, Virginia, Federal Area Development Authority. She remembered, "Muffie Brandon knew everyone in the county—a big Democrat from Boston. Her father was a Chinese professor at Harvard and had houses in Plymouth, and so on. So she knew Ted, she knew Jackie, she knew Ted's wife, Joan, and just about everybody else. . . . What she asked Jackie to do was get a book published. I was hired as the curator for a national traveling exhibition, and Professor De Pauw was hired as the academic historian. And the two of us together wrote the book."

Hunt described the watershed moment of history that gave birth to the book and informed the collaboration. "Remember that was nineteen seventy-six—the ERA, the whole nine yards, Betty Ford, the conference in Houston to get it passed, and so on. So that was a movement that was gaining. . . . The whole *Remember the Ladies* project came together in nine months, like birthing a baby. And then it traveled for two years. It was one of the official bicentennial exhibitions by the American Revolution Bicentennial Commission. And Muffie raised a million dollars. She got the most incredibly diverse group together. If they had all ever been in the same room, they would have killed each other. She had the Mount Vernon Ladies' Association, and the National Organization for Women, the Kennedy clan, and hard

Right Republicans as sponsors—it was just a hoot. And it was a very big success.

"We had one editing session in New York. . . . We worked primarily with an editor named Barbara Burn, who did most of the work. And Jackie came in during this session. What we were doing was design layout, and we were all down on the floor. And in she comes. Much shorter than I thought she was. Of course you always think Jackie O should be six feet tall. That funny little voice, wonderful sense of humor, and very, very interested in what we were doing. . . . The designer was talking about having the captions flush left, ragged right. And Jackie said, 'Now walk me through what you mean by that, these various design editing terms.' She wanted to know about the type style that would be used, and so on."

Released after resounding victories by crusaders for civil rights and women's rights, it was a sign of the time that the book and exhibition celebrated not only colonial pioneer women but also enslaved women of color and Native Americans. While incorporating a minimum of text, the book achieved considerable impact through the artifacts it displayed, and extensive captioning of those objects.

Remember the Ladies is an early example of how history was being transformed by advances in alternative scholarship, and Jackie was to play a leading role in this enlightened revisionism. The proliferation of slave narratives that were hardly known by earlier generations would become a recurrent theme in several later works that she undertook to develop and publish. She knew very well that history can only be accurate if all peoples are included. With lessons accumulated from her own past, Jackie was prepared to bring that kind of critical awareness into book after book, despite the entrenched resistance that she sometimes had to contend with along the way.

2

In the Russian Style, by Way of Paris

As she adjusted to her work schedule in the fall and winter of 1975, a typical day when she was not in the office found Jackie shopping at Bloomingdale's, perusing the shelves of the Gotham Book Mart, having her hair done at the Kenneth Salon, or just sitting by herself over a hamburger at Leo's coffee shop on Madison Avenue, with all eyes fixed on her. She also might have been seen enjoying an omelet at P. J. Clarke's or indulging her sweet tooth at Serendipity. On Friday afternoons, Jackie often drove her little green BMW ("jellybean green," as she described it to friends) out to her getaway home in the horse country of Somerset County, New Jersey, for a long weekend with her children and riding, although she often took manuscripts with her.

Becky Singleton charted Jackie's progress after her plunge into Viking. "By the end of the year, things had quieted down to something that approached normalcy. Jackie had become a familiar figure in the halls. Her relationship with Bryan Holme had progressed to the point where he seemed to view her as a colleague. He would often call or come to my office to ask

Jackie's whereabouts, as this project or that had arrived on his desk and he wanted to get her thoughts. She was also working as coeditor on books with some of Viking's senior editors—Elisabeth Sifton, Barbara Burn, and Cork Smith.

"The ease with which she had integrated herself into Viking's casual, friendly atmosphere seemed to have won over those who'd had misgivings about what impact her daily presence might have on the existing workplace environment. For Christmas that year, I gave her one of our standard-issue Viking Press T-shirts, which was the outfit du jour at softball games and company picnics, along with a note that said, in effect, now it's official—you have been a pleasure to work with and we enjoy having you around."

One of the books that Jackie later remembered having a hand in early at Viking was a Bryan Holme coffee-table production (eventually published in 1979) of Abraham Lincoln daguerreotypes. This book, *The Face of Lincoln,* was compiled and edited by James Mellon, from the legacy of archival images by the pioneering photographer Mathew Brady. One can well imagine why the forlorn but stately figure of Lincoln attracted the attention of Jackie, even beyond the obvious assassination parallel with JFK. She understood how a singular character could define an era.

The book's prime mover, James Mellon (a descendant of Andrew W. Mellon, the Pittsburgh industrialist and banker), wrote, "In Lincoln's face, as in the story of his life, every American can see something of his country's toil, something atavistic, for Lincoln remains the nonpareil example of the American character as it formed, and sought to define, itself." The book visually captured that essence of the man, and Jackie treasured the memory of even the small role she played. While two of the book's editors, Barbara Burn and Elisabeth Sifton, had no recollection of Jackie's having worked on this project, Becky Singleton informed me, "Jackie often mentioned this book to me. It was obvious that she took special interest in it . . . Jackie probably contributed to the book in an informal way, but her contribution must have been sufficient to cause her to feel 'part of the team.' "

During her first year at Viking, Jackie's friendship with Tom Guinzburg flourished, and they often saw each other socially. She offered him moral support through a divorce. They were simpatico in many ways and moved in the same social orbit, with publishers and writers at its center. Guinzburg remembered the challenge of dodging the paparazzi during a vacation that he shared with Jackie, Caroline, and John Jr. "We were in Jamaica, and the *National Enquirer* snuck this fellow in to follow her. We knew about him. He was a good-looking guy. And the problem was not so much Jackie and me, because we could avoid him—or she could avoid him on her own—but there were the kids.

"Our children were about the same age, and for all we know they could have been off in the woods smoking ganja, so I was just terrified the *National Enquirer* was going to snap a picture of them. But it was fun, because it was Jamaica, of course, and we had our little stratagems: the car that was supposed to have Jackie in it going off without her, and I would go off in one direction, and then she could go relax someplace. . . . There was a lot of that, but she never seemed flustered by any of it."

That same year, Guinzburg, while maintaining his role as publisher, sold Viking to the British conglomerate Pearson Longman Ltd, merging the house with Penguin, and the family enterprise began to take on a corporate identity. An aspiring editor at Penguin, David Zinsser, knew Jackie through the son of her Vassar roommate and longtime best friend, Jessie Wood, the daughter of the French writer and Paris hostess Louise de Vilmorin. It was through Wood's mother that Jackie met André Malraux in 1961, and together they had masterminded the loan of Da Vinci's *Mona Lisa* from the Louvre to the National Gallery and the Met. After the two of them pulled off this feat of French-American diplomacy, Malraux quipped, "Who had the better smile, Jackie or the *Gioconda*?"

David Zinsser and his friend Jessie Wood's son, Cabell Bruce, once stayed as guests at Jackie's apartment, and attended the movie *Nashville* with her and Caroline after it opened in September 1975. The film, directed by Robert Altman, presented an instance in which Jackie was unable to avoid being confronted by her past. Zinsser told me, "I don't think Jackie knew, and I certainly didn't know, the extent to which the movie was kind of a parable about the Kennedy assassination. And when the woman in the movie said, 'And *her* in her little pink suit,' I practically jumped out of my chair. We went back to the house afterwards, and I remember having tea, and she didn't really talk about that part of it. I guess she was anxious not to at that moment because Caroline was there, too. . . . It was so heavy, because we were experiencing it the way [Jackie and Caroline] did."

In the years to come, as Tom Guinzburg foresaw, Jackie would use her social networking skills to lure a number of authors to the publishing house. Elisabeth Sifton noted, "My hunch was that her principal means of acquisition, her line into getting a book, apart from hotshot agents who submitted things to her thinking that she was the appropriate receptor, was that she would go to dinner parties with very interesting people who would tell her interesting things. And then she would say, 'That's so interesting! You must write a book about that.'"

Another one of Jackie's editorial assistants, Delfina Rattazzi, was an heiress to the Agnelli Fiat fortune and then a recent graduate of Columbia University's School of Journalism. In her mid-twenties, she embraced the opportunity of having Mrs. Onassis as a boss and "grew to love and respect her." Rattazzi told me that on occasion during this period, "Jackie was out at high-level parties where her privacy would be protected." One of those gatherings was a party for author Jean Stein, recorded by Andy Warhol in his diary in an entry dated Wednesday, April 13, 1977.

Warhol wrote, "I was going up for cocktails and then dinner for Jean Stein at her sister Susan Shiva's apartment in the Dakota. . . . The first person I saw when I walked in the door was Jackie O., looking beautiful. Then Norman Mailer. Jackie was talking to Jean's boyfriend who works for the Smithsonian. Delfina Rattazzi who still works for Jackie at Viking was there with such a complete new look I didn't recognize her—curly hair and sexy dress. . . . had the first really nice talk with Jackie O., but I don't remember too much what it was about, the Magic of People in the Movies, or something."

Rattazzi also remembered, "People were always trying to use her. Peter Beard would drop by the office, and since I knew him I would step in to say hello. But once she said, 'I love Peter, but he is always trying to use me.' . . . Once she told me her son John was raising a python in the bathtub, which made her angry, but we laughed anyway. I remember her inviting me for an informal dinner at her apartment on Fifth Avenue: Warren Beatty and Diane Keaton, Jim Wolfensohn, a lot of people who had talent, even if finance was their business. She was very private. The one thing which amazed me about her was her capacity to pick up friends whom she could really trust, who would not say one word about her."

John Jr. spent a summer working in the reptile wing at the Bronx Zoo, thanks to Jackie's friend John Pierrepont, who was a trustee. Becky Singleton offered a slightly different take on John's snake story in light of Jackie's offbeat sense of humor. "Having heard many tales about John from Jackie, I would not rule out the idea that the python actually existed. I think John actually told this to a reporter. However, John seemed to enjoy tweaking his mother a bit and she knew this, although she always pretended to take him seriously. Jackie also pretended to be determined that John was going to date my twelve-year-old sister, who was a math whiz and quite unsophisticated. What she meant by this was, your sister is the type of influence I want to see in John's life. He's sixteen years old and I'm being driven half-crazy by the type of girls he is going out with."

While Jackie continued to move in colorful circles, one special friendship was destined to lead her into several fruitful book projects. In 1972, she had contributed to a fund to help cover the salary of Diana Vreeland as a consultant to the Metropolitan Museum's Costume Institute, enabling the fashion maven to land on her feet after having been fired as editor in chief of *Vogue*. Jackie and Vreeland had an even longer history, dating from 1960, when Jackie wrote a ten-page handwritten letter asking for Vreeland's advice on fashion, as Jackie felt that her own preference for French couture would be inappropriate for a First Lady.

On May 28, 1975, Jackie penned a letter to Vreeland expressing her feelings after receiving a gift of flowers. She wrote, in part. "Your tuberoses are so beautiful—when I walk through the living room I close my eyes and smell them and think I'm back with Proust. I *know* you are my friend as I am so deeply yours—and knowing you has taught me more than you could ever know—your spirit."

At Viking, Jackie would collaborate on two books with Vreeland, both associated with exhibitions that Vreeland organized at the Costume Institute: *In the Russian Style*, published at the end of 1976, and, the following year, *Inventive Paris Clothes, 1909–1939*, which featured photographs by Irving Penn, covering designers Poiret, Vionnet, Callot, Molyneaux, Paquin, Chanel, Schiaparelli, and Alix. Penn fell in love with the mannequins and costumes and rendered a series of exquisite images that perfectly complemented the exhibition.

Diana's son, Frederick (Frecky) Vreeland, a former diplomat who served as U.S. ambassador to Morocco, described his mother and Jackie during this time as two "widowed career girls in the swirl of New York." Frecky, who had also been a roommate of Tom Guinzburg's at Yale, met Jackie at least ten years before she and his mother crossed paths. Frecky explained to me in an e-mail, sent from his present-day home in Rome, "Mom came late and separately to JO, who had been a friend of mine since we met as teenagers. She was at Vassar College at the same time as my fiancée and together we frequently visited Jackie in Northern Virginia at her mother and step-father's house. It was there that she introduced me to a gawky young congressman on crutches who later became Senator and her husband."

Frecky Vreeland suggested that his mother and Jackie "undoubtedly had great respect for each other's enormous talents and saw each other as social and intellectual equals, each intent on maintaining her special identity in an otherwise highly-charged competitive world. Without having to spell it out, each intuitively understood the other's finely-tuned psychology. Each one nurtured a secret they didn't have to keep from each other. Jackie tended to keep each of her friendships distinct and so there was never any cross-current between Mom and myself in our continuing relationships with JO. I just remembered a conversation with JO when I once (stupidly) remarked on her habit of biting her nails. She said yes, that she went through life bearing an over-bearing mother—and added that this was something we probably both shared."

Tom Guinzburg described Diana Vreeland as a force of nature. "I don't think anybody in the world ever brought Diana to any office unless she marched in herself. She was a family friend I knew reasonably well. In fact, the first time I went off to play with her son, Frecky, in Brewster, New York, and I came back, I remember my mother was gardening out in the country, and she said, 'How's that Vreeland guy?' I said, 'Well, he's okay, Mom, but listen, let me tell you something.' She says, 'Well, tell me about him.' I said, 'He's a nice kid. We got along fine. Mom, listen to me.' She says, 'What are you going on about?' I said, 'Mom, Mrs. Vreeland has a phone in her bathroom!' "

Ferle Bramson was Diana Vreeland's assistant in the 1970s, and she, too, described the relationship between her flamboyant boss and Jackie as an intimate friendship. Jackie was one of those whom Vreeland would telephone in the morning from her bathroom. "They spoke all the time when this Russian exhibition was going on," said Bramson, "and they worked closely together as far as the book was concerned. Mrs. Vreeland always worked from home in the mornings. . . . They'd talk on the phone because Jackie lived across the street from the museum."

At the Met, Vreeland had Jackie's full support and brought her informally into the curatorial team that mounted the Costume Institute exhibitions. Most of the staff that Vreeland employed volunteered their services, while she enjoyed the support of the Met's director, Thomas Hoving, and his protégé, Philippe de Montebello, who would take over as director later that year. Like Hoving, who exhibited the flair of a dynamic showman as well as being a scholar, Vreeland held the view that the museum should appeal to people with grand theatrics, while preserving and celebrating the splendors of history. Hoving was the charismatic museum innovator who popularized the blockbuster show and enjoyed a tumultuous reign at the Met, from 1967 to 1977.

Vreeland's grandson, Nicholas, today runs the Tibet Center in Manhattan, but in his youth he worked with Diana and Jackie on a number of exhibitions and book projects. Describing the bond between Jackie and Diana, Nicholas Vreeland told me, "They were very, very close friends. I really witnessed it when living with my grandmother in New York in the early seventies. There was this mutual trust and love and respect. As my grandmother did the exhibitions, Jackie was involved. These exhibitions, one a year, were a time when all sorts of friends from all walks of life came together to make them happen. And the atmosphere was very much like before opening night at the theater, as people contributed what they could. And Jackie was definitely one of the people who really gave what she could to them, and it was those books."

Rosamond Bernier, the glamorous lecturer on high culture whose engagements were for many years much anticipated highlights at the Met, first met Vreeland in the late 1940s through their connections with *Vogue* and the fashion world. Bernier recalled, "We were always friendly, and I believe that after she was fired from *Vogue*, I was getting over a divorce, and we would meet quite often—she lived very near me—and have little shots of vodka, and talk about how we felt the world had behaved badly for us." Bernier believes that Jackie's formal education endowed her with more "culture" in the French sense of the word than Vreeland possessed, even given the latter's prescient instincts and personal flair. "They came from different directions. Indeed, I think probably each one had, to a certain extent, what the other did not have." Frecky Vreeland suggested that his mother's remarkable character and intellectual gifts more than made up for any deficiency in formal education.

Another volunteer who assisted with the Met extravaganzas was André Leon Talley, who later became creative director of *Vogue*. In his memoir, *A.L.T.*, Talley described one of the cultural passions that Jackie and Diana shared:

> Mrs. Vreeland loved just about anything from Russia (which she pro- nounced *"rush-hour"*) and obsessed on that country's extravagance. . . . I think her entire interest in Russia stemmed from a tale she once heard that Empress Catherine the Great had five thousand dresses. Mrs. Vreeland had the chance to inspect a trove of them in person when she went to the Rus- sian Museum's archives in Moscow to research the show *Russian Style* for the Costume Institute.

As Vreeland and others from the Met assembled this exhibition devoted to the artifacts of czarist Russia, Jackie scoured private and public sources to create a companion volume. She assembled jewels, objets d'art, litho- graphs and early photos, and, most of all, clothing, from the waist-high leather wading boots of the gargantuan Peter the Great to the silver and gold brocaded dresses favored by Catherine the Great. Some of the more elegant costumes were to be presented in color photographs taken in the actual Winter Palace where they were once proudly worn and passed down from generation to generation.

Judith Straeten was an assistant curator at the Met and worked on cataloguing acquisitions for the exhibition. Reminded that Jackie was called upon to help secure the Russian contributions in the summer of 1976, after Vreeland had traveled to Moscow when first planning the exhibition the previous year, Straeten said, "The Russians were not very impressed with Mrs. Vreeland. That was a nightmare from ground zero. There were a lot of things that she wanted that the Russians didn't want her to have until Mrs. Onassis stepped in. They sent them to us because of her. When Mrs. Vreeland had put in her final list of requests and the Russians had said no, Thomas Hoving was on it with Jackie, and Jackie persuaded them."

Vreeland arranged for Jackie and Hoving to meet in Paris and travel on together to Moscow to negotiate acquisitions from the Soviets. As the journey began, Hoving and Jackie dined out one night in Paris in late July on the Left Bank. The press had been alerted to Jackie's visit and surrounded the restaurant, pouncing on her arrival by taxi, screaming to get her attention, "Jackie! Jackie!" Hoving told Diana Vreeland's biographer, Eleanor Dwight, that after entering the restaurant that night, "I thought Jackie was going to crawl under the table. She was shaking." Jackie then voiced her concerns about traveling on to Russia and threatened to cancel the trip if she was going to run into that kind of frenzy in Moscow. Hoving allayed her fears. He explained, "The one good thing about Communism was that the state-controlled press would take one photo on arrival and one on departure—both times only after her permission."

Not surprisingly, the tabloids were soon trumpeting that Hoving was Jackie's new secret lover. They traveled to Moscow and Leningrad, viewing the Winter and Summer palaces. Hoving later recounted Jackie's contentious encounters with the Soviet Union's apparatchik ministers of culture and the coup that she managed to accomplish in the Russian-U.S. détente exchange: "She was really intent on gathering everything for the exhibition and book. . . . When she got onto something, she was inexorable. She wanted the costumes of the late Czar Nicholas and Czarina Alexandra, and she just either absolutely hammered them or stepped back and nudged. It was still a huge political issue, the czar's murder. . . . They finally gave her a sleigh of Nicholas and Alexandra's, and led her to a large trunk with Alexandra's costumes. They didn't let her take it, but she did get to try on the czarina's white coat!"

Jackie also managed to acquire a green velvet lap robe that had been used on sleigh rides by Princess Elizabeth, daughter of Peter the Great and Catherine I. Interviewed by *Newsweek* in 1994, Hoving remembered, "We were having a big dinner hosted by the American consul in Leningrad, who was a stiff individual who did not like the Russians. He looked at the people I had invited—artists and some bad-ass curators—as a bunch of Tartars. One of the Russian guests made a toast and said Russians had a tradition of throwing their empty glasses at the paintings on the wall. The counsel froze stiff in horror and thought there was a serious threat to one of his paintings. Jackie turned to me and whispered, 'If you don't get me out of here in five minutes I'm going to have the biggest nosebleed in Soviet history.'"

Jackie later described her work on the book, saying, "It was an example of publishing that literally took you into the world." Becky Singleton told me that she could not repeat what Jackie had confided to her about the trip to Russia, because her remarks "would probably reignite the Cold War if they saw the light of day!"

The companion book for the exhibit was produced by Bryan Holme, with the assistance of his son, Christopher, who said, "Jackie was very interested and involved in the layout, and the typeface that was chosen to go with *Russian Style*." Gael Towey described working with Jackie on the book. "I kept disappearing to go do Photostats, and she would say, 'Gael, where are you going?' And I'd reply, 'To the stat machine that's making all these pictures.' She said, 'Well, I want to see how that works.' I told her, 'Well, you really shouldn't come in here. The chemicals are horrible, it's smelly.' She said, 'No, no, no! I want to know everything that's going on.' I have to say that just that little exchange was something that really showed me how curious she was about everything. . . . When we were working intensely on all of this, she would go around and take lunch orders. She'd say, 'Gael, would you like a tuna fish sandwich?' With her whispery soft voice, she'd make a tuna fish sandwich sound like it was the most exotic thing in the world."

To help with the effort, Jackie consulted two Russian expatriates who had served in the last court of the czar: Serge Obolensky, a descendant of Catherine the Great's commanding general, and Vava Adelberg, son of the governor general of St. Petersburg. Jackie also invited one of her old friends from her Vassar days, Suzanne Massie, to lecture at the Met on the subject of Russian art and cultural history. Suzanne's husband, Robert K. Massie, had written the highly regarded *Nicholas and Alexandra,* a biography of the last czar of Russia, Nicholas II, and his wife, Alexandra of Hesse. Suzanne would later serve as a consultant on Russian affairs to President Reagan. Jackie introduced Suzanne to Vreeland, and while preparing *In the Russian Style,* Jackie tenaciously picked Suzanne's brain on the subject.

Massie described one work session with Jackie at her home: "I visited and went over a lot of things with Jackie—pictures, and captions—and she kept plying me with Dom Pérignon; and every time I'd get up to go she'd say, 'Well, now, just this one more picture. Let's go over this one.' So I thought that she was the most determined creature that I ever saw. Everybody's talked about her as being sort of shy; but she was not at all! And in the end I was completely bombed by the time I left—and I didn't leave until about two in the morning."

The night of the exhibition's opening at the Met was a spectacle of society figures dressed in original designer fashions from the likes of Oscar de la Renta and Yves Saint Laurent, showing off modern designs that would mirror the Russian imperial and peasant themes on display. Many society guests turned up looking like members of the Russian royal court.

However, that evening Jackie and Diana dressed with tasteful simplicity and together worked the receiving line, along with Russian dignitaries and the Met powers that be. It was a glorious show orchestrated in a grand setting, far more substantial without the Hollywood glitz that the Costume Institute's annual spectacles have relied on in recent years under the direction of *Vogue* editrix Anna Wintour.

Under the guidance of Jackie and Diana, the book and exhibition conjured the regal world of Peter and Catherine the Great while also displaying the less lavish garb of the "rich" Russian peasantry. By all accounts, the opening was indeed a paparazzi-worthy party, and yet with more emphasis on culture and art than glitterati. From room to painted room, each a unique glimpse into history, the atmosphere was filled with the scent of Chanel's Cuir de Russie ("Russia Leather," revived by Chanel for the event). The floors were strewn with furs ("to give the idea of savagery," Vreeland told *The New York Times*); the music of Tchaikovsky, Rimsky-Korsakov, Borodin, Moussorgsky, and Glazunov played on tape. Balalaika players performed in the main hall, and ballroom dancing continued into the wee hours. Vreeland stationed herself in front of the bookshop, flourishing the *Russian Style* book and hawking it to the crowd, crying out, "Buy a book. Buy a beautiful book!"

In the Russian Style was more than just an exhibit catalogue, featuring illustrations and contextualizing captions, and Jackie had the editorial good sense to provide quotations from contemporary accounts of czarist life, taking the reader through a kind of Russian-lite history. The book contrasted the Slavic influence of Russian folk art with the Francophile influence that held sway among the bourgeoisie and royal entourage. Embroidered fans, samovars of silver, bejeweled music boxes, imperial flatware, malachite vases, snuff boxes of gold and opalescent enamel, shimmering chandeliers and elaborate furniture rounded out the collection, creating a luxurious portrait of a long-gone era.

In the Russian Style was one of only two books published during Jackie's editorial career that carried "Edited by Jacqueline Onassis" as a credited byline. She often expressed her aversion to using her name to sell books. As she once remarked, "One of the things I like about publishing is that you don't promote the editor—you promote the book and the author." At a press conference to promote the exhibit and book, improvising and perhaps uncomfortable with her promotional role, Jackie made light of the costumes, saying, "You love to see it, the way you love to see *Gone with the Wind*. But wouldn't you rather wear your blue jeans than wander about in a hoop skirt?"

She also described another Russian project she was working on at the time, a book entitled *The Firebird and Other Russian Fairy Tales,* for which she would write an introduction. It was published in 1978. With characteristic enthusiasm, Jackie said this project "meant working with a Russian translator and doing research in the New York Public Library's Slavonic room. I love doing illustrated books—a great art book can reveal a whole world to the reader. This was the rediscovery of the work of Boris Zvorykin, a member of Diaghilev's circle. He was a master of decorative art, yet virtually forgotten."

Boris Zvorykin (1872–1935) was a Russian illustrator who produced stunningly beautiful images for children's books, in an elaborate Russian style that featured a wide palette and complicated, fractal-like borders. The owner of the Gotham Book Mart, Andreas Brown, brought an unpublished French folio version of these illustrations to Jackie's attention at the International Antiquarian Book Fair held at the Plaza Hotel in March–April 1977. She immediately grasped the unique nature of Zvorykin's renderings and commissioned a book that featured them in English-language retellings of four seminal Russian children's tales. The most renowned of the stories was "The Firebird," immortalized in music by Igor Stravinsky and in ballet by George Balanchine, a mythical romance reminiscent of various "Phoenix" tales. Jackie undertook the translation herself from the French source, and Viking reportedly paid Brown five figures for the book. This is the other book on which she was credited on the cover as editor.

Jackie was for many years an ardent collector of fine books. She often visited the Gotham Book Mart and turned to Brown for assistance in locating books for herself and her children. Over the years, Gotham's distinguished clientele had included Arthur Miller, John Updike, Tennessee Williams, Ezra Pound, J. D. Salinger, and Katharine Hepburn. Brown recalled that in the early 1970s Jackie bought books "almost every day, hundreds a year. . . . Her taste is eclectic—fiction, nonfiction, history, art—and she's fascinated with current social issues." Describing her position at Viking, Brown added, "She's not window dressing there."

Christopher Holme worked on the Zvorykin book with Jackie and told me, "With *The Firebird,* she would come in and look at proofs from the printer, and I guess previous to that she worked on the layout. And when the book was printed, she wanted to go to see it on press and see the operation, which was out in New Jersey. So I got to drive her out to New Jersey in my parent's Chevrolet Vega, which is far from the type of vehicle you'd expect her to be in. We went out, and the press run went as most of them did, with no major surprises, but they were all of course instructed that she was there just like anybody else, and no one was to make a fuss."

Jackie contributed an essay to the catalogue for Vreeland's next exhibition, *Vanity Fair: Four Seasons of Fashion from the Costume Institute,* which opened December 11, 1977. The exhibit featured garments and accessories selected from the Costume Institute's collection of more than thirty thousand articles of clothing and various ornamental accompaniments. The title was borrowed from *Pilgrim's Progress* by John Bunyan, and Jackie dedicated her essay, "A Visit to the High Priestess of Vanity Fair," to "Diana Vreeland, whippet-boned, with black lacquered hair, looks like a high priestess, which in a way she is, and her temple is on the ground floor of The Metropolitan Museum of Art." Jackie would continue her literary collaboration with Vreeland in grand fashion during the years ahead.

On October 28, 1976, Jackie wrote a memo to Alan Williams to recommend a manuscript she had read by Lawrence Durrell for a book entitled *Sicilian Carousel*, which was based on the author's somewhat embellished bus tour of the island. Williams in turn wrote to Durrell, attempting to lure him to Viking by quoting some of Jackie's memo, which reads in part:

> This is a book that I just cannot bear the long waiting for until it appears. Durrell can evoke place better than any writer I know. . . . I loved . . . [*Marina Venus* and *Prospero's Call*] before I ever saw a Greek island—When you know them, every white pebble, every olive tree, every character and all the history he weaves in and out. Of course everyone is going to the Greek islands now—so it would be the standard book that they buy as they take off with their sun-oil and instamatic cameras—just to be crass and commercial. I mean I think it would have an audience that perhaps Durrell's books do not always reach. To those who love Durrell—what a joy to sit down with this and just savor it. . . .

Jackie described Durrell as one of the masters of the art of travel writing, likening him to Kazantzakis, Patrick Leigh Fermor, and Flaubert. Jackie's praise was welcomed by Durrell, and his book was published by Viking in September 1977.

Looking back in a syndicated story in 2002, Jimmy Breslin, a Viking author, wrote that he had run into Jackie in the hallway outside her office after she first started as an editor. He offered her a new book idea on behalf of a friend. "I had just been in Chicago, where I had been with Eugene Kennedy, a priest who was at Chicago's Loyola University. He wanted to write and he talked about a book on Mayor Richard J. Daley. I told this to Onassis and she went into her office and started it off. She was a working woman. He was a working priest, professor, and, given the chance here, he became a working writer."

Breslin told me that his relationship with Jackie went back to the early days of the Kennedy White House as well as the nightmare of the JFK assassination. "There was one scene I remember about her. She was in the Parkland Hospital in the lobby there. Kennedy's dead inside, in the room, and she's talking to the priest. The priest was—I saw him, what the fuck, I went to his rectory and talked to him. He's in the clips. He was giving Kennedy the last rites, and she asked him, at the end, 'Is it a valid last sacrament?' She asked him that. And he assured her it was. Because you have a period of time, according to their faith, that the soul does not leave the body and you can say a prayer for it before it goes. That was what she was dealing with at the end, and that's bone Roman Catholic faith. That's the way she went through the rest of her life—*bone*. Get up and go to work."

Taking Breslin's suggestion, Jackie contacted Eugene Kennedy, and expressed her interest in his doing a book about Mayor Daley, the rotund, Machiavellian Chicago mayor. Kennedy, who was not related to the Massachusetts Kennedy clan, told me, "I had written a piece, 'St. Patrick's Day with Mayor Daley,' because I spent St. Patrick's Day in 1975 on the reviewing stand with him. I got the idea that nobody had ever done a book about him. It is true—Jimmy Breslin and I have known each other for a long time, and it was Jimmy who put us in touch with each other."

Jackie would cultivate a close relationship with Gene, as she called him. He said, "I remember Jackie and I had a long talk one afternoon in her apartment at 1040 Fifth Avenue—it was quite a place; I went there many times. She served cucumber sandwiches for lunch, and she sat on a couch in her library. Behind her was this shelf of bound volumes, all of which had printed on them, JBK & JFK, and they were all memoirs and so forth of her years with Jack. And I could really feel—there was no doubt in mind—that her love for him had never ended. We had a lot of talks about that and about loss. She was not a woman who missed anything, nobody was throwing anything past her."

Kennedy remembered that Jackie worked with the highly regarded editor Corlies (Cork) Smith, Breslin's editor, on the Daley biography. Becky Singleton recollected, "Jackie was listed as coeditor on the Eugene Kennedy book. She told me some quite amazing tales about a luxurious monastery and Catholic retreat located on an island in the Great Lakes near Chicago. As I recall, she speculated in a humorous way that Father Kennedy might have spent a good bit of time there. This was actually sort of a compliment—we both saw him as being a remarkably urbane and elegant priest."

Eugene Kennedy took a PhD in psychology and taught at Loyola for many years before retiring. He wrote many books on the intersection of psychology and religion, and has long argued for reform among the ever-diminishing Catholic priesthood. Jackie recognized that, although born in New York, Kennedy, having lived much of his adult life in Chicago, had a special perspective as a priest and, later, as a Catholic activist on how the ethnic Irish, Italians, and Eastern Europeans were knit into a fragile coalition by Mayor Daley and his associates. Entitled *Himself! The Life and Times of Mayor Richard J. Daley* and published in 1978, Kennedy's book won the Carl Sandburg Literary Award and the Thomas More Medal.

Kennedy's portrait showed that Daley was not always the Neanderthal that the mass media made him out to be after his ugly side surfaced during the 1968 Democratic Convention and the attendant battle for the streets of the city by protestors and Chicago police. The book offered a key revelation about JFK's relationship with Daley. There are many who still believe today, more than fifty years later, that JFK would not have carried Illinois (the key to his razor-thin margin of victory in the election) had it not been for the strength of the Daley machine, an electoral juggernaut so powerful that it could allegedly make the dead rise up and seek out their polling places. Eugene Kennedy found the truth to be otherwise.

"Jackie knew Daley, of course," said Kennedy. "She told me that he had a lot to do with Jack's election. He didn't really do anything illegal; that's the odd thing that people don't understand. The real stealing of votes was always done downstate by the Republicans. He did something very unusual that election night. What the Republicans in our state always did was to wait for the last returns from Chicago to come in. At that time, they were still using cardboard boxes and paper ballots, and they would plant enough votes downstate to overcome the last votes from Chicago." Kennedy recalled that during his research on the book he learned that Jackie was right with her speculation, that "a week before the election Daley had asked Joe Kennedy for a million dollars to have poll watchers at every poll downstate to prevent the Republicans from stealing the election. Therefore the votes were not votes he made up; they were votes that in fact had been cast. He was blamed for stealing votes out of nowhere; but he never did that. . . .

"Jackie wanted to come to Chicago once. She said, 'Now, I don't want any special treatment, you know. . . . And what we do,' she said, 'is we walk fast, or everybody will surround us.' She said, 'I want you to take me to lunch when I get to Chicago.' I said, 'Do you want to go to some elegant restaurant.' 'No,' she said, 'I want you to take me to someplace that's low-down and dirty. . . .' What she wanted to see was a real Chicago restaurant where all these characters were hanging out. Though she wasn't able finally to come to Chicago, she was very interested in all of that, and that's why she was interested in the books she was doing. . . .

"I was her escort at the Democratic Convention in 1976. You read accounts of that convention, and a lot of people say that they accompanied her. But I have a picture that was taken of us together that night. She had talked to me in advance about going with her and whatnot, and it was quite an experience. I was traveling with Mike Royko and a group from the Chicago papers. What occurred that night, first, of course, we came into the hall, and it was mayhem as soon as she entered. She was extremely calm, and I walked with her, and I didn't have my collar on or anything like that, and I went to these seats that had been reserved for her. And her sister was there. And then all these people came streaming over to say hello to her—the actor Lorne Greene and the Carter family came down. Everybody wanted to be seen with her. It was highly amusing, in a way, because you could see why she did want to walk fast. . . .

"Here we were at the heart of the Democratic Convention, and she had asked to meet Daley, who was a delegate. We talked to the guy that was the chairman of the party then, Robert Strauss, from Texas. So he set up this meeting, in a lower level of Madison Square Garden, in some subterranean chamber. And here's Dick Daley in his blue suit, and I knew the way Daley would react. She went over to talk to him, and he just listened, very happy to see her. But even to her, whom he idolized, as far as a book, he was very self-protective and protective of his family. She wanted him to know she was having a book written about him. She was very straightforward. She told him that she had commissioned a book, and he said something like, 'We'll look into it.'

"He died the next December. Now while he was alive, nobody would talk. They feared for their lives and their jobs and so forth. It was very interesting, the control he exerted. After he died, I ended up talking to dozens and dozens of people, who knew him in various ways, some of them in a very intimate way, and they were very helpful. Jackie was fascinated by all this, and her support never wavered. Before Daley died, it didn't matter to her that he wasn't going to give any direct support. She understood, if you were on to something, if she felt you were on the right track, she would encourage you to keep going along that track. If she thought you were diverging from it, that's when she would intervene and say, 'Well, I'm not sure about that.' She did it so nicely."

Assessing Jackie's sensitivity as an editor, Kennedy later wrote that she "understood that writers, like fine china being prepared for shipment, need to be packaged gently and supported strongly for the long journey from blank paper to publication day. Her style was encouragement, that of a coach prompting as good a performance as possible out of a long-distance runner."

Kennedy married a former nun and psychiatrist, Sara Charles, in September 1977, while working on the book. He told me, "I remember Jackie met my wife, and she was so happy that we had gotten married, actually. She said, 'Oh, you're so fortunate. You're so *equal*.' That was really a wonderful thing to say."

Another Viking book—a work of historical fiction about Thomas Jefferson's relationship with his slave mistress Sally Hemings—proved to be a thorny challenge for Jackie and her colleagues, one that would lead to some contentious exchanges with the soon to be acclaimed author, Barbara Chase-Riboud, then the wife of photographer Marc Riboud. This was the first novel that Jackie acquired and played a role in editing, and it was to be a learning experience, a balancing act undertaken while negotiating the tightrope that extended between a neophyte author and a fledgling editor.

Chase-Riboud was an African American sculptor, poet, and aspiring novelist based in Paris who had met Jackie during her marriage to Ari. A native of Philadelphia with a master's degree in fine arts and architecture from Yale, Chase-Riboud's sculpture had been exhibited internationally since the 1960s, and her first book of poems, *From Memphis & Peking,* had been edited by Toni Morrison at Random House. In 1996, she would be knighted by the French government, receiving the Chevalier de l'Ordre des Arts et des Lettres.

When Chase-Riboud's *Sally Hemings* was published, in 1979, before the science of DNA promised to unearth secrets that had long been thought safely entombed, it created stirs of protest and grumblings from proud Jeffersonian scholars who were loath to admit that the first statesman from Virginia and our third president, a slaveholder, might have had a relationship with one of his own slaves—a relationship that seemed loving and constant, and which produced issue. The romanticized image of Jefferson as one of the "good" slaveholders prompted Jefferson defenders to deny the likelihood of such a relationship, one that had been noticed by John Adams and gossiped about even during their lifetimes.

The lesson that controversy sells books was not lost on Jackie, though she would not live long enough to see the book and her author vindicated. In 1998, the British science journal *Nature* published an article by a team led by Eugene A. Foster comparing the Y chromosomal haplotypes of the male descendants of Jefferson, both free and enslaved. While these tests could not conclusively establish Thomas Jefferson as the father (his brother Randolph could have possibly been instead), these findings, along with the preponderance of historical evidence, seem to have turned the tide among historians. In 2000 the Monticello Society published a white paper validating the DNA findings, which led to reunions of Jefferson descendants at Monticello. The credibility of Chase-Riboud's historical fiction has risen accordingly, with the novel republished in 2009 by the Chicago Review Press to mark the book's thirtieth anniversary.

As a witness to the civil rights movement as it had affected both JFK and RFK, Jackie surely appreciated the fact that Sally Hemings was an unlikely heroine. Hemings accepted her status as a slave, even when she joined Jefferson in Paris in 1788 as a maid-in-waiting for his daughter, and was told by her older brother, also in Jefferson's service, that slavery had been outlawed by the French. She used her special relationship with the master of Monticello to secure elevated status for herself, and even persuaded him to build a secret room for her on the second floor of Monticello, so that visitors to the mansion would not see the nightly trips she took to Jefferson's bedchamber as "mistress of Jefferson's wardrobe." But her devotion to Jefferson led to the freeing of all of the Hemings clan after his death, and it was the written accounts of two of her sons, Eston and Madison, that led to the genealogical digging that occurred two centuries later.

In her book, Chase-Riboud deftly weaves this story together using flashbacks and alternating between Hemings's voice and the vantage point of an omniscient narrator. She does not flinch from details that might make Hemings or Jefferson seem less elevated than history characterized them, and demonstrates how impossible it was for a man like Jefferson to serve two masters—the call from his heart and the privileged positions he held as a founding father of the country and slave owner simultaneously. She depicts their relationship as one of passion, inflamed by its very prohibition.

Interracial marriage during this era was considered a felony and punished by fine, prison, and exile from Virginia; to free a slave, even one's children, meant their exile from the state. Proximity to Jefferson transformed Hemings in an era when it was illegal for blacks to go to school or learn how to read. Not only did she master these disciplines with his explicit encouragement, but she also learned French during her stay in Paris. Intimacy with one of the most brilliant statesmen America has ever produced paid dividends, and upon her return to rural Virginia, Hemings maintained echoes of the French lifestyle. Given Jackie's deeply felt Francophile predilection, Sally Hemings captivated her, as did Jefferson.

During her White House years, when the famous Jefferson portrait by Rembrandt Peale was donated and placed in the Blue Room, Jackie wrote, "I'd have liked to study architecture . . . like Thomas Jefferson. Now there was a man! . . . He could do so many things. Jefferson is the president with whom I have the most affinity." Her esteem for Jefferson appears not to have altered even when the more complex picture of the man emerged with the Chase-Riboud novel, which drew on primary historical sources, as well as Fawn M. Brodie's 1974 biography, *Thomas Jefferson: An Intimate History.*

During a recent Skype call from Paris, Barbara Chase-Riboud told me, in a lilting, mellifluous voice, "I had met Jacqueline for the first time in Greece, where we went for vacations. I think it was seventy-four or seventy-five that I was spending the summer with our friends who were from Philadelphia, in their house on a nearby island. And she would call her old roommate [Jessie Wood], who was my friend as well, to come over to the island, to Skorpios. And every year we would say the same thing. It was too hot, it was too far, one of the ten kids was sick. And that year, for some reason or other, I said, 'I don't know about you guys, but I'm going.' I had decided to ask the only woman I knew who could tell me what it was like to live with an American president.

"We arrived at the island, and I started talking to Jacqueline about the presidency and power and love and her life in the White House, and how these men operated on that level of worldly ambition and vision. It's unbelievable now that I tell the story, but it actually happened that way. There we were, sort of lying on the beach in Skorpios, watching the paparazzi go around the island in speedboats, and trying to figure out what Thomas Jefferson and Sally Hemings could have done and said to each other. It was really amazing, and it went on for three days. I told her about my doubts at being able to bring these iconic characters to any kind of life. We talked about that, and finally she said, 'You know, Barbara, you've got to write this book.' And I said I didn't know anything about writing a novel. 'I'm a poet, a sprinter, not a novelist, a long-distance runner, and I don't know . . .' She said, 'You've got to do it. Nobody else is going to do it for you,' in her unique breathless voice, and so on. She sort of convinced me in the end that I should do it, and this was before she had anything to do with publishing.

"Earlier, I had already proposed the idea for *Sally Hemings* to Random House and my editor was Toni Morrison. Toni said, 'The way you see it, I can't get any advance for you whatsoever. They want a big historical novel, and you're giving me a long epic poem. This is not going to work. They don't want it.' Then I asked her to do it. [I asked] practically every writer I knew . . . to write the story. And everybody was busy. Nobody took it up, and I had sort of dropped the whole idea."

Chase-Riboud recalled that Jackie, after joining Viking, "called my agent, Lynn Nesbit, every week to check on the progress of the novel. . . . I had decided to write it as a novel, but, you know, being very clear that it was based on documents and research, and that I believed that this story was true. That's how it began. Fawn Brodie had stayed more or less in the realm of academia. She simply raised the question in one chapter, and that was enough for me; but that was also enough for the Jeffersonians to get their shotguns out for me.

"It sort of ties in with Jacqueline's whole persona and her whole concept of history, her honesty and directness, and her empathy for this woman and for what she represents. Jacqueline practically forced me to do this book. We became very good friends almost immediately. It was sort of love at first sight. I loved her wry humor—her self-deprecation . . . her chic and her charm. . . . And she was often in Paris. I was often in New York. We would see each other, usually not in public, usually at her flat or someplace where nobody was taking any pictures. It lasted. She was the one who sort of got me through my divorce, as a matter of fact. She told me not to come back to New York a divorced woman. She was there when I needed her, and we remained friends until the time that she died. . . .

"People just did not faze her, and I think they didn't because she had spent the first part of her life—let's put it that way—building this kind of network of empathy, which also kept people at a certain distance. She could always look at herself from outside, and most of the time she could laugh, whatever happened. She was very brave in the heroic sense, but she was also brave in the domestic sense. I think of Michelle Obama like that as well. She has a kind of courage, which makes great women, but she also has that kind of down-to-earthness. . . . If you could go through the books and see what kind of women she empathized with—you would get a real sense of her, I think. The kind of women that she published books about is the kind of woman that she actually was."

Chase-Riboud writes, in her afterword to the revised edition of the book, "Viking embarked on a series of perversities that threatened to derail the book." She told me, "Once Jacqueline had left, I felt like an orphan; Viking got sold, the editor in chief got fired, a new president came in, it seemed nobody was there who had been there in the beginning; someone decided that nothing happened in the second part of the book. At that point I grabbed it back, and I gave it to a writer friend of mine who is also an excellent editor, and we holed up in the Algonquin Hotel for a week without ever going out, with a pile of greenbacks on the night table. And I said, 'When these are gone, this book is finished, because I can't afford to pay you any more than this.'

"The book jacket came in with Jefferson on the cover in an open-to-the-waist shirt with a wineglass in one hand and his other arm around a wind-swept, buxom, flowing-haired Sally Hemings in a torn dress. Mary McCarthy put me on a plane to New York clutching the illustration. Then the Jeffersonians weighed in. It was bad enough that Hemings had escaped academia and their Wite-Out; now even before the book was published, it had been sold to the movies, the first of eleven options. It was going Hollywood!"

The movie was never made, but Chase-Riboud described the book's later success: "The DNA was not the only vindication for her first novel acquisition as an editor. The book sold a million and a half copies in the United States and almost as many in France and the rest of Europe and South America. It went on to win the Janet Heidinger Kafka Prize and was translated into ten other languages, with more than thirty different editions." Chase-Riboud also noted, "In the earliest drafts, I had Sally Hemings die at the end of the book, but Jacqueline said, 'There is no reason for her to die.' So, I allowed her to live beyond the novel—which she has truly done."

In the latest edition of *Sally Hemings,* the author characterized Jackie's unnamed assistant as "an unreconstructed West Virginian: this woman claimed to 'know how to handle these people,' referring to me, the only black writer in the house." Becky Singleton has vivid recollections of the conflicts that took place during the editing process, which eventually led Jackie and Singleton to defer to the husband-and-wife editing team of Jeannette and Richard Seaver. The Seavers took over the final round of editing. Singleton, who is from West Virginia, takes strong exception to Chase-Riboud's apparent characterization of her. "Good heavens, what can I say? Of course I didn't make the remarks Barbara attributes to me."

Singleton offered a lengthy recollection of their exchanges, suggesting that the racial issues masked other editorial conflicts. "Barbara is an extremely gifted writer. No one at Viking ever questioned her talent, although she may not have felt that way. . . . From the start, nothing was easy with Barbara. Tom [Guinzburg] must have sensed a bad situation when the completed manuscript arrived—about eight hundred pages typed on legal-sized paper—because he asked Ed Kennebeck, Viking's senior copy editor, to take a look at it.

"Tom was adamant that Viking could not . . . publish the novel in its current form. The question in everyone's mind was how to get Barbara to make the necessary changes. . . . It was decided that Jackie and I would deal with the issue at a customary sit-down editorial conference. . . . I made a list of our objectives, and Jackie and I talked about how these might be most tactfully achieved. Since the novel was much too long, we had marked passages for possible exclusion. If Barbara agreed to the cuts, the entire issue could be resolved. . . .

"On the day of the meeting, Jackie and I began by giving Barbara lots of praise—and in truth, many of the passages she had written were moving, lovely, and powerful. Then we slowly began to raise the issue of historical inaccuracies. . . . Due to past associations, both Jackie and I were well-grounded in the history of Old Virginia. We had found many inaccuracies of the sort that could diminish the impact of her narrative, but could easily be corrected. The 'bad cop' role went to me, in that I actually voiced the specific alterations we felt were needed. Then Jackie . . . offered Barbara a constant massage of encouragement, even as she gently reinforced the need for the revisions.

"Barbara wasn't impressed by our efforts to be tactful. She was hostile to the idea of making any changes, even minor ones. Her responses to our suggestions seemed to question the notion that a publisher might actually ask for revisions rather than embrace the artist's completed work, as written. After an hour or so . . . Barbara leaned forward dramatically and announced that she wanted to make a statement. What she said went something like this: 'The two of you might think that this meeting is taking place as two people against one. That's not true. I am not alone, because I am speaking not only for myself and Sally Hemings, but also for the entire black race and their suffering throughout time. . . . They, rather than you, are the only ones qualified to judge the accuracy of my portrayal of plantation life in Old Virginia. . . .'

"Momentarily, we were left speechless. . . . After that, we tried to move forward . . . Jackie's responses to Barbara had become noticeably more cool. As for me, being delegitimized as an editor due to race was a new experience and I found it disheartening. . . . Barbara was clearly angry that we continued to talk about revisions. . . . The conference had already lasted several hours and we'd made virtually no headway.

"In the end, I was forced to inform her of Tom's verdict—namely that her novel could not be accepted for publication by Viking in its current form. From her reaction, it was clear that Barbara had never considered this possibility. The moment I mentioned it, she erupted in fury. . . . I glanced over at Jackie and she immediately took the lead. She tried to calm Barbara down by reminding her of our glowing praise for many sections of her book and then made what I considered to be a lovely appeal to Barbara about what the world would miss, if she chose not to work with a publisher to create the best possible book. Barbara was having none of it. . . . She conveyed this to us in terms that were rather unpleasant and then stood and swept from the room. . . . Jackie and I briefly discussed the wrecked situation. We felt badly about the outcome but couldn't think of anything we could have done differently.

"Sometime later, Jeannette Seaver came down the hall, looking very amused. She said she'd spoken to Barbara. 'She's very upset with both of you,' she said merrily. She told us that her husband, Dick, had agreed to take the manuscript home with him to see if it could be published as a Seaver Book. Jackie and I said fine, fine. We would have agreed to anything at that point . . . and also thought that Barbara might respond differently to a male editor." With regard to the conflict, Tom Guinzburg shared Becky's sentiments, saying, "We all thought that Barbara Riboud was one of the most difficult authors we had ever dealt with."

Jeannette Seaver, whom Chase-Riboud credited as her editor, characterized the experience as "a nightmare." Jeannette said, "I inherited the book out of default. Tom came into my office and asked if I could take it over, and I did. And therefore, it bore the Seaver imprint on it. It was no reflection on Jackie at all. She left just at the time that happened. . . . She was the one who brought the book in. I can only say that as a colleague she was reproachless, she was polite, one could count on her. . . . Because they had been friends, I sought her to help with the promotion . . . and she was extremely helpful. . . . This was just at the beginning when she was learning to become a publishing soldier. I worked very hard on that manuscript. Dick and I put in a great many devoted hours to, how shall I say, make it better, or humbly so? She owes me, Barbara, a whole bunch. She never so much as thanked me . . . but she went on to good things, so what can I say?"

Chase-Riboud remembered the friction working with Jeannette. "Once, she dumped the whole manuscript on my agent's desk. There was one legendary scene where everybody thought one of us was going to fly right out of the seventeenth-story window ushered by the other when I said I couldn't publish a book about slavery where nobody worked, as she had cut the only work scene in the book. There was also an argument about the strict use of 'Sally Hemings' instead of 'Sally' as a means of equalizing the two historic figures. She insisted, 'It doesn't matter if a few Sallys slip into the text.' [As for] the real Jefferson quotations at the beginning of each chapter in which he condemned himself in his own words . . . [Jeannette] said [that they] slowed down the book, and [she] wanted to eliminate [them]. But [this] was a device which captivated both critics and public"

Barbara Burn described the lesson Jackie learned as far as dealing with authors: "The best authors always are the ones that are willing to be edited. The worst ones are so defensive about their writing that they fight with every change, you know. And Jackie was aware of that." Whatever the challenges Jackie faced with the Sally Hemings book, she never lost her belief in it. Jackie's friend the historian William Howard Adams recalled, "I was a trustee at Monticello and had worked on Jefferson history, including *The Paris Years of Thomas Jefferson*. Jackie was fascinated with the Thomas Jefferson–Sally Hemings relationship and was always bringing up the subject, including the novel. She adored Jefferson and spun out all kinds of romantic fantasies. She insisted that it all happened according to the novelist's imagination and that it was an air-tight case."

Jackie maintained her friendship with Barbara Chase-Riboud over the years. As a favor, in 1988 Jackie submitted the manuscript for another one of her novels, *Echo of Lions* (published by William Morrow in 1989), to Steven Spielberg's company, Amblin Productions, for consideration as a film project. In 1997 Barbara filed a $10 million copyright infringement lawsuit, contending that Spielberg's movie *Amistad* had lifted material from her novel. Both the book and the movie recount events surrounding an 1839 revolt aboard a slave ship bound for the United States.

Spielberg's lawyers tried to turn the tables by arguing that Chase-Riboud had lifted material for her book from a 1953 novel by William A. Owens, *Slave Mutiny* (later entitled *Black Mutiny*). The latter book had been optioned for a film in 1984 by Debbie Allen, one of the producers of *Amistad*. While the case was eventually settled, during the legal proceedings, Chase-Riboud was interviewed by *The New York Times* and explained her point of view, arguing that, as a writer of fiction dealing with historical subjects, she had the right to appropriate reference material from the public domain. "I have a technique of sort of weaving real documents and real reference materials into my novel and making a kind of seamless narrative using both documents and fiction."

Thanks to her well-honed technique and the early success of *Sally Hemings*, Chase-Riboud has enjoyed a long career writing historical fiction in addition to pursuing her other artistic endeavors. Becky Singleton characterized the experience as a victory. "When the Sally Hemings novel was finally published, I was delighted to find that nearly all of the revisions Jackie and I had originally suggested had been incorporated. . . . What's important in the end is that a good book was made to happen. To me, this harrowing episode offers a telling portrait of 'the real Jackie' at work. She was willing to take whatever came with being an editor in order to make good books happen. From the start, she seemed comfortable with the idea that in publishing, editors do not get carried around on little white satin pillows. She was willing to get into the trenches and knew how to handle herself when she got there. I like to think that she 'earned her stripes' at Viking and that the confidence she gained by doing this sustained her for the rest of her career."

3

A Tale of Two Houses

After almost two years with Viking, Jackie was coming into her own, thriving in her work life and seemingly at home with her colleagues. The casual style she brought into the office earned her the affectionate nickname "Earth Shoes." Becky Singleton explained at the time, "Earth Shoes is cute, but it doesn't say it all about her. She's out to prove herself as an independent working person and doing it well. Jackie becomes desperately involved in her projects. She's likened it to the birth of a baby. It's like being there for the delivery; she's pushing and pulling and tugging."

Former Viking editor Amanda Vaill remembered meeting Jackie in March 1977. "Certainly by the time I got there . . . she'd been there for a year, two years. . . . She was really part of the group, and it was very collegial, and she was pretty well integrated into the fabric, and she came to editorial meetings. That's where I met her the first time. In fact, my very first editorial meeting, I was early because I was the new girl and I was gonna be prompt, and she and I were the first people into this dimly lit conference room. The whole place looked just like *Mad Men* offices. It was on Madison Avenue and there were a couple of ad agencies just below us.

"And Jackie materialized out of the gloom in this conference room, and I looked at her and said, Oh my God, there she is—it's her! And I had never been next to anyone so famous in such a small space, and with it being only her and me. . . . I said, 'Hello, I'm Amanda Vaill. I'm the new editor.' And she reaches out her hand and says, 'Ohhh, hi! I'm Jackie Onassis.'

"There was something so touching about her manner; she had beautiful manners. Everybody knew that. It was kind of a confiding quality of her voice. Her lack of—*of course, you know who I am-ness.* . . . She knew what was appropriate in any given circumstance, and it didn't have to do with her, it was about the other person."

Vaill was struck by Jackie's aplomb and fashion sense in the office. "She had such beautiful style. She was always exquisitely dressed. Very glamorous working girl. Cashmere trousers and silk shirts and beautiful pumps. A gorgeous tweed jacket, it would be Gucci or Chanel or whomever. I mean you wouldn't know except that it was so perfectly cut. She always looked impeccable and not showy. She lent a style to the whole place and everybody kind of tried to emulate her in their own way. It was like we had to dress in the marked-down version.

"I think she would engage with the author at the level of the manuscript, instead of just at the level of the idea of the property, the marketing. Viking was actually a very good school for anyone who wanted to learn. You would read copies of all the correspondence that Cork Smith or Alan Williams or Elisabeth Sifton or Jackie had sent to their authors. You would see how people did their work, and how they engaged with the people they worked with. So you got this extraordinary sense of how an editor did her or his job. . . . For Jackie, I think it must have been invaluable."

Longtime friends like Tish Baldrige and George Plimpton noticed how Jackie had taken command of her life. Baldrige told *People* magazine in 1977, "She has pulled herself together lately. She's become more independent. . . . Work is good therapy for anybody." And Plimpton, who was later to work with Jackie on two books, agreed, saying, "I sense a change in her. She's very much more like the girl I first knew, who had a great sense of fun and enthusiasm. It must be an electrifying, extraordinary thing for her to be on her own—she was always somewhat diminished by the men around her."

Jackie later observed, "It has helped me to be taken seriously as an editor, for my own abilities." Jackie's old friend Peter Duchin also witnessed a change in her outlook that he attributed to progress with her career. "I think it gave her a lot of self-confidence . . . a kind of a peace within herself, because I mean it's one thing having lunch with Louis Auchincloss, but another thing to work with him. And I think that had a big meaning to her. . . . When people praised her, it wasn't just because she was Jackie Onassis or Kennedy. People praised her seriously because she'd done something constructive, and she loved that. . . . Don't forget, people on that level—well, there are very few people on that level—most of them that I've met are dying to be taken seriously. . . . Obviously as First Lady that's taken seriously enough, but I think to do something on your own the way she did, especially after the period of time with Ari, when she was cruising and out there and doing that, I think to be taken as a really good editor meant a lot to her."

Duchin explained that he and Jackie shared a certain attitude about their backgrounds. "We were really very, very close friends. She was godmother of one of my kids, and that kind of stuff. Jackie once said to me, 'You and I are both outsiders.' What she meant by that in my case was that I had been brought up by surrogate parents, the Harrimans, because my mother died when I was born, and my father died when I was thirteen. . . . But I was not really of that blueblood variety—I was half-blueblood and half-Jewish.

"And about her being an outsider, I think she meant that she had had the Newport Janet, her mother, but [Jack] Bouvier was a different sort. Hugh D. Auchincloss, who was Janet's second husband, certainly was not the real father, as it were. There was that Catholic background. And I think Jackie always felt that she wanted to be a professional woman, and that was why she became a reporter. . . . And yet she had had that society in Janet. One of the odd reasons that we were very close was that Janet was a classmate and a very great friend of my mother's at Spence. So there was that kind of society bond, and Jackie also realized that she and I both thought of it as total bullshit. She was also knowledgeable enough to know that we both sort of used it in a certain way."

There were many writers and artists like Duchin whom Jackie consorted with socially over the years, following the same instincts that led her into editing. Looking back, she explained that her decision to go into publishing was based on "the obvious reasons—I'd majored in literature, I had many friends in publishing, I love books, I've known writers all my life." While Jackie attended public events with a number of male escorts, seemingly playing the field, during 1977 she was seeing a great deal of the *New York Daily News* columnist Pete Hamill, though he was involved with Shirley MacLaine and publicly denied rumors of a romance with Jackie. Hamill's relationship with her was strained almost to the breaking point when Rupert Murdoch's *New York Post* republished disparaging articles that Hamill had written for the *Post* back when Jackie married Ari (including the line "no courtesan ever sold herself for more").

While Jackie devoted herself to various Viking projects that year, including the books that she had under way with Chase-Riboud and Eugene Kennedy, there was one project that she stayed away from, in accord with an agreement she made with Tom Guinzburg. This work was a novel entitled *Shall We Tell the President?* It was written by former British MP Jeffrey Archer, a controversial figure who was to achieve enormous commercial success as an author of pulp fiction. Later, after taking a fall in the rough-and-tumble of British politics, Archer would do two years of prison time for a perjury conviction, and yet manage to continue his literary career.

Archer's book for Viking was inspired in part by Frederick Forsyth's 1971 bestselling novel *The Day of the Jackal,* which featured an assassination attempt on Charles de Gaulle. Archer constructed a similarly fanciful storyline, set in the then uncertain future of 1983, involving a plot to assassinate a fictional American president explicitly based on Jackie's brother-in-law Ted Kennedy. In the book's published form, Kennedy's role had been reduced to a cameo—he barely appeared in the book, with most of the plot revolving around a junior FBI agent and his efforts to foil the assassination plot. Nevertheless, the premise alone was enough to raise Kennedy eyebrows and arouse ire.

There are at least two contradictory versions of this particular Jackie episode, which was a classic he-said-she-said tale that would bring Jackie into collision with the Kennedy family and her publisher employer. When Archer's book was published, in October 1977, critic John Leonard's *New York Times* review ended with a not so subtle indictment of Jackie for her implied involvement with the project. "There is a word for such a book," wrote Leonard. "The word is trash. Anybody associated with its publication should be ashamed of herself."

The critic, not one to conceal his pomposity, later told the *Times* that his attack had indeed been directed at Jackie. "Of course, I was partially referring to her. She should have objected. She could have stopped its publication if she wanted to."

Unbeknownst to Leonard, Jackie had been shielded by Guinzburg from having any direct involvement with the book. Everyone agrees that the churlish review caused all hell to break loose and set into motion a series of events that quickly led to Jackie's resignation. In a statement provided to the *Times* during the week just after the review appeared, Jackie said, as quoted by her longtime secretary, Nancy Tuckerman, "In the spring, when told of the book, I tried to separate my lives as a Viking employee and a Kennedy relative. But this fall, when it was suggested that I had something to do with acquiring the book and that I was not distressed, I felt I had to resign."

Tuckerman ("Tucky," as she was called by Jackie) was a former Vassar classmate and a friend of Jackie's since their prep school days at the Chapin

School, where they first met, and at Miss Porter's School, in Farmington, Connecticut. Jackie brought Tuckerman into the White House as her social secretary, and Tuckerman later landed a job at Doubleday, Jackie's future employer, as an assistant to the publisher. While Jackie was at Viking, Tuckerman continued to serve her part-time in a secretarial capacity, even though they were working at rival publishing houses. No one suggested there might have been a conflict of interest with these two competing houses in the picture as the Archer scenario played out with Jackie caught in the middle.

As the official gatekeeper, Tuckerman was always dignified and extremely tight-lipped. She never married and over the years devoted her life to Jackie. The former publisher of *Women's Wear Daily*, John Fairchild, told biographer Sarah Bradford (*America's Queen*) about an encounter that he had with Tucky. "One day I said to her, 'Why don't you go out and have some life? Why are you devoting your life as a slave? What is the future for you?' She said nothing." After coauthoring a book on Amy Vanderbilt's rules of etiquette in 1995, Tuckerman told *The New Yorker*, "Mrs. Onassis cherished her privacy, so I did have to reject a lot of questions." It was Tuckerman who would one day be burdened with the monumental task of organizing Jackie's funeral.

Doubleday editor Lisa Drew, who in 1976 published Jeffrey Archer's first book, *Not a Penny More, Not a Penny Less*, was also a friend of Jackie's at the time Archer's second book was acquired by Viking. A highly respected editor whose Doubleday credits included Alex Haley's *Roots*, Drew offered author Carl Sferrazza Anthony her account of the events surrounding the unseemly controversy that was to engulf Jackie. Most of the testimony about this particular interlude, which appears in Anthony's book *As We Remember Her*, including Lisa's recollections, is based on hearsay regarding events now more than thirty years past, with all who were involved putting words in Jackie's mouth.

Recalling a lunch date with Jackie and Nancy Tuckerman, Drew told Anthony, "Several days before we met, I'd heard that in the middle of February, Viking had purchased a novel which I had turned down at Doubleday, by Jeffrey Archer, called *Shall We Tell the President* [sic]. The premise was an attempted assassination of Ted Kennedy. I was appalled and told the English agent it was totally tasteless and I wouldn't have anything to do with it. With Jackie being at Viking, and their buying it—I was dumbfounded. At our lunch, I said to her offhandedly, 'How about this Jeffrey Archer book that Viking bought?' And she said, 'Who's Jeffrey Archer? I don't know anything about it. What's it about?'"

According to Drew, she explained that the book was a "political thriller" involving Ted Kennedy as a character. She decided not to pursue the subject further with Jackie, sensing it might be delicate. After the novel was published and Leonard's review appeared in the *Times,* Drew recalled, "Jackie called me at home that night and said, 'I don't know what to do, but I think I'm going to quit. Nancy said you were outraged,' and I said, 'Well, I'm quite outraged because frankly, a week or so after Viking bought the book, I mentioned this to you at lunch, and you'd never heard of it.' And she said, 'Oh, is that the book you mentioned? . . . I went to Tom Guinzburg after our lunch, and I said I just had lunch with Lisa Drew, and what is this book by some guy named Archer that's about Ted Kennedy. He said, "Don't worry about it. It's not anything you're going to have anything to do with." So, I thought, fine. I'd known Tom a long time, and I thought he was looking out for my interests with respect to this, so I paid no attention. Now, here he is on the front page of *The New York Times* saying that I knew all about exactly what happens in this book, and I didn't know about it at all!' She felt awful. About two hours later, Nancy called and said, 'She's resigning, and sending a handwritten letter to Tom Guinzburg by messenger tonight.' "

Drew's recollections and Jackie's statement related to the press became the official version of the story. Drew insisted, ". . . the truth of the matter is, she first heard about it from me—after they bought it." Yet there are several minor inaccuracies in her account, including the fact that Guinzburg was not quoted on the front page of *The New York Times*. The only article to appear on the front page was the subsequent report on Jackie's resignation. Moreover, Guinzburg never suggested in that article or any other that Jackie "knew all about exactly what happens in this book"; rather, he said that she had been apprised of the novel's subject matter but had played no part in its acquisition or editing. Drew claimed that she knew Viking "had purchased" the Archer novel, but she never explained how she knew that or if she knew when the contract was signed. She was apparently repeating gossip that she heard after she passed on the book with Archer's agent.

Like Viking, Doubleday was a family operation, owned by Nelson Doubleday Jr., who took the reins after his father and grandfather put the company on the map with trade book publishing and related ventures. Doubleday's publisher and president at the time, Samuel Vaughan, remembered hearing Jackie's point of view on the Archer affair related after Jackie resigned, at a meeting with her and Doubleday chairman John Sargent Sr. at Jackie's apartment: "Tom Guinzburg, when he approached publishing the book about [the plot to kill] Edward Kennedy that got him in trouble with her . . . lost his friends and editor thereby. Now everybody thinks because he decided to publish this book that she went along with it. He did talk to her about it, I gather. But what really got her unhappy . . .

was Tom's letting the impression get abroad that she had okayed the publication of the book, that she had more than acquiesced to it."

Jackie's interpretation of events was later added to a story by Jack Anderson and Les Witten for *The Washington Post* that ran on December 14, 1977. While the subhead declared, "Jackie Speaks," the writers stated in the article that Jackie spoke only through her unnamed "spokeswoman," presumably Tuckerman. Published two months after the resignation, this article appears to be an effort by Jackie to distance herself from Viking once and for all and further placate the Kennedy family. Jackie found herself in a position wherein she had to denounce the book and its publisher in order to maintain her delicate and guarded relationship with the family.

Anderson and Witten wrote that Guinzburg

insisted to us that he would never have purchased the novel without her explicit consent. That necessarily would have been before Feb. 13—the date Guinzburg agreed verbally to purchase rights to the thriller. But Onassis— who has remained virtually mute on the controversy—informed us through a spokesperson that the first she heard of the book was on March 2, when two luncheon companions disclosed the existence of the novel. . . . Not until then, Onassis recounts, did she ask her boss, Guinzburg, about the book. Only then did she learn that the novel portrayed the last of the Kennedy brothers as an assassin's target. His comment to her, she remembered, was "we have a great story." Onassis "categorically" denies approving the book or that Guinzburg even asked for her approval. She described his claim of a "generous and understanding response" as simply untrue.

The Kennedy clan had given Jackie plenty of flak, more than enough reason for her to feel compelled to repudiate the book and discredit Guinzburg. Still, some niggling questions persist. Did Jackie ever actually express any strong disapproval of the book? How would her lunch companions have known whether or not Guinzburg had approached Jackie in some fashion before the decision to publish was made? Would Jackie have remembered the details of such a noneventful meeting in which Guinzburg assured her that she was to play no role with the book?

It may well be that Jackie acquiesced to the book's publication in an initial conversation with her boss without even wanting to know the details, not even giving the initial exchange with Guinzburg enough heed to recall the name of the author at her subsequent lunch with Drew and Tuckerman. Nevertheless, the allegation was that Guinzburg had essentially published the book behind Jackie's back. His story remained consistent through the years insisting that he consulted with Jackie about the book before he agreed to the deal. Former Viking insiders all agreed that Guinzburg adored Jackie, and found it hard to believe that he would have risked her displeasure over such a questionable book.

Guinzburg recounted for me the chain of events that began early in 1977. "Jeffrey Archer's agent was a woman named Debbie Owen. She was married to David Owen. He was an up-and-coming British leader [Owen founded the Social Democratic Party and was foreign secretary from 1977 to 1979], and Debbie was the daughter of Kyrill Schabert, who ran Pantheon. . . . She offered me the manuscript while I was visiting London. We were friends. She said, 'We have a big offer, but I'd like you to read it.' So I read it in the next couple days and I called Debbie and said, 'Well, it's a pretty good yarn, but there are some problems.' She said, 'Yeah, I know, all that Kennedy stuff. . . .' There was all this early scenery in the book around Hickory Hill and the Kennedys playing touch football. I said, 'For openers all of that would have to come out.' She said, 'I don't see any problem with that. Why don't you meet Jeffrey and see how you get along.'

"Jeffrey took me on a wonderful evening's expedition up the Thames River to some swell little restaurant, and we got along fine. We talked about the book. I said that I'd be delighted to publish it for him *if*—as he would have to understand—if I could clear the whole business with Mrs. Onassis. He said, 'I understand,' but I didn't think he really did understand, so I went back to Debbie Owen and said, 'Look, I'm going home Sunday, and Jackie takes Mondays off. I'll see her Tuesday morning in the office and I'll talk to her about this. If it can work, I'll call you at home that evening and we'll go from there.' We weren't going to fight about the money. It was a couple hundred thousand dollars, and that was a lot then. She told me that she already had an offer from Random House. That's exactly what happened, and after I returned to New York, I went into Jackie's office and I closed the door."

In our exchanges, Guinzburg stood by the version of the conversation with Jackie that he gave to Jeffrey Archer's biographer, Michael Crick, and repeated it to me almost verbatim, as follows: "I said, 'I've got a problem with a manuscript,' 'How?' she asked. 'It's a caper-thriller novel by an Englishman named Jeffrey Archer.' She said, 'Tell me about it.' I said, 'Like many of these things, this has a gimmick—an assassination plot.'"

Jackie asked him, "What are you getting at, Tom?" Guinzburg told her, "In this case it's Ted Kennedy, and the year's 1983." Remembering that exchange, Guinzburg said, "It was just as though I hit her; she winced. She muttered something about, 'Won't they ever stop?' And I didn't say anything. Then Jackie visibly collected herself, and said, 'Is it really a pretty good book?' I said, 'It could be, if he does some rewrites. There's a lot of extraneous Kennedy stuff and we can move it out, but it depends on that situation; it really does.' She thought again for a few more seconds. 'Will somebody else take this if we don't?' I said, 'Oh, sure they will, but that shouldn't be a consideration for you.' "

Guinzburg continued his account, saying, "Then she said something really very sweet: 'I know how many books you've turned down, because you are always so protective of me and of the president, and I know that you've been absolutely terrific. Maybe the time has come when you ought to make a little money.' . . . Then she paused again and said, 'I wouldn't have to have anything to do with editing or publishing or whatever?' I told her, 'Of course not. Once you and I have finished this conversation, we don't have to discuss this book again, and you don't have to have anything to do with it.' "

According to Guinzburg, "That was the end of the conversation. I called Debbie that evening in London and repeated it to her. Debbie said, 'Let's go ahead then.' "

For an oral history Guinzburg contributed to Columbia University's Butler Library in 1980 (in deference to Jackie's feelings, made available for research and publication only after her death), he recalled telling Jeffrey Archer at their dinner meeting in England, "People are going to say that you are going to stimulate some crazy guy to go out and shoot Ted Kennedy, and that's the worst of it, that's the basest, meanest aspect of this whole situation . . . and you are describing Ted Kennedy as being fat, and you are describing Teddy as having had too much to drink and so forth, and all that has to come out, because that's just cheap and you don't need it. . . . But that's not going to satisfy the people who will not like you for using him as a target of an assassination." According to Guinzburg, Archer told him, "I would certainly agree to tone it down so that there's nothing in there that is injurious to the family or to Ted himself."

Archer worked with Cork Smith on the book, who had him cut much of the offensive Kennedy material. Smith, courteous and soft-spoken, had edited Robertson Davies, Muriel Spark, and Thomas Keneally, but he was also adept with more commercial fiction. As he put it, "I have a good nose for vanguard fiction, I handle all the sports books, and I have a golden touch with commercial crap."

Confirming Guinzburg's account of their exchanges about the Archer book, Deborah Owen told me, "Plenty of crappier books have been published. This was a good, readable, page-turning book. . . . And I had said to Tom, 'Look, I don't want you to take this book unless Cork's prepared to edit it,' because I knew that no one would be better than Cork in New York—no one. He was the king, in my eyes.

"And God knows what was going through Tom's mind—but I'm darn sure between the two of them they would *not*—repeat, *not*—have kept it from Jackie until after the deal was done. There's no way he would not have thought of her first. I think Jackie could have been creative with her version of the story after the event. I really do, and I think Tom, because of his deep affection for Jackie, would have been, if anything, overly protective of her. And I would bet my last dime on Tom's version.

"Where we all might have been naive—and I mean *all* of us, and very much me included—is that we didn't understand that this was ripe pickings for newspapers because anything with Jackie's name in it sold. So they blew up something . . . after the John Leonard review. . . . And we were maybe naive not to have understood that this might happen, and therefore, even if she had absolutely nothing to do with this book, she still would be linked to it by the very fact of her being an editor at Viking. Jackie had a heck of a burden on her. The press really went for her."

As Jackie's brother-in-law (married to Jean Kennedy) and the Kennedy family's point man on such issues, Stephen Smith told *The Boston Globe* that he had informed Guinzburg the book was an "act of venal commerce and in bad taste." Guinzburg confirmed to me that Smith, whom Tom had known over the years, had contacted him and expressed that opinion, but he said that Smith did not respond until after the book's publication and the Leonard review. For Jackie's part, she had months before the book's publication to voice her strong disapproval of the book's publication, but had not done so. Meanwhile, Guinzburg was desperate to speak with Jackie, but other than one brief telephone conversation during which he pleaded with her to meet, he was put off from further contact by Nancy Tuckerman. Recalling the receipt of Jackie's letter of resignation, Guinzburg said, "I tried to call her at home after I got it, and she would not take the call."

Guinzburg then told *The New York Times,* "After being friends for more than half our lives, I more than ever deeply regret Mrs. Onassis's decision to resign from Viking Press without a personal discussion of the incident which resulted in her decision. . . . My own affection for the Kennedy family and the extremely effective and valued contribution that Mrs. Onassis has made to Viking over the past two years would obviously have been an overriding factor in the final decision to publish any particular book which might cause her further anguish."

Deborah Owen has no recollection of Lisa Drew communicating her high-minded objections to the book, but suggested, "We were asking for more than they [Doubleday] wanted to pay, so maybe she rejected [the book based on] the amount of money that I was asking for."

Ten years before Cork Smith passed away in 2004, he told Michael Crick about his take on Archer's book, saying, "I thought it was a viable commercial novel that needed work. But the question was: 'How will this sit with Jackie Onassis?' Guinzburg said he'd take care of that."

Guinzburg told members of his staff that he had discussed the book with Jackie as a courtesy before agreeing to its publication. Amanda Vaill had a meeting with him in his office just after he had agreed to purchase the Archer novel. Now an acclaimed nonfiction author, Vaill told me, "When I was interviewed by Tom at Viking in February of '77, before I was hired, he told me about this book called *Shall We Tell the President?* that's coming up, and he explains that he has spoken to Jackie about it and asked if it was okay if he published the book. And he told me that she'd said, 'I don't want to know anything about it. Don't ask me—you wouldn't ask anybody else here if it's okay to publish this book or any book. If you wanted to do it, you would just go ahead and publish it. So don't treat me any differently than you would treat anybody else. I don't want to know anything more about it than what you've just told me.' And that's what he told me in February before there was any reason for this to matter."

Not only was Jackie informed about the subject of the novel, at least in general terms by both Guinzburg and Drew, but prior to publication, copies of the book were sent to Ted Kennedy (whose office reported to the *Times* that he had "flipped through the book") and to Stephen Smith, with whom Jackie had a cordial relationship. It was Smith who communicated the family's outrage to Jackie after the book came out, and he would have put her on the defensive as far as the role she had played in its publication.

Of course, memory can be a traitor, especially with emotionally charged events in the distant past. Jackie suggested much later, in the last interview of her life (with *Publishers Weekly,* in 1993), that she had never been consulted by Guinzburg about the Archer novel. As she was not specifically quoted on the subject but paraphrased, it may be that she was misunderstood during the interview. Whatever she may have said, it was clear that for the rest of her life Jackie was distressed by the memory of her ungraceful exit from Viking.

Becky Singleton told me, "On the morning that Jackie left the firm, Tom called me into his office and gave me a brief description of what had transpired. . . . He seemed genuinely stunned, which was understandable. In the version of events that those who spoke for Jackie were promoting as fact, Tom had supposedly acted with callous indifference, which went completely against the grain of the way he had actually treated Jackie for the past two years. The outside world couldn't possibly know how often Tom had taken action that was designed to protect her best interests—but Jackie knew. She and Tom had a history. She knew that he had consistently made a special effort to shield her from the media and to resolve circumstances that might have caused her professional embarrassment. If she'd been with the firm for only a few weeks, her reaction would have been easier to understand. But she had been at Viking for nearly two years. In many ways, what was now being said and what was happening—it just didn't make sense."

Ever since the publication of William Manchester's book about the JFK assassination, Jackie had been under siege in various ways related to her Kennedy past. During 1977, congressional hearings reviewing the Warren Commission findings were under way, and Judith Exner's memoir recalling her illicit affair with Jack Kennedy was published that same year by Grove Press. Two unauthorized biographies of Jackie (by Kitty Kelley and Stephen Birmingham) were to be published the following year. Guinzburg had demonstrated that he possessed the sensitivity and ethical compass to steer Viking away from any involvement with books that he knew would be potentially embarrassing for Jackie.

Becky Singleton was troubled by the circumstances under which Jackie tendered her resignation, without saying good-bye to her colleagues. "The unexpected lack of civility in her departure had shaken me to the point that I was second-guessing a lot of my previous assumptions about our relationship. . . . At the time, I interpreted the breach of etiquette as evidence of a mass indictment that suggested little had been valued during her time at Viking and much was now disdained. If I had been older and more seasoned in the ways of the world, I might have considered the possibility that she simply felt embarrassed about the way things were being done. In hindsight, this does make sense. I wish I'd thought of that at the time.

"The blow that may have struck hardest at Tom was the fact that she chose to resign through her social secretary. She must have known that to many this deliberate slap would appear to be an act of justified retaliation made in response to reprehensible conduct on his part. So, in many ways—in what was being said and how things were being done—Jackie's exit from Viking wasn't a traditional parting of the ways. It was more like a blow-torch ending to a personal relationship, the kind when one person not only stalks out, but also rips up the rugs and carts off the furniture."

Singleton also suggested that Jackie may have been misled. "Jackie wasn't subservient, but she often chose to be deferential. . . . What I'm trying to say is that she had a yielding nature. Friends like Nancy Tuckerman and Lisa Drew would certainly have been able to [take advantage of] this." Singleton added, "I'm convinced that Jackie's friends, Nancy and Lisa, played a pivotal role in her departure."

Regarding the allegation that he had betrayed Jackie, Guinzburg said, "I was really upset that my friends just assumed that for some reason I would have done something like that, and they were my good friends.

They were the George Plimptons. Well, this is Jackie Onassis. It was her word against mine, and it was just as much my fault. I was pretty staunch for a while that morning with all these reporters calling, but *The Boston Globe* was the one who got me . . ."

The *Globe,* publishing in the heart of the Kennedy family homeland, left out Guinzburg's explanation that Jackie had not been in any way involved with the book's acquisition or publication, though the article did quote the publisher as saying when he first informed Jackie about the book that she "didn't indicate any distress or anger." That quote was enough to put the Kennedys on the warpath. Jackie's relationship with the family had been strained ever since her marriage to Onassis. Intent on maintaining her relationship with Ted and the family, Jackie apparently caved in to that pressure with her blanket denial that she had been consulted.

In his defense, Guinzburg said, "Do you really think I would have taken the chance of losing Jackie's friendship and her participation at Viking, which was of inestimable value . . . over one silly book? I mean, we can always find another book. Any publisher can."

Reminded of the Archer novel and the furor it caused, former Viking editor Barbara Burn said it was "a horrible book, but it was John Leonard that caused the whole problem with his review, which was clearly a blow at Jackie. And Tom made a fatal mistake, which was that he chose to speak for her to the press. Jackie was up in Hyannis Port at that point, and they couldn't reach her, so he told the press, well, this is how she felt about it. And he should never have done that. That's really the crux of it."

Elisabeth Sifton agreed that it was a deplorable situation and might have been avoided. Archer's novel "would have been published no matter what . . . Tom wanted to publish Archer and keep Jackie. He did the correct, open, transparent, straightforward thing. She agreed with it. But both of them had neglected to take into consideration the wrath of the Kennedys and the way the press would distort it."

As head of publicity and public relations, Rich Barber was on the front lines when the flood of press inquiries hit Viking. Barber told me, "I was sort of deputized to make sure that copies of the book went out to Steve Smith and Teddy Kennedy's office way ahead of publication. In hindsight it's always twenty-twenty on these things, but nothing really blew open until the John Leonard review. That was one of those bad days where I left my office to sit in Tom's assistant's chair all day answering the phone. Tom's point of view was, and it was relatively simple, that this is going to be published, it's going to be a good-selling book; but at least if we do it, we can control how it's presented. The Kennedys had had plenty of time to raise the Jolly Roger or whatever, and had not done so. . . . And I think actually Nancy Tuckerman went ballistic when she saw the John Leonard review. And I think that colored everything that happened thereafter."

Archer's book received mixed reviews around the country, and the publicity about Jackie's role spurred sales to some extent, although the book spent only one week on the *Times* bestseller list. Archer himself was on a book tour in the United States when the novel was published and was distraught over Jackie's reaction, offering to return to New York from the West Coast to try to help defuse the situation with her. He told me his sympathies were with Tom. "I am unable to believe that Tom would have purchased the book in the first place if he thought it would offend the Kennedy family. That never added up. That's my first point. My second point is you're dealing with such an honorable man and such a fine man in Tom that when the outburst came it was a total surprise to me. I mean, I was shocked. I thought, how can this possibly happen when they're close friends?"

Archer recalled that within a year after Jackie's resignation, Guinzburg was fired from his position as head of Viking Penguin. "Here is a much better story for you of what happened because of Jackie Onassis's decision [to quit]. Tom had sold Viking to Penguin at the time, before my next book was just being presented to Tom. With my admiration for him, and my thanks when I was in financial trouble, I offered him my next book, *Cain and Abel*, for $400,000, which he jumped at. When he was, whatever word you want to use—sacked, removed, thrown out (and by the way, he was treated disgracefully by Penguin)—they behaved like hooligans."

In fact, Guinzburg was relieved of his duties unceremoniously by the Pearson group just before a scheduled board meeting in New York, in September 1978. He was at home convalescing from a recurrent health problem (a blood clot in his leg) when he received the news. He was devastated. Thirty Viking employees gathered in his bedroom to hear the news and express their sympathies. Guinzburg told publishing veteran and former Book-of-the-Month Club executive Al Silverman, "I remember telling the housekeeper, 'Get out every bottle of booze we have, because it's going to be a long day.'"

Jackie did not entirely forget her Viking friends, but the episode had surely been traumatic, and she kept her distance from Guinzburg and her former colleagues in the aftermath. She was soon making plans to land on her feet by changing houses, with encouragement from Tuckerman and Drew. Guinzburg remembered trying to contact her a few months after she left, hoping for some acknowledgment, if not a reconciliation. "I let it go. I thought, let it die down, and then in December I was trying to think of something to do around Christmastime. I knew I was going to write her a letter, and I was planning on sending her something that would have some kind of meaning. And I happened to be in Sherry-Lehmann's . . . the liquor store—and I saw some magnums of something called Perrier-Jouët Champagne, and since Jackie had pretty much singlehandedly started the Perrier craze around New York, I thought, aha, that's clever, Tom. . . .

"First I went home and wrote her the letter . . . and brought it back, and put it inside one of those gift boxes, and they sent it up to her apartment—this was mid-December—and I didn't hear anything, and I thought, well, that's that. Finally, just after New Year's I got one of those Jackie envelopes—you can tell them, with their distinctive handwriting."

Jackie's note offered only a terse thank-you and wished him a happy New Year. It was signed, "Sincerely." Tom suggested it was "a sad way to end that up."

Becky Singleton also made an effort to reach Jackie after her departure. "A year or so after Jackie left the firm, I received the first of several calls from supposedly legitimate authors who were writing supposedly reputable books about her. One particular person, whose name I can't recall, obviously was looking for dirt. I told him that I never cooperated with a journalist and never would, which pretty much ended the conversation. Then I called Nancy Tuckerman because I'd always done this when I worked for Jackie, when something like this came up. Wow, did I get a frigid reception! She curtly acknowledged my message, then practically hung up on me. At the time, I took this as another gesture that said, 'We want nothing to do with you.' Now I wonder if Nancy was simply acting on her own."

In 1990, Studio Books wunderkind Bryan Holme died, and Rich Barber recalled Jackie paying her respects. "I remember sitting with her when she came to his funeral at that Episcopal church called the Little Church Around the Corner—where is it, Twenty-ninth Street?—and she came, and she was feeling kind of lost, and there was a little gang of Vikings sitting there. And I went over and got her to join up with us. It was Cork Smith, Barbara Burn, and a whole bunch of people. Jackie had arrived and literally was looking quite forlorn. Bryan was somebody who was very special to her."

Jackie and Tom Guinzburg continued to run into each other because their social circles overlapped. Within a month of her resignation, *The New York Times* reported on an exhibition at the Wildenstein Gallery, a charity to support books and an event that attracted New York's elite. But after the gallery opening, Jackie and Guinzburg attended separate dinners, undoubtedly reflecting Jackie's intention to avoid him. According to the *Times,* "John Sargent, president of Doubleday, gave his dinner jointly with Jacqueline Onassis, who recently resigned from the rival Viking Press. They invited the Orin Lehmans, the senior John Loebs . . . the historian Brendan

Gill, the Louis Auchinclosses, Ahmet and Mica Ertegen, Cheray Duchin and Ted Sorensen. Peter and Ellen Paine (she is president of the library's council) invited the Douglas Dillons, Enid Haupt, and Thomas Guinzburg, Mrs. Onassis' former boss, to their dinner party."

John Sargent Sr. and Jackie would soon become a publishing item, and she was to be his prize acquisition at Doubleday.

The October 24, 1977, issue of *Time* reported that Jackie was now unemployed, with a headline that read, "Situation Wanted, References Available." The following year she would join Nancy Tuckerman and Lisa Drew at Doubleday as an associate editor, working three days a week with a yearly salary of approximately $20,000, almost double her salary at Viking. Drew remembered meeting Jackie for another lunch date and encouraging her to make the move. "We talked about Doubleday. She gently raised the question about working there. I said it would be a safe haven. Nancy was there, and she had known John Sargent, the CEO. She felt there were enough people there to protect her, that it was safe to risk exposure one more time. I asked her later why it took her a few months to decide. She said, 'I just really wanted to be careful. I'd made some mistakes in my life by reacting too quickly, and I really wanted to be sure I was doing the right thing.'"

Sam Vaughan remembered meeting with Jackie and John Sargent Sr. to discuss her coming to Doubleday. "John Sargent was the chairman of the company, and I went to call on her with him. It was his idea and based on his friendship with her after she left Viking to see whether she might like to find a position with us. Everybody assumed that it was all Sargent's doing, and I couldn't give you any percentages, but I can assure you that both Nelson and John were arm in arm on this. John and I went up there one afternoon to her apartment on Fifth Avenue, and we had an amiable talk. If fact, it was quite a productive talk because we sort of got to a lot of little details that were better sorted out before she decided than afterwards. Nancy Tuckerman was in the picture all along, and was cooperative, and I think she was in pretty good shape herself at Doubleday."

Jackie reported to work February 13, 1978, at the company's offices at 245 Park Avenue, just a few blocks from Grand Central Terminal, which she had been crusading to preserve as a landmark and architectural treasure—a successful campaign that culminated with her leading a delegation to Washington, D.C., on the famous *Landmark Express* train in April of that year. At her new publishing house, she again worked hard at being a team player with her colleagues, eventually blending seamlessly, if not quite invisibly, into her new workplace. She was given a modest windowless office, and told John Sargent, "Oh, that's all right, John. I've got lots of windows in my home." She later told author Eugene Kennedy, "Like everybody else, I have to work my way up to an office with a window."

Commenting on Jackie's initiation at Doubleday, John Sargent Sr. once said, "At first there was some resentment—a feeling that perhaps Jackie wasn't all that serious. She was not full-time, and she had everything in the world, so naturally there was that perception among the troops that this was just a diversion for her. But she was so relaxed and so unaffected—not at all the wildly extravagant, ultraglamorous figure she was made out to be—that her coworkers couldn't help but be charmed."

Former copy editor Glenn Rounds said, "We had a wonderful woman called Rose who was in charge of the canteen for a number of years. When Jackie walked in for the first time, of course there was a lot of conversation, and then it was suddenly dead silence. Rose was a very matter-of-fact, down-to-earth kind of person, and she said, 'Well, what will you have, Jackie?' So that broke the ice."

Former editor in chief of Anchor Books and now literary agent Loretta Barrett also recalled Jackie's entry at Doubleday. "I was there when Jackie arrived. I remember going in to her office one day, trying to get in touch with someone, very well known. I was so embarrassed, and she said, 'Well, let's look in the phone book.' And we found this person, and I was thinking Jackie Onassis had this Rolodex of everybody in the world who could breathe and talk. She pulls out a telephone book! I couldn't believe it."

With her office as a shelter a few days a week, Jackie settled into a routine that ensured her a modicum of privacy behind the continual barrage of publicity. The media was often unreliable in reporting on Jackie's activities. NBC News announced early in 1979 that she had boarded a plane for Australia to pursue negotiations with the Earl of Snowden, the royal photographer who had recently divorced Princess Margaret, for a tell-all memoir that promised to "blow the lid off the British royal family." Jackie was able to laugh off the patently false story, as it was revealed that she was in reality vacationing in Jamaica with John Jr. at the time. The press would also report that after failing to interest Princess Diana in writing a memoir, Jackie had offered a $2 million advance to Camilla Parker Bowles for a royal tell-all. But according to her Doubleday colleagues, while Diana may have been pursued with a letter of interest, the offer to Bowles never happened and she was never considered by Jackie for a book.

The move from Viking to Doubleday was a major change in scale and corporate culture for Jackie, with a marked shift in publishing company policies. According to Tom Guinzburg, "It was like going from a PT boat to a battleship." Viking had two hundred employees, while Doubleday was one of the largest and most successful houses, employing three times that many, with bookstores and book clubs under its umbrella, though its trade division had been suffering, as was the case at many other houses. Doubleday's books were viewed as schlocky in terms of the physical layout—cover, paper, typography, etc—as their printing operation cut corners. Jackie was going to face a serious challenge as she demanded the highest production values for her books.

Guinzburg recounted a bittersweet reunion with Jackie several years later under the auspices of her new house, where he would be retained as a consultant. "Jackie went to Doubleday, which was the obvious thing for her to do because she was a good close friend of John Sargent's in those days, and he was running Doubleday. And John Sargent was a good friend of mine; we'd been friends forever, since we were kids. So when they later suggested that maybe I would come over there to Doubleday . . . I said, 'I can't come over there unless Jackie thinks that there won't be a problem.' She readily consented, and we did see each other. We didn't go out anymore, we didn't spend intimate time together—that part was finished. But it was inevitable that I would see her; we had lots of friends in common, and there'd be dinners and I would run into her at various functions."

John Sargent was a frequent escort of Jackie's, and there were rumors of a romantic affair. His only son, John Sargent Jr., who also went to work at Doubleday and is now the head of Macmillan, told me, "They were friends. My dad will no doubt take it to the grave with him; if they were anything more than friends, none of us ever knew it. He was a very popular guy in those years. He dated tons of women, and he was always on the list of 'New York's Top Ten Bachelors,' and this, that, and the other. We could never figure out what exactly the Jackie relationship was. But I believe she was simply a friend and confidante; Dad hired her at a moment that that was important for her."

Despite her friends and welcome entrée at Doubleday, Jackie did not make an easy transition to her new corporate family. Former Doubleday VP and executive editor Patrick Filley recalled, "In the early months, they came close to stifling her enthusiasm." Carolyn Blakemore, one of Jackie's early editorial colleagues, told me, "When she came in, I outranked her. I had the corner office and she had one next to me. I think Jackie was hired by higher-ups without necessarily consulting the people whose budget would be affected. I think it was John Sargent probably, and Nelson. Of course, Patrick Filley was of the social class of all those people and would have had a different sort of edge on it than maybe some of the rest of us did. But I remember once Jackie said to me, 'I suppose I'll have to do what they want me to do for that'—for some function. And I said, 'Absolutely not. Don't do anything you don't want to do.' "

There was one routine task Jackie would have to do. In order to win approval for acquiring a book for the house, she now had to face weekly meetings with an editorial and marketing committee. This was a relatively new modus operandi in the publishing world, with its newly emerging megaconglomerates. This was to be an increasingly adverse environment for Jackie. Former Doubleday executive and senior editor Betty Prashker described these changes in publishing for Al Silverman, who chronicled the period in his book *The Time of Their Lives*. "In the beginning, in the forties and fifties, the editor was at the top of the pyramid, supported by the administration, the art department, the sales department, the promotion department. There was basically no business department. . . . But gradually over the years that pyramid ended, and the editors wound up at the bottom."

Interviewed by Silverman for his book, Lisa Drew described the early 1970s at Doubleday before Jackie's arrival. "It was slow going for women then. Doubleday was not prone to promoting women into editorial jobs. . . . There were only three women who preceded me as editors. . . . You got to a certain level and then you left. But of course, they hired tons of men out of college, and made them editorial assistants, then six months later, made them editors. A year or two later they were gone, because they didn't know how to be editors. So when all of that got sorted out around 1970, give or take a year or two—when the whole industry began to change—women, as well as men, began coming in at the assistant level."

Jackie's position as a part-time associate was exactly that kind of entry-level position, but she had some female predecessors, such as Lisa Drew, Betty Prashker, and Kate Medina, who had worked their way up the editorial ladder and inspired others to follow their footsteps. They had cracked the publishing house glass ceiling with their talent and tenacity. The men in the house sometimes referred somewhat derisively to those distinguished female editors as "the brides of Doubleday." Those editorial "brides" would serve as mentors and role models for Jackie as she struggled to find her way. She worked closely with both Prashker and Drew. Nancy Stauffer, who headed the subsidiary rights division at Doubleday during the 1980s before becoming a literary agent, took umbrage at the expression, saying, "'Brides of Doubleday' was obviously pejorative and not flattering to those women, and unfairly so. They were very bright, capable, accomplished women."

Harriet Rubin, who would later become one of Jackie's editorial colleagues, described her impact on the company, "Her becoming an editor was a tremendous vindication of the struggling book business. I think she regarded books as a form of magic. Temples are built upon scrolls and sacred texts, and she was going to produce modern magic formulas for opening people's minds, for revealing hidden wisdom." Rubin included Jackie as "one of the Brides of Doubleday," noting that "they shaped the cultural conversation through the books they edited. Editor is a formidable stealth position: An editor can launch twenty books a year into the culture, a writer maybe one every few years. Bloggers need reminding that books change lives and societies. . . . I think that Jackie found she could have a conversation with the elite or leadership class, and sometimes the rest of us, through her books.

"What I most remember is how she would operate in weekly editorial meetings. She attended maybe once a month. When her turn came to present her ideas, she trilled about projects that would have gotten anyone else fired for being ridiculously uncommercial: a collected Pushkin, an American Pleiade, an illustrated children's book based on a tale in Vasari of Leonardo crafting artificial insects. She lost these battles."

Describing the weekly editorial meetings, another former Doubleday editor, James Fitzgerald, told me, "Jackie didn't have a billion projects lying around. But as an editor she was one of us. We had these kind of *Gong Show* publishing boards that you had to go to. And there would be a line of people up on a dais, and sometimes Nelson would come in, and other people who were way upstairs and you didn't even know who they were. And you'd present books, and you'd have to get all these forms together—I mean it was a pain in the ass, you know—all these financial forms, and then circulate them, before we had e-mail and all that. And Jackie would come down and complain about that, as we all did. But she would go into those things and she'd get shut down and cut down on some projects. She was just like the rest of us. There was total democracy on that floor."

The editorial process may have been democratic, but Doubleday was very much a boys' club, and in those days, there was a lot of carousing and partying under the regime of Nelson Doubleday. Fitzgerald said, "That was an interesting crew, boy, I tell ya. Ever go to Tuckerman's house for a drink? Oh. You hit the long ball there, boy. But everyone at Doubleday did. It just went with the territory. It was a very exciting place because everyone worked very hard and everyone played very hard."

Former Doubleday editor Les Pockell said, "Doubleday was a little time warp kind of thing. Women were kept down, and the men ran every major department. If you look at most major book publishers today, women run most of the major departments. In those days, even the publicity, and rights, and everything was run by the men, and then they basically had their assistants whom they treated like secretaries. But imagine, someone like Jackie Onassis was like a queen. She was a special, special case. In most cases the women editors were . . . tolerated, but they weren't really taken that seriously. But Jackie was taken seriously because of who she was more than anything else obviously."

Explaining the challenges that Jackie faced having to adjust to her new work environment, Loretta Barrett said, "It was a very difficult time at Doubleday. There were a lot of incompetent people in charge, so, forgive me, a lot of us almost left. It was a very difficult time in that company with people that eventually were all fired. So it wasn't just the system, believe me. It was more than that. I didn't know Jackie terribly well at this point. I knew her only professionally, but I was very fond of her. I'm one of twenty-nine first cousins, and so I understand the Kennedy family, and I know a lot of them, the kids, so sometimes our conversation was very tied to that. People think of Jackie as a super-WASP, but there was an ethnic side to her which I got because of my background. She was Catholic, and there was an enormous prejudice against Catholics during that period. Vassar wasn't terribly welcoming, she told me.

"But one thing she said which was very interesting, back to the Doubleday situation. She had never known women who were bosses before. She was speaking of Lisa Drew and Betty Prashker. . . . I can't remember the structure, but she reported to Lisa and Betty. And she said it was the first time in her life she had ever worked with women who were bosses, and how wonderful it was. Whatever year this was, she had gone to see the movie *9 to 5*. Her daughter had told her to go see it when that film came out [1980]. And we were laughing about the movie; but she said she had never known women in professional positions, or worked for women. . . . I remember in that movie, they tied the guy up and kept him prisoner. Believe me, we could have done that with some of the guys at Doubleday and been very happy.

"There might have been frustrations at Doubleday, but it was with some of the management, whom I had enormous frustrations with. And it was a period when there were guys that were making one decision after another that were bizarre. Jackie was a very savvy woman, believe me. And she knew who the winners were and who weren't. I'm not talking about John Sargent, who seemed to be a real gentleman. I'm not even talking about Nelson, who was my first boss and was wonderful to me. There were a lot of drinking problems in that whole company. But they weren't the problem. It was down below, as the company got bigger and bigger.

"When I first came, Nelson was head of the publishing division. Then he moved up and John Sargent [Sr.] moved up. Remember, they owned the book clubs. They owned television, they owned radio, they owned the Mets. So those guys were not involved in the daily operation of the publishing division, and it was turned over to people like Patrick Filley, and on and on. . . . So no, they weren't the problem. They were the problem only in the sense that they became absentee landlords; there wasn't enough oversight."

Doubleday's art director, the affable, urbane Alex Gotfryd (who designed my first book and has since passed away), told biographer Christopher Anderson (*Jackie After Jack*), "Some people thought she was out of her depth at the beginning, but she was really just shy." Former editor in chief Sandy Richardson said that when Jackie first went into editorial meetings, "She turned to the person next to her and in that famous little-girl whisper asked what she was supposed to do." According to a former Doubleday editor who spoke off the record, it was Sandy Richardson who encouraged a policy of total confidentiality with employees who had exchanges with Jackie, what amounted to a vow of silence. Sandy's widow, Sally Richardson, also worked at Doubleday for five years during her early editing career. Now publisher of St. Martin's Press—which is part of the Macmillan Holtzbrinck group under John Sargent Jr.—Sally shared her impressions of Jackie from that era. "I remember Sandy and John Sargent [Sr.] stepping in and attracting her, and I think John Sargent was a huge motivator for her to go to Doubleday. He was a great, elegant man. I was a kid when I worked there, and he was the president and very kind and very big-minded, the world at his fingertips and he loved every inch of it. And he tried to share that kind of love. He was a larger-than-life guy, the kind you seldom see anymore. He had the power and he had money so he didn't have to be mingy about anything. As time goes by, Jackie's is a nostalgic, bygone era story for many reasons. Of course, her death and unique situation, but, I mean, just look at the way the book world has changed."

Loretta Barrett also noted how the business of publishing was moving in the direction of the corporate bottom line, not only at Doubleday. "My way of looking at it, all of publishing changed. When I first came to Doubleday it was the biggest house in the United States and was extremely commercial. We were doing *Airport* and *Wheels* and *Roots* and things like that. But all these companies were privately owned, and the philosophy was you took that money and you could gamble on other books. And what shifted in publishing was that instead of doing an overall profit-loss–style list, they did it on every title. It wasn't just Doubleday; it was a shift in the industry. . . . It was a philosophical shift and a business shift, and the accountants took over. Everything moved into marketing and sales, and part of that was the rise of the [bookstore] chains."

Barbara Burn noted, "That was the transition. It was a little bit after Jackie left Viking, I think, that it became more important to get Michael Jackson's book written by anybody than it was to do really high-quality books, and I think that was always a disappointment to her. Publishing started being increasingly difficult, and now it's just even more difficult, which is really a shame."

Observing that "publishing is often an extremely negative culture," Daniel Menaker, former executive editor in chief at Random House and *New Yorker* fiction editor, writing for the *Barnes & Noble Review*, described how the role of the editor was changing, a reality with which Jackie would have to reckon in the future: "The sheer book-length nature of books combined with the seemingly inexorable reductions in editorial staffs and the number of submissions most editors receive, to say nothing of the welter of noneditorial tasks that most editors have to perform, including holding the hands of intensely self-absorbed and insecure writers, fielding frequently irate calls from agents, attending endless and vapid and ritualistic meetings, having one largely empty ceremonial lunch after another, supplementing publicity efforts, writing or revising flap copy, ditto catalogue copy, refereeing jacket-design disputes, and so on—all these conditions taken together make the job of a trade book acquisitions editor these days fundamentally impossible. The shrift given to actual close and considered editing almost has to be short and is growing shorter, another very old and evergreen publishing story but truer now than ever before."

In his portrait of the world that editors inhabit, Menaker observed, "You're more likely to be 'right' if you express doubts about a proposal's or a manuscript's prospects than if you support it with enthusiasm. . . . The inevitable competitiveness among acquisitions editors will incline them to cast a cold eye on others' projects. The 'team' metaphor fits the editorial departments of publishing even less well than it fits other competitive businesses, though almost all businesses use it as a means of covering over the implacable Darwinian dynamics that keep the heart of capitalism pumping. And this is only the beginning of the negativities that editors must face. Barnes & Noble doesn't like the title. Borders doesn't like the jacket. The author's uncle Joe doesn't like the jacket. The writer doesn't like the page layout and design. Your boss tells you the flap copy for a book about a serial killer is too 'down.' The hardcover didn't sell well enough for the company to put out a paperback. . . . The *Times* isn't going to review the book. And so on."

While finding her bearings in her new position, Jackie was once again deluged with book submissions from agents, most of which she rejected. Manhattan agent Mary Yost tried to interest Jackie in a biography of Marcel Duchamp, but Jackie was unable to sell the project at Doubleday.

In a letter dated May 3, 1978, typical of many of Jackie's rejection letters, she wrote, "While I enjoy reading anything about Duchamp, I am afraid the feeling here is that the writing isn't original enough to market it very well. What a shame, because the author has obviously worked so hard and done so much research. . . . Thank you again . . . and I do hope you will send me other manuscripts in the future."

Sam Vaughan, who vaguely resembles Jimmy Stewart, was at Doubleday from 1952 until 1985. He described himself to me as "Jackie's boss," as he was third in command under Nelson Doubleday and John Sargent Sr. "The structure was that the corporation consisted of a number of divisions—five, six, seven, something like that. Where Jackie and I worked was in the publishing division. . . . She was hired to be an editor, and I was head of the division. I will say that she and other people involved in the arrangement were so cooperative and understanding that it didn't take too much getting used to. Doubleday had a history of hiring people from outside who hadn't been trained there but who got to be really an important part of the place. . . . Jackie was exceptional, it's true, but she also was part of a tradition. Doubleday was somehow an open place. It was thought to be a WASP-y place; it was thought to be not a place for Jewish people, all of which characterized that time. But we were a fairly cooperative community, and I think she sensed that going in.

"And somebody had to be in charge of everything, so they gave it to me since I'd been an editor for quite a while and I had other jobs, too. Jackie was a special case and we never pretended otherwise. Sargent and I said to her during our first afternoon visit that we were trying to work towards some ground rules: Your time is your own. You don't have to be there. We're interested in the books you're interested in. We're interested in you participating in as much of the company business as possible, but you don't have to be there at eight or nine, and you don't have to leave at five, because we knew she had other obligations in the way of family, travel, and so on.

"Doubleday was a family company, and Nelson took pains about that quality, because he was proud of his ancestors, and Jackie I think could just fit in if she wanted to. She didn't take many wrong steps or put her foot wrong in many cases. Also, there were people to surround her in a protective way, and I think that's one of the keys to understanding why it worked for as long as it worked. She didn't try to be a one-woman show. The books she chose were hers, as we say in publishing—they're really the author's but . . . in the house they were hers, and everybody respected that, and offered help. . . . Now, people like Nancy Tuckerman and especially Lisa and an assistant she had, Shaye Areheart . . . often helped right in the right spot. . . .

"Jackie would come in and talk about books she wanted if she hadn't talked about them in a meeting prior to that. She had an obligation, as I did, to tell Doubleday what we were doing. . . . We had a publishing meeting once a week where the editor who had a project ready to propose would bring up the book. . . . But the real decision, the day-to-day decisions, theoretically stopped with me. But the fact is that any book that cost a certain amount of money beyond the normal, or any book that presented a certain number of practical problems out in the world, would have to have Nelson's okay, or Sargent's.

"Now, Sargent was strictly a very light-handed executive, and in that respect a very good one. Nelson was much more, how shall I say, he felt more passionately about a few books, and didn't give a particular damn about others. Jackie seldom had to go through Nelson or to Sargent with the project itself. I saw her in the hall one day, or she saw me, and she stopped me, and she said, 'I've got this wonderful book coming in.' I can't remember what the book was, I'm not happy to say; but she said it was a lovely book, and she went on about it. I smiled throughout, and at the end of her talking, she said, 'What do you think?' And I said, 'I think it sounds wonderful. I think it will sell about three copies.' It was as if I'd thrown cold water on her book, but it was partly in fun. I don't think she pursued that one further. We always admired smaller houses like Viking, where by legend you could get acceptance for a book if you mentioned it on the stairs, or in the elevator. . . . She did have an edge, after all. But if she was interested in doing a dictionary of Transylvanian folktales, even Jackie would have to get approval. She was a full-fledged working editor in that sense also.

"We had to be careful in the sense that Doubleday was a family company and a commercial company at the same time and liked to make money, and did not like to hide beneath the more literary books published there. We published a lot of fine books, but we didn't take refuge in the snob value. . . . So you frequently got into disputes about whether this will sell, or will it sell a lot, or a little, and we did turn books down that we didn't think were suitable for the company. . . . But fortunately Jackie's tastes, though they seemed to be all carriage trade and such, were fairly broad."

Jackie later suggested that her wide-ranging literary tastes were shaped by natural curiosity and a lifelong intellectual quest. "What I like about being an editor is that it expands your knowledge and heightens your discrimination. . . . I'm fascinated by hearing artists talk of their craft. To me, a wonderful book is one that takes me on a journey into something I didn't know before." She added, "I'm drawn to books that are out of our regular experience. Books of other cultures, ancient histories."

It is not unusual, for an editor changing publishing houses, to bring certain favored authors along. After leaving Viking, Jackie brought Diana Vreeland to Doubleday for a book of photographs entitled *Allure*. Nicholas Vreeland described the collaboration of Jackie and Diana as a shared labor of love. "I watched Jackie work with my grandmother on the *Allure* book, and she would come over to my grandmother's apartment, and they would sort of put things on the floor, and just go through the maquette of it, and decide how to do it. They really did it together. . . . What's astonishing is that it was not really designed by a designer; it was designed by them."

Diana and Jackie made clear in this elegant photo collection, mostly of celebrities exhibiting some unusually tantalizing aspect of personal style, that appeal and physical charm are not the same as "allure." As conceived by the two collaborators, allure can be shockingly disjointed and ugly, or artfully composed and beautiful, but the phenomenon is usually triggered by some fascinating piece of visual detail that makes it difficult for the viewer to take his or her eyes from the image. Wry commentary by Vreeland was interspersed between high-fashion photos taken by Edward Steichen, Richard Avedon, Man Ray, Irving Penn, Bert Stern, Sir Cecil Beaton, Deborah Turbeville, and others.

From Arletty to Audrey Hepburn, from the Duchess of Windsor to the Queen Mother, from Coco Chanel to Gloria Vanderbilt to Rudolf Nureyev and Martha Graham, the famous and the elite in this book parade before the viewer's eyes in images that seem candid and spontaneous rather than formal and posed. The photos strive to capture an essence of something almost indescribable, like the aura of mystique left by the presence of each exceptionally charismatic figure. Vreeland explained the concept for the writer of the introduction, Christopher Hemphill, defining allure only in vague terms: "I think it's something around you, like perfume or a scent. It's like memory . . . it *pervades*."

The inclusion of three photos of Maria Callas in the book was surprising given the opera legend's rather scandalous affair with Ari Onassis that continued during his marriage to Jackie. But the Callas photos served to underscore Vreeland's contention that style and allure are inherent possessions, not an add-on that the well-off whimsically don and discard. One particular photo catches Maria Callas coming out of a stage door, just having been ambushed by a process server. Callas's face is distorted in a grimace of horror, like a caricature of herself, yet she carries a power and a grace that transcend the ugly situation.

Jackie's then-assistant Marcia Jacobs remembered reviewing the photographs with Jackie: "All of a sudden there was a photo of Maria Callas that kind of popped out, and she made a very funny comment, and it certainly wasn't bitchy or anything like that. She said, 'We'll keep this photo in the book. It has to be in there.' . . . I think she was just so dignified and so above all of it."

For Jackie, the book involved a number of other collaborators in-house, including art designer Alex Gotfryd and his assistant, Peter Kruzan. In addition, one of Jackie's new Doubleday friends, editor Ray Roberts, brought his considerable experience to bear on the text. Jackie developed a close friendship with Roberts. He later bequeathed letters and memos that Jackie wrote to him to the Harry Ransom Center at the University of Texas. Letters, of course, are the revelatory lifeblood of biography. Though not always perfect with her spelling and often freewheeling with her punctuation, Jackie's handwritten and typed missives were typically playful and witty, and even flirtatious at times with Ray, as with a red heart-shaped Valentine she gave him, signed "Guess who?" This was a close relationship that blossomed in the office, unreported and invisible even to Jackie's biographers.

In one memo to Roberts, Jackie tried her hand at writing promotional copy for the Vreeland book suggesting that Flaubert should have written her copy, which read in part, "The worlds of royalty, fashion, high society and superstars are here to be dipped into like a gorgeous box of chocolates."

In another memo to Roberts, she wrote, "Ray baby—look at these fabulous quotes for *Allure*. I hope they will help you put it over the top!" Jackie accompanied her note with promotional blurbs she had collected from Gloria Vanderbilt, Yves Saint Laurent, Lauren Bacall, Truman Capote, and Andy Warhol (who offered only a quip: "It's a lot better than my book"). Jackie also expressed her mystification to Ray when George Weidenfeld, cofounder of the British publishing house Weidenfeld & Nicholson, decided against publishing the book in London, suggesting that it would be too costly. On June 17, 1980, Jackie wrote, in part, "What went wrong here? Is Weidenfeld being unreasonable . . . I'd like to learn for the future!"

Erudite and courtly, Ray Roberts worked with such authors as John Fowles, Ansel Adams, Greg Mortenson, and Martha Grimes. Jackie often accompanied him on outings to gallery openings, films, and museum exhibits, always with an eye to books that might be acquired. In a memo dated November 2, 1978, about an opening they attended, Jackie wrote, "Janet Malcolm wrote a marvelous piece [in *The New Yorker*] on the Avedon exhibit. . . . & I thought she might be a writer for the dance book? Can we sign that one up before Bob Gottlieb does?"

Despite Jackie's enthusiasm for the subject, she and Ray failed to interest Doubleday in a book based on the International Center of Photography exhibit "Fleeting Gestures: The History of Dance Photography." Jackie's friendly competitor on the proposed dance book, Robert Gottlieb, served as editor in chief at Simon & Schuster and Knopf, and later at *The New Yorker*. While for many years Jackie served on the board of directors of American Ballet Theatre, Gottlieb was on the board of New York City Ballet. In this vein, he published several books by stars from the dance world, including Mikhail Baryshnikov and Margot Fonteyn, who was friendly with Jackie, as was Fonteyn's frequent partner, Russian defector and ballet icon Rudolf Nureyev, with whom Jackie would later collaborate.

The dance book with Janet Malcolm went no further, but Jackie suggested other projects to Roberts. In an October 4, 1978, memo, Jackie suggested to Roberts an Indian photographic book that had been proposed by Senator Patrick Moynihan's wife, Elizabeth. Jackie often passed along third-party letters to Roberts that she had received and copies of letters she had written, soliciting his opinion and offering suggestions. On November 14, 1978, she forwarded to him a memo from a producer friend at CBS News, Gordon Hyatt, who was also an ally in her preservation efforts. Hyatt was attempting to involve Egyptian president Anwar Sadat in a documentary on his country's ancient and modern history and what Hyatt called "the legacy of the Nile." Jackie predicted that Sadat would not cooperate, and indeed, neither the film nor book ever came to fruition.

Responding to a memo from Roberts, Jackie offered praise for a book proposal submitted by Morrill Cody, described by Roberts as "one of the last survivors of the Lost Generation." Jackie and her colleague were unable to sell Doubleday on Cody's book, entitled *The Women of Montparnasse*, which was published by a small house in 1983. Jackie wrote, on March 1, 1978, "I love the idea of this book—The period has such poignancy for so many—and the woman's angle should give it a double audience—If you need a name for the introduction, what about George Plimpton, who breathed in Paris as a young man like Morrill Cody did, and who started *The Paris Review*?"

Roberts and Jackie also pursued an art book by Thomas B. Hess, who had been an early champion of Willem de Kooning and the editor of the influential *Art News* journal. In the end, the project failed to sell to any major house. In the spring of 1979, a proposal from William Howard Adams led Jackie and Roberts to a rare book entitled *Diary of a Scotch Gardener at the French Court at the End of the Eighteenth Century,* by Thomas Blaike. The book had been published in London in 1931 and was no longer in print. On April 24, 1979, Jackie sent Roberts a copy with a memo asking his opinion, but that book was another that failed to elicit support at Doubleday. In a postscript to her memo, Jackie queried in passing if Roberts knew anything about the progress of Diana Ross and a writer she was working with. Diana Ross and Michael Jackson had costarred the year before in *The Wiz,* and Ross was now exploring the possibility of a book with a ghostwriter under Doubleday's aegis. But her memoir, *Secrets of a Sparrow,* would not be published until 1993, by Villard.

In a memo written in late May or early June 1979, Jackie asked Roberts to suggest a figure for an advance offer that she might pass on to her friend the art critic John Russell, who she was hoping would agree to an illustrated book on historic American houses. She informed Roberts that she had an upcoming lunch date with Russell, during which she planned to win him over. But in the end, Russell backed out of the project.

A few weeks later, on June 21, 1979, Jackie informed Roberts about a book proposed to her by Elizabeth Katz, the wife of Jackie's friend at the Met, Karl Katz. The proposal suggested a biographical portrait of Giovanni Belzoni, the Venetian explorer of Egyptian antiquities. That book also fell by the wayside.

The following year, on May 14, 1980, Jackie wrote to Roberts about a book opportunity that summons memories of one JFK scandal that overshadowed Camelot. In that sense Jackie's recommendation is surprising: "MARILYN MONROE!!! Bert Stern is doing a book called *The Last Sitting*—his 3-day photographic session with Marilyn 6 wks before she died. . . . $50,000–$100,000 for it. . . . Are you excited?" This was another book that eluded Jackie, despite her eager enthusiasm for the Monroe portraits. Stern's photographs were published by Morrow two years later

In the spring of 1980, Jackie and Roberts both were surprised and dismayed to learn that Doubleday was letting him go. Jackie sent a memo to the longtime executive who made the decision, Robert Banker (copied to Sam Vaughan), pleading for Roberts's job. Jackie wrote, "I was so stunned when you told me about Ray Roberts that words failed me. But all weekend I have had thoughts that I feel I must share with you. . . . Working closely with Ray has made me aware of his many qualities which are special and which cause me to have the deepest feelings of esteem for him. I have never worked with anyone as closely and I have rarely enjoyed anyone as much."

Jackie went on to list all the projects that she and Roberts were planning, including future tie-in books with the Met and ICP, a retrospective of Berenice Abbott's photography, an illustrated book on Central Park with text from Paul Goldberger, a work devoted to Boris Godunov, a tell-all memoir by Hollywood director George Cukor, and a book by Philippe Petit, the young man who had walked a tightrope between the World Trade Center Towers.

Jackie then described the illustrated books that Sam Vaughan had encouraged her to do for the house. "These are the books I love most. . . . They take more time than a written book (and make less money I know!) . . . one is always dealing with at least 3 prima donnas . . . but when you look over the years at a shelf of them, they are books . . . which . . . bring joy and knowledge, and I hope credit to the company. Ray has taught me to say No to marginal projects. . . . It is work-effective to be on the same wavelength as your co-editor, and it is difficult to imagine having the same rapport with another person."

Jackie's plea was rejected. Though their professional collaboration at Doubleday ended and Roberts moved on to Little, Brown in Boston, the two would continue to correspond and meet for lunch dates in the years ahead. During that time Roberts gave many books to Jackie as gifts. In a thank-you note in which she voiced some envy of Roberts's house, which had recently published John Fowles's *Mantissa* and *The Noël Coward Diaries*, Jackie wrote, on October 30, 1982, "What staggeringly wonderful books! How I would have loved to be in a house that did them."

The following year, on October 15, 1983, she wrote, "It's Autumn in New York and you are Santa Claus—I can't believe the marvelous pile of books you sent me—Julia, Coastal New England, Balthus, Karsh—they are all treasures. . . . I just never think of sending Doubleday books to you!"

Jackie's passion for gardens and French history led her to another book in 1978, while Roberts was still her coeditor, a work devoted to Eugene Atget, the innovative French photographer (1857–1927) belatedly acknowledged as one of the masters of the art form. Atget was a failed actor and painter who did not begin using a camera until he was about forty but then worked prolifically. Using obsolete equipment until the end, Atget produced more than ten thousand images. He took black-and-white photos of France's royal parks and gardens, many of which documented the shabby state into which these outdoor areas had been allowed to devolve. Underappreciated at the time, Atget is now regarded as one of the medium's first social documentarians. Jackie's work with author William Howard Adams on *Atget's Gardens,* featuring seventy-one of Atget's photographs, would contribute to the photographer's long-overdue recognition.

Jackie was sensitive to the fact that beauty can emerge from the ravages of time and neglect. She wrote an eloquent introduction to the book lauding the photographer: "It is not just the fading romance of something that is about to disappear that he gives us, but rather a new statement now framed within his photograph that transcends the evocative beauty of the gardens themselves." Some of the Atget photos, like those of Saint-Cloud and Sceaux, represented royal parks wherein the chateaux no longer exist. Of the latter subject, citing a phrase by pioneer photographer-inventor William Henry Fox Talbot, himself a chronicler of ruin, Jackie wrote, "By 1900 'the injuries of time' had made it a mirage of history that can hardly be believed. Could the intrigues of the Duchess of Maine, the malicious smile of Voltaire have quivered here, in this image that seems a wild Greek island with terme and tree torn by wind, in this one that shows a sorcerer's wood? The wildness has been largely corrected now by careful civic restoration, so that Atget's record of Sceaux at its greatest moment of decay is a unique historical documentation. In the city parks we feel Atget's humanity. He photographs with tenderness and melancholy."

One early admirer of Atget's was his Montparnasse neighbor Man Ray, who published unattributed Atget photos in *La Révolution surréaliste.* Atget may have been denied credit, but this exposure introduced him into the fine arts movement of the surrealists. It was an assistant of Man Ray's, photographer Berenice Abbott, who became enamored with Atget's work and rescued much of it from the shadows of obscurity, placing a large collection of his photographs with the Museum of Modern Art in the 1960s. Jackie would be photographed with Berenice Abbott attending the opening of the London exhibition of Atget's photographs in November 1979 at the Royal Institute of British Architects (RIBA), timed to coincide with the book's publication on both sides of the Atlantic.

William Howard Adams told me, "Jackie and I had been friends socially and so on for a stretch, and we shared an interest in things French. And she was always very adventurous about new projects. I told her that I had written a book when I was a fellow of Dumbarton Oaks Garden Library on the history of the French garden. And she was very interested in this. I told her that while I was doing my research, to my surprise in the Bibliothèque, when they would bring you a working file on a particular arrondissement, or garden, there would be these original Atget photographs of these places at that time. She thought that was just amazing. And I said that I had discussed this with the RIBA in London—a friend of mine, John Harris, was head of the collection. It was where they held all of their manuscript drawings, architectural drawings, and all kinds of things in relation to architecture; it's one of the great collections. They had come up with the idea maybe of doing a small exhibition of the Atget photographs. I guess I told Jackie something about this. And she said, 'Oh, what a good idea! Why don't you do a book?'

"I first said, 'I don't want to do a book.' Then I said, 'Well, I'll think about that if you'll do the heavy lifting on keeping the records straight'—on going through all the massive numbers of photographs. . . . She said, 'Oh what a great idea! Of course I'll do that.' So the next day I knew we were on our way, and she said, 'Well, I'll talk to the International Center of Photography in New York and see if they would take it, too.' That was the genesis of it. We were going to have to go off and go to check other collections in Paris. . . . And so that's what we did, and she really wanted to participate in this way.

"It was a moment when she could get around Paris without being noticed—with her usual scarf on and glasses. She liked the idea of being a kind of researcher manqué. And for her it was a real payoff. After all, the great seventeenth-century diarist of Versailles, the Duc de Saint-Simon, was one of her favorite writers. She told me she had carried a copy [of his memoirs] with her during the presidential campaign in Wisconsin, to escape the tedium of the campaign trail of endless shopping malls."

Adams continued, "The director at Versailles was someone that I knew, and she'd said early on she wanted to visit Versailles sometime, just unofficially. She had her great visit there when de Gaulle had this dinner. I said, 'Well, while we're there I'll see if the director can give us a key one day, and we'll just go out there and have the place to ourselves—no guides, just a concierge.' That's what we did. It was cold as hell. We went all over the place and particularly all the back rooms and the apartments. That was just a great kind of adventure for her. . . .

"Near the Marly, which is not far from Versailles, Louis XIV's private retreat—the chateau is long since gone—but on the edge of this forest was an eighteenth-century sort of folly, a park with a number of buildings in it. It wasn't really a chateau, but it was basically a place to go off for the weekend. So she knew about it, and she wanted to see it. I said, 'Well, look, I know an architect who's been involved with it. I know it's off-limits. It's privately owned, they don't want anybody intruding there. They even have watchdogs. All of that of course just egged her on, so we also included that in our research. We went up in mud and rain, and we got stuck, couldn't get the car out. She just loved every minute of it.

"One time we were going someplace, and she said she had to go into Doubleday. And I said, 'Oh, why don't you just get your own imprint? Then you wouldn't have to put up with all this stuff.' And she laughed at me and said, 'What do you think I want to do, sit home all day and smoke cigarettes?'

"She seemed to be pleased with the book. In fact we laid the book out on the floor of her apartment, literally, took copies of the photographs, Xeroxes or whatever they were, and actually rolled up the rug and laid it out on the floor—better space. I want to emphasize the professionalism. Obviously the social part of it figuring in, because she knew how to use that; but when it got down to the work and what had to be done, and how things should go, she was really professional. I've worked with many editors, and I couldn't have gotten any better.

"The other little footnote to this whole adventure was that we got Berenice Abbott to come over for the opening in London. Jackie loved the idea of the legendary Berenice Abbott coming—a specter out of the nineteen-thirties and forties—when she arrived for the opening in London. It was such fun."

With trips to Moscow and Versailles already behind her, editing had now become a passport to the world for Jackie. And her life continued to come together in other ways as she opened herself to new challenges. In line with her quest for independence, she had acquired approximately 365 acres of prime real estate on Martha's Vineyard in 1978 and commissioned a Washington, D.C.–based architect, Hugh Newell Jacobsen, to design her dream house on the sea. Jacobsen had been recommended by Jackie's friends I. M. Pei and Bunny Mellon, and Jackie provided Jacobsen with her own detailed specifications. He recalled, "She laid the whole house out in string on the beach in Hyannis so that she could walk from room to room." Construction would continue over the next three years while Jackie continued to adjust to life at Doubleday. The Vineyard was only a short plane ride to the Kennedy compound in Hyannis Port, but far enough for Jackie to keep the family at arm's length.

Jackie's friend Ashton Hawkins told Sarah Bradford, "I think she was very proud of that property . . . it made her very happy, sort of reminded her of a lot of good things, but it wasn't connected with the Kennedy family in any way. . . . I remember feeling that she was extremely proud of that. That was maybe the first place she built on her own."

Jackie would share her homes with a new companion. Before the close of the decade, she established an intimate relationship with a successful Belgian-born diamond merchant and financier, Maurice Tempelsman, who would provide an emotional base of support that would sustain her for the rest of her life, even though he was a married man whose devout Jewish background he shared with his wife, Lilly, prevented a divorce. Tempelsmen had known Jackie since Jack Kennedy's days in the Senate, and attended various White House functions during those years. After Ari's death, Jackie and Maurice became close, with Tempelsman handling Jackie's finances and eventually turning her settlement from Onassis into a much more substantial fortune, multiplying it tenfold over the years.

Ted Sorensen, whose Manhattan law firm (Paul, Weiss, Rifkind, Wharton & Garrison) represented Jackie on occasion, described Tempelsman as "one of my closest friends and clients . . . warm, wise and supportive . . . their mutually caring relationship gave me many more opportunities to see Jackie socially." According to Sorensen, Tempelsman had to overcome some early reservations that Caroline and John Jr. harbored about him. Another friend of Jackie's said simply that Jackie "adored Maurice. I think he brought her peace of mind." Tempelsman was indeed Jackie's perfect match—attentive and cultured while possessing the wit and intellectual qualities to keep Jackie engaged and on her toes. I met him only once, when he accompanied Jackie to London to attend a ballet. He appeared confident and secure in his role, exuding a warm, low-key charisma. It was obvious that she doted on him, and vice versa.

At Doubleday, Jackie continued to cast about for new projects and occasionally brought people into her social circle on the off chance that a literary project might evolve out of the association. "That is part of an editor's job," Jackie wrote for *Ms.* magazine, "You keep asking everyone—friends, authors, agents, experts; anyone with access to a particular world—if they know of a person who should be published or a subject that should be treated."

Another Doubleday project that Jackie touted for Gloria Steinem's magazine readership in 1979 was a book entitled *How to Save Your Own Street,* by Raquel Ramati. Jackie said of the author, "She's a brilliant architect and a Sabra. I went to Israel with her last year. Her book shows how to fight decay in neighborhoods and streets, and preserve the quality of urban life. It's going to be extremely valuable to the average citizen and to the professional planner. And Saul Steinberg is donating one picture for the cover—because he cares so much."

Raquel Ramati first met Jackie through their involvement in the movement to support landmark preservation and neighborhood renewal. She recounted for me the fortuitous circumstance that led to her book and relationship with Jackie. "I was working for the Department of City Planning, and I did a presentation to the Forty-second Street Redevelopment Group, who did work to improve Forty-second Street. When I did the presentation, apparently Jackie was impressed with me. I mean, I didn't know that. She was there; she was part of the board. And the next day I got a call from her, directly from her, not from her secretary, asking me if I would like to go to Israel with her—I nearly fainted. I was born in Israel, and I'm both an Israeli and an American citizen. I couldn't believe it.

"And she said, 'I'd love you to come with me to Israel. I'm going to the opening of the Diaspora Museum—and I'd love you to come. But the only thing is you'll have to meet Maurice, and he'll have to approve it.' And I didn't know her or anything, I just saw her once. And I met Maurice, and we had an incredible ten days. And we got very, very friendly. We went to Israel . . . and I introduced her to a lot of the people that I know. . . . We took a helicopter and flew to the Sinai, and we met Moshe Dayan, and we met Begin, we met Golda Meir, and Jackie met my mother, and my mother made her a cheesecake. So she came for the opening of the museum, and it was really through the initiative of Karl Katz. And we sat there when the president inaugurated the Diaspora. We were sitting with the president of Israel and his wife in the second row. There were speeches for forty-five minutes in Hebrew. I was bored to death. Jackie didn't move. You'd think she understood every word. She was so focused. . . . It all was really a fantastic trip, and then she invited me to go with her to Paris, and we were in Paris a few days."

Karl Katz had interested Jackie and Ray Roberts in a Diaspora book, which was part of her motive for visiting Israel, but Ramati suggested another idea to Jackie. "On that trip, I told her about this idea that I had about a book, because it was a time when, like now or worse, when real estate was in terrible shape. I did work on communities, which was not too popular at the time. Now there are community boards and everybody talks community. . . . She was very interested . . . and she said, 'You know, I think it would make a good book.'

"Then when we came back we started—I gave her what I was doing . . . and she brought it to Doubleday. Now obviously it wasn't one of these books that was going to be a best seller; but it was a book that might be important. It's out of print now. But the interesting thing was that she's the one that recommended the cover, which is a Steinberg cover. We went together to Steinberg's studio, and we picked that drawing, which is a very beautiful drawing. Jackie was a pleasure to work with because she had a wonderful graphic sense. From the point of view of publisher, probably it would have made more sense to do a black-and-white book and sell it for $4.95, which is the way it would have gone to the people that should read it. But we both were so interested in the graphic part of it, and we wanted it in color and so forth.

"Another thing, by the way, before we went to Paris: This is gossip, but it's really important. Because everybody thought that she married Onassis for the money, but when we were in Israel, every single thing reminded her of him. We would go to Caesarea, and there was a good Greek restaurant, and she would say, 'Oh, Ari would have loved it.' And I think she really cared about him. I said to her, 'Would you like to come and see the monument for Jack,' and she said, 'Well, maybe later,' that kind of thing. She said, 'To be married to a Kennedy was to be married to a family.' "

Ramati informed me that Jackie didn't do the line editing on her book, which included detailed assessments of several model communities like Mulberry Street in Little Italy and Newkirk Plaza in Brooklyn. "I think she didn't feel that she knew much about the subject. . . . She was interested in urban development . . . urban preservation; so therefore she saw this book as an important book. It was at a time when there was a real economic crisis, and . . . nobody was building anything. Somebody else would be doing the line editing. But she did get involved in seeing whether it's . . . beautiful enough. In other words, she was a conceptual person. And what I think is unknown about her is that she showed me once—I think it was a diary or journal that she had. And she had extraordinarily beautiful drawings that she did herself. They were really amazing."

Ramati recalled that the visit involved roughing it, including the use of public showers. "We were very intimate when we were on the trip because of the way the trip was. You know, we took flights to places, to the Sinai, and so I sat very close to her. But after that we would see each other many times for lunch, and I was at her house for the Christmas parties. But there was something strange that—I think two things: One, I sometimes felt very close to her, and other times, she was completely changed, like she would take a distance, you know, because maybe she was afraid of people getting close to her, you know, and needing something, which I never did."

Karl Katz offered his recollections of the trip to Israel to Carl Sferrazza Anthony, saying, "I took her through the old city of Jerusalem and to archaeological sites that I had excavated like Gath and Caesarea. She really loved the [Jewish] Diaspora Museum . . . and we also went to the place I helped build, the Israel Museum, where she was very interested in the archaeology of the Bible. She visited an Israeli kibbutz and talked to students in a class. . . . She was always asking questions. You never ran out of questions with Jackie."

Jackie was drawn to another historical project on a subject in which she had a keen interest: the Civil War. The project took the form of a narrative of an affecting wartime romance. It was undertaken after Jackie received an overture from William (Bill) Walton, a gay journalist turned painter whom she had known for years. Walton had been a friend of JFK's during the 1950s and was appointed by Kennedy to be chairman of the U.S. Commission on Fine Arts in 1963. Later, he would serve at Jackie's behest as a trustee of the John F. Kennedy Library, assuming the position just before his book was published.

Early in 1979, Walton shared a family heirloom with Jackie, a packet of letters his grandfather, Edwin Weller, had written as a soldier during the Civil War to Walton's grandmother, Antoinette (Nettie) Watkins. Jackie immediately saw the potential for a book and championed the project at Doubleday, with the aid of an editorial colleague, Michael Ossias (who did much of the line editing), and additional assistance from Lisa Drew, whose correspondence to Walton survives in the JFK Library archives.

Technically credited on the cover as editor of *A Civil War Courtship: The Letters of Edwin Weller from Antietam to Atlanta,* Walton described in his introduction how the letters came to him. "Edwin's letters were preserved in the conventional family manner—in the attic—by his descendants, of whom I am one. When Nettie died in 1929, her daughter Helen Louise inherited the letters and stuffed them into a battered iron safe hidden under the curving staircase of our house in Illinois. After her death, my sister Helen Hackett became the owner of the old safe, magpie treasures and all. Now I have unfolded those crumbly pages to learn something about the enigmatic bearded face always referred to as 'your Grandfather Weller who fought in the Civil War.'"

In presenting his grandfather's letters of courtship to his grandmother, William Walton explained that Weller, then twenty-three, was among the first to answer President Lincoln's call in 1862 for three hundred thousand volunteers to enlist in the Union Army, so that "this unnecessary and injurious civil war" could be brought to an end. The letters cover the period from the bloody battles at Antietam and Gettysburg in 1862 and 1863 to Sherman's march through Georgia and Weller's subsequent return to civilian life in late 1865. They constitute half of the correspondence; none of the letters from Watkins to Weller were preserved, though they were continually mentioned by the latter. Most of his letters start off with a kind of formality that seems stilted today, but which reflected the conventions of the time: "Dear Friend Nett." They are signed, "Ever your friend, Ed." In the early letters, there is sometimes a joshing tone, as though Weller were acknowledging that Antoinette might have other suitors. During the brutal

Georgia campaign, his attitude toward Antoinette changed, such that he was able to write, "Now Nett I can say with truth and sincerity that I love you."

With this book, as with others, Jackie was attempting to preserve a kind of literary virtuosity that she sensed was already in peril, long before the age of the Internet and e-mail. It is difficult to imagine such a nuanced letter on so critical and heartrending a subject committed to paper by our current generation. The art of circumlocution possessed by a simple army private (subsequently promoted to lieutenant) during the Civil War exceeds the ability of many college graduates today.

Just before the book was published, Jackie collected promotional blurbs from a number of old friends, such as Theodore H. White and Arthur Schlesinger Jr. The latter wrote, on January 20, 1980, "I have read Bill's book, and, if a plug would help, you may quote me as follows: 'This fine series of Civil War letters gives a rare, honest, touching portrait of war, death and love.'"

In the same letter, Schlesinger also shared his political analysis of the election year with Jackie, writing about Ted Kennedy's challenge to Jimmy Carter, hoping "to put Ted over" for the nomination. That year Jackie would campaign for Ted in the primary, but his liberal rogue initiative was unable to defeat the incumbent, Jimmy Carter, who in turn was unable to prevail against Ronald Reagan. Jackie's loyalty to Ted and efforts on his behalf, as well as a number of her topical books, belie the assumption that she had no interest in politics later in life. David Halberstam got it right when he once called her a "supple political animal," adding, "She played the game exquisitely."

On October 20, 1979, Jackie and Ted met in the Boston suburb of Dorchester for the dedication of the John F. Kennedy Library, with the contretemps of Jeffrey Archer's book safely behind them. Per Jackie's specifications, the library's high glass walls and stunning white futuristic contours, designed by I. M. Pei, overlook Dorchester Bay. There are small-scale replicas of the Oval Office and other White House rooms, while the library collections contain the country's most extensive research archive devoted to John Kennedy. At the dedication ceremony, Ted announced his presidential campaign. With Jackie standing at his side, he was viewed as the heir apparent to JFK's legacy. (According to Jimmy Breslin, after the dedication, Jackie lampooned some of those in attendance, saying, "I think they really wanted Caroline to come out skipping in a little girl's dress.")

While still working on the Walton book, Jackie recruited another first-time author into the Doubleday ranks, Stephen Appelbaum, a psychiatrist whom she met through Peter Beard. According to his widow, Ann, and son,

Eric Nicholas, Appelbaum, who was on the faculty of the Menninger School of Psychiatry in Kansas City, acted as a consultant for one of Beard's books. His son recalled hearing Appelbaum describe his association with Jackie: "He talked about Jackie a fair amount. I think he got kind of a kick, as one couldn't help but do, from his proximity to such fame. And I think he genuinely really enjoyed talking to her, too. You could tell he was tickled to death."

In a letter dated November 7, 1977, written on Jackie's behalf, Nancy Tuckerman had invited Appelbaum to a dinner benefiting the International Center of Photography, indicating that Jackie wanted him to be seated at her table. Jackie cultivated a relationship with Appelbaum for several years, though it was destined to wane. A few years before his death, in 2000, engaging in some armchair analysis after the fact, Appelbaum told biographer Edward Klein (*Just Jackie*), "Jackie and I had a sort of friendship, and met a time or two in New York for social reasons, and corresponded and talked on the phone. She had an interest in just about everything, but how deep it went was hard to tell. I don't want to call her deceptive exactly. She was quite open and receptive. But she was also strangely opaque and unrevealing. Free as she was up to a point, beyond that point you did not learn anything."

Appelbaum continued, "There was, of course, some special circumstance in her relationship with her father that made her have relationships with various powerful men. But leaving it at that would be selling her short, and be one-dimensional. She had an independent, managerial, controlling streak. Her sibling position—she was the firstborn and the older of two sisters—made her by nature controlling, a person who took the initiative.

"She was the kind of person who would say to me when I was discussing a manuscript, 'Use my house as a drop,' as though she was a gun moll. I detected a certain tactile strength there. So it would be a disservice to call her overall a dependent person. She wasn't. She was no clinging vine. If a woman has, as women do, something missing in the sense of power, they can get it by affiliating themselves with powerful men. They are adopting for themselves the power they are close to. It's a method of being strong and independent. You can live through men, like Jackie, and have a lot of iron."

Appelbaum's choice of the "gun moll" image is off the mark. Using her "house as a drop" sounds more like the language of a spy, suggesting a conspiratorial sense of collaboration that Jackie adopted with many of her authors. Appelbaum's book, *Out in Inner Space: A Psychoanalyst Explores the Alternative Therapies,* would be published in 1979. All manner of user-friendly variations on therapeutic self-improvement were cropping up at the time, and Appelbaum provided a survey of these, from the perspective of a classically trained psychoanalyst, wooing Jackie with his erudition in a field that intrigued her.

After dismissing with withering contempt such non-Freudian techniques as primal therapy, Gestalt therapy, behavior modification, EST, Silva mind control, Rolfing, Reichian regression therapy, and biofeedback, Appelbaum pulled back in the book and admitted his conservatism. Evidently, Jackie held off on trying to temper Appelbaum's prejudices. Though he later submitted ideas for several other books, she put him off with a cordial rejection letter.

By the end of her first year at Doubleday, Jackie had initiated a half dozen projects that showed the range of her eclectic taste. One of her early acquisitions was a novel by Nancy Zaroulis, which Jackie suggested was going to be "an extraordinary book." In an interview in *Ms.* magazine, she explained to Gloria Steinem, "It's the story of a girl working in the mills of Lowell, Massachusetts, in the nineteenth century. The manuscript seemed to weigh about twenty pounds, and I thought: My God, it will just depress everyone. But once I started to read it, I couldn't put it down. I realized that the story would illuminate a period of American history and the lives of a whole group of American women. One of the good things about working for a publishing house like Doubleday is its size: somewhere among its different divisions, there is a place for almost every subject and kind of book."

While Zaroulis did not wish to be interviewed, she did tell me in a letter that she didn't really collaborate with Jackie, because her novel "was published as I wrote it." With her grasp of history, Jackie was aware that women only became useful cogs in the economic machinery of human labor and capitalism after the onset of the Industrial Revolution. Before that, they were the uncompensated labor force that held families together and provided the social glue for lower-class nuclear families. The Zaroulis novel celebrated the pioneering contributions of the Lowell mill women, assembly-line seamstresses and garment makers who took the raw bales of cotton picked by slaves and transformed them into salable commodities, using river and steam power. *Call the Darkness Light* tells this story in the form of historical fiction. It succeeded because the author refrained from troweling the bathos too thickly, something that Jackie detested and often communicated to her authors.

Just before her fiftieth birthday, in July 1979, Jackie attended a book party for Zaroulis, whom she had previously talked with by phone but never met. The festivities were held at a hospitality suite on the fourth floor above Doubleday's bookstore on Fifth Avenue, at Fifty-third Street. Jackie's longtime paparazzo nemesis, Ron Galella, was camped on the sidewalk in front of the store awaiting Jackie's arrival, despite a restraining order she had won against him in court in 1975 intended to keep him at a distance.

The month before, Galella had stalked Jackie and Caroline, then twenty-one, following them to Andover, Massachusetts, where they attended the graduation of eighteen-year-old John Jr. from Phillips Academy. On the night of the book party, Jackie managed to catch Galella off guard and slipped by unmolested. A *Newsday* reporter suggested that Jackie "was celebrating her biggest personal success as a working woman," noting that the paperback rights to *Call the Darkness Light* had been sold to New American Library for $500,000. The novel was also a Book-of-the-Month Club selection, with profits from the sale of foreign rights putting the gross near $1 million. The same reporter callously suggested that the only sign of Jackie's age was that her hands were "slightly gnarled."

In the Doubleday suite, Jackie was the instant center of attention. She lit a cigarette in a long holder, and mingled with literary agents and a group from *Publishers Weekly*. Upon meeting her new author for the first time, Jackie took Zaroulis by the hand and whispered, gushing, "Are you excited?" Before the young woman could reply, Jackie paid her a compliment, "You're so pretty." Zaroulis replied, "May I say—so are you." At that point, a photographer approached the two, and Jackie, after some encouragement from a Doubleday publicist, overcame her camera-shy reticence and consented to a picture with Zaroulis to help promote the book.

Zaroulis later described their exit from the party, recalling that she and Jackie were jostled by the crowd that had gathered outside the bookstore. "We literally had to link arms to get through the crowd to a taxi. I admire Jackie for being able to maintain her interest in work despite things like that. . . . I'm just old-fashioned enough to think a former First Lady deserves a certain amount of respect. . . . Jackie just remained perfectly calm, looking straight ahead, not reacting at all."

When asked what kind of challenge it would be for a fiction writer to turn Jackie's life story into a novel, Zaroulis said, "It would take a genius to make anyone believe it was a true story." Alex Gotfryd once recalled that after a visiting author beat a hasty retreat from Jackie's office, she asked him, "Why do they all run like scared bunnies?" Without waiting for a reply, she said, "I can't blame them. When I think of my life, *I* have a hard time believing it. It seems like it all happened to someone else."

4

An Office with a Window

As Jackie became more comfortable with the demands of her editorial role and with her colleagues, she brought a mischievous sense of fun to the office. She and her fellow editors often wrote witty, affectionate notes to each other and left them on the seats of their office chairs. These were the kind of charming, handwritten interoffice memos that were common before e-mail came to dominate the workplace. With her shoot-from-the-hip eloquence and love of epistolary, Jackie (who was also an aficionada of the game of charades), would pass impish notes to her colleagues to break up the withering formality she encountered in the conference rooms. Privately with friends, she would offer wry send-ups of some of her more stilted colleagues. According to then deputy publisher Bill Barry, "If she had someone into her office who was haughty and arrogant, she was capable of doing a fair imitation after the meeting."

Former Doubleday editor Paul Bresnick told me, "I was sitting next to Jackie at the big conference table where we held our weekly editorial meetings. I made an impassioned presentation about a novel by Hunter

S. Thompson that I wanted to acquire. After I finished my spiel, Jackie slipped me a note: 'I would give up lunch to publish Hunter Thompson.' I fantasized about having lunch one day with the two of them. Alas, I didn't get the book."

Bresnick also remembered a day that Jackie appeared at his office door, long before smoking was banned in the workplace, and asked if she could get a light. After pulling out a matchbook from a desk drawer and handing it to her, he noticed ("to my horror") that JFK's face was featured on the cover of the pack of matches. "There was the tiniest flicker of recognition on her face as she looked down at the matchbook, but nothing more than that. I just thought, God, this must happen to her *all the time*. Even the most quotidian human interaction is necessarily *fraught*."

Bill Barry recalled an incident exemplifying her whimsical side that he related to their mutual friend, George Plimpton, who later enjoyed repeating the anecdote: "I remember Bill Barry . . . telling me a story about her— that the two of them had taken the shuttle to Washington, the last to get on, and the two of them had walked the length of the plane to find two seats together in the rear, the passengers gawking at them as they passed. In fact, according to Bill, a number continued to turn and stare over the backs of their seats as the plane taxied down the runway. Jackie couldn't resist it. She leaned over and whispered to him, 'Oh, Bill, they all *know* you!' "

Barry served as a special administrative point man for Jackie. He was to put out any fire that ignited involving her. John Sargent Jr. said, "Bill was the guy who, when there was an issue with Jackie, you know, like salary and things like that, he was the guy who was dispatched. He was close friends with her. . . . So, when it came up, oh, God, we gotta talk to her about this new policy—Bill would go talk to her."

Jackie's assistant in the late 1970s, Hope Marinetti, described herself as "a nice Italian girl from Rochester who moved to the big city knowing two people and ended up working with arguably the most famous woman in the world. . . . Her skill at making you feel comfortable and included was so highly tuned. Grace is not a word I use often but she was quietly yet deeply gracious. Combined with her intelligence, wit, and tenacity, she could have been formidable and undoubtedly was with those she perceived as a threat. But to a lowly editorial assistant, she was always patient, kind, and compassionate. I think she liked the fact that I treated her like any of my friends, not like she was a hot-house flower. . . . I remember sometimes we would go through *People* magazine to see if there were any pictures of her, as a joke. She would say, 'Oh, look at that one!' Her kids she wanted to keep out of the limelight as much as possible, but of course that never happened. What a lovely, incredibly intelligent woman she was. . . . I've never wanted to talk about her because I didn't want to add to the crap out there."

Marinetti, who now works in design, offered a few disparate recollections: "When I was having trouble with a boyfriend at the time and was crying in the bathroom, she happened to come in and we ended up talking quite seriously about how hard it was to meet nice men. I remember thinking she was so much more beautiful in person than any picture I ever saw. I hadn't met too many elegant women yet and she was the definition of the word. Early on, she thought I was a nice girl. I was young, and we got along great. . . . I walked into her office one day, and we had a problem with some royalty check going to one of the authors. She said something like, 'Oh, yeah, the check is in the mail,' and before I even knew what I was saying, I said, 'Oh, yeah, and I promise I won't come in your mouth.' She leaned back in her chair and cracked up; she was laughing so hard she almost hit her head on the wall. She said to me, 'I underestimated you. You're not so much the girl next door, are you?'

"From then on, we really kind of opened things up, and I treated her like I would any of my friends. She had dinner at my house one night. I lived in Chelsea, which was not nearly as nice a neighborhood as it is now. I had this tiny little studio, with practically no furniture. She came and sat on the floor with me and my two best friends. We had a great time, and it was very nice of her to do that. She went out of her way. And I used to go to her apartment and she always sent food home with me. I was making nine thousand dollars and living in Manhattan and starving."

Marinetti played the role of gatekeeper for Jackie. "Full moon, the nuts would come out of the woodwork with phone calls and people coming up to the office saying they knew her. . . . There's a reason why when you see pictures of Jackie in public, she's got that kind of glazed look on her face. That's because she had to, unlike many celebrities in New York. I mean, New Yorkers are pretty hip. They let people kind of have their anonymity. But people would just stop and stare at her. And when we would leave the building together, I thought to myself, Oh my God, if I ever thought I wanted to be famous, this just killed it. I would never want to have this kind of scrutiny.

"I remember the trend in those days, I remember we used to read unsolicited manuscripts, and those of us who were in the young editorial staff would have those authors that we really wanted to publish, and we knew it wasn't going to be a huge best seller, but it was a well-written book. The trend was so much toward star biographies and crap that was going to make money. . . . I thought it was going to be about a reverence for words, and it wasn't. The MBAs took over.

"Jackie actually got me my job after I left Doubleday. After I left editorial, I went to the publicity department for a little while. Then I was thinking about moving on, and she called me and said that she had a friend who was looking for an assistant and would I be interested. I said, 'Sure,' and it turned out it was Mike Nichols. And the day of my interview, it was pouring cats and dogs, and she called me and said, 'My God, you're never gonna get a cab, and you don't want to take the subway. Come on, I'll meet you downstairs and you can ride in my car.' That's the kind of person she was. It was just typical of her to be so thoughtful."

Having endured numerous trials by fire in the Doubleday editorial meetings, and having learned about the political gamesmanship that was played in the house, Jackie came to have a certain irreverent attitude about the corporate hierarchy. Peter Beard told me, "She became more cynical." Expounding on his experience with Jackie and the publishing world, Beard continued, in typically outspoken fashion, "The publishers are shits! We brought one of my best diaries, a couple of the really good ones, and we had an uproarious afternoon with the art director, whom Jackie knew very well. He knew what a complete fuck-up the company was.

"We just kept sitting there making jokes about them, because there was no chance of them taking the book. But we liked going through it and discussing the fact that there could never be a book like that or, in fact, any decent book. They're just incredibly incompetent. I can't tell you more strongly. She knew damn well they were just big fat political job climbers. . . . They had no interest in the books they were working on. . . . I sound very negative today, but I am very negative." Beard was characteristically acting the part of provocateur with his comments, but, at least to some extent, in her own way, Jackie agreed with his harsh assessment.

One of Beard's Yale classmates studying art in the late 1950s was John Loring, who later became design director of Tiffany & Co. Starting in 1979 and continuing the collaboration until the end of her life, John worked with Jackie for fifteen years on an illustrated series of six Tiffany books. The first was *The New Tiffany Table Settings*. Loring, who collaborated on more books with Jackie than any of her other authors, remembered how Jackie often had to wage a struggle against the editorial and marketing bureaucrats. "Some people had called an editorial meeting to get us to do certain things that she and I did not want to do with the book we were working on. And she said, 'We have to psych them out on this one. You know, we're not going to argue. We're just going to psych them out.'

"She did her homework thoroughly before the meeting, and she knew what every man and woman was up to, and what they were trying to put over, and who was siding with who. . . . And she knew how to tip the balance at the right moment in a meeting. . . . We were sitting across the table from these people who were proposing these unacceptable things, and she leaned over and whispered to me, 'Look at them! They're all so vile, so vile! They think of things every minute that we couldn't imagine in a lifetime.'

"She had a strategy. Jackie said, 'Let's sit down and write the script.' And literally you would sit down with her and you would write the script of how you were going to psych them out: 'You are going to say, and then I'm going to say, and even before I'm through saying that, you're going to say this, and then I'm going to appear very surprised.' She would write these little scenarios. . . . And then she would instruct you to send testy letters to Doubleday . . . about things that she was testy about. Then she was going to take the letters and say, 'You see!' Remember, she was married to a politician, and I think she picked up a few tricks along the way."

Loring, a polished, soft-spoken gentleman enjoying his retirement, told me over lunch in Midtown Manhattan during 2009, "She was super— almost a ventriloquist. . . . She could look straight ahead at something else, and it wouldn't appear that she was speaking; but you could hear very clearly what she was saying. . . . so that was one of the psych-them-out ceremonies. She did not mince words when she spoke privately. Publicly everything was absolutely perfect—no flicker of what she really thought. But privately she'd come out with these hysterical things which she obviously passed on—these asides were typical of Jackie. They were sort of whispered in the air, but you heard it. . . . What we were saying was not necessarily something that charity would have recognized."

The designer of several of the Tiffany books, J. C. Suarès said, "Jackie and John Loring were very friendly. It was the two of them, and they always whispered to each other and we never knew what they were saying. But he's a good guy, and he's got great taste, and his ideas for books were wonderful . . . beautiful stuff. They weren't real books. It was vanity publishing. They were financed by Tiffany's. We spent a fortune."

Loring explained, "They were subsidized by Tiffany only in the sense that we paid for all the photography. Those were books that were fun to do and would have been impossible to do under any other circumstances. Some of the books were commercially more successful than others. The wedding book is still used by wedding planners in the United States."

Loring credited the charismatic head of Tiffany's, Walter Hoving, with initiating the book series at a meeting in 1979. A Swedish-born businessman,

Hoving had a history with Jackie, her family, and the Kennedy family. In 1960, Hoving met then president-elect John Kennedy in the Manhattan store and assisted him in purchasing a brooch for Jackie by designer Jean Schlumberger, a dazzling piece studded with rubies and diamonds. Hoving possessed a flair for public relations, and the Tiffany coffee-table books were to be one of his coups. Loring told me, "He put this together. I had been writing for magazines, notably *Architectural Digest* . . . and Mr. Hoving said, 'I'm paying you to be the design director of this company, but also the advertising director . . . and you're also going to write for me.' "

Referring to Jackie's mother, Loring continued, "Mr. Hoving said, in his own way, 'You know, Janet's daughter is an editor at Doubleday, so the two of you are going to write books for me, and so I suggest you put together a proposal. . . .' Mr. Hoving had known Jackie since the day she was born, so he had this kind of parental attitude, and he was a very close friend of the mother, Janet Auchincloss. . . . Mr. Hoving called the two of us into his office one afternoon, sat us down on his sofa like two children being scolded about something. It was the funniest thing I've ever seen. Here's Jackie sitting there, and Mr. Hoving had this sort of amazing presence. I mean, he's a real prince amongst men, wonderful. And if you were in that space with him, it was his space, not yours. So Jackie and I are sitting there like little dutiful children, and that's how it all started.

"Of course, you instantly think she's not going to do this, because the ex-First Lady is not going to lend herself to promotion. Well, she cleared that up very quickly. She said, 'No, of course I'm not lending myself to books as promoting Tiffany, which I love, or anyone else. . . . I see this as a great opportunity to write a series of social documents, documenting the development of American culture, not just in the decorative arts, but in society, business, sports, government . . . because Tiffany & Co. after all has been there in the middle of all that since 1837. . . . Tiffany has been not only witness to, but standing in the center, and it's a terrific vantage point from which to document the development of this country. . . . That is why I'm doing this.' "

Although the Tiffany books were among her favorites over the years, Jackie never allowed her name to appear in the books, not even in the acknowledgments. She told Loring, "I absolutely cannot have my name put into a commercial venture."

Loring said, "I think she must have told Doubleday the same thing— they were going to have the books on her terms, or she wasn't going to do them, period. And I remember when we did the second book [*Tiffany Taste*], it required a trip around the world to get all the props and photographers for that one book. Nobody has any idea what that book cost to produce. There were two budgets. Nancy Holmes, who is not with us any-more either, was then the head of public relations of Pan American Air-ways. So Jackie and I had this idea of this book we wanted to do with a trip around the world. The question was who's going to pay for this? Clearly Doubleday was not, and Tiffany was not. So God sent us Nancy Holmes, who admired Jackie tremendously and was a great buddy of mine, and was very adept at wheeling and dealing. And so at lunch at Le Cirque one day I explained the project to Nancy, and she said, 'I'll make you a deal. You have four first-class tickets for one year anywhere in the world to do this book, provided one of the tickets is for me.' So we said, 'Deal, Nancy, deal!'

"Nancy enabled Jackie and me to do the book we wanted to do, because without four first-class tickets, how do you get me, a photographer, and the equipment to all these places, like to the border of Nepal and India? So Jackie was thrilled to bits and so was I. . . . This was outrageous spending on the part of Pan American Airways. Jackie would look at what was going to happen and where people were going to go, and she'd say, 'Well, I've never been there. I'd love to go.' And then you'd try to say, 'Well just do it,' and she'd give you that look. . . . That was not going to happen . . . but she definitely had a vicarious pleasure in our travels. . . . And she very much encouraged parts of the writing that she liked. She said, 'Well, what I want to see in this writing, I want to feel that I've met these people and been there.'"

Loring continued, "She had a wonderful sense of . . . humor, but it's not really repeatable . . . because it was all situational. She sized up a situation instantly and came out with these absolute whoppers that only related to that moment. . . . She was very tolerant, very charitable, very open-minded towards everybody. But if people started behaving badly, that would not escape her notice. . . . She had a thing that if you knew her well, you could see when she smelled a rat. She had this expression . . . she would just move her face about a sixteenth of an inch to the left. . . . The movement was so infinitesimal . . . it was the knee-jerk to a rat approaching. And then you knew that the rat's game was over because she had smelled the rat before they'd even got within six feet of her. . . .

"With the books, she liked everything that told a story about things that she liked. . . . She'd select photographs and say, 'Oh, look what they did with that! That's very original. You think of something to say about that.' On the back of *Tiffany Taste*, there are four silver beakers I brought back from a trip to Nepal, holding watermelon squash. They cost ten dollars each in a street market. And she said, 'Oh, I'd give up iced tea and drink watermelon squash all summer if I had those cups.'" Loring remembered placing the cups in a cardboard box and sending them to her office by messenger. Jackie called and told him, "You created quite a stir here. Security thought the package contained a canister bomb, and that someone was trying to blow me up."

Loring told me, "She also, working with you, would really pay very close attention to things outside of what you were doing in the work. In editing and talking to you, the editing was more than just editing what you were doing at the time. She'd sometimes stop and say, 'Now I want to talk to you about'—and she'd tell me something that she observed me doing in certain situations that she didn't think was the right thing to do. She'd say, 'I think you want to think about what you do in that situation. Jack would have done this.' And she would explain what she meant and then say, 'And I think Jack was right, and that is the way to do it.' Or she would say, 'Ari would have done this in that situation, and I think he was right.' She used examples like that, which showed how much respect she had for both the president and Aristotle Onassis, which many people don't realize. So she was editing your writing, your photography, your personal behavior, your way of thinking. . . .

"She was deeply involved with her friends and with those she was working with. And she was not involved with herself. There wasn't any real vanity or self-involvement at all. . . . She demanded complete respect from her friends, and she gave in return complete respect back. And that's very rare in this day and age. There was no pretension at all. It wasn't a tactic; it was the way she was. But that brought the best out of everybody. She made them her partner, and they turned in a better performance. And how about those calls at two o'clock in the morning, when she'd say: 'I just wanted to check if you're still working.' "

Loring recollected that Jackie at a certain point altered their working lunch routine. They had been accustomed to sitting on the floor with Styrofoam containers of iced tea, takeout deli sandwiches, cole slaw, and potato salad. He called her one day and asked, "Where do you want to meet—your office floor or my office floor?"

Jackie replied, "Oh, can't we just go to a restaurant like normal people?"

"You're kidding!" said Loring. "You mean just go to a restaurant and eat lunch like everybody else? Where shall we go?" He thought for a moment and said, "I've got an idea. How about Le Cirque? It's a safe place to go."

Jackie loved the idea. She knew the owner, Siro Maccioni, who would seat her at a table in the corner and command the waiters to guard her privacy. Loring said, "It was straight to the corner in Le Cirque, and that was where we had our meals. This was part of the lifting of all these ghosts of her past. In the beginning, she still seemed very haunted by things. Then it was suddenly, 'No, I'm not going to hide in the office and eat nasty things from delis. I'm going to stand up like a normal person and walk into a restaurant with you, and eat lunch, and walk out again. I don't care if paparazzi jump out and take pictures.' "

Loring observed that Jackie "changed a great deal over the years," and became "a happy camper," as her children matured and her relationship with Maurice Tempelsman continued to flourish. The designer-author noticed that she gave up her trench coats and the scarves she often wore over her head in public. "Sometimes she'd walk down Fifth Avenue in the middle of the day, and people would do a double-take, and then you would see their faces cloud over, and they'd be saying to themselves, 'No, it couldn't possibly be.' You could see on the person's face, 'Oh my God, there's Jacqueline Kennedy,' and then two seconds later their face would cloud over and say, 'Well, of course it isn't. It's just somebody who looks like her.' So they paid no attention, and she learned that disguise wasn't really necessary, that she could go wherever she wanted and do whatever she wanted to."

Now in its third century, Tiffany & Co. is among the leading producers of luxury goods, from its legendary jewels and flatware designs to the stroke of luck that the film *Breakfast at Tiffany's* conferred upon it, creating an everlasting association with that most regal of actresses, Audrey Hepburn. Jackie embraced the idea of publishing the Tiffany style books as social chronicles, while the store's CEO knew they would appeal to the haute bourgeoisie, their intended client base, who would see what the super-rich were doing to entertain themselves. Walter Hoving's idea was that the striving classes would imitate the icons of style whose settings and drawing rooms were featured.

The New Tiffany Table Settings (1981) invites the reader to dine with the elite. The dining rooms and table settings of Brooke Astor, Jacqueline de Ribes, Ann Getty, Diana Vreeland, Andy Warhol, Lily Auchincloss, Letitia Baldrige, Bob Hope, Mia Farrow, Julia Child, and Lee Radziwill grace the pages. The level of detail that the color photographs depict is stunning, and a savvy viewer can see the hours of preparation that went into creating the perfect table presentation.

Tiffany Taste (1986) is a more generic rendering. Details of entertaining are presented, along with how to compose menus, arrange cookery, decorate, and set tables. This book does not limit itself to domestic situations. While elegant settings in the Texas Hill Country and Nantucket are present, so too are settings utilizing local color in Kathmandu, Hong Kong, Dublin, Venice, and the Versailles of Louis XIV.

The Tiffany Wedding (1988) presents "an idealized portrait of the American wedding from Tiffany's perspective." While this book, like all the others, has splendid color photography, it also stands as a how-to book, covering topics as disparate as the proper font for wedding announcements and the creation of a personal trousseau. How does one budget a wedding? How should the sticky question of prenuptial agreements be approached? What gifts are appropriate for attendants and for the officiating clergyman? What do the tiers on a wedding cake symbolize? How are the wedding rehearsal and breakfast best handled? What happens after the honeymoon? All these questions and more are addressed in this book, with Jackie drawing on her own experience with her daughter's wedding to museum exhibit designer Edwin Schlossberg in July 1986.

Tiffany Parties (1989) is a book that economist Thorstein Veblen could have used to illustrate his concept of "conspicuous consumption." The book basically documents forty-five different parties, some commemorating the dedication of public institutions (the New York Public Library, the Central Park Zoo, the New York Philharmonic, Union Station, in Washington, D.C.), others celebrating historic events (the Reagans' final state dinner, Irving Berlin's one hundredth birthday). All are lavishly photographed, demonstrating place and table settings, invitation décor, and a host of other party staples.

What better tribute could there be for a food and fashion book than *The Tiffany Gourmet Cookbook* (1992), which provides table settings and favorite recipes from many in the world of haute couture? Legendary designers Valentino, Yves Saint Laurent, and Bill Blass, celebrity chefs such as Wolfgang Puck, socialites such as Betsy Bloomingdale and Mrs. Cornelius Vanderbilt Whitney, and artists such as Françoise Sagan and Deborah Turbeville, all contribute recipes and arrangements that reflect their own individual personalities.

Tiffany's 150 Years (1992) is a compilation volume led off with a "Dear Tiffany" love letter signed by "your devoted friend, Audrey Hepburn." Louis Auchincloss contributes an introduction, after which the book travels decade by decade, from 1837 to 1987, vividly illuminating "a century and a half of the marriage of wealth and decorative arts in America." This is probably the best introduction to Tiffany that an art-obsessed reader could find.

While the writing in these books is consistently straightforward and informative, it is the detailed photographs that make these tomes worth keeping and prominently displaying, just as Jackie and John Loring intended. To this day, collectible copies of each volume continue to show up in eBay offerings.

Describing one her books in progress to Gloria Steinem in 1979, Jackie revealed her lifelong interest in journalism: "In the works is *Men and History,* by Don Cook of the *Los Angeles Times,* one of that disappearing breed of foreign correspondents. He pairs ten statesmen and ten events that have shaped European history since the war: de Gaulle and the Fifth Republic, Adenauer and the Bonn Republic, Jean Monnet and the Schuman Plan, and so on. I initially heard about him from Teddy White, that most enthusiastic of all foreign correspondents."

It is a commonplace that journalism is the first draft of history, and as Jackie noted, Don Cook was a veteran journalist who had covered the endgame of the European theater of World War II and its postwar reconstruction aftermath for a variety of American newspapers and magazines. Published in 1981, *Ten Men and History* was his anecdotal account of the events and statesmen who shaped postwar Europe from 1945 to the end of the 1970s. It is not a complete history of the era, in that it focuses only on three countries—Great Britain, France, and Germany—and on their leaders. But what it lacks in comprehensiveness is made up for in the way it personalizes history and reveals how individual quirks affected policy decisions.

This was the era when France got its democratic government back from the Nazis and Germany was partitioned according to the dictates of the victorious Allies, as prelude to the Marshall Plan, NATO, and the European Common Market. Cook offers biographies of ten leaders: three English (Ernest Bevin, Harold Macmillan, and Edward Heath), four French (Jean Monnet, Charles de Gaulle, Georges Pompidou, and Valery Giscard d'Estaing), and three German (Konrad Adenauer, Willy Brandt, and Helmut Schmidt).

In her previous role as First Lady, Jackie had met at least two of these world figures, de Gaulle and Adenauer, and had enough exposure to the world stage to know that the hidden backstories of history can often be more fascinating than the official version. What is remarkable is that she commissioned a book that still is informative and readable three decades later. The beauty of this book, even today, is that it explodes the popular mythologies of the period and demonstrates how momentous decisions sometimes rested on the shoulders of men temperamentally unprepared to make them.

With *Ten Men and History,* Jackie seized on the concept and placed her confidence in the author without having to contribute much in the way of editing. By all accounts an affable, amusing man with friends all over Europe, Don Cook told *People* magazine in 1984, eleven years before his death, "I got no requests for line changes. Jackie sent me lots of flowery, handwritten notes on how much she liked the book. And I got two lunches with her, one at '21' and another in her apartment."

The violent news stories of the early 1980s took their toll on Jackie's psyche, inevitably calling up her own dark memories. Madmen tried to assassinate President Ronald Reagan and Pope John Paul II, and terrorists murdered President Anwar Sadat of Egypt. Meanwhile, conspiracy theorists investigating the JFK assassination managed to have the body of Lee Harvey Oswald exhumed to try to prove their theories. Jackie was also deeply disturbed by the murder of John Lennon in Manhattan by a demented stalker assassin. Lennon's death led Jackie to a book project early in 1981 that was a joint venture published the following year by Doubleday and Rolling Stone Press.

Entitled *The Ballad of John and Yoko,* the book is a compilation of all the coverage that John Lennon, Yoko Ono, and the Beatles received from *Rolling Stone* magazine over the years. *Rolling Stone* was founded in 1967, just as the Beatles were becoming megastars. John Lennon graced its first cover, dressed in combat gear for his role in *How I Won the War.* The book's credited coeditors, Jonathan Cott and Christine Doudna, state in their preface, "*The Ballad of John and Yoko* was taken from that special issue of January 22, 1981, which was put together by the staff of *Rolling Stone* in the eight days and nights following Lennon's death." The book contains some of the freewheeling journalistic style of the magazine. There is a section in which various celebrities recall their feelings when Lennon was gunned down; and there is the final interview that Lennon granted the magazine, conducted by Cott for the December 5, 1980, issue.

Rolling Stone founder Jann Wenner notes in his foreword to the book that his relationship with John and Yoko began as a journalistic acquaintance and morphed into friendship as years passed. As editor, Jackie made demands on Wenner, with whom she also cultivated a friendship for a time. She insisted that he rewrite the first draft of his introductory essay to make it a more impassioned piece, and he complied. Joe Armstrong suggested that Jackie's attraction to Wenner was initially based on "commerce and curiosity." Christine Doudna told me the book "probably came out of Jann's and Jackie's relationship somehow. I mean Jann totally adored, idolized her, and I think she found him amusing." Years later, an exasperated Jackie would call Wenner a "bully" when she clashed with him over the cover of a commemorative book, *The Best of Rolling Stone* (published by Doubleday in 1993).

As a collection of previously published material put together in a rush job dominated by the *Rolling Stone* editorial staff, *The Ballad of John and Yoko* was not among Jackie's more hands-on titles. Her main contact was with Cott, who was the author-editor working with Doudna. Pulling out a copy of the book recently, Jonathan recalled that in the book's acknowledgments he thanked Jackie, crediting her "for having faith in and sponsoring the project." He also told me, "Jackie was really, really fascinated by and interested in John Lennon and Yoko Ono." The book was the first serious look at Yoko Ono and her world, one seemingly discordant with the pop-star lifestyle of her husband, but an essential piece of knowledge for anyone following the Beatles. The book also reproduced many classic photos of the era, such as John and Yoko staging their famous "bed-in" in Toronto, capped off by a portfolio of color shots by Annie Leibovitz.

While Jackie had her issues with tabloid journalism (what she once called "the river of sludge") and paparazzi invasions, she often waxed enthusiastic about her favorite serious journalists. She once observed, "Before I was married, I worked on a newspaper. Being a journalist seemed the ideal way of both having a job and experiencing the world, especially for anyone with a sense of adventure." At a Christmas party at her apartment in 1981, Jackie greeted Edward Klein, then editor in chief of *The New York Times Magazine,* and cooed, "Oh, Ed. I'm so glad you could come. Journalists are the most interesting people in the whole world!"

That same year Jackie had a hand in two books by the French historian and scholar Olivier Bernier, the stepson of the Met's lecture diva Rosamond Bernier. Jackie was to play a role in five of his books. The first was a work entitled *Pleasure and Privilege: Life in France, Naples, and America, 1770–1790,* an immensely engaging discourse on the twenty years preceding the French Revolution. Although she did not edit the book, she campaigned to have Louis Auchincloss contribute an introduction, which would inspire another long-term collaboration.

At his Park Avenue apartment in 2009, I interviewed Auchincloss, who was the only relative Jackie edited. A former Wall Street lawyer and prolific writer of both fiction and nonfiction, he was an elegant man, with a patrician beak of a nose and a lilting, high-pitched voice that suggested his Brahmin background. Jackie admired his probing intellect and gentility. He provided me with an essay about her entitled "Belles Lettres," which he wrote for *Quest* magazine, a niche journal serving Manhattan's social elite and real estate circles. Auchincloss has been described as "the last of the gentlemen novelists." His insights into Jackie's character and early life cast a revealing light on the various talents that she later exploited to great advantage working with him as editor:

> My friendship with Jackie flourished largely in the years of her second widowhood and was primarily based on our relationship as editor and author in

the preparation of several books we produced together. My acquaintance with President Kennedy had been of the slightest; I chatted with him briefly on a couple of family occasions. Her second husband I never met.

Yet I had known Jackie much further back. Her stepfather, Hugh D. Auchincloss (known as "Hughdie"), and my father, Howland Auchincloss, were first cousins, and the house where Jackie spent her girlhood summers, Hammersmith Farm, in Newport, had been built by my grandfather, John Winthrop Auchincloss, and sold, when he suffered financial reverses, to his brother, Hugh D., Senior, who could well afford its upkeep, having just wed Emma Jennings, a Standard Oil heiress. The place was inherited by Jackie's stepfather in 1942.

Until Jackie had passed her debutante year, I saw her hardly at all. I was a dozen years older than she, and the young are rigidly age-conscious. But my brother, John, who lived in Washington, saw a great deal of Jackie's mother and stepfather, and when I visited him there I got to know her and became, as did everyone, subject to her charm. She had no public persona, of course, in those days, but when in after years she developed one, it amused me that it was so soft and gentle. Indeed, she could demonstrate those qualities, and delightfully, but there was another side of her nature that made her an even more interesting and vital person. She could be very strong, even willful.

For example, one summer when she and I both happened to be in Paris, she invited me to go out to Chantilly in a small car she had rented. Her sister Lee accompanied us. Jackie was driving at breakneck speed when I observed down the road an ancient woman in black who seemed to be debating whether she had time to cross in front of us. She obviously didn't, but her sense must have been dull, for to my horror I saw her step forward and cried, "Jackie, for Christ's sake!" Jackie slammed on her brakes, and we lurched across the road and back, landing, harmlessly enough, in a ditch. The old woman was frantically crossing herself. Jackie simply observed: "She should be thanking my good brakes and not the good Lord. And by the way, Louis, we don't mention this to Cousin Hughdie when we get home." On we drove, and at the same speed.

Not long after this episode, in 1952 or 1953, when I was visiting my brother in Washington, Jackie came to dinner with her mother and Hughdie, and we were told she was engaged to a young man called Husted. John broke out some champagne, and we drank to the couple. But after dinner, sitting with me in a corner, Jackie expounded on what her life would be as the wife of a respectable young businessman in New York. She seemed to think it would be peaceful but dull. I had just published a novel called *Sibyl* about such a woman's life, and Jackie kept saying em-

phatically, "That's it. That's my future. I'll be a Sibyl Husted." I remember
vividly my sudden, inexplicable conviction that the woman telling me
this was destined for a very different fate. Jackie's mother, Janet Auchincloss, was against the marriage, and only days later, we learned the en-
gagement was off. . . .

I found an undated letter from Jackie, probably from the 1960s, for it
was hand-delivered in New York, in which she responds to a letter I had
written her about some article on the Auchincloss family that must have
misquoted me as saying something indiscreet about her. She protested that
I mustn't be upset. For how could I have helped it? "One doesn't expect
people to behave dishonorably, but I'm afraid, as I have learned this winter,
that when money is involved, they often do. I expect this to be the rule
rather than the exception now, so do you know what the nice thing about
it was? Your writing to me. That was a very touching thing to do."

Could anything be more graceful?

In 1980 our professional relationship commenced with my writing for
her a preface to Olivier Bernier's *Pleasure and Privilege,* which she claimed
I "had finished writing before one had finished asking you."

Auchincloss later shared a few observations for a PBS documentary
that he repeated for my benefit. "She gave enormous encouragement to
her writers, and that's a very great thing because an editor becomes kind
of like your mother. You expect love and encouragement from an editor.
She knew how to hand it out, and at the same time she knew how to make
her objections stick and make her writers change to meet her demands."

Regarding his foreword to Olivier Bernier's book, Auchincloss told me,
"That's when it started. She asked me to do an introduction, which I was
very happy to do. I liked the book. I liked him. He's gone on to have a very
successful life. He runs tours. He's a very agreeable man. I used to think he
was rather superficial, but he's not. He wrote a very good biography of Lafayette, and he's adored by all these rich women who tour. He takes them to
lunch at castles, and so on."

Describing his work on *Pleasure and Privilege,* Bernier recalled, "I
knew Louis Auchincloss, and I also knew Jackie, but at that point in fact
it was Jean Anne Vincent who was my editor and who also was the editor
for *Louis the Beloved.* Then she retired and I guess Jackie asked for me. I
would have asked for her if I had known ahead that Jean Anne was retiring.
But anyway, it worked it out, and she then became my editor.

"I first met her not actually because of the books, but because Rosamond Bernier, my stepmother, and John Russell, her late husband, were
great friends of hers. So I had actually met her before I ever met her

professionally and found her exactly the same. There wasn't one social persona and then another different professional persona. She was who she was, always.

"She was the editor for *The Eighteenth-Century Woman* because it was a coproduction of Doubleday and the Met, and she was the editor at Doubleday who was involved with a production with the Met. . . . The book was meant to come out, as it did indeed, together with the show, and it was Diana Vreeland's show. I specified that if we were going to do this book, and furthermore an illustrated book, we ought to have some actual costumes from the Met collection. And that was very much up to Diana, and when the time came, I asked her if she could please arrange to have some dresses put on mannequins so that we could look at them, which in fact she did.

"Jackie was the most enormous help because when a book is being done by several—well, in this case two—large organizations, things have an unfortunate tendency to not get done. . . . I kept asking questions—'Do we have this? Do we have that?'—'Well, no, we don't.' 'Well, weren't we supposed to have it two weeks ago?' 'Oh, were we?' I found that I could— and this was in the summer—call Jackie on the Vineyard, and invariably get her. I mean, if she was out sailing, two minutes later the phone would ring. She would call back as soon as she got my messages, and she would then see to it that whatever we needed actually got done.

"*Louis the Beloved* came out at a time when Doubleday was having financial problems, and therefore it was printed on really bad paper. The margins were miniscule, and the quality of the print really left a lot to be desired. So when we were talking, after I had handed in the manuscript for *Louis XIV,* I said, 'Look, please, Jackie, can we do something to see to it that this book looks decent, that it's got decent margins, that it's good paper, that it's got good design.' And she said, 'Absolutely.' She called down, because he was on a floor below, and made an appointment with the designer for the book.

"And so I went back that day, she and I went down together, and I watched her make him melt. It was wonderful to watch. She stood about five inches from him, and looked straight into his eyes, and said, 'Oh I know we're going to have a beautiful book'—you know, the voice. 'I know you're going to do an extraordinary job.' And she went on. And I watched that designer melt. I think he was transfixed. And we got a decent-looking book.

"She had, as you know, enough charm to knock over a large building, and she knew exactly how to apply it when she chose, and when she applied it, it was completely irresistible. . . . Her heart really was in what she was doing, and she did clearly feel very protective of her authors. . . . I did *At the Court of Napoleon* because she asked me to. It was her idea, and not mine. The other books were my ideas. But she really was interested. And I was very struck, for instance, by the fact that when I was at her apartment and we talked about something, and she mentioned a book, she would go to her bookshelf and know exactly where it was. Well, it seemed to me to indicate that she read the book in question and that she cared enough about it to make sure she could find it again easily. . . .

"She was, I always thought, incredibly nice. When *Louis XIV* came out, for instance, there was a book party, and she gave me a very pretty mother-of-pearl. It must have been originally, I think, the kind of little mother-of-pearl [box] in which young women kept, oh, I don't know what, their ball cards—that sort of thing. But then when I left Doubleday and did a book with Little, Brown on the French Revolution, and there was a book party for that, not only did Jackie come to the book party, but she again produced a present, which I thought under the circumstances was extraordinarily nice of her. She cared about the eighteenth century or the seventeenth, for that matter, and she obviously cared about France a great deal, and she was also herself really very knowledgeable. . . . I've forgotten which book, I'm afraid, but one day she looked at me and she said, 'Oh, your books are just like drinking champagne!'

"I've just remembered what I think is really an extraordinary case of her complete commitment to her authors. Very little time before she died, but when she was already ill—and I didn't realize how ill she was until she died very soon afterwards—she called me because she wanted me to write a blurb for a book she was just publishing. . . . We just spoke on the phone, and she was exactly the way she had always been. And then, to my horror, literally days later, there it was in the newspaper about her being deadly ill. So she must have been already very unwell when she called to ask me to do that, and the fact that, knowing what she must have already have known, after all, she still, to the very last moment, really, was looking after her authors. I mean, that's very remarkable."

As Jackie knew well, for connoisseurs of the sweet life, the pampered courtiers whose last gasp occurred just before the French Revolution inhabited a different world. Etiquette had replaced coercion as a motive force, and the flutter of a regal hand or wrist could alter a family's prospects for generations to come. Paris was the supreme example of a bourgeois heaven on earth. It was supremely civilized in various ways, featuring beautiful architecture, immaculate gardens, and endless gustatory pleasures. The king could do pretty much what he wanted, and so could the aristocracy, as long as they maintained their seeming obeisance and discretion.

Bernier the historian writes like a novelist, a quality that Jackie appreciated and did her best to encourage in all of us writing nonfiction. He extracts passages from diaries and letters, and uses these to bring the highly stylized rites of the French royal court into focus for modern readers. By focusing on the twenty years preceding the French Revolution in *Pleasure and Privilege,* Bernier knows he is writing about a doomed society, one that will be stripped bare and demonized once the Jacobins come to power.

Some of the hallmarks of prerevolutionary France were embodied by the aristocratic women whose machinations heavily influenced the court at Versailles. This is why *The Eighteenth-Century Woman* is such a fitting companion to *Pleasure and Privilege.* Both concern the same period. *The Eighteenth-Century Woman* was the companion volume for an exhibition that opened at the Met in December 1981. By showing the shrewdness of Madame de Pompadour and the secret schemes of Queen Maria Carolina of Naples, by illustrating the chic fashion trends of the Musicale and of the elegant fan made of mother-of-pearl and silk that no self-respecting grande dame would go without, by describing how games of chance and divertissements obsessed the idle rich, Bernier adds color to the more straightforward word game that is history. Using painting as the photography of its time, he amply demonstrates how the nobility lived, while hinting that this conspicuous consumption might have also triggered the violent reactions against them.

Jackie's enchantment with the French court enabled Bernier to mount another book on the subject, *Secrets of Marie Antoinette* (1985). In the context of the intricate web of etiquette and social politesse that consumed the court and the widening gap between the royal family and the French citizenry, Marie Antoinette would come to symbolize this abyss. As Bernier chronicles in his book of epistolary "secrets," for more than a decade after her arrival in Paris in 1770, Marie Antoinette wrote her formidable mother, the Empress Maria Theresa. With their correspondence and the parallel letters of the Count Mercy-Argenteau to the empress, Bernier provides a glimpse into a dying era just before modernity would change the world forever.

Seventeenth-century France is even more distant, alien territory, half medieval and ruled by customs that no longer make sense or comport with contemporary values. The divine right of kings was still in force, and concepts such as liberty and freedom had meanings other than those they came to have after the French and American revolutions. Reading a biography of Louis XIV becomes problematic if the author does not carefully present the cultural context in which the Sun King reigned. In *Louis XIV:*

A Royal Life (1987), Bernier understands this dilemma and provides explanations that make the larger-than-life figure of Louis XIV comprehensible. In line with her own reading of history, Jackie was sensitive to the fact, as related by Bernier, that during the reign of Louis XIV sites such as the Tuileries gardens and the palaces at Versailles were created not for the upper classes alone but as enduring symbols of "la belle France."

Setting the stage for another French chronicle instigated by Jackie, Bernier tells us in *At the Court of Napoleon* (1989) that Napoleon inherited a bloodthirsty revolution that repulsed him; so he returned to the courtly intrigues of the Bourbon kings in a deliberate gambit to reassure the French ruling classes that he, as self-proclaimed emperor, was not going to assume the Jacobin mantle. A number of other Corsicans migrated to Paris to take advantage of the status they acquired when he took power. One of these was a sixteen-year-old girl, Laure Permon, who would later become Laure Junot, the Duchess d'Abrantès. She established herself as one of the world's first gossip columnists, encouraged by the novelist Honoré de Balzac, writing the "inside dish" about the peccadilloes and endless affairs and betrayals inside Napoleon's court.

Bernier edited the duchess's memoirs and provided interleaved glosses for them. They stand as one of the most insightful documents illuminating the Napoleonic era, peeling back the scrim of rectitude that official histories often hide behind. Just as Bernier's *Secrets of Marie Antoinette* uses that queen's diaries to create a portrait of the last of the Bourbons, so too does the author render a parallel portrait here of a short-lived dynasty that appeared, for one brief moment, to threaten to take over the entire civilized world of Europe.

Recalling Jackie's editing of the book, Bernier said, "For *At the Court of Napoleon* she suggested, and rightly too, a lot of cuts. . . . I wrote that introduction and those bridging passages, but otherwise I pretty well translated the text, and Jackie said, which was quite right, that it was much too long, and suggested the places where she thought cuts could be made. For my other books it was really . . . the only line suggestion that I can think of was, it must have been . . . I don't remember; I suppose it was about *Louis XIV*. At any rate, I had evidently written something that made her say, 'You should really change it because it sounds as if you're talking about Nancy Reagan.' So I changed that."

Shortly after Bernier's *The Eighteenth-Century Woman* was published, in February 1982, Jackie was promoted to the position of senior editor. While she was moving up the ladder and eventually given a corner office with a window view on the forty-third floor, some of her colleagues, such as Betty Prashker, were experiencing frustration with house politics. According to Al

Silverman, "Betty Prashker had finally been granted a vice presidency and had become editorial director of the division, but in 1981 she left Doubleday in disenchantment."

Prashker moved on to Crown, while Sam Vaughan later moved to Random House. In reporting the personnel changes, Silverman noted, "The golden age at Doubleday had come to its end." But Jackie stuck it out— she had every opportunity to follow her colleagues, but she was on the ascent at Doubleday and chose to stay. At the same time, her family life was a picture of rock-solid, if unorthodox, stability. Maurice Tempelsman left his wife and moved into the Stanhope Hotel, on Fifth Avenue, just a few blocks from Jackie's apartment (he would not move in with her until 1985). John Jr. was beginning his junior year at Brown University, and Caroline was working in the film and television department at the Met under Jackie's old friend Karl Katz. And there was to be another welcome development. In March 1982, Jackie was relieved to win a court case against Ron Galella, who was cited with contempt and ordered to pay $5,000 in damages, though he had not yet snapped his last shot of her and would again invade her privacy.

Jackie's literary influence already extended well beyond the books she published at Doubleday. While working with Bernier on his excursions into French history, Jackie encouraged Louis Auchincloss to make a fictional foray into the Bourbon court. The result was the novel *The Cat and the King,* an arch tour de force purporting to be the memoirs of the second Duc de Saint-Simon. Published in 1981, the book was well received by critics, and Auchincloss conveyed to me that although Jackie played no role in its publication, he expressed his gratitude with his dedication, which reads: "For Jacqueline Kennedy Onassis, who persuaded me that Versailles was still a valid source for fiction."

Even before her promotion, Jackie had recruited one more author from her days at Viking. Eugene Kennedy would give her two novels exploring political themes that would help solidify her fortunes at Doubleday. She was always looking for authors who would embark on a series of books, which she would pursue regardless of the commercial success of their first work. For Jackie, the authors themselves were works in progress, and she was committed to helping them develop and refine their talents.

Kennedy's first novel, published in 1981, was *Father's Day,* a muckraking potboiler set against a realistic backdrop of Illinois and Indiana. Kennedy recollected, "It came about when I had the idea to write the novel. . . . It came upon me when I was driving through South Bend one day. Jackie had been at Viking and I went there and had a meeting with some of the people there. . . . despite all the folderol at Viking, they were very enthusiastic about it. But they had some idea I might write a different kind of book, more about Father Hesburgh [then president of the University of Notre Dame], whom I knew quite well.

"And I talked to Jackie on the phone. I said to her, 'I think I'd rather work with you on this.' So she said she was very delighted that I'd made that decision. . . . I just felt more comfortable sticking with her and going to Doubleday. I think she did spoil us in a way. I worked with a lot of different editors, and most of them deal with you with a sort of a calculated indifference."

Jackie shared the editing of *Father's Day* with Lisa Drew. Kennedy suggested that Jackie didn't do the line editing. Rather, he described her at this stage of her career as more of a "conceptual editor," which was what the project needed. An accurate history of the complicated entanglements between the Catholic Church, Notre Dame, the mob, and the political machine of modern Chicago could land a historian in trouble. The beauty of this kind of fiction is that a novelist can tell the story as a thinly disguised roman à clef and win praise from the very people who might order up cement shoes for an offending investigative reporter. *Father's Day* is a multigenerational saga of the Kinsellas, an Irish Catholic family whose story parallels the twentieth-century growth of the Second City, mixing real and imagined characters. One can imagine Jackie's guilty pleasure when she commissioned the story. She had undoubtedly witnessed parallel events in another predominantly Catholic city, Boston, after marrying the son of kingmaker Joseph Kennedy.

Jackie lauded the book and author to Ray Roberts, giving him a copy of the manuscript and suggesting, in an undated note, "Be sure to read the Notre Dame pages first. They set everything in focus—We have a little François Villon on our hands." Describing Jackie's editorial approach to the storytelling, Kennedy explained, "The things that she would talk about or want to change or question were whether the character would really react in this way or not react in this way." Kennedy later recalled, "She would surprise you with a phone call, as she did me once on a Fourth of July evening, to tell you what she liked about your manuscript that she had spent several hours on that day. 'No woman would react that way to a man,' she once said of a female character who had responded passively to male indecision in *Father's Day*. 'A real woman would kick him all over town.'"

While cast in the same quasi-fictional mode, Kennedy's second novel, *Queen Bee*, posed a different set of challenges for the author and his editor. This roman à clef is about Chicago politics and the Daley machine. Mayor Richard J. Daley is Mayor Cullen in this novel that could have only come from the mind and pen of an insider. The book evolved from a meeting with Jackie and Lisa Drew after Kennedy had published an article in *The New York Times Magazine* about Chicago mayor Jane Byrne. "They suggested that I write a novel about that article," said Kennedy. "Naturally the character in that book is very like Jane Byrne, believe it or not."

The book charts the rise of Anne Marie O'Brien, an ambitious woman whose husband is missing in action in some unspecified war. She becomes a protégé of Mayor Cullen. When Cullen succumbs to a fatal disease, O'Brien becomes the first female mayor of Chicago, at the same time starting a dangerous liaison with a handsome television reporter, a move that almost guarantees scandal to come. Kennedy characterizes her as a magnet for men, a natural queen, not unlike his editor.

But in nature, the queen bee has less freedom than any other member of the hive, a fact made clear by Kennedy's choice of a valedictory passage preceding the story's onset. Citing Frank C. Pellet's *The Romance of the Hive,* makes it clear that the hive's survival depends upon the queen's fertility, so while she is accommodated, she is also a prisoner of her own status and of the needs of the worker bees. This is the situation that would-be mayor O'Brien finds herself in as she struggles to the top, slipping on the grease and grime of big-city politics.

After Jackie's death, Kennedy wrote a reminiscence about his editor that he invited me to include here. "It was by her professionalism that she earned her window at Doubleday. . . . She understood the rules, demands and discipline of selecting a book, editing it and even making it sound more worthy than it was at sales conferences. . . . She did her homework well. I recall her bundling ten books on Russia into a satchel as she left her office one evening. 'I got these from the library,' she explained, 'to prepare for a book I'm going to work on next.'

"Her consistent efforts to master the levels of an editor's calling did not make Mrs. Onassis into somebody else, of course. But they did give her an opportunity to be who she really was, a fiercely bright and talented woman with great artistic sensibility. Her eye for the telling details of existence had once motivated her to be a photographer. It served her, and her authors, well in the editing process. For most writers, being edited is like handing your firstborn over to a doctor you don't trust for delicate surgery you don't think is necessary in the first place. But I will always be grateful for her incisiveness. . . .

"I remember her best after a book party, standing alone in the middle of Fifth Avenue at ten o'clock at night, laughing as she hailed a cab in classic New York fashion to take her home. She was unafraid, it seemed to me, to head home in the dark. It held no secrets and no fears that she had not faced a long time before."

5

Unseen Vistas and Avant-Gardens

At Doubleday, even after becoming a senior editor, Jackie lost more battles than she won running the editorial and marketing gauntlet. Over the course of her career, there were countless books that she proposed for which she was unable to win support. She never had complete freedom in choosing her books, though she was at times coddled by the powers that be, who realized she was a considerable asset for the house and didn't want to risk losing her. With some of her projects, they simply acquiesced in order to placate her.

With books that Jackie managed to acquire, there was another challenge to be faced down the line: rallying support for each of them with the in-house sales reps and publicity department. After leaving Doubleday, Sam Vaughan described the hurdle that routinely confronted Jackie and her colleagues. "You see, in effect, a book gets bought by a house more than once. The first time is when the contract is offered. Then it goes off everybody's screen except the editor's, for the year, or two years, or five, or ten, it takes the author to write it. It comes back, and, despite the fact that you have a contract, and that the contract may be big, it has to be sold again, in a psychological way. Now, if you've put out a lot of money for a book, and everybody knows it, it makes the editor's task a bit easier. All the flags fly when the book comes through. But that's for a very few books. The other books have all cost money. But whether the book costs fifty thousand dollars or two hundred thousand dollars, that fact, by and large, does not persuade anyone in the house. They've got to be persuaded, by the manuscript itself, ideally."

Jackie wooed the company's sales reps with calls and memos and even contacted bookstore buyers to promote her books. While she had considerable entrée with celebrities of all stripes and while by dint of her position she attracted overtures from various Hollywood and political figures, most of the book projects thus solicited never came to fruition. After watching actor George Hamilton talking about his life on a TV talk show, Jackie expressed interest in having him write a memoir. Hamilton hired a ghostwriter to put together a book proposal, but when it was delivered, it was overblown, presenting him as a major historical figure, with stories spanning the globe. According to Lisa Drew, Jackie then balked at the idea, saying, "Hmm. He's George Hamilton—not quite Alexander the Great."

Jackie later saw a story in a gossip column about a memoir that Dolly Parton was planning, which Parton described as "sort of exaggerated with a little bit of truth, a little bit of humor, and a little bit of dirty stuff, to make it sell." Jackie's reaction was, "Well, it sounds like another cultural watershed."

Gloria Steinem later submitted a novel to Jackie entitled *The Beholding,* written by her friend Kenneth Pitchford, who was also a published poet and playwright. After reading his manuscript, an intriguing exploration of a circle of 1960s relationships, sexuality, and various interpersonal crises that evoked the era, Jackie contacted Pitchford by phone to let him know that she wanted to publish the book. She invited him for a meeting at her apartment along with her fellow editor Michael Ossias, who also supported the book's acquisition. Pitchford brought Steinem with him, and when they arrived, they ran into Jackie on the sidewalk outside her building and accompanied her inside. According to Pitchford, Steinem had an agenda in addition to offering him her support for his book: She hoped that Jackie might lead her to another *Ms.* magazine story. "Steinem had her own ax to grind," Pitchford recalled. "She was trying to reach Joan Kennedy after her divorce from Ted Kennedy to find out how the new divorcée was faring."

Pitchford recalled being welcomed into Jackie's apartment and the break-the-ice small talk that followed. "The walls and ceiling of the study were covered in a bright yellow print, a quilted paisley fabric that had been used to upholster the sofa as well. I was ushered to an armchair, also in quilted splendor, and we all sat down. The first thing that Onassis decided to do was to display her liberal views on gay issues. I need to point out that this was still only a few years following Stonewall. The anecdote she told could not have been more retro to a gay radical such as I. She spoke of a lavish mock wedding that had occurred recently in Grosse Pointe, Michigan, between Christina Ford and Imelda Marcos. . . . When asked if she had attended the wedding herself, Onassis said no, but [she said that she] had heard all about it from her sister, Lee, who *had* attended."

At that point, Jackie shifted her focus to Pitchford's book. "Onassis walked over to me and sat down at my feet. Cross-legged on the Persian rug, she looked up into my eyes and said, 'Mr. Pitchford, you are a great writer and I'm going to publish your novel.' Talk like that can turn any writer's head." Jackie told Pitchford that Ossias would handle the book, and suggested a few plot changes. The author inwardly recoiled in silence. Referring to one of his novel's central characters, Jackie said, "You mustn't let Delia marry that awful man!"

Their discussion came to an end with Pitchford assuring Jackie that he would "think about" her suggestion. He noted, "Now, at the end of our meeting, having been careful not to step on my one-to-one with Onassis, Steinem asked if Jackie could be of help in reaching Joan Kennedy for a cover story in *Ms.* magazine. 'We're not in touch,' Onassis said, and that was that."

In fact, Jackie was still very much in touch with Joan Kennedy and wrote to her, offering counsel on her breakup with Ted. According to published reports, while Joan was struggling with the ill-fated marriage, Jackie advised her, "This is the twentieth century—not the nineteenth—where the little woman stayed home on a pedestal with the kids and her rosary. . . . Your life matters—as much as him—you love him—but you can't destroy yourself. . . . Forbidden fruit is what is exciting. It takes much more of a real man to have a deep relationship with the woman he lives with. The routine of married life can become boring." Some years later, Joan Kennedy would write a book about classical music that was published by Doubleday, and she often stopped by to visit Jackie at her office, though according to her former colleagues, Jackie played no role in acquiring or editing the book.

Kenneth Pitchford's book was ultimately turned down by Doubleday's editorial board and not published for more than twenty years (despite

Jackie's enthusiastic presentation and the fact that poet Adrienne Rich called it "truly a remarkable book, utterly original, serious and beautiful"). The author remembered, "In due time, I received a touching personal letter from her [Jackie], which I still have, saying that the board's decision went against me, allegedly because of the length of the book, my relative obscurity as a writer, and the complexity of the writing. However, she made it clear that reading the book had meant a great deal to her personally. . . . In her last words to me in the study, Onassis said she hoped I wouldn't mind that some pages had been disfigured by spaghetti sauce spilled on them at the beach by her negligent son John, whose rooms at Brown she was helping to decorate."

Jackie's assistant during the early 1980s was a young woman named Marcia Jacobs, the daughter of the late Australian poet and memoirist Jacob Rosenberg. After studying for her master's at NYU, Jacobs took a typing course and ended up working in Doubleday's personnel department. She was soon invited to replace Hope Marinetti, but she was reluctant to work for Jackie, as she had recently married and didn't want to take on the pressures that she thought the job would entail. Jacobs remembered her interview with Jackie. "I went up to her office. . . . I had black tights on and a little tight skirt, and I just walked in and I sat down. I don't even remember what we chatted about, but it was a very short conversation. And she said, 'Oh, you're adorable. Would you like to work with me?'

"And I was sort of taken aback. Not, Would you like to work *for* me?— but, Would you like to work *with* me? I said, 'Okay.' I couldn't say no to her. . . . I wasn't in awe of her and I wasn't intimidated in any way. And I turned out to be right in the sense that she was so motherly and so kind, and I saw how she cared about her children, and how she was interested in my life. I mean, I was just this kid from Australia.

"I was a young girl, and really inexperienced in terms of corporate life. I've been a teacher and I've been an academic most of my adult life. . . . I came in at a time where Doubleday was going through some real economic hurdles. . . . It was just so commercial at Doubleday, everything was about money. . . . I remember the chief editor was fired. I think his name was Sandy Richardson, and I remember him storming out of the office. He just left all his stuff on the desk and he just walked out. I mean, it was really pretty dramatic. . . .

"I have another story I'm just remembering. Richard Avedon called, and I felt so completely stupid. I didn't know who Richard Avedon was. I realized afterwards that all of New York and the whole world knew about Richard Avedon, but I just didn't know. Why would I have known? I was a girl from Melbourne, Australia. And he rang into the office, and I made him spell his name out. I had to be very protective of her, and I had to be very careful. He was not amused, but I got him to spell his name. I told Jackie the story because I felt like such an idiot. She was roaring. She was laughing. She thought it was great. I'd never seen her laugh like that. She was just doubled over."

As with Jackie's other assistants over the years, when Jacobs was ill, Jackie insisted, "You've got to go and see my doctor." Jackie later told her, "Don't worry. I've got a doctor for every part of your body." Marcia said, "Other people and other bosses who I had along the way certainly weren't as humble as she. She never threw her weight around. She was gentle, sensitive, and she was just remarkable. I knew that she had a tough time with the press. The press would make up stories about her, as they tend to do. There were obviously several areas of her life that she compartmentalized. I imagine, looking back, that her period in the publishing industry probably made her feel normal, and then she was just propelled in that very interesting world. It's a real privilege to go to work, and I think she realized that. That's why she was just so good at what she did."

Jackie operated within a kind of self-protective emotional moat, with her social and professional lives compartmentalized, but she was proactive as editor and relished taking the initiative to launch her projects. She loved the process even with its inherent frustrations, and she was soon pursuing another ambitious endeavor that would take her back to France. For this coffee-table production, *Unseen Versailles,* she enlisted the talents of avant-garde fashion photographer Deborah Turbeville, whose captivating, irreverent work had been included in Diana Vreeland's *Allure*.

Unseen Versailles is a visit to the royal Bourbon palace long after the French Revolution had altered its importance, its appearance, and its soul. Louis Auchincloss summarizes in a lengthy introduction the meaning of Versailles then and now, rehabilitating its haunting topicality. Turbeville's photos are tinted, heat-seeking missiles for the ghosts of the eighteenth century. Headless statues of granite rest on the floor, and derelict debris collects in every open passageway and forlorn corner. According to Turbeville's grand design, models wearing elaborate French period costumes inhabit the private apartments of Madame Du Barry and Madame de Pompadour, the cunning, art-loving mistress of Louis XV whom both Jackie and the photographer greatly admired. This was not the Versailles of the tour guides but a darker, more solemn place where, to use Percy Bysshe Shelley's phrase, "nothing beside remains."

Jackie consented to write a short, elegant editor's note: "Another photographic book of Versailles? Are not the coffee tables groaning already? But wait. While it is perfectly true that the gardens and state rooms have been done and redone, in classic, splendid images formal and glistening, no one has yet seen the palace and its environment as Deborah Turbeville has seen them. . . . We wanted to match Louis Auchincloss' formal portrait of Versailles with Deborah Turbeville's dream; to unite a master of the precise and a mistress of the poetic."

In August 1979 Jackie wrote a note from Hyannis Port to Ray Roberts suggesting that Louis Auchincloss was "very keen" on contributing to the project, expressing her hope that he would follow through, and closing with the lines, "Hot spit! Keep your fingers crossed." Auchincloss recounted how Jackie convinced him to write the introduction. "Jackie's proposal that I do the piece was couched in her usual beguiling fashion: 'Only a writer at home in the period could do such a text. I can just picture popping you down in the Galerie des Glaces, and I can imagine what you would say to everyone there.'"

Auchincloss explained his and Jackie's approach to the text: "I had deliberately sought to balance the artistic boldness of the pictures in the book with the conservatism of the introduction: a fusion of romantic and classical. Jackie liked this, but it worried her. She thought we needed a paragraph to deflect criticism, to explain that the difference in tone between the text and photographs was intentional. As she explained to me, what she was trying to say to the reader was: You are getting such a double-barreled treat here, and you better realize it—a brilliant, structured history of Versailles in words, and a fragmented impression of it in photographs and collage."

Describing how the project fell into her lap and the subsequent "frustrations of production," Deborah Turbeville told me, "Jackie Onassis had a very special way of working, as you probably know, as an editor. And she always liked to connect her books. And so she'd been doing books on Atget, or Atget's Versailles, things like that. So she yearned to do another book about Versailles, and she was taken by—I think his name was Howard Adams, who was the head of the bicentennial—on a tour of the private rooms in Versailles. . . . And she fell in love with these rooms, and had the idea to do a book on the *petits appartements,* and to convey through text and evocative photographs what it could have been like at that time. So she thought of me to do the pictures. And it was kind of connecting Atget's Versailles with a young photographer who Vreeland had used in *Allure,* bringing about another book with this new photographer on Versailles. . . .

"And then it was really funny, because she called me. And I used to hang out in the loft of a friend of mine when I came back to New York because I didn't have a permanent home here anymore. So I was staying with friends who were up in the country, and I was free to use their, what do you call it, little machine which has messages—message machine. So one night I came home, put on the messages to hear if there's anything for me, and I hear this voice, the most famous voice in the world, saying, 'Does anybody here know where Deborah Turbeville is? This is Jackie Onassis, and I'm searching for her because I want to talk to her about doing a book with me.' I couldn't believe it because I had no warning that she was going to propose this.

"So then I called her back, and she just went on and on about how great it could be, and dadadada, and then she said, 'You go off and think about it. We have plenty of time.' It was the middle of the winter. And then I came back in the spring, and she invited me over to a lunch in her apartment with Howard Adams, and we chatted for a few hours over this project and plotted how it could be done. And I was to meet Howard Adams in Paris, and go with this curator who had shown him the back rooms, and see what Jackie had seen. And then we'd go from there.

"So I went back, and I saw the rooms and everything. In the midst of all of this—it was a kind of funny thing—the guy who was the curator there . . . held the whole thing up. . . . Jackie was getting more and more anxious. She was afraid she'd lose the project, it wouldn't go ahead, because she knew how it was better to strike while the iron is hot kind of thing. She had them interested at Doubleday but, you know, other things come up. Finally she called me one day and said, 'You know something? I think that this is ridiculous. Why don't I just call my cousin Louis Auchincloss, and I'm sure he would be available to do the introduction, and he would do a great job.' So that's what she did, and that's when the book got started.

"And then she and I flew over to Paris to get the permission to shoot from the curator . . . which wasn't easy. It was a lot of protocol, and he was skeptical, and they were nervous. It was very bureaucratic. . . . She of course went separately, and she stayed at the Crillon, and I stayed at my apartment. . . . So we went out the next day, and the whole thing was like a fairy tale. The whole fairy-tale quality of Louis XV's Versailles was what captivated both of us. And then, I mean, Jackie in the limousine was leaning out of the window when the driver pulled beside the guard. It was like a Monty Python thing. We proceeded into the inner sanctum of Versailles and then we had the meeting with the curator. He was so charmed by her that he said, 'Okay, okay, okay, you can do it.' And that was it. It was unbelievable!"

Never at a loss for words or spirited ebullience, Turbeville continued, "Then Jackie was calling me constantly in Paris to find out how it was going. I'd never photographed empty rooms before, and I was a little nervous about how that could be done. I didn't have the confidence I have now, after doing it for so many years. Then I thought, I don't know if a book with just me taking pictures of empty rooms is going to be anything. And it was an awful challenge, because I kept thinking, Here's me assigned to do a book by Jacqueline Onassis, and if I don't do it I'll regret it for the rest of my life, and if I do it, I may make a terrible blunder, it may be an awful thing. So I was caught between the two.

"I had a marvelous French stylist who did costumes for the theater and had lots of expertise, and she and I went to Versailles and got very discouraged because we really felt like we couldn't pull it off. And we sat in the café across from Versailles talking about what in the world we were going to do. It was very bleak, and I kept telling her stories about what I could see in the rooms. And she said, 'But you have to use people, Deborah. You have to use models. You have to ask for permission to use models.'

"So I put it all behind me and called Jacqueline, and made the proposal. And she said, 'Oh, Deborah, it's so precarious, I doubt that they would okay it. They might even throw us out if you start making waves like that. I don't think so'—all this kind of stuff. And I just said, 'You know, but I have to insist, Jackie. What am I doing? I'm not doing anything, just putting a few nice people in the pictures to illustrate it a little. Any painter does that. Why can't I?' Finally she acquiesced and said, 'Okay, I'll call the curator.' And so she called, and she finally talked him into it.

"So we proceeded. Oh, but the kind of things that I did!—like hiring pets, like trained monkeys and owls and I don't know what else, and all the entourage, and a crazy British hairdresser, who insisted on using these huge white wigs that were dyed and insisting that it was authentic—shocking pink wigs, and you name it—all this stuff, the paraphernalia going up and down the stairs, and it was the middle of winter, and there was no electricity, so we had to use artificial lights at times, and then poke around and try to get it done as best we could on one small electrical outlet. Then coming down at nine o'clock at night with two guards at my elbow all the time, holding on to the candelabra, because there was no light to get downstairs with all the entourage."

The daily routine included providing Polaroid photos of the sessions in progress to the curator for his approval. "The thing of it was," said Turbeville, "he flew into a rage and started spreading kind of funny reports around, and got after Mrs. Onassis. He told her that he heard that this

'Lady Hamilton,' the photographer, was making porno—he got me confused with David Hamilton, who did soft porn—because I had models in petticoats with paniers and things like that. So Jackie said, 'I assure you, dadadadadada,' and then she was calling me at midnight on the phone saying, 'I have to tell you this story! He thinks that you are David Hamilton. Can you imagine, Deborah? We sat in his office, and I mean he's got that old Boucher painting up above his head where the guy's sticking his hand right up the girl's crotch.' I thought, Oh my God, if this international conversation is heard by any operators who recognize her voice—It was so funny! 'How dare he say that when he's sitting under that painting!' You probably know, Jackie just said what she thought. . . .

"It was just one hilarious story after the other. Jackie was always there in the background, never far away. She was on the phone, and she kept saying, 'When are you coming back? We have to sort this out. I don't want to lose any more time. I'm afraid they might put it on the back burner,' and all this stuff. I've never worked with an editor who was like that, who was so involved at every level of the whole thing. You never get that now with editors. . . ."

Turbeville continued, "Jackie knew her history backwards and forwards. As a matter of fact, she made me go back afterwards and hire a guide and go through all those rooms, and get all the furniture, the period. It turned out that of course they were all scrambled up and you'd find in a Louis XV room a Louis XVI desk, and all this kind of stuff, because they just grabbed what they could from the flea market. And she said, 'Now I want a rundown of all this stuff, what was in the rooms. And get the story about the hairpins, the story of Marie Antoinette's hairpins and the day of the revolution.' I was terrified that I wouldn't get it right. . . .

"To make a book like that I had to break all the rules in order to have it be anything. . . . I remember in my bedroom I had this long bulletin board, and I stuck up each day as I went along the progress. I had to begin to try to figure out how to make all that nonsense I had been photographing work together in one book. . . . I had two sets of layouts, one very traditional and classic, and the other one the way I thought the book would be more interesting. So I said to Jackie, 'I'm going to show two, but I'm hoping that the art director, Alex Gotfryd, goes for what I've done.'

"I was out staying on Block Island, and I came in just for the meeting, so she had never seen what I had in mind. And then she saw it for the first time in his office, and she loved it, and he loved it. Jackie, I think, had a very good relationship with him, and they saw eye to eye on everything. When we got in there she already had spoken to him, talking to him about me. And then Alex looked at the layouts and he said, 'Well, there's no question in my mind. That very special thing you've done with it is what we should run with, and we just have to get you a very special book designer to make it all happen.' So that was how we got Michael Flanagan. But it was Jackie backing me up one hundred fifty percent that did it."

Turbeville remembered that Michael Flanagan had beautiful handwriting and wrote captions for the photos that were quotes drawn from primary sources. The captions, as snippets of history, were Turbeville's idea, but she had to overcome Jackie's resistance, as the editor worried that the captions might upset Auchincloss, who was responsible for the rest of the text. Flanagan provided me with excerpts from an unpublished manuscript entitled "Famous" that recounted his collaborations with Jackie over the years after he first met her in 1980.

One day out of the blue I was hired by Alex Gotfryd, Doubleday's senior trade art director, to design a "special" book of Jackie's, called *Unseen Versailles*. I had only designed one or two photography books before, and I felt like a novice. . . . Alex explained over the phone that he had chosen me for Versailles because, as he put it, Jackie wanted it to be designed by a "real artist . . ."

A few weeks later we had a planning session at Doubleday for *Unseen Versailles*. Besides Deborah Turbeville and myself, several staff people were there, including Alex and of course Jackie. . . . When Jackie and her assistant entered the room, Alex introduced us. As I shook Jackie's hand, I had the impression of looking into a face I already knew. A face we all think we know. The image on a million magazine covers, as iconic as Abe Lincoln or Marilyn Monroe.

"Gee," I said. "You look so . . . familiar!"

She smiled forgivingly.

I liked her for that; but I wasn't ready yet to admit that I wanted her to like me too. I spent the first fifteen minutes of the meeting deliberately ignoring her. As if to prove what? That I couldn't be seduced? Eventually when I looked at Jackie's face I studied her guiltily, greedily, secretly—as though I expected her features to reveal something more, something beyond the mere topography of flesh and blood.

But there was nothing more. Only an attractive woman dressed for business, with a pair of nondescript reading glasses looped around her neck, carrying a handbag and yellow legal pad. She settled into a chair beside me. She took notes during the meeting. The table was strewn with photographs. Jackie unwrapped a Tootsie Roll from her purse, and passed it around. "Does anyone want some?" An hour later we took a coffee break, and Jackie poured. . . .

We were supposed to be laying the groundwork for the book: deciding on the binding, trim size, page signatures, plate-making, inking, printing, et cetera. Nobody seemed flustered by Jackie's being there; yet I found it irritating. Such politeness among us, such decorum! As if there was nothing strange about being in that airless room, sharing Tootsie Rolls with the most famous woman in the universe. . . .

Jackie made no secret of her fascination with aristocrats. She took an infectious delight in their lunatic foibles. She read Saint-Simon's journals and other accounts of 18th century French courtly life in search of juicy quotations for our book. . . .

"Versailles is full of ghosts," Jackie said.

I confessed that I'd never been to France.

"Oh, you must go some day. You will go."

Louis Auchincloss described Jackie's wry take on his 'partnership' with Turbeville. "Jackie was pleased with the book when it was finally printed, and she even exceeded her usual hyperbole when she wrote in my copy: 'Your text is splendor.' But the contrast between my prose and Deborah's photographs seemed to suggest to her an amusing dissimilarity in our personalities, for she added, 'I predict a whole series from the two of you shackled at the ankle, hopping around the world together interpreting great monuments of the past. Maybe next time she will let you dress up and be in some of the photographs.'"

While Turbeville and Auchincloss actually had little direct contact—as she put it, "We each did our own thing"—with Jackie's encouragement, they agreed to work together on another book, entitled *Newport Remembered*, with photographs and text devoted to the gilded society Mecca of historical Rhode Island. Turbeville said, "I asked Jackie to do that book, and she couldn't do it. It was at a time when Doubleday wasn't too keen on doing books like that, and they weren't interested. So she felt badly, and she recommended me to another man who was head of Abrams. He said yes and he was delighted."

While the Versailles book was still under way, Louis Auchincloss approached Jackie with an idea for another book that had deep personal significance for him and his wife, Adele, an artist. With this book, Louis and his wife agreed to have their family privacy invaded under Jackie's guidance. He wrote, "Our next project was *Maverick in Mauve*. I had discovered the diary of my wife's grandmother, Florence Adele Sloane, written in the 1890s. . . . As she was a member of the Vanderbilt family, the diary provided an interesting 'inside' view of the belle epoque in Manhattan, with all its gilt and trimmings. Jackie agreed with me that the diary was a sociological document of some value and determined to publish it, but she had some trouble with the Doubleday board, who found it a bit on the weak side but who finally agreed to go ahead if I would supply an extensive running commentary to go with the entries, which I was glad to do.

"Jackie and I clashed over the illustrations. I wanted it to be a strictly historical document, with each family photograph (I had many albums) carefully related to a particular episode in the diary." While Auchincloss wanted to adhere strictly to the chronology of the photos as they related to the text of the diary, Jackie preferred to go with photos that appealed to her regardless of the dates they were taken. When he objected, she said, "Do we have to be so technical?" and gently taunted him, saying, "Oh, Louis, don't be such a PhD!" With a mischievous grin, Auchincloss told me, "Then I realized that when you have an editor who's a former First Lady of the United States, you lose those arguments." He also noted, more seriously, "In retrospect, I think she was dead right. The pictures tell the story quite as well as the text."

Maverick in Mauve is three books in one: the diary of the romantic age by one of its privileged participants, a scrapbook of eighty-plus period photos depicting turn-of-the-century urban life in Manhattan, and the modern commentary supplied by the novelist. Florence Sloane herself was the granddaughter of Cornelius Vanderbilt, the railroad tycoon who was at one point America's richest man. Her diary begins in 1893, when she was seventeen, and chronicles the frustrations of a well-to-do teenager whose family reins her in more than she would prefer. It's a tantalizing and affecting glimpse into that opulent era.

Being a Vanderbilt had its advantages. The Vanderbilt family decided to survey the extent and health of American forestland, and hired conservationist Gifford Pinchot to conduct the assay. The young Sloane struck up a correspondence with Pinchot and thus became aware of things outside the more circumscribed realms of the so-called Four Hundred, referring to the four hundred powerful industrialists and financiers like the Vanderbilts who were thought to control the country at the time. More important, it inspired her to create a diary. She was infatuated with Pinchot, but, alas, it was a one-way passion. Her diary records her courtship by and eventual marriage to James Abercrombie Burden Jr., a Harvard man whom Miss Sloane found "intensely interesting" and "perfectly wild about this country."

Her diary indicates she was more inclined to another of her suitors, Frederick Beach, but he was fifteen years older than she and not socially acceptable. Duty called, even as she wrote an appraisal that would have resonated with Jackie: "If I marry a society man, it will narrow my life down to that set tremendously, and I will probably be very little thrown in with the sort of people whom I thoroughly enjoy talking to. I like discussions and good arguments. I like talking of books and a hundred other things, and I would miss it fearfully if I would not have it. But I will have it." Adele and her husband sailed to India and Japan on their honeymoon, with a trip around the world at least some consolation for a marriage founded on a bond other than love. Adele's diary continues episodically until the loss of her firstborn daughter.

Adele rarely mentions issues of money or class, as these things were not discussed in polite society. What her diary does achieve, with the interpretive help of Auchincloss's commentary, is an explication of the values and mores of the privileged class of early industrial Americans. Listening to him, it was easy to see why Auchincloss was attracted to this window into his past through his wife's family, and perhaps even more understandable are the similarities the book's editor would have seen between Florence Adele Sloane in the 1890s and her own early life in Newport in the late 1940s and early 1950s.

According to Auchincloss, Jackie was "haunted" by the diarist heroine, and surmised that the book would have a special appeal for women, saying, "I was captivated by her. I, as well as many women today, am constantly fascinated with what my forebears were thinking, feeling and doing." Auchincloss provided me with the text of one of Jackie's memos to him that he had published in 1997 that showed her keen editing skills as well as her sensitivity. Challenging the author gently, Jackie wrote, "Could you describe what was going on in the world then, to set the reader in historical time. Who was president, king? What were national issues, scandals, headlines of the day, what was being written, what was being read? Who were popular and avant garde artists? Did they have electric lights yet, cars or horses and carriages? What were wages, hours of work, size of household staffs at various economic levels, etc.?"

Jackie's lengthy memos indicate that she was quite specific with regard to particular lines that he had written in his manuscript. For example, with a line that began, "With Harry in New Haven," Jackie wanted to know more about the young diarist's life and the customs of the era: "Did she go for a college weekend? What about chaperones? You could discuss courtship rituals of Florence's set."

Jackie's editorial notes reveal why she identified with Florence and had such great affection for her. "She feels shut in and stifled in New York City. Only in Lenox does she feel free—the wild horseback rides and picnics, her rapture with nature. How confining life was in the city—even her clothes.

"Again, love is the only adventure. She reminds me of Natasha.

"Would you want to discuss in another part of the book if any birth control was available to women then?"

Shortly before the book was released, in the fall of 1983, Jackie suggested to her author the idea of having a publishing party at the Museum of the City of New York. Auchincloss was then the president of the museum and expressed his willingness to pay for the occasion, albeit reluctantly. He remembered, "I said, 'Yes, we can have the party right at the museum. They've got a lot of photographs of the period.' I said, 'I'll pay for it. It's just a question of a bunch of thumbtacks to put the photographs up.' Well, you know, we would have to put a couple of thousand dollars into it— Jackie was very stingy, and you never got a penny out of her. But I didn't want to pay for the party. I tried to get Johnny Sargent of Doubleday. He was reluctant, but when I finally said, 'We're going to have paper cups,' he said, 'Oh you can't do that.' And so we arranged the party.

"Then that woman, what's her name, Nancy Tuckerman—who I thought had influence on Jackie. She had none. She was a slave. She called me up and said, 'Jackie says they're going to be photographers at that party.' I said, 'Photographers! As many as I can get!' I said, 'Jackie wants a publicity party. Now don't tell me Jackie doesn't know what publicity is.' And Nancy said, 'Well, anyway, she says she'll feel like a fish in a fishbowl. She's not coming.' I said, 'Nancy, she got me into giving this party. She got me to pay for this party. And if she doesn't come I want you to tell her that I'm writing her a letter saying, This is an act of non-friendship.' The whole idea was to publicize the book, and how were we to do that without the press? Well, of course, Jackie came early, stayed late, and made the party. If you tell her that she's being a shit, she was right there good as gold when you put it to her."

At the party, Jackie quickly found a quiet corner and chatted with Auchincloss family members and friends who attended. At a certain point she had a lengthy conversation with journalist-author Marie Brenner, who published a piece for the *Los Angeles Times*. Jackie's focus was entirely on the book, and Brenner noted her identification with the diarist, which Jackie communicated without any hint of irony with respect to the parallels with her own life, such as her own experience with miscarriage: "What was so moving to me was the spirit of this woman, and the dignity with which she lived her life, and her basic character. That her life would seem to be ideal, and then tragedy would strike her—losing her child, for example. And that her life was not going to be so perfect after all, that she was going to have enormous difficulties, but somehow her spirit and her character would carry her through. You realize, especially when she writes so movingly about the death of her child, how difficult her life could be."

Continuing his reminiscence, Auchincloss recalled, "She was pleased when I informed her that I had another book, *False Dawn* (1984), a series of biographical essays on women of the seventeenth century, that I hoped she would publish: 'I am so happy that we still have *False Dawn* ahead of us, as every step of *Maverick in Mauve* was such a joy. I have terrible withdrawal pangs and feel the depression people do at the end of making a movie—all the fun and excitement over, back to everyday plodding. Doing books with you has been the greatest treat, and you have been so patient and amusing through it all. At least there is still one (and I will always be racking my brain for more) to go.' "

This book was subtitled *Women in the Age of the Sun King,* which implied a discourse on the status of women during the reign of Louis XIV, but it was really an account of the various royal women who circled around the court of the Sun King, not an examination of gender inequity. The book makes clear that noblewomen were bargaining chips in the games of royal succession. Their marriages were predetermined, their opinions belittled or ignored, and their options few—either go along with the machinations of the ambitious aristocracy, or enter a convent and direct their hormones to the service of the Lord, to whom they might consider themselves wedded.

Auchincloss provided short essays on fourteen remarkable seventeenth-century women, all of whom lived in the shadow of Louis XIV. Each of these women used her wit or piety or sexuality to affect the course of history, sometimes aiding the reigning monarch, sometimes diminishing his influence or advancing the schemes of one noble house or another. One of the insights of this short book is how it demonstrates the complex royal genealogy that spanned the boundaries of countries. The rulers of England, France, Spain, Holland, Italy, Austria, and other countries were related, to one degree or another, and many of the wars and truces were shufflings of the royal gene pool for real or perceived advantage.

It was the author's argument that the late seventeenth century allowed for the first tentative flowering of feminism, albeit under clever guises to avoid royal suppression. Hence the title *False Dawn,* a necessary precursor to feminism's real emergence two centuries later. He may have overstated the case, but he made an intriguing argument that was consistent with Jackie's reading of history. Auchincloss noted, "She read the book and got down to business, as shown by another . . . work sheet she sent me," advising him to train a penetrating lens on his subject:

> The most uncomfortable thing I have ever had to do is edit your immaculate writing. I hope and expect that you will object vociferously and that I will learn a lot from you in the process.
>
> Please realize that one gets obsessive and nitpicking when editing a manuscript filled with facts, in a concentrated session. I did yours in a day and a night at Martha's Vineyard. It isn't at all like reading a book for pleasure, and I may have been overzealous.
>
> . . . This is what I have decided I feel; it is a little too concentrated in spots, more for an English audience than an American one. Could you get a little more air flowing through it in places where information is more tightly packed? Could we have some lovely stories, some waspish stories?
>
> Would it distort an occasional essay to give an anecdote here and there, to more fully describe a person, a place? I have always thought that Henriette d'Angleterre must have been one of the most enchanting women who ever walked on this planet. Could we have more about her? And Sarah Churchill finding in her dead husband's desk her hair that he had saved. I only know the obvious anecdotes. You know so many more. I would like to know what Anne of Austria looked like. Do you want to describe her horrible marriage to Louis XIII and the conception of Louis XIV? I know this is a tired old bone to you, but it is anecdotes that readers love and remember.
>
> The Grande Mademoiselle is my favorite chapter [the story of Anne Marie Louise d'Orléans, Duchess of Montpensier, Louis XIV's cousin]. I think it is a tour de force. I can see and hear everyone in it as I write this, feel the cold when she is by the fire with Lauzun, sense the excitement on the ramparts, see her big red nose and ungainly walk. . . .
>
> I want every chapter to be a novel so that I can know more about these people and imagine them in their settings, and of course, that is impossible in an essay. I do look forward to our lunch and am prepared to be told I am an utter dolt.

After enumerating the details of Jackie's memo, Auchincloss posed two questions: "Doesn't that show why she was a writer's dream as an editor? Where would you find her today in a world of megapublishers?"

On a lighter note, Auchincloss couldn't resist sharing one more story, which he related with bemused glee, about his doing the introduction for Tiffany's 150th anniversary book. He said, "I went down to Tiffany's every day for some weeks and worked with John Loring in the library. And it's a perfectly respectable book I did. But Jackie was very funny once, because it was a grandson of Tiffany's, or a great grandson of Tiffany's—what was his name, I've forgotten [Harry Platt]—and he used to give a biennial ball at the St. Regis, a beauty ball for society beauties and so on. And that had to be covered in the history. Jackie produced a whole mass of photographs of the beauties, and I got bored with that, and I said in the text, 'It was a relief to turn from the pictures of the grandson's *balls* to something else.' And then Jackie said, 'I think perhaps we need another word.' "

Jackie's ambivalence about the press and the requisite Doubleday book parties continued through the years. She often tried to get across to her writers that she did not want to use her name to promote their books, and though she did make exceptions, there were lines that could not be crossed. Jackie's initial reluctance to attend the pub party for *Maverick in Mauve* may have stemmed from an unfortunate series of incidents that took place some months before. She had befriended a young novelist, Richard de Combray, whose book *Goodbye Europe,* was published by Doubleday in 1983. According to Marie Brenner, writing in the *Los Angeles Times* that year, the author had "insinuated that there was a romance between them."

Indeed, there was a story in the *New York Post* under the headline, "The dashing writer in Jackie O's life," and the tabloid *Star* later reported "JACKIE ONASSIS finds handsome new love, writer Richard de Combray." De Combray told me in 2009, "Actually, I don't remember specifically where or why I met her. All I know is that . . . we did go out a few times to places, bookshops and stuff like that. I'd been to her house and met her new man . . . Tempelsman. He was just a nice guy with a nice suit. I think I saw him two or three times with her. It was clear that he was very involved with her. It was all pleasant stuff. We were out on Third Avenue having lunch one day in an ordinary place, which is still there. We talked about things. We'd gone to a museum together. And while we were walking down Third Avenue, some guy came along with a camera. Well, I mean, she'd certainly been photographed many times, and I mean, people have taken my picture, so big deal. Anyway, she said, 'Let's get out of here.' And we went into a shop. . . . We stayed inside, and then as soon as he was gone she got into a taxi. And I don't know what went wrong. . . .

"There was something in the newspaper. That picture was on the front page, and I have the clippings. I kept them because I was so angry about what happened. I mean, the *Post* is terrible. . . . That's what they do. Anyway, she would never speak to me again. And I hadn't done anything. . . . It was the *Post*'s business to create that story. And it was very hard for me, and I got a lot of phone calls. I was alone. And I said, 'Look, I don't really want to get into this thing, because I don't understand why this thing is happening.' They wanted to come up to interview me."

By fleeing rather than simply denying the story, de Combray sealed his fate with Jackie. "And so I got into a plane and went to stay with Lillian Hellman. She was in California. I said, 'Look I'm getting out of here because I'm not having a good time and I don't know how to deal with this.' And I stayed with her."

On a descriptive page of de Combray's Web site, referring to his novel, he notes, "In the book of short stories, *Goodbye Europe*—which my glamorous editor, Jacqueline Onassis, urged me to call a novel (they sell better)— was actually a series of short stories that semi-fictionalized many of my own experiences here and there on the continent."

When I spoke with de Combray, he couldn't remember if Jackie had actually been the editor of his novel. In fact, he said, "I never knew that she had anything to do with it, frankly." He credited one of Jackie's colleagues, Shaye Areheart, with doing most of the editing. Knowing Areheart, who also worked on all of my books with Jackie, I suspect the suggestion to call the book "a novel in six parts" rather than a collection of short stories probably came from her.

De Combray's book plays fast and loose with the notion of a novel. None of the stories bear any organic connection to the others, and aside from the unnamed first-person narrator, there are only two or three characters that carry over from one story to another, and these do so through only a passing reference. The only unifying theme is the restlessness of American expatriates abroad. Critic Stephen Koch wrote a favorable review for *The Washington Post,* suggesting, ". . . there have been relatively few good novels about the subject of Richard de Combray's *Goodbye Europe*—namely, that wave of Americans who went (I almost said fled) to Europe between, say, 1952 and 1965, refugees from the suburban movement and the age of conformity."

Prior to the contretemps, Jackie held de Combray's writing in high enough regard to offer him another project, though he has no recollection of it. Jackie commissioned a book from fine art photographer Robert Farber, and de Combray was to write the text. Farber explained, "Well, my literary agent at the time called me and said that she got a call from Doubleday because Jackie Onassis likes your work and she'd like to see what you're working on. And actually the pictures I was working on were mostly a lot of pictures around the Riviera. And then I remember Jackie turned and said,

'Why don't you take pictures all over and call it *By the Sea*. Can't you smell the clams cooking, and the lobster?' I remember the words."

After Farber signed his contract with Doubleday, Jackie sent him a note that he framed as a keepsake. It was dated February 29, 1984, and said, in part, "I'm happy that we will have *By the Sea* on our list, and I'm sure it will be a very special book." Alas, it was not to be. De Combray had been slated to write the text, but was dropped after his falling-out with Jackie. Jackie's editorial cohort, Shaye Areheart, worked with Farber on the book, but after delays with the text dragged on over two years, Farber withdrew the project and eventually published the book with a small art book publisher.

While Farber's book was still in the works, Jackie impetuously commissioned one of her more unlikely books involving her old friend George Plimpton. She wrote a nostalgic reminiscence to mark the twenty-fifth anniversary of *The Paris Review,* recalling her visits with Plimpton in Paris during the early 1950s. "All the most brilliant and romantic young men were involved with the magazine and all the girls were vivid. We were discovering a city, discovering Europe, literature, and *art sur place*—slight expatriates all, determined that our lives would not be mundane. . . . I remember sitting with you in an airless hole of a nightclub on the Boulevard Raspail. You, rather pale in a black turtleneck sweater, told me how the blue notes of saxophones through smoke-filled haze ushered in the dawns for you, and how you would walk the gray Paris streets in the first light back to a strange bed."

More than thirty years later, Jackie found herself sitting with Plimpton over lunch and was struck by an outlandish idea for a new project. With that moment in mind, Plimpton recalled that his first book with Jackie, *Fireworks: A History and Celebration,* "was inspired by a fireworks show fired from behind the Metropolitan Museum and which she'd watched from her Fifth Avenue apartment across the avenue. We had lunch the following day. I told her that as the fireworks commissioner for the city I was partly responsible for what she'd seen—that the fireworks were Chinese manufactured and had been selected to herald one of Diana Vreeland's Costume Institute openings at the Metropolitan. She immediately suggested a book on the subject—delighting me for sure but also leaving me somewhat skeptical: how could a reputable publishing company ever be persuaded to sign up a book on *fireworks*? I have often speculated on the scene—the number of dropped jaws around the conference table when Jackie gave her presentation. I should have known better. They were persuaded. For the editorial work on the book—the layout, the selection of photographs and paintings, which she was largely responsible for—I prize it above all my other works."

Of course, George Plimpton would not write a conventional history of fireworks. He used fireworks to unlock long-forgotten memories of childhood and to speculate on why humans have loved watching big bangs since the invention of gunpowder. Plimpton postulated that July Fourth was a far superior holiday than, say, Christmas. And he described the ever-escalating passion that starts out with a sinuous snake made of ash or a multihued sparkler on a front lawn, and quickly moves to cherry bombs and M-80s, the juvenile Molotov cocktails of choice. On Independence Day, and Halloween, we are allowed to play at being terrorists, even as we are lectured about the apocryphal neighborhood kid who lost three fingers out behind the barn.

Plimpton figured out how to prolong these explosive rites. He did in fact become the self-appointed, unofficial fireworks commissioner under Mayor John Lindsay's benign sufferance, a title he mock-seriously held for the rest of his life. He began to immerse himself in the history of controlled explosions. He became involved in planning for the Central Park extravaganza that caught Jackie's interest, and started to meet the few family-owned businesses that produce fireworks for the domestic market.

Plimpton later wrote, "Thinking back on it, I think one of the curious pleasures of doing a book with Jackie was that one felt part of a conspiracy—that somehow she had infiltrated into enemy territory and was there to guide her writers through the barbed wire and across the trenches. The editorial relationship was very personal. Her voice over the telephone was certainly conspiratorial: 'I'm going to get you more money, *but don't tell anyone!*' " The author also noted that Jackie possessed "a kind of oblique way of looking at things that was never in the least solemn, as if humor was the best condition to face almost any situation."

While working with Plimpton on *Fireworks,* Jackie took on a far more ambitious illustrated book, one that would take her on an extensive journey to India in January 1984. The publication of Naveen Patnaik's *A Second Paradise: Indian Courtly Life, 1590–1947* was planned to coincide late the following year with another one of Diana Vreeland's annual Costume Institute exhibitions, "Costumes of Royal India," which would open in December 1985 (along with the Met's "Festival of India" exhibit, with a catalogue entitled *India: Art and Culture, 1300–1900*). Later embarking on a political career, the author of the book, Patnaik, is now the chief minister of Orissa, India. His sister, Gita Mehta, is also an author and the wife of Sonny Mehta, editor in chief of Alfred A. Knopf.

As cited by Carl Sferrazza Anthony, Gita Mehta described Jackie as "really an extraordinary, nineteenth-century type of editor. I watched her do *A Second Paradise*. . . . Jackie sent Naveen pages of research material annotated by herself. It was obscure research. I know as a writer to have that kind of attention by a commissioning editor is quite rare."

British author and former *Vanity Fair* writer Sarah Giles, who would later do a book for Jackie on the life of Fred Astaire, told me that Patnaik was a "favorite of Jackie's. She adored him, and she nurtured him, and did all kinds of things she didn't do for other people, like their publication parties. When it came to publicity, as you know she wasn't there to perform. But she was for Naveen, and she loved him, and she loved India."

Jackie had first visited India when she was First Lady, traveling with her sister, Lee, in 1962 on a goodwill tour. She had immersed herself in Indian culture and history while the guest of Prime Minister Jawaharlal Nehru. Upon her arrival in New Delhi, she was greeted by one hundred thousand people who lined the road. Throughout her travels, she was followed by dozens of international journalists, including a young Barbara Walters. At Jackie's invitation, the journey was chronicled by the French artist Jacqueline Duheme, a friend of Matisse and Picasso. Her paintings were later included in the book *Mrs. Kennedy Goes Abroad*.

American ambassador John Kenneth Galbraith remembered her visit. "My wife, Kitty, and I planned Jacqueline Kennedy's trip to India. We re sisted a proposal that she visit the ancient temples of Konrak, where her viewing of explicitly erotic statuary would have greatly attracted media attention. President Kennedy's reply to his wife's viewing sensuous statuary was 'Don't you think she's old enough?' " Personal connections with India's royalty and political leaders that Jackie cultivated during her goodwill tour, including the maharaja and maharani of Jaipur, would serve her well on the extensive collaboration that that came to fruition with Patnaik's book.

For that project, Jackie enlisted the aid of Harvard professor and India art expert Stuart Cary Welch, who wrote the foreword and who would accompany Jackie to India on her 1984 visit (and again in 1989). She recruited Patnaik, a founding member of the Indian National Trust for Art and Cultural Heritage, who served as her guide, and an Indian miniaturist court artist, Bannu, to contribute to the endeavor. It was Bannu's task to capture costumes and their surroundings in original illustrations that aped the painting styles that India developed over the centuries.

Bannu is survived by a son, Shammi Bannu, who is also an artist in Jaipur, following in his father's footsteps in a family tradition of court painting that goes back centuries. I spoke with him via Skype and he remembered making tea for Jackie on the day she and Welch visited his home to hire his father. "I was thirteen years old at that time. My father had his own style and popularity of his work here and abroad. . . . He had a friendship with Mr. Welch from the Boston museum. . . . And then Mrs. Kennedy was to do a book based on Jaipur and the British period to the contemporary period. And they want a person who can paint that idea what she had in the mind. . . . And that was just like dream come true when she walked in my old house. My father don't have any words; he just say welcome to my house. . . . They discussed in the eight hours what she wanted to do, what kind of a book she wants. . . . And she told my father, 'There's a writer, a Mr. Patnaik, he will come to you and he will write the book which I am going to publish.' "

Patnaik later told Dominick Dunne, "Jackie was fascinated by India. At the suggestion of Diana Vreeland, she came to see me. Her son, John, was studying here in New Delhi at the time. She was frightfully independent. She used to wander off on her own, and I would get nervous. She was able to go unrecognized for the most part, but when she was, she was completely grateful if people asked her for her autograph. We traveled to several very grand kingdoms. She literally had with her only two pairs of slacks, dark glasses, and one gold jacket for evenings, which she wore to even the grandest places. She had an aesthetic sense for anything beautiful." It was Patnaik whom Jackie advised, "If you produce one book, you will have done something wonderful in your life," and he later wrote of her visit: "Dear Jackie, traditionally people come to India in search of their gurus. It was my good fortune that my guru came to India."

The book was to cover two distinct artistic styles, Mughal and Rajput. It contrasts the early days of princely India with the later period, when the princely states either rose or fell according to whether or not they cooperated with the colonial British. Mughal painting began in the sixteenth century and drew its initial inspiration from Persian miniaturists. Rajput painting was a spin-off of Mughal, with each Rajput kingdom having its own distinctive style; some were miniatures, but large wall paintings illustrating the Ramayana and Mahabharata were also commonplace. In the published book, these depictions of Indian court life are lush and complicated, so it comes as a visual shock when photographs from the British period show these princes and their retinues appearing more like bedraggled European royalty than like the rajas and ranis of yesterday.

Under Jackie's supervision, the Indian artwork had to be tracked down and photographed, and Diana Vreeland's grandson Nicholas lent his eye and camera to the cause. He said, "I was involved in the one on princely India, and I remember going with Jackie to the apartment of James Ivory. He wasn't there, and Jackie and I, we were let in by their scriptwriter, Ruth

Jhabvala. Well, she let us in, and Jackie and I sat on the wooden floor of this very sparse apartment, which was in the east lower fifties and First Avenue. . . .

"I was asked to photograph the images. I was there with a large-format camera. . . . I remember she had the ability to crouch. We put the images on this wooden floor, and it was a collection of old photographs and maybe some miniatures, maybe some photographs that had been painted on. And together we decided what would go into this book. What was remarkable, what was really lovely, was that she was in no way proprietary. She was very willing to have me participate in this process."

Ten years before Cary Welch died, in 2008, he spoke to biographer Sarah Bradford about the friendship that he and his wife, Edith, established with Jackie. Like many of her friends during her later years, the Welchs better understood the woman they knew in the present by keeping a perspective on and safe distance from what she had lived through as the historical figure she had been in her past. "One realizes that she had a kind of genius for friendship," said Cary Welch. "I guess you must have found out that she had more friends than you'd ever heard about. . . . I also think that she was very much drawn to men who were father figures rather than lover figures.

"Knowing her well only in the last decade of her life, our view of her therefore is based on the person who had already suffered terribly. So the person we knew was someone who had been through all that and who had enormously wisened and who had gained in breadth and depth because of those miseries and who had become much more herself. Cleansed by fire, but terrible fire."

For the India project, Jackie and Alex Gotfryd again turned to designer Michael Flanagan. They had to overcome his initial resistance due to the fact that he was busy at the time with other projects. Recounting his involvement, Flanagan wrote:

I was on West Broadway, sitting at a table at the Odeon, sharing a salad of "hand-foraged greens" with Alex and Jackie. Alex kept my wine glass filled while Jackie talked.

"This book," she exclaimed breathlessly, "it won't interfere with your art work, it will help you. I promise. I just know it's going to be a great book. It will make us famous!"

"But you're already famous."

"Well, then we can both be famous."

Alex gave me a wry little smile. It didn't take much to make me cave in. The next day a messenger delivered a bottle of champagne and a postcard from Jackie—a photo of the dancer Nijinsky with his arms raised in a weird, ecstatic posture.

As a painter, Flanagan had to complete some of the artwork that was left unfinished by Bannu. Jackie told the designer, "Michael, this will be our secret. No one will ever know." After the artwork and photographs for *A Second Paradise* had been collected, the production process began, with Jackie once again hitting the floor and looking over the shoulder of the director of the Doubleday trade production department, Albert Yokum. Yokum told me that Jackie was involved every step of the way. "During a meeting in which we were reviewing all the slides the Metropolitan Museum of Art had made for producing her book *A Second Paradise* . . . after viewing them on a light table, I would hold up those that seemed too dark for reproduction purposes. To my disbelief, with the names of each facing me and invisible to Jackie, she instantly knew each one by sight and could enunciate the Indian names perfectly . . . able to rattle off . . . 'Maharao Raja Raghubir Singh Bahadur of Bundi,' 'Rao Ram Singh I of Kotah,' or 'Prithvi Singh of Kishangarh.' I dare anyone to try it with the labels in front of them."

Yokum said, "I mean, she knew each piece of artwork. . . . She was a hands-on editor, and she worked hard, and was dedicated, and was as much of an editor as, if not more so than, any other I have ever worked with. . . . She wasn't removed, she wasn't above it, she was in it. She was in it up to her elbows!"

By the time the Patnaik book came out, Jackie already had rolled up her sleeves with signed contracts for two more books—one with pop sensation Michael Jackson, and another with ballerina Gelsey Kirkland and me as coauthors. Neither would be easy books for Jackie to deliver, and each would try her patience as an editor. Yet both books were destined to become bestsellers—thanks, in part, to her unflinching tenacity.

6

Moonwalk *and the Power of Myth*

In January 1984, *The New York Times* reported that Michael Jackson had suffered an accident while filming a Pepsi-Cola commercial in Los Angeles that resulted in second-degree burns on his scalp when his hair was set on fire by an exploding smoke canister. Tacked on to the end of the article was a brief announcement that the ascendant pop icon had recently signed a deal with Doubleday: "A book by Mr. Jackson, combining autobiography, how-to and more than 100 color photos, is to be edited by Jacqueline Kennedy Onassis. Doubleday said it was scheduled to be published in 1985. The writing is to be done by Mr. Jackson, a Doubleday spokesman said." The advance paid to Jackson was reportedly $300,000, but his motive for doing the book had more to do with his editor than with money, which he didn't need—his 1982 album, *Thriller*, had already sold forty million copies, almost twice the sales of any other album in history at the time.

Jackie and editor Shaye Areheart had visited Michael at his home in Encino, California, the previous fall in order to entice him to write the book. This was before he established his Neverland sanctuary, and before the music video for "Thriller" was released. Areheart had worked her way up Doubleday's editorial ladder and as Jackie's protégé enjoyed a very special relationship with her. Although Shaye had her own list of titles, she served as a partner with Jackie on quite a few books over the years, including the three that I coauthored. Shaye became an integral part of Jackie's Doubleday team, and they shared editorial assistants. The team was later dubbed "Jackie's SWAT Team," and part of their responsibility was to shield Jackie from the intrusive public while avoiding contact with the press other than approved book promotion forays.

Scott Moyers, one of Jackie's editorial assistants, told biographer Sarah Bradford that there was a division of labor among the editors and that Areheart was often responsible for tasks that were considered "dirty work . . . negotiating the fine points of contracts, presenting books in marketing and sales meetings, writing the fact sheets the sales reps used, so that she [Jackie] was really only doing the interesting stuff, acquiring and editing." Much of the "dirty work" on the Jackson book was given to Areheart, who welcomed the opportunity.

One of Jackie's colleagues at the time, Karen Van Westering, remembered that Jackie "helped younger editors. She was supportive of the younger kids coming up—Shaye in particular, but also others. She dealt with big-name authors, and she was a big name herself; but she was not beyond lending support and advice to younger editors who were getting started." Loretta Barrett also commented on Jackie's relationship with Areheart, saying, "Shaye Areheart was so close to her. She was like a daughter, and Shaye would never talk. And Lisa Drew was very, very close to her. . . . At Doubleday when we were all there, we just never ever talked about anything. It was the unwritten rule. So Jackie was very open and sharing as a result with all of us, and we all had enormous respect for the woman, and fondness."

Areheart is one of those confidantes who took a vow of silence with regard to Jackie, insisting she would never betray that confidence, but she made an exception recently, writing an afterword when one of her own Random House imprints, Harmony Books, reissued the Jackson memoir, *Moonwalk*, in 2009. Apparently, Areheart couldn't tell the whole story, as that might have jeopardized the commercial success of the book's republication in the wake of Jackson's untimely death. Her sanitized reminiscence paints a rosy portrait of Jackson without revealing the prolonged series of conflicts that took place between the superstar and Jackie during the more than four-year ordeal before the book was finally published, in 1988.

According to Areheart, at their first meeting, Jackson gave her and

Jackie at her Viking Press
office, New York City,
January, 1977.

Jackie the working
woman: her first day on
the job at the Viking Press,
September 22, 1975.

In the Viking Press offices, publisher Thomas Guinzburg poses with the newly hired editor and former First Lady, September 22, 1975.

Jackie with the Viking Press/ Studio Books mentor Bryan Holme in the company offices as they look over their book, *In the Russian Style,* January, 1977.

Top: Jackie and her friend Karl Katz arrive at "The Glory of Russian Costume" exhibit opening, Metropolitan Museum of Art, December 6, 1976.

Bottom: Jackie and author-artist William Walton arriving at the International Center of Photography for the opening of the exhibition "Fleeting Gestures: Treasures of Dance Photography" at the International Center of Photography, November 6, 1978.

Opposite, top left: Jackie and Doubleday president John Sargent at the Doubles Club, Sherry Netherland Hotel, February 18, 1976.

Opposite, top right: Jackie attends the Broadway play *Amadeus*, January 2, 1981, at the Broadhurst Theater, January 2, 1981.

Opposite, bottom: Jackie and her author/stepcousin Louis Auchincloss at the Metropolitan Museum of Art for the New York City Mayor's Award of Honor for Art and Culture, November 27, 1978.

Above: Jackie arrives at her daughter Caroline's wedding to Edwin Schlossberg in Centerville, Massachusetts, on July 19, 1986.

Top: Jackie supporting the fight against Manhattan Tower developers, July 30, 1987.

Bottom: Jackie and Maurice Tempelsman walking under an umbrella on their way to a John F. Kennedy Library fund-raiser, January 1990.

Right: A Jackie sighting in New York City, circa January 1990.

Below: Jackie with Maurice Tempelsman and journalist Bill Moyers, November 3, 1992, prior to the publication of *Healing and the Mind.*

Above: Then President Bill Clinton with Jackie and John Jr. during the opening ceremonies for the newly redesigned John F. Kennedy Library in Boston, October 29, 1993.

Below: John Jr. and Caroline after their mother's death in Manhattan, May 22, 1994.

Jackie a tour of his Encino house that was highlighted by his introducing one of his favorite pets. "Jackie and I were looking around, admiring some beautiful birds in cages, oblivious to what Michael was up to, when suddenly he turned from the terrarium and said, 'Here, Shaye, you want to hold Muscles?' Languishing across his outstretched hands was a pretty boa constrictor. I took it. It felt like damp silk and, much to my surprise, began to move sideways, so that I was in danger of dropping it. . . . Michael protectively retrieved his snake with a look of abject disappointment on his face. It was only much later, when he teased me about it, that I realized he was hoping—wildly hoping—for a shriek from me and, maybe, a hysterical dash out of the room. He was a kid at heart—then and always."

In a radio interview in 2009, Areheart suggested that "Michael was so easy to work with." Speaking of Jackie's relationship with Jackson, Areheart told the press that year, "They got along very well. . . . She thought he was so sweet." According to several other insiders and my own discussions with Jackie, that was hardly the case.

To have lured such an immensely popular celebrity into writing a book that was likely to be a bestseller was initially viewed as a major coup for Jackie. John Sargent Jr. told me, "I remember the level of hoo-ha about that book, and it was huge!" But the alliance of Jackie, Areheart, and the "kid at heart" was never an easy one, and as work on the book dragged on year by year with postponements, the situation became what Jackie later described to me as "a professional embarrassment." As Jackie's frustration with Jackson became obvious to her colleagues, some of them speculated that the project had been foisted on her by higher-ups in the house. In fact, Jackie had taken the initiative both in recruiting Jackson and selling the idea to Doubleday.

Loretta Barrett said, "I'll tell you exactly how that book came about. . . . Doubleday had what they called a pub board. And I went to pub board for Anchor, and Betty [Prashker] would go, and sometimes the editors would go. But Jackie's children told her who Michael Jackson was. And she came into the editorial meeting saying, 'My kids!' Remember, this was when Michael Jackson was this innocent young boy. And she came in, and then at the financial meeting half of them didn't know who Michael Jackson was. I said, 'How could you not know who Michael Jackson is?' It would have been like saying you didn't know who Diana Ross was. . . . But it was Jackie's kids, and it was Jackie who came in with the book idea. I remember saying, 'That is a fabulous idea.' The older guys and the sales guys didn't know who she was talking about.

"What happened was then he never delivered, and she was caught in the endless morass of it. But initially it was one of these brilliant editorial ideas. . . . She understood popular culture. . . . Like Caroline telling her to go see *9 to 5*. That's what generations do."

James Fitzgerald, who had edited music and pop culture books by stars like David Bowie, agreed that Caroline and John encouraged Jackie. He told me, "She listened to her kids." Fitzgerald also recalled a day when Jackie visited him in his office: "She came in and she said, 'Do you think Michael Jackson is the new Fred Astaire?' And I said, 'Yo! What are you doing?' And she said, 'Well, I saw this tape of the Motown show, and I think he's marvelous.' . . . Another character got involved with this, because the book evolved a little bit during its creation. He was a designer by the name of J. C. Suarès. He came, and I think the three of us met once. But at one point I realized it was really a battle of egos—this was Jackie and Michael Jackson, and that was the real big thing. And the book evolved from kind of a picture thing, to a text thing, to a this-and-that."

Jackson would eventually dedicate the book to Fred Astaire. Sam Vaughan, then Doubleday's president, remembered Jackie coming to him to plan the first trip to California to close the deal with Jackson. "We handled a lot of people who were in show business, from Noël Coward to Somerset Maugham, so we weren't flummoxed by star power. . . . One day Jackie and two or three other young publishing people gathered around my doorway and talked about the fact that she was ready to go to California and spend some time with Michael Jackson. . . . This was before the Michael Jackson hair-burning incident. Michael Jackson was, to some people, like me, who didn't respond to his music or his stage persona, not the big name he would be the next day. So she and this group crowded around my doorway, hollering their enthusiasm, and talking about the trip to California, and I said, 'Hold on a second. Who is Michael Jackson?' In a tighter place I probably would have been fired."

Vaughan nevertheless approved the California junket. Joe Armstrong recalled Jackie's reasons for undertaking the project as she expressed them to him, which was exactly the way she later put it to me: "You know, Jackie wasn't involved in that because that was an interest of hers, or a passion of hers, or a curiosity of hers. She said she did it 'to be a good citizen' at Doubleday. Those were her words. Because she said if she helped with that, it let her have the ability to do the kind of special books she truly loved."

Areheart wrote that the project was initially planned as "a coffee-table picture book with a lot of text." From the publisher's standpoint, the most commercial type of book was an autobiography rather than an expensive picture book, and that distinction soon became a source of conflict. The first ghostwriter to work with Jackson, longtime *Los Angeles Times* music critic and author Robert Hilburn, told me, "The reason he signed to do it was that Jacqueline Kennedy Onassis was the editor, and he was flattered. But he didn't want to do a biography, it turned out. Once I got on the road with him I found out he wanted to do a picture book. He wanted to get all his pictures together and have maybe a caption about them; whereas she wanted a revealing book. But Michael . . . felt that the less you knew about people, stars, the more you were fascinated by them. He would say to me, 'Elvis never did interviews. Howard Hughes didn't do interviews.' And that was the framework he used. . . .

"So we spent weekends on the book. The frustration kept getting more and more intense because he'd pick up these pictures, and he was so much against telling anything about himself. I remember, we picked up a picture one time of an older man, maybe somebody who looked like he was eighty or ninety. I said, 'Michael, who is this?' And he said, 'Oh, that's my grandfather.' I said, 'Let's see, what can we say about him in the caption? Did you like your grandfather?' 'Oh, I loved him!' I said, 'Oh, great, we'll say that.' And he said, 'No, no, no! That's too personal.' And so it was really very difficult. Finally there was a showdown. Jacqueline Kennedy Onassis came out to Los Angeles, to his house, to kind of sit with us to discuss this book that's not going right."

Jackie was accompanied on that trip by J. C. Suarès, who had worked on four of the Tiffany books, was both the art director of *The New York Times* op-ed page for many years, and design director of *New York* magazine. Suarès told me, "We traveled to see Michael in California several times together. And then it became kind of a difficult project, and we met at her house or different places in order to get this thing done. It took forever. It didn't work because Michael had hired a ghostwriter [Hilburn] . . . and the guy wanted to stay in Michael's good graces, so it was all . . . pontificating nonsense. And when Jackie got the manuscript, she decided it was just no good. So we decided to go to California and face Michael."

Suarès provided me with the first draft of the manuscript that Jackson and Hilburn submitted to Doubleday, a scant eighty-seven pages filled with Shaye Areheart's handwritten critical notes asking the ghostwriter to "expand" and "embellish," to deliver Jackson's personal story and the genesis of hit songs like his "Beat It" anthem. The narrative did provide a few details of Jackson's life, and he and Hilburn dutifully found a sentence or two to describe each of the talented siblings. For example, "Janet is a tom boy and she's been my best friend in the family for years, so I was sad at first when she got married in 1984. We used to do everything together, almost like twins. . . . We enjoyed the same stuff. I adore her." Before he is through, he also "adores" Diana Ross, Gregory Peck, Steven Spielberg,

Fred Astaire, Katharine Hepburn, and just about every other celebrity he mentions.

The manuscript also eventually took on more weighty issues, like Jackson's proclivity for cosmetic surgery and his sexual orientation, but never in a way that revealed anything. The ghostwritten narrative was more about damage control than revelation. If a steady stream of backstage encounters with celebrities and inane frustrations with organizing details on road show tours were your cup of hemlock, this might have been the manuscript for you. Clearly, Jackie was not pleased, and she would travel west for the first of several contentious meetings with Jackson, firing Hilburn along the way.

In a preface to his 1994 book *Uncommon Grace,* Suarès wrote, "What she didn't anticipate was that getting a real book out of him—one in which he would share his innermost thoughts about serious matters such as his family troubles, his alleged fixations on children and pets, and his sexual ambiguity—would prove out of the question. So secretive was he that just prior to our beginning work, Michael had arranged a press conference at which his manager, Frank Dileo, read a statement warning that Jackson would sue any publication that spread false accusations about the star's personal life."

Suarès also told me about their first confrontation with Jackson. "So here we were, in Encino, California. We talked about it, and we talked about what she should say to Michael—something to the effect that nobody is going to take him seriously, and if this was a good book, there'd be other books, and so on. This was before Neverland, which is kind of like Michael Jackson purgatory. . . . This was Jackie and Michael and I in a room, and Jackie says to Michael in her whispery tone that the book is empty of anything important, and that people are going to make fun of it, and that he has to do something about getting some more important stuff in it. And he's looking at her and nodding his head. And he has no idea what she's talking about because he didn't write it, he's got this guy writing it. So he agreed.

"And then later on I'm talking to Jackie and I say, 'You know, you reminded me of Bette Davis in that scene in *The Little Foxes*—where her husband or somebody is dying, and she just watches him die.' So she called me later, and she said, 'Really? You *really* think I was like Bette Davis?' I said, 'Yeah, you're just like Bette Davis.' She said, 'Oh, you made my day!'

"So the book turned out to be highly visual. It started as a large coffee-table book and ended up something about the size of *Reader's Digest,* because it was all nonsense and we didn't think it was going to do well. I spent a lot of time with Michael trying to get pictures from his archives. He had a full-time photo editor, and he kept pictures of everything. We put together a very graphic book. I named it *Moonwalk*."

Of Jackie's relationship with coeditor Areheart, Suarès told me, "I remember a conversation with [Shaye] where she mentioned that Jackie had come to her house a number of times and knew her kids. I got the feeling that she equated those visits to having the Mother of Christ herself appear at her door." The designer explained Areheart's extreme secretive stance as "a quasi-religious kind of thing in reverence to Jackie. Jackie had a contagious phobia about the press and publicity of any kind. . . . People became converts to the atmosphere she created."

Jackie appreciated Shaye's loyalty and had the highest regard for her talents. When I once questioned Jackie about Shaye's role in editing my books, Jackie said, "Shaye is your editor, too, and you wouldn't believe how little she is paid." Most of the editorial notes that I received over the years were in Jackie's handwriting, further distinguished from Shaye's notes by the various colors of the pencils they used. Years later Shaye told me that she remembered spending long nights at Jackie's apartment working into the wee hours on manuscripts that they coedited. Jackson's book would require that kind of overtime devotion.

With regard to Jackie's attitude about Jackson's pets, Suarès remembered, "Jackie and I were alarmed at the way the animals were treated. There was a llama and a sheep in a small cement pen with nothing else in it. There was the huge boa constrictor, Muscles, and a poodle desperate for attention in a playpen in an empty room. Jackie joked about calling the ASPCA. She felt sorry for the lonely animals, but did not voice these sentiments until later, over lunch at the Beverly Hills Hotel."

According to the designer, as the work on the book continued, Jackie became increasingly disenchanted and by the end held a low opinion of Jackson. "She took the whole thing as a pain, from having to fly to California to stay at the Beverly Hills Hotel, to having to go to his house and try to deal with this nonsense. . . . She could be a snob, and Michael wasn't cultured, he didn't have an important job in the government or anything like that. He was out of her radar. . . . Jackie thought that Michael was a freak. She didn't like him. . . . Now Michael's compound was one of the strangest places you've ever seen. There was a gate with a guard, and then a main house that was huge, with Michael, his mother, and his sister La Toya living there. There were paintings of clowns everywhere—you know, those paintings of clowns with tears, crying clowns—and huge chandeliers, mostly kind of Venetian copies. A very gaudy kind of place.

"We got to see Michael's bedroom, and it was surreal. It was a large bedroom with a huge bed. . . . But everywhere in the bedroom there were life-sized models of people, mannequins, fully dressed, like cloth figures. They looked realistic; they weren't too heavy, but they were huge. And there was one of a man kneeling next to a little girl. Who was the man? Who was the little girl? We weren't sure about Michael's sexual orientation at the time. And Jackie would ask me, 'Does he like girls?' That was her way of saying, 'Is he straight?' So I would always say, 'I don't know.' But the driver of our limo, who was a wiseguy, said, 'Well, I had Michael and Brooke Shields in the car a few nights ago.' And we said, 'Well, what happened?' He said, 'She sat on one side, and he sat on the other side, and they never spoke; they just shook hands at the end.' That was his proof that the guy was not interested. So Jackie made a prediction. At the time, he was in his twenties. And she said, 'When he's thirty-five he'll marry an eighteen-year-old girl child.' " Suarès added, "She was almost right, but things got much more complicated for Michael after that.

"The only high point of our visit to California the first or second time was that I invited Martha Stewart to join us for lunch. And Martha came an hour late to a restaurant, then the best restaurant in L.A., called Ma Maison. There was nobody there. We were waiting and waiting and waiting for Martha. And Jackie said, 'Do you think I should wear my sunglasses?' I said, 'No, because there's nobody here.' Jackie and Martha had a charming exchange but didn't really hit it off." Suarès explained in his book, "Although she appreciated Martha's style, Jackie did not quite understand how it had become an entire industry: She assumed that most people knew how to arrange roses and polish old silver and that those who didn't had gardeners and maids who did. After that day, she could never remember Martha's name and referred to her as 'that pretty girl.' I don't think they ever spoke again."

To attempt to get Jackson to tell his story in more detail, Shaye Areheart was dispatched to Australia to conduct interviews with him while he was on tour, and then another ghostwriter, Stephen Davis, was hired to finish the book. Davis told me, "I did the whole thing with Shaye. I didn't meet Mrs. Onassis until after the book was published, at a party at Carly Simon's house. My agent called me. I was working on a book with Fleetwood Mac and I was out there, and they weren't having any luck with Robert Hilburn's stuff or Shaye's stuff. . . .

"So I went and met him, and he was very shy. . . . And I said, 'Look, Mrs. Onassis sent me. Do you want to do this? Is this going to happen? Because I don't want to put my life on hold for a year to do this.' He was totally enthusiastic about it, and especially when I reiterated the magic word 'Onassis.' He told me later on that she was the only person in America who could call him and have him pick up the phone. That's how it happened. To this day I don't know how much they paid him. I tried to find out. While he was in the bathroom, I was snooping around the bedroom, using my sharply honed journalistic skills trying to find out what was really going on there.

"I think he just wanted to have her on the other end of the phone and be his editor. And then of course he put her through this thing at the end where he was going to kill the book unless she wrote a foreword. And then all of a sudden they put a very heavy deadline on me and my brother [Christopher], who was pulling this text together. . . . And so we sent this to them expecting to be fired, because, you know, this was not in any way a publishable manuscript from what I was used to submitting to publishers; and two weeks later we started getting proofs. We couldn't believe it, actually. And Shaye did a new ending. Other than that, that's the book that we sent in. *Moonwalk* is unique in my career and in publishing history. . . . I just know he had absolute power over what happened with that thing and that people at Doubleday were afraid of him because he had more money than God, and he was litigious."

Alberto Vitale was the CEO of Doubleday, which had been bought by the German conglomerate Bertelsmann AG. The company had been renamed Bantam Doubleday Dell. Vitale recalled that Jackson made an effort to pull the plug on the book at the eleventh hour when it was ready to go to the printer. "He was such a problem, you have no idea. . . . We had to go and have a meeting with him, you know. At the last minute, he didn't want to publish the book. I gotta tell you that was some historical meeting. Quite an experience, at his hotel room here in New York. We got him to say okay, to publish the book. At the end I didn't know what to say. I told him, 'Well, you know, this book is going to be published, a legacy to humanity.' "

Writing the introduction for the book continued to be a challenge for Jackie that she postponed right up until the end. Suarès said, "She wanted me to write it, but I didn't know what to say, either. She kept referring to it as an 'envoi,' not an introduction or preface. . . . I told her what to say in it, and she finally wrote it. It was much shorter than what she was supposed to do."

Indeed, Jackie's introduction was but a succinct homage, but it caught the attention of the critic who reviewed the book for *The New York Times Book Review,* NPR rock critic Ken Tucker: " 'What can one say about Michael Jackson?' asks his editor, Jacqueline Kennedy Onassis, in her introduction to this autobiography by the world's most famous living pop star. Since Mrs. Onassis' introduction takes up all of one short paragraph, the

implied answer would seem to be 'Not much,' and indeed the same question seems to have stumped the book's author, who fills pages with drab
show-biz cliches and aimless anecdotes. Had it been written by anyone else,
Moonwalk . . . could be dismissed as an assiduously unrevealing, frequently
tedious document. Ultimately, however, these are precisely the qualities
that make it fascinating."

A sanitized self-told tale of the life and accomplishments of the androgy-
nous King of Pop enigma—perhaps even more enigmatic than his editor—
was a reasonable publishing proposition back in early 1980s, before his
terminal weirdness had surfaced and at a time when he still had a large
youthful following. Slightly more than two decades later, Jackson had endured financial humiliation and scandal and had been vilified for alleged
child molestation. His actions may or may not have amounted to a somewhat innocent reaching out to children whom Jackson thought were facing
the same predicament that he had faced, a family obligation enforced on
him to continue being a "meal ticket" at a time when most youngsters are
still worried about acne and schoolyard bullies.

Today, many of the passages in this book carry a different meaning.
Jackson recounted his first appearance at the Apollo Theater, turning it
into a coming-of-age tale. "I had seen quite a few strippers, but that
night this one girl with gorgeous eyelashes and long hair came out and
did her routine. She put on a great performance. All of a sudden, at the
end, she took off her wig, pulled a pair of big oranges out of her bra, and
revealed that she was a hard-faced guy under all that make-up. That
blew me away. I was only a child and couldn't even conceive of anything
like that."

Of course, he could not have had a normal childhood. He was world-
famous before he hit his teen years, and allegedly abused by his father. His
first "date" was with Tatum O'Neal. The young superstar couple visited
Hugh Hefner at the Playboy Mansion. He tells how Astaire singled him
out for his dancing talents and encouraged him to dance with anger and
ferocity. Acutely aware that his core audience was teenage girls, he made a
point to deny a chauvinism that some critics detected in a few of his songs.
"If this song ['Heartbreak Hotel'], and later 'Billie Jean,' seemed to cast
women in an unfavorable light, it was not meant to be taken as a personal
statement. Needless to say, I love the interaction between the sexes; it is a
natural part of life and I love women." It may not take an O.E.D.-licensed
grammarian to note the unnatural phraseology. The "interaction between
the sexes" reads like it was taken from a teenage sex manual written by
cloistered nuns.

The only new information was Jackson's assertion that he learned more about singing and performing on stage from Jackie Wilson than from anybody else, and more about acting from Marlon Brando, who became a father figure for Jackson. The book indicates that he was treated like a blank slate during his Motown years—he had to learn grammar, table etiquette, and all manner of practical things before he could be loosed upon the world. The Motown relationship turned ugly when Jackson suggested that he might write his own songs and establish his own publishing house. Motown's founder and chief impresario Berry Gordy, who would later write another introduction for the reissued book, would not allow this independence, even when it meant losing one of his biggest stars.

Jackson did end up owning his own publishing company, and proved himself a keen businessman when he purchased the Beatles catalogue of songs. But in many ways, this book remains unsatisfying, even after his tragic demise. He addressed his transformation from a dark-skinned African American to a much paler man, a metamorphosis noticed by legions of his fans, in an unbelievable manner, blaming his condition on a rare skin disease and denying ever having had plastic surgery on his nose, despite published photographic evidence to the contrary. It would not have been lost on Jackie or Areheart that mostly he comes off as insincere, more interested in what he thinks is expected of him than in actually plumbing his own inner depths. This was not Jackie's finest project, though it elicited a great deal of interest given the subject.

Despite the book's banality, it shot to the top of the *New York Times* bestseller list in June 1988, though its time on the list was destined to be short-lived, as word of mouth and less favorable reviews had an impact on sales. There was never a paperback edition published in the United States. Still, the book made money for the house with worldwide sales. Jackie was never pleased with the outcome, despite Areheart's suggesting that "Michael was very happy and proud of the attention the book was receiving and so, of course, were we." Jackie flatly refused to be involved in Jackson's next book, *Dancing the Dream: Poem and Reflections,* which was edited entirely by Areheart and published by Doubleday in 1992—apparently more dirty work.

Ghostwriter Davis remembered an encounter with Jackie that revealed another side to the story: "I never met Mrs. Onassis until three or four years later, because we were neighbors on Martha's Vineyard. Finally we wound up at the same party, and I said to Carly Simon, 'Listen, I did Michael Jackson's book for your friend Jackie. Do you think you can introduce me to her?' And that's how I met her. And as I said, 'I did *Moonwalk*. I worked with Shaye,' she just rolled her eyes way back into her head. 'Oy, *Moonwalk!*' "

When I started working with Jackie in 1984, she was in the final stages of publishing another of her illustrated works, *Drawings of the Northwest Indians,* which was aimed at preserving the work of the nineteenth-century artist George Catlin. With this facsimile volume, Jackie outdid herself, sparing no expense for its production. Featuring reproductions of Catlin's drawings on rich, thick paper and in full size, the book sold for more than $100, an unusually high figure for that time. Catlin's sketches were an ethnologist's dream, accurate and realistic portrayals, preserving facial markings, headdresses, and clothing styles of his Native American subjects. He did not embellish or romanticize in an era when frontier exaggeration was the norm.

The Catlin book included a foreword by Stuart P. Feld and Robert D. Schonfeld, of the Hirschl & Adler Galleries, which was located on the Upper East Side and had a collection of Catlin's albums. The gallery's exhibition, "A Festival of Western American Art," coincided with the book's publication. An introduction was written by Peter Hassrick, who was the director of the Buffalo Bill Historical Center, in Cody, Wyoming. The president of the gallery, Stuart Feld, had been a curator at the Met and had known Jackie for a number of years. While he was the one who proposed the project, in a letter to Jackie at the end of 1982, he told me that he didn't have much contact with her while work on the book was being completed.

Jackie later wrote to the gallery's vice president, Robert Schonfeld, to outline her ideas on how the book might be promoted. Her letter read, in part, "This is the marketing plan which I think is good—because it is high-powered, and approaches people who should be approached for a book—like this—The poor trudging salesmen aren't really the way to go with such a special project." Pleased with the outcome of her efforts, she later wrote glowing letters of appreciation to the gallery directors.

Jackie continued to try to interest various celebrities in doing books. Before the Jackson book was published, Lisa Drew recalled Jackie saying lightheartedly, "Is there anybody else that you'd like me to try and get? Because people do sometimes take my phone calls." Drew suggested Barbra Streisand, and though Jackie wasn't a Streisand fan, she did arrange an exploratory meeting with her in Los Angeles. Afterward, Streisand never followed up, but Drew told Carl Sferrazza Anthony, "About a year later, after I had left Doubleday for another job, Jackie called to say, 'I got a message that Barbra Streisand called, but I wasn't here.' An hour later she called me up, laughing, and said, 'Well, I've talked to Barbra.' And I said, 'Well, what? What?' And she said, 'She isn't interested in doing a book at all. She wanted the name of a good libel lawyer. I told her I didn't have one because I don't sue for libel.' "

Jackie also considered acquiring a book from the controversial author Jerzy Kosinski, who was introduced to her by J. C. Suarès. Kosinski and Suarès shared a passion for polo, and Suarès thought that might be a subject for a book. He said, "The story begins with Jerzy being in dire need of money because the *Village Voice* did an exposé of the way he put books together. And he asked me to help him out. So we went to Jackie, and we were about to go into a meeting. . . . She said something to the effect that polo was very dangerous, and he started a whole argument to the effect that in fact we're all dying anyway. . . . The more he talked, the more unlikely it was that this book would ever happen. Jackie called me out of courtesy to say, 'There's just not enough of an audience.' "

The polo audience may have been limited, but the ballet audience at the time was enormous, and Jackie was an impassioned fan, having studied ballet in her youth. The 1960s and 1970s heralded a "ballet boom," with regional companies sprouting up everywhere and a national audience rivaling that of professional football. There were ballet superstars and acclaimed stage partnerships like the Royal Ballet's Rudolf Nureyev and Margot Fonteyn, and American Ballet Theatre's Mikhail (Misha) Baryshnikov and Gelsey Kirkland. All of them attracted their share of media attention and appeared on the covers of *Time* and *Newsweek* magazines, with Soviet defectors Nureyev and Baryshnikov garnering special attention at the height of the Cold War.

Jackie was friendly with both Nureyev and Fonteyn, and she was also an admirer of Gelsey Kirkland, who recalled, "I first met Jackie at a gala in the early eighties, when I was seated next to her at a formal gathering after a performance. It was arranged by the ABT management to put us together, since her support of the company was crucial to its survival. When Jackie first came over and sat down, the first thing she said was, 'Gelsey, you're probably nervous about meeting me, but I'm even more nervous to meet you!' "

Jackie was enthralled by Gelsey's artistry, and later broached the subject of writing a book, though initially without success. For several years before I met Gelsey early in 1984, she had been caught in a self-destructive spiral of eating disorders and drug abuse. Anorexia, bulimia, cocaine, and Valium were threatening her life, to the extent that one of her fellow dancers described her as "sliding down the razor blade of life." Indeed, she was in danger and had even performed onstage on occasion under the influence. Both ABT management and her fellow dancers were well aware of the problem, but no one intervened. At that point, though she was still a major box-office attraction, she was in no condition to tell her story.

Gelsey was a brilliant, articulate, tormented artist, arguably the greatest ballerina of her generation, a perfectionist whose demands in the ballet studio and onstage led to conflicts and daily bouts of anguish that she attributed to her troubled childhood and early training at choreographer George Balanchine's New York City Ballet and its school.

In the early eighties, Gelsey's tempestuous offstage romance with her frequent partner Baryshnikov ended badly, and she had to endure working for him (and dancing with him) while he was the artistic director of ABT. Ballet was then a male-dominated enterprise, though you would never know that watching the 1977 classic PBS film of *The Nutcracker,* danced by Baryshnikov and Kirkland to great acclaim. As far as the public knew, everything was still beautiful at the ballet. In that period of turmoil, drugs for Gelsey were not recreational but a way to dull the pain and parry the abuse she encountered in her excruciating routine as a dancer. When challenged by concerned friends, she would say defiantly, "I'm an addict, I'm going to die, and there's nothing you can do about it!"

At the time, I was working in film as a reader for the story department at 20th Century Fox, and I met Gelsey by accident at the door of an unsavory drug dealer in Midtown who catered to various high-profile artists and their hangers-on, the Studio 54 crowd. Within a few whirlwind months, she and I became romantically involved and, in shared desperation, moved upstate to take rufuge and clean up our acts, motivated at first simply by our fear for each other's lives. Our idea was to escape the self-indulgent cauldron of Manhattan, with all its fashionable temptations. We went through a surprisingly painless withdrawal, immersing ourselves each day in Shakespeare, Renaissance art, and classical music, an unorthodox stint of our own self-styled rehab that by some miracle just happened to work for us. The dangers of relapse passed and we never looked back.

While Gelsey resumed her ballet discipline, giving herself class at the barre each morning and preparing for a return to the stage with the Royal Ballet, we accepted Jackie's offer to write a book that would chronicle her life and career. At the time, Gelsey was thirty-two years old and, since the age of eight, had spent her life in the cloistered dance world. From the outset, Jackie gave Gelsey the freedom to relate her experiences with no holds barred. My job would be to record interviews and then translate them into a literary voice consistent with her personality. Every word had to meet with Gelsey's approval, and with Jackie's.

I remember the first meeting we had with Jackie and Lisa Drew, which took place at La Petite Ferme, a cozy French bistro on Manhattan's Upper East Side. Over lunch, Gelsey gave a rambling account of her life in the ballet world and had all of us in tears. Jackie was obviously quite moved and also thrilled with the prospect of having Gelsey tell her story, knowing full well based on what she had just heard that it was bound to be contro-versial. As editor, Jackie had no reservations about that, though I suspect she may have underestimated just how scandalous the book would be. At the end of our meeting, Jackie said, "Greg, I've been taking a course on computers. They're really amazing, what they can do. Do you think you might want to borrow one to work on the book?"

At that point, Lisa Drew, to whom Jackie deferred on business matters, leaned toward her and whispered, "Jackie, they'll be able to buy a com-puter after we give them their advance." Jackie then enthused, "Oh, of course, they will!" In the weeks that followed Gelsey and I put together a proposal and rough outline that Jackie used to pitch the book at Double-day, and we eventually signed a contract in August 1984, accepting an ad-vance of $125,000, Doubleday's preemptive offer to discourage us from shopping around for bids from other publishers. The initial offer communi-cated by Jackie was $100,000, but she immediately told us not to worry and promised to get us more money, before we even had the chance to ac-cept.

We delivered a chapter every couple of months, and Jackie would call or write and offer such effusions of high praise that it was difficult to take her seriously, and then we would take a two-hour train ride from the quaint river town of Hudson into Manhattan and meet for lunch. At that time, our discussions were mostly about the book and the work under way, though Jackie also loved to hear and offer gossip about the dance world. Because she was on the board of ABT, she knew many of the char-acters we were writing about. But she was also interested in what was going on in our lives and our plans for the future. She was delighted when Gelsey and I were married in May 1985, and equally supportive even when we parted amicably eight years later. Jackie never wavered. When I first suggested the title of the book, *Dancing on My Grave*, to her one night on the phone, she said, "Oh, that's perfect! Gelsey has been like a little bird banging against a window all these years, and now she's found herself and has a home. She *is* dancing on her grave, and she will have the last laugh."

As Jackie went through each chapter, she gave us specific suggestions for line edits and revisions. She knew exactly how to deliver constructive criticism while cheering us on. At one point, she wrote:

> The reader is with you, heart in throat, as you unfold your story. . . . Whenever your characters speak, it rings so wildly true. Oh Boy, some of those lines will go down in history. . . . You were overly conscientious starting out to write your first book. . . . And you were too intent on showing what you

had learned through study. . . . As in dance, we shouldn't be able to tell what you got from which teacher. It's great when it looks effortless. . . . The most important thing I have to tell you is that your book is TRULY GREAT. Soon the world will agree—much love, Jackie.

Gelsey remembered, "There was the war of chapter four, where we fought over Stravinsky. It must have taken us three rewrites." We had included some harsh criticism of composer Igor Stravinsky, because in her youth Gelsey had a difficult time dancing to his discordant music in the Balanchine ballet *Firebird.* She eventually rebelled against the Stravinsky/Balanchine neoclassical aesthetic, and defected from the New York City Ballet to join ABT, devoting herself to its more dramatic and classical repertory. Jackie loved Stravinsky—he had been one of the first artists she and JFK invited to the White House. With great patience, our editor instructed us to tone down and soften the invective, and we relented, only later realizing how right she was.

In one of her many manuscript notes, Jackie wrote, "Delving too deeply into philosophy here? Cut.—Especially quoting Stravinsky. Readers won't be coming to this book expecting such a polemical work, and will be alienated. Include only as much as illustrates Gelsey's developing creative attitudes and contributes to the story. Keep *story* in mind and omit anything that seems unnecessary. The reader, by this time, understands that Gelsey and Balanchine have inharmonious attitudes. Any more is overemphasizing the point. . . . 'I was trying to be a classical dancer on a modern stage.' This encapsulates the point very well. The 20 preceding pages could be summed up with this one concise sentence."

Jackie was also right on the mark when she later cut the first draft of our six-hundred-page manuscript almost in half, though Gelsey and I found that awfully difficult to accept at the time. I remember wanting to argue with Jackie at times on the phone, but then being repeatedly disarmed by that voice of hers. Her most frequent editorial note, written over and over in the margins of our manuscript, was "Concision!" It was a lesson that we slowly took to heart, and which made our future collaborations much easier. We began to understand, as far as the editing was concerned, how her mind worked.

Jackie always knew how to deftly and gracefully cut to the chase. For instance, she advised us,

Early anecdotes: Watch out for ones that aren't needed, that detract from the impulsion of the story. . . . What you don't want to do in the first part of the book is slow it up, turn the reader or reviewer off before they come

to its heart. Any autobiography that starts from childhood has this problem. What the first chapters do is: introduce you, your background, your
temperament as a child, the family influences that shaped you—and then
take us through the first part of your fascinating relationship with Balanchine. If this happens with fluidity, the reader will be HOOKED.

Jackie loved both the cerebral challenge of working with us and the vicarious thrills. Her mirth at our lunches and on the phone was irrepress-
ible. She loved our youthful bluster and irreverence even when she disagreed
and we tested her patience. We regarded her as our special friend and ally—
our own fairy godmother and prodding mother hen. She always kept her
promises, and as with many of her authors, she made us feel like what we
were doing might actually be important. She constantly defended our interests with the publishing house and offered us financial advice, coming
through with early payments on our advance money when we were in need,
while swearing us to secrecy.

While the fate of the book was still uncertain, Jackie's generous support gave us the stability and security to travel to London in the fall of
1986 in order for Gelsey to make a comeback with the Royal Ballet's production of *Romeo and Juliet.* We somehow continued the writing while
Gelsey took class and rehearsed all day. We were surprised and deeply
touched when Jackie and Maurice Tempelsman traveled to London to attend Gelsey's first performance at the Royal Opera House in Covent Garden. We thought that was an extraordinary gesture and vote of confidence
on Jackie's part, but she wouldn't allow us to include that episode in the
book. The performance was to receive sterling reviews from every London
critic. When the curtain came down, I saw tears in Jackie's eyes.

While we were in London, Diane Sawyer and a crew came over to interview us for *60 Minutes,* producing an affecting piece that would later
be nominated for an Emmy. Jackie was a friend of Sawyer's and of her
husband, director Mike Nichols, but according to the producer of the *60
Minutes* piece, Jan Legnitto, it was Doubleday's public relations person at
the time, Ellen Mastromonaco, who arranged for the segment. Still, I've
always believed that Jackie's involvement had to have been a factor for
Sawyer.

We did have a few peevish skirmishes with Jackie, as we had our own
headstrong agenda with the book and were overbearing. Gelsey remembered, "We were always stubborn and standing our ground so it must
have been hellish for Jackie at times to get us to budge." For Gelsey, telling
her story was a catharsis that was a long time coming, so every passage in
the manuscript was discussed intensively with Jackie. When there were

disputes between Jackie and Gelsey, I was thrust into the role of mediator, in the middle of the crossfire. Gelsey later recalled, "When Jackie gave me the opportunity to write my autobiography, she helped me recover my life and career. . . . She was both an editor and a friend, and whenever the two roles came into conflict, the friendship always won out."

There were more challenges when the book had to be vetted by the Doubleday lawyers. Apparently unaware that he had died some years before, they were concerned that George Balanchine might sue us. While we were reviewing the proofs of the book, Baryshnikov's lawyers threatened legal action, and Jackie convinced us to make a few word changes to appease them. She advised us in a letter to substantiate many of the potentially defamatory assertions in the book, as requested by the lawyers.

Invasion of privacy was also an issue Jackie explained: "This is what I found out that is scary. It usually isn't the public figures (people whose names have been mentioned in the press) who sue. It is the little people. . . . It costs them nothing. They get a contingency lawyer and if they win, they split the money awarded. And YOU are liable, not Doubleday." Jackie added, "When it sounds like nit-picking, don't get annoyed. . . . Don't panic and think you have to eviscerate your book. Back up your assertions. Where it's prudent change a name, leave out a word like 'lesbian' or 'toilet-training.' Change a first name when it is dangerous."

At a certain point, shortly after Gelsey had appeared on *60 Minutes*, at the behest of Doubleday's publicity department, Jackie called and insisted that Gelsey had to do additional press interviews. Gelsey balked, hating the idea of publicity, and we finally had to break off the conversation, rudely hanging up. The next day Jackie sent a gigantic bouquet of roses and apologized, telling Gelsey, "I remember when Jack was running for the Senate, and they wanted me to do more publicity appearances, and I finally refused. That's exactly what you did, Gelsey. I'm so sorry I tried to push you too far."

In October 1986, while we were in London, the book was published, and we received a steady stream of congratulatory phone calls and telegrams from Jackie keeping us up to date on the book's progress. There was a firestorm from the critics, who were either laudatory or hostile, pretty much evenly divided. In *The New York Times Book Review*, Deborah Jowitt called the book "hot stuff" and a "bizarre and terrifying volume," concluding with the line, "However sensational the material, however baffling, contrary and still not entirely wise to herself Ms. Kirkland may be, she has provided an unnervingly vivid statement about the perils of a profession in which your instrument is yourself."

We returned to New York in November and met Jackie for lunch, just after a review in *Vanity Fair* appeared by James Wolcott that included a not-so-subtle smear of our editor. Wolcott wrote, referring to a graphic description of Gelsey's addiction nightmare and drug-induced seizures, "Is this the place to note that the book's editor is Jacqueline Kennedy Onassis? I guess not."

While Jackie was unperturbed as far as we could tell and continued to send us copies of reviews from around the country, Gelsey was vulnerable and hurt by some of the more vicious slings and arrows. In an effort to console her over lunch, Jackie said, "Oh, Gelsey, you just have to ignore the critics. Don't allow them to hurt you. They are all fickle, and they will eventually change their minds about you. You'll see. When Jack and I were in the White House, it was Camelot to everyone. But later, after I married Ari, I was the traitor. At the time people couldn't understand why I needed that sanctuary. And now, suddenly, I'm the world's greatest mother!"

We and our editor were all the more consoled by the fact that the book stayed on the *New York Times* bestseller list for several months, and repeated that performance the following year when the paperback edition came out. As our book appeared two years before the Michael Jackson book, it was Jackie's first bestseller. It was also heartening over the years to see that some ballet companies were making efforts to provide support systems and therapeutic options for their dancers to deal with health issues that Gelsey had raised publicly for the first time.

Jackie's encouragement led to two more books for us over the next seven years. We would meet for lunches, and she would clap her hands and say excitedly, "What are we going to do next?" Our ballet-theater journal entitled *The Shape of Love* was published in 1990, the title referring to the physical ideal of the nineteenth-century classical ballerina. And a children's book, *The Little Ballerina and her Dancing Horse,* came out in 1993. The latter was based on specific instructions that Jackie gave us to write a story about two of her childhood passions—ballet and horses. We put together a saccharine tale about a little girl who had to decide between studying ballet and horseback riding, initially entitled *Side Saddle Ballerina.* Jackie loved it and wrote me a letter saying that she was reading it aloud to all the children in her life. That was in 1993, not long before she became gravely ill.

Back in 1986, even when Jackie threw a gala book party for us in the Doubleday Fifth Avenue suite to celebrate the publication of *Dancing on My Grave,* I wasn't aware of how important that particular book was for her professionally and how she relished it as a personal victory. Of course, she complimented Gelsey and me in florid terms and said how proud she was of us. That may explain why she continued to work with us, even though our next two books weren't as successful commercially. When I asked if she was disappointed that our second book hadn't become a best-seller, she just chortled and said, "Oh no, Greg, sequels are usually not as successful as the first book. Don't worry about it. It's a wonderful book."

Another one of Jackie's authors, David Stenn, a biographer and television writer, started his collaboration with Jackie in 1986. Stenn told me, "Jackie would say, 'David, promise me I get first dibs on your journals.' I said to her, 'If I publish my journals I'll never work again'—because here I was, this twenty-two-year-old hick suddenly writing for *Hill Street Blues,* and she got a kick out of hearing my stories. She'd tease me about being 'sweetly depraved' and refer to me as 'my little mogul.' "

David continued, referring to his journal while we conversed. "At the time of our first meeting, *Dancing on My Grave* had just come out. Jackie told me that she was treated differently by the other editors now that she had a best seller. She also said that despite the furor over its more salacious material, the book generated heartfelt response from dancers, and that made her proud. She felt she got it right.

"So I was meeting her in a different place than she'd ever been as an editor. She had a little more confidence, having extended her turf to best-selling material, which she also felt contributed to the culture—and as long as I knew her, that was always a concern. She worried about the dumbing-down of mass culture. She told me, 'Our culture will become like it was during the medieval times when there truly was a cultural elite. The rest of the people will just watch television, which will be their only frame of reference.'

"It wasn't snobbery; she just felt there was a reason the classics were classic. I remember we both happened to be reading the same book: *The Secret History,* by Donna Tartt. I asked Jackie what she thought. 'I like it a lot,' she told me, 'because the characters are classics majors, so they're intelligent.'

"She made a point of saying, 'Both my children read a lot as kids and still do.' So reading—the act of reading—was really important to her. To me, that explained her passion for editing: She was fostering a cause she advocated deeply in her own life, with her own family, and for the general public. If she could keep someone reading, then she was succeeding.

"And yet she was smart enough to understand that you can't force-feed people. If they're reading about a silent film star, they're obviously not reading a classic. But they're *reading*—and if the book is well written, and interesting, and moving, that's an achievement. And I was young enough, and green enough, to feel I could accomplish that—chiefly because Jackie told me I could. Having her as an editor was the ultimate confidence-booster. In moments of self-doubt, you'd remind yourself: 'Jackie Onassis believes in me, so maybe I'm right to believe in myself.' "

David's first book with Jackie, *Clara Bow: Runnin' Wild,* was published in 1988; he followed up with *Bombshell: The Life and Death of Jean Harlow* in 1993. Thanks to the talent and compelling voice of the author, the two books read like companion volumes, though the two subjects are quite different in terms of character and historical point of view.

While Jackie had a book under way on Fred Astaire, she had not published any Hollywood biographies, which made David all the more appreciative of her support. "I think, in my case, Jackie was cultivating an author more than a subject. She'd call me in L.A. [where David had returned to write and produce shows like 21 *Jump Street* and *Beverly Hills, 90210*] and say, 'I can't wait! What's our next book going to be?' She seemed to see me as a long-term investment—and words can't convey how much that meant. I never felt like a writer until Jackie treated me like one. . . . I'd never written a book, never written a magazine article. . . . If I hadn't had a true editor, I would have been in serious trouble."

David recalled Jackie's advice on the concept of his first book, and how she took an active role in promoting it. "She said she wanted the Clara Bow biography to be like a Bach fugue. I had no idea what that meant. But what I did know, right then and there, was that she had a *vision* for this book.

"In our second meeting, she said, 'The Doubleday publicists are deadbeats. We have to do this on our own.' She told me to write her a memo selling my book, 'doing all the things you don't usually do, like dropping names.' Which was anathema to me, and I figured she'd feel the same. But she said, 'Do it—because we're going to have to create our own publicity campaign.' "

Jackie also tried to drum up support for the book with her colleagues in-house by arranging for a screening of one of Clara Bow's films. David said, "At one point I remember asking Jackie, 'Do you think anyone will care?' Because at the time, Clara Bow had essentially been forgotten, and I was pouring my heart into this project. And she said, 'David, you're going to *make* them care. You'll see when the reviews come out.' So I just figured, Okay, that's right.

"Now I look back and think, who ever counts on their reviews? But I didn't know any better, and that was the beauty of it—I was in a bubble, because of Jackie. If she said something, I trusted her so thoroughly that I believed it. And the funny thing is, she was right: The very day that book was published, *The New York Times* gave it a rave."

Indeed, the eminent British critic and author John Gross wrote the review for the *Times* and credited the author for rescuing Clara Bow from obscurity: "David Stenn has found out as much about her as it is given to mortals to know; he takes an intelligent approach, neither too solemn nor too flip." Now more than twenty-two years after its initial publication, *Clara Bow: Runnin' Wild* remains in print, though no longer published by Doubleday.

While Jackie's publishing fortune's were rising, Doubleday was in decline, commercially running a distant third to houses like Simon & Schuster and Random House. The president of Doubleday when I started working with Jackie was lawyer Richard Malina. He sent Gelsey and me a congratulatory note before *Dancing on My Grave* came out, saying, "I've finally had the opportunity to read your book, and I know now that the excitement within Doubleday and all over is very well-deserved." We had no further personal contact with any Doubleday executives, as the atmosphere in the house changed dramatically that year with the takeover by Bertelsmann.

The family company took on a more regimented corporate identity, which we felt each time we visited Jackie at her new office on Fifth Avenue and Fifty-second Street. Dick Malina was replaced by Nancy Evans, who came over from Book-of-the-Month Club at the behest of Alberto Vitale. Her qualifications for the position were questioned both in-house and in the press. While *The New York Times* described Evans as "someone with no book-publishing experience," Vitale credited her with bringing "new blood" and "boundless energy" to the company.

Harriet Rubin described Jackie's singular position in the house and the impact of the regime change: "What was most impressive was the effect she had on the Doubleday culture. She was there when the company was bought by the German firm, Bertelsmann. It's hard to believe this today, but the idea of Germans buying 'America's publisher,' the publisher of *Roots*, rocked the media world. This was a cultural invasion. The Germans were going to dumb us all down and then take over America. Jackie's presence kept the house resisting the tide toward schlock. The company that employed Jackie had to maintain a classy presence in the marketplace or they'd lose her. She was the last visible standard of highbrow in the company, maybe in the industry. Nobody wanted Jackie resigning in a public relations huff. . . .

"As open as she was to ideas, I once got the paparazzi swat when I found her in the ladies' room in a cloud of jasmine. 'Jackie, what is that amazing perfume you're wearing?' She barely hesitated and said something about my looking like 'the daughter of the regiment' in my gold-buttoned Chanel suit and walked quickly out, taking the mysterious jasmine and leaving a burning rebuke. Was she afraid I'd sell the information to *People*? It made me realize Jackie wasn't really an employee of Doubleday like the rest of us. She worked for high-minded Camelot; she published books there."

Rubin also described the new CEO, Alberto Vitale, who would eventually take over the reins at Random House: "Alberto was brilliant.... He loved smart, beautiful women, loved to have them around, and his adoration was like a free pass to be oneself. Jackie had to have been a prize to him. But Doubleday had a majority of, forgive me, idiot savants, editors who stepped into piles of golden shit or BS'd Alberto and so rose in the hierarchy. They don't know a colon from their colon. Quality scared them. Ideas scared them. Colleagues who were independent thinkers scared them. The idiot savants won in the sense that their projects and style of publishing prevailed. I hope your book deals with the dark side of publishing in which Jackie got caught. The woes the news media now face were present first in book publishing."

Jackie knew the "dark side" of publishing as well as anyone in the trade. What she made clear to me after the Bertelsmann transition was that she regarded the executives as an adversarial challenge. She played them all with her wiles and charm, but they were without exception the corporate "enemy" that had to be conquered in order for her books to be acquired and published on her terms. In the years ahead, her frustrations would increase, as it became increasingly difficult to sell some of her more arcane and extravagant books to the house. While she claimed not to think about success in terms of sales, she told me on more than one occasion that the books she did that made the bestseller list were necessary in order for her to be able to publish those books that were less commercial.

Recalling a project in which Jackie became briefly involved, her former colleague Les Pockell said, "She was kind of a magnet for people like that who wanted to do certain kinds of high-profile celebrity-oriented books. . . . But then not everything was right for her, so she would . . . kind of pass it off to other people. . . . I was in the special interests group, and she was in the general group. I did a book with . . . a Hungarian [Bertalan de Némethy] who was a major figure in equestrian training. . . . Her only involvement was she knew this guy many years before. She wouldn't have published that book in the area that she was working in, so she sent it to us." *The De Némethy Method: Modern Techniques for Training the Show Jumper and Its Rider* was published in 1988 with an introduction by William Steinkraus, then captain of the U.S. Equestrian Team.

With regard to the tribulations that Jackie and many fellow Doubleday editors experienced after the advent of the Bertelsmann era, Pockell noted, "By that time, Bertelsmann had changed the company in very, very drastic ways. I mean, we used to be at this really kind of fine old building on Forty-sixth Street and Park Avenue, and that was a real publishing company with real publishing offices. And then we were forced to move over to 666 Fifth Avenue temporarily, because that's where Bantam was, and Doubleday just became an adjunct of Bantam. It was Bantam Doubleday Dell. Jackie never had the same feelings of connection with the corporation as it had evolved at that point. None of us did.

"And while she was there nobody from Doubleday was happy—I think I can say that categorically—with the new setup. . . . But she was a darling over there. . . . You knew that she was around because you could smell that expensive perfume in the aisles. I mean, really, she left a cloud of whatever it was. You knew it was her. She didn't put on airs or anything, but she was just a very, very special person to have around, and I think Doubleday regarded that as an incredible ornament, as I'm sure Bertelsmann did as well, but they just didn't do such a good job of managing it."

From her favored position in the house, Jackie persevered, despite the challenges of working under the new management regime headed by Nancy Evans. Jackie soon undertook a project that reunited her with one of the personalities associated with her Camelot years, Stewart Udall, a former congressman who served as secretary of the interior from 1961 to 1969 under both JFK and LBJ. Udall's book, *To the Inland Empire: Coronado and Our Spanish Legacy*, was conceived as a celebration of the golden age of Spanish exploration in the American Southwest by Francisco Vázquez de Coronado.

The Udall book would take Jackie to an area of the country that she had avoided since the assassination in Dallas. Udall teamed up on the book with photographer Jerry Jacka, a longtime contributor to *Arizona Highways*. Jacka told me how he became involved in the project: "Stewart said, 'By God, Jerry, I think we're going to get Jackie out here and do a book.'"

Udall and Jacka had already been researching Coronado's history in anticipation of a magazine presentation. The full-length book, published in 1987, reveals that Udall's interest in the subject was personal. He grew up in rural Arizona, near the route that the conquistador Coronado had taken in 1540 during his search for the seven golden cities of Cibola. Attending a road-naming ceremony near his ranch as a child, Udall heard locals grumbling that this was not really Coronado's trail, that the real one was actually to the west, running across an Apache reservation. This disconnect between official history and local knowledge fascinated the young Udall, and would intrigue his future editor. Udall and Jacka, who retraced Coronado's trek together, created a series of "Coronadoscapes," large-format photos that captured the grandeur that Coronado must have felt as he wound his way through the desert.

Jacka recalled Jackie's visit to Arizona to participate in researching the book with Stewart and his wife, Lee, and Jerry's wife, Lois. "The Coronado story had been told over and over again, but not from the perspective that Stewart wanted to tell it, and no one to our knowledge had camped along the area that we felt was Coronado's trail. But we had some very good reference material . . . some of the letters from Coronado when his men went back to Spain and Mexico. And that shed a lot of light. We camped along the route, so that's where it all started, at a campfire.

"A year later, Stewart called my wife, Lois, and me and said that Mrs. Onassis was coming out to Arizona, and he would like for Lois and I to join Stewart and Lee, Mrs. Udall, and Jacqueline Kennedy Onassis and Maurice Tempelsman on a little junket, and that he wanted to show her actually where we felt a portion of this route went, and kind of get her excited about the project."

Jacka continued, "We took her to some extremely rugged terrain. Stewart and I, having camped and researched, we felt that there was a crossing at the Black River that divides San Carlos and the Apache Indian Reservations. . . . So we took Jackie there [in] a four-wheel-drive 1984 Chevrolet Suburban; and it wasn't even a road. We were just bouncing where the wagons used to go over boulders. And then Stewart stopped and served a little wine, a tailgate wine gathering at the river. And he read poetry . . . and we had a little cheese and crackers. Then we all waded the river with Jackie in tow. And the river was fortunately not too high at that time. . . . She was just a charming, wonderful gal. She was down-to-earth, and she and Lee Udall and Stewart were reminiscing of the White House days, and it was fun for Lois and I to eavesdrop on that.

"Stewart had arranged for her to visit Zuñi Pueblo and an old Catholic church there. . . . We wanted to take her up the old stone stairway that we felt was probably the stairway that Coronado used as he and his army ventured up into Acoma Pueblo. Acoma is called the Sky City; it's up on a very high plateau. And so we accessed that by this stairway, and she just really enjoyed it."

After the book was published, Jackie gave Jacka and his wife an inscribed copy that read, in part, "With admiration for one of the greatest poets the Southwest has produced—the poet of the camera."

While Jackie was putting the wraps on the Udall book, she commissioned another illustrated work. Sarah Giles's *Fred Astaire: His Friends Talk* evolved from a *Vanity Fair* article published by the magazine's then-editor, Tina Brown, shortly after Astaire's death in June 1987. Jackie had Giles expand the number Astaire's friends who contributed. Composed primarily of interview excerpts rather than narrative, the book was divided into sections that covered "The Artist," "The Astaire Women," and "His Private World."

Giles acknowledged to me that to some degree the book reflected the interview format that was established by Jean Stein and George Plimpton in their 1982 book about Warhol muse Edie Sedgwick (*Edie: American Girl*). "I think I split it up into sections like that because, you know, we all knew *Edie*. . . . And that's really what the original concept was, when Tina Brown and I got up to do this. We just copied; but it was a good formula, and she [Jackie] liked it."

The book party for the Astaire book afforded Jackie the opportunity to meet Giles's friend at *Vanity Fair,* author Dominick Dunne. In an article he wrote for the magazine, Dunne recollected, "The only time I ever actually had a conversation with her was at a lunch party at Mortimer's to celebrate the publication of a book she had edited about Fred Astaire. . . . I had always longed to meet her, but when the moment came, I couldn't think of a single thing to say. 'Oh God, don't let me go mute,' I prayed. The slight smile on her face indicated that she knew that people sometimes had that feeling in her presence. Of course, she saved the day. She mentioned a quote of mine in the book and asked me something about Fred Astaire, whom I had known because his daughter was a friend of mine, and suddenly I was off and running. Only later did I realize that I had done all the talking. She had just given me the subject."

Jackie had a capacity for forbearance and was able to embrace even the most eccentric personalities among those artists she worked with. She inherited one book and its photographer-author, William Eggleston, from her colleague James Fitzgerald when he was planning to move on to St. Martin's Press. Fitzgerald explained, "One of the things that happens when an editor leaves, they have books already under way. I had a book that I was quite excited about. . . . I remember buying the book, and people coming by. And Jackie came by and went, 'Lucky you!' So when I left I had all these books to dole out to people, and I thought, Who better than Jackie for this? And I went over and asked her, and she said, 'I'd be honored.' Just by chance Eggleston was coming to New York, and I thought, Fun, we'll get them together. . . . And Eggleston came in, and we went down to Jackie's office, and I introduced them. And she went, 'Ohh, I've been wanting to meet you.'

"Eggleston was not awed by anything. He had riding boots on, and a leather coat. He's kind of a character. . . . We were planning to go have lunch, and it was about eleven, and I was in the midst of getting out. So I said, 'I'll leave you two to talk'—Jackie had the pictures there; I mean, it was pretty much well on the way. . . . I came back, and when I walked in the office, Eggleston was standing on top of her desk showing her how Prussian soldiers would about-face. She was fascinated. . . . It just kind of went with the territory, as far as she was concerned."

Eggleston's book, *The Democratic Forest,* was published in 1989. The book's title suggests that views of rural America somehow characterize the spirit of democracy. But the photographs included are more limited in scope. A talented photographer fascinated by the commonplace, Eggleston set out to capture rural Americana with its quaint storefronts, highways, and parking lots, but strangely confined himself to the southeastern quadrant of the United States. His color photos of the misty mountains surrounding Chattanooga and of rural homesteads in Alabama and Mississippi are evocative, and the introduction written by the celebrated southern novelist Eudora Welty further reinforces the regional vision that this volume represents.

Fitzgerald remembered working with Jackie earlier on another exotic adventure book, *The Search for Omm Sety,* written by Jonathan Cott. "He came to me," said Fitzgerald, "with something that I thought, and I still think to this day, is a very interesting story about a woman in England [Dorothy Eady]. I just think Jackie was interested in the subject, she was mad about ancient history, and I mentioned it to her. . . . It led to meetings up at her apartment, her pulling out these maps and books."

Jonathan Cott told me that he regarded Jackie and Fitzgerald as co-editors, and he later referred to them in the book as his editorial "guardian spirits." Cott's interest had been piqued by a 1979 *New York Times* article by Christopher Wren that told the story of Dorothy Eady's fateful journey from England to Egypt and her mystical transformation into Omm Sety. Whatever her eccentricities, this strange British woman, who was born in 1904, also became a highly regarded Egyptologist in her day.

Cott clipped the *Times* article, and some years later brought it with him to his first meeting with Jackie to discuss the book. He recalled, "When I sat down across from her, I felt pretty nervous. For me, she was more like a universal anima figure than a prospective editor! But then, after a few minutes, my projections melted into air, as Jackie made me feel that there was no need to stand on any kind of ceremony since we shared a common fascination with this remarkable twentieth-century English-Egyptian priestess of Isis."

It was to be a serendipitous meeting. When Cott showed Jackie the *Times* clipping, she pulled out the very same article from her own files. Recalling that moment, Cott said, "Emily Dickinson once wrote: 'The incredible never surprises us because it is the incredible.' While working with Jackie, nothing was ever surprising because everything was incredible."

Recognizing Jackie's "great knowledge of and love for ancient Egypt" from the outset, Cott recounted that Jackie "told me that she herself had met Omm Sety, who had lived in a mud hut in the Upper Egyptian village of Abydos until her death in 1981, on a trip she had taken down the Nile in the 1970s. Ever since then, Jackie said, she had been fascinated by this woman, and she talked to me with such intensity and passion about the book I was in the process of writing that it seemed as if she were dreaming it herself.

"When I had completed the first draft of my manuscript, Jackie asked me to come to her office, where she had brought from her home a score of books on ancient Egyptian history, art, and religion, including one of the enormous twenty-four volumes of the *Description de l'Egypte* commissioned by Napoléon, with its incomparable engravings. Listening to my editor's wonderfully knowledgeable ideas about ancient Egypt and to her enthusiastic but specific comments about my manuscript, I soon began to imagine that, like Omm Sety, I, too, was entering the world of ancient Egypt, conversing with an Egyptian queen who was as beautiful as Nefertiti. . . ."

Cott continued, "And then I came out of my little trance—back from Thebes to Fifth Avenue—and Jackie was pointing to a page of my manuscript, saying, 'A diminishing sentence. Pull out the stops. Make this passage more dramatic. . . . Let us understand what it meant for Dorothy . . . to come to know the meaning and purpose of her life. . . . Don't let her just be an English eccentric. Dottiness was her cover-up. *Say she was a witch!*' "

Having chanced to meet Dorothy Eady when traveling on a tour of Egyptian antiquities, Jackie was once again drawing on connections from her past. Eady seemingly had more access to sacred relics than the local Egyptians did and, by the time Jackie met her, had become a self-taught expert on Egyptian hieroglyphics and the many dynasties that flourished around the Nile before the Common Era. Dorothy Eady adopted the name Omm Sety only after she became convinced that she was a reincarnated consort of Pharaoh Sety the First.

As Jonathan Cott revealed in his book, it turned out that this particular Dorothy had been seeking her own peculiar Oz since she was three years old. Eady eventually made her way to Egypt, but spent many years on the outskirts of Cairo, near the tombs at Giza. By the time she finally moved upriver to the village at Abydos, she had learned Arabic and had already assisted in translating hieroglyphics for the local scholars.

These may have been the actions of a charming eccentric, a particularly British type, except for the secret life that Omm Sety was pursuing after dark, when her lover Sety the First would come and visit. Dorothy kept diaries of all these encounters, and reading these diaries clarifies why Cott chose "Reincarnation and Eternal Love" as his subtitle. This was the resurrection of a three-thousand-year-old love affair. How could Jackie not be seduced by such a tale? In his acknowledgments, Cott thanked his editor "for reminding me, in the words of an ancient Egyptian scribe, that to speak of the Dead is to make them live again."

At her apartment on occasion, Jackie regaled Cott with stories about old friends like André Malraux, France's minister of culture under de Gaulle, who years before had led the international movement to save Egyptian monuments that were threatened by flooding due to the construction of the Aswan Dam. Jackie told Cott that Malraux, who seemed to have had a crush on her, had dedicated his autobiography, *Anti-Memoirs,* to her. After she married Aristotle Onassis, he pointedly removed his dedication to her from the book's second edition.

Jackie shared her grand view overlooking the Met with Cott, who told me, "She took me to the window and said, 'You see, there's the Temple of Dendur.' Of course, you can see it through the glass ceiling of the museum. And she said, 'Do you want to know how it got there?' I said, 'Sure.' And she told me this incredible story (though I shouldn't have been surprised) about how she was personally responsible for getting it. She had gotten Jack Kennedy to give money to Egypt . . . and Nasser, the president of Egypt, wanted to return a favor to Kennedy and to the United States, so he asked Kennedy what he would like from Egypt. And he apparently said to Jackie, 'What should we ask from Nasser?' And she said, 'What about a temple?' And Nasser sent the Temple of Dendur to Washington."

In fact, Jackie had initially wanted the temple to stay in Washington as a tribute to Jack after it arrived; she had wanted it to be located on the Potomac. But the Met later managed to obtain it.

Returning to the subject of his book, Cott said, "Jackie didn't do detailed line editing on my book, but she wrote wonderful and illuminating comments throughout the whole manuscript. She read my book as if she were a besotted teenager reading some kind of supernatural mystery story with her mouth agape. Her comments were sharp, witty, and always on target. Not one could be dismissed.

"The New York publishing world has always had an amazing number of brilliant book editors, but with Jackie, you felt like you were talking to someone who was your friend, because she really was obsessed with the things you were obsessed with. I know it seems incredible in this day and age, when marketing departments generally have the final say in whether or not a book gets published, but Jackie seemed to be immune to those kinds of commercial pressures."

Cott continued his alliance with Jackie on *Isis and Osiris,* which was published in January 1994. The author explained that the second book came about "because the Isis and Osiris story was at the heart of the Omm Sety book, because Omm Sety had performed the role of Isis when she was a girl, a teenager. Abydos is the center in Egypt where Omm Sety lived—was the ancient center for the Isis and Osiris mystery play, where that was performed.

"So we were talking a lot about Isis and Osiris, and I found out about the Fellowship of Isis at Clonegal Castle, in Ireland, where an archpriestess named Olivia Robertson held court and from where she kept in touch with, and greeted visitors from, more than fifteen thousand followers of the goddess in sixty countries. So I told Jackie that I wanted to go to visit the castle and talk to the archpriestess. And I also found out about two Canadian psychologists in Edmonton whose patients reenacted the Isis and Osiris story as a kind of group therapy. I would wind up connecting with all kinds of other Isis and Osiris devotees, as well as two Egyptologists who talked to me about the Isis cult and placed it in a historical context. And one thing and person led to another, and everything soon fell into place.

"Jackie was really enthusiastic about the project, and after the book was published, she sent me a note—it was around Christmastime—in which she wrote: 'May Isis watch over you throughout all of the holiday season.' I mean, to me, Jackie turned out to be a kind of avatar of the goddess herself—and I'm half-kidding but also more than a bit half-serious!"

Using mythological interpretation, Cott demonstrated how the Horus-Isis-Osiris triangle became the precursor for the Christian iconography of holy father, virgin mother, and sanctified and resurrected child. *Isis and Osiris* was as fascinating as author Joseph Campbell in its mythic analysis, and Cott quoted Campbell approvingly, suggesting Isis and Osiris was a tale that expressed "the immanence of divinity in the phenomenal forms of the universe." This, too, would turn out to be a rich vein of esoteric scholarship, as elaborated by Campbell, for Jackie to mine and turn into another unanticipated tour de force.

In 1987, Jackie commenced a series of books with her old friend Bill Moyers, whom she had known since her White House days. Moyers had served as a Peace Corps administrator under JFK and as press secretary under LBJ. The first book, published in 1988, was Joseph Campbell's *The Power of Myth,* which was the companion book to Moyers's PBS series that presented a series of interviews with Campbell. Jackie's assistant Scott Moyers (no relation to Bill) told Carl Sferrazza Anthony that Jackie "had known about Joseph Campbell having been a Svengali figure at Sarah Lawrence College, and Doubleday took a chance on *The Power of Myth* and—boom—it sold millions."

Bill Moyers's chief collaborator on the book and consultant on the PBS series was Betty Sue Flowers, PhD, an enormously resourceful polymath who would later become the director of the Lyndon Baines Johnson Library and Museum. The book was Flowers's brainchild. She instigated the project and was credited as editor. She in turn acknowledged the role played by Jackie, "whose interest in the ideas of Joseph Campbell was the prime mover in the publication of this book."

There was plenty of credit to be shared with such a multifaceted collaboration. The book had to have involved deep meaning for Jackie, though her editing role appears to have been limited primarily to the project's acquisition, along with arranging for the illustrations. In the book's introduction, her role after Dallas was highlighted: Campbell called her organizing of JFK's funeral "a ritualized occasion of the greatest social necessity." He observed, "Here was an enormous nation, made those four days into a unanimous community, all of us participating in the same way, simultaneously, in a single symbolic event." Moyers suggested that the universal news coverage and the images of Jackie mediating the event would forever "line the walls of our interior system of belief like shards of broken pottery in an archeological site."

Betty Sue Flowers explained how the book evolved from the film. "I had never edited film before, and so I began by doing a paper cut on the transcript, which I thought was pretty good. But when I saw the actual interview, on tape, I could tell my paper edit wouldn't work at all. Film is like music—there are energy levels and sound and light that have to be matched—it's not just the words and ideas. Because there are so many constraints in editing film, including the timing, I could see that a lot of the interview would literally end up on the cutting room floor. So I kept working with the transcript, in a way that was very different from working with film editing, and in spite of knowing that Joe [Campbell] never allowed the publication of transcripts of his lectures or interviews.

"I began by putting together everything in the interview related to what I thought of as a spiritual journey. I sent that first chapter—the second chapter as it appeared in the published book—to Joe, and he sent it back to me with his own edits and no other comments. I never asked Joe if I could do a book—I just kept sending him edited chapters, and he just kept returning them with additional edits of his own. So I began working with Joe's publisher [of his previous books]—and then, before the series aired or the book had been published, Joe died. And suddenly, the publisher was no longer interested in the book. So I took the manuscript back to Austin, not knowing what to do.

"One day, I was at home, grading student papers—I was an English professor at that time [at the University of Texas]—and the phone rang. A voice said, 'Would you hold for Jacqueline Onassis?' I said, 'Sure!' I thought it was some kind of student hoax. And then I heard her distinctive voice saying, 'I understand you have a manuscript related to the Moyers interviews with Joseph Campbell.' I said yes, I did. She said, 'Two of my heroes are Bill Moyers and Joseph Campbell, and I'd like to do this book, but I don't know if there's time. Can you come to New York in forty-eight hours, with one hundred black-and-white illustrations and seventy-five color illustrations and the book?' And I said yes and hung up, not knowing how in the world I would do this. The reason for the rush was that in order for the book to appear on PBS as a tie-in book, it had to be on the shelves by the time the series aired.

"I flew up to New York and spent the next forty-eight hours in a hotel room creating a notebook with descriptions of what each illustration and caption should be. I took it to the meeting room where her design team was assembled. She came in, and it was very lovely to meet her. All the many years I worked with her, she always wore the same thing: a very elegant cashmere black sweater and black slacks. After we settled down, she asked for the illustrations, and I said, 'Well, in forty-eight hours there was no time to get them, but I have a list with the captions.' My idea was that someone looking at the book would be able to tell what it was about by reading the captions for the illustrations.

"She said, 'Well, it's got to be done in ten days, so we're going to have to find someone who can get all of these permissions and actually find usable images.' And I wondered how that was going to happen because it would take a person with a certain kind of education to know, for example, what I meant by the instruction 'Find a picture of Icarus and Daedalus, with the emphasis on Daedalus.' The next day I met the person Jackie had found . . . I never saw her again after that day, but she found exactly the illustrations I was thinking of and finished by the deadline.

"I so admired the way Jackie was willing to go with the flow in this really intense project. You have to remember that before the series appeared, the response to the proposed project from funders was 'Are you crazy, Moyers? You've lost it! Six hours with an eighty-three-year-old mythologist?' No one thought there would be any interest whatsoever in this. So Jackie went way out on a limb with Doubleday because to publish a book with that many illustrations represents quite a risk. She was so focused and so courageous. She had an image of what the book should look like. It wasn't just a little book of transcripts. She made the book beautiful, she really did, with her insistence on it being fully illustrated . . ."

Flowers also recalled, "When we finished our work, she would always walk me back to the elevator. I'd get into the elevator, and then turn to the front, and as the elevator door would close, she would—I don't know how to describe this—she would *let me in*. I don't know how else to say that. Her eyes would become intimate, not just kind and charming, and then she would just say my name. She'd say "Betty Sue." It was so sweet. . . . It wasn't an invitation to become a personal friend, but it was a very personal good-bye as the elevator doors closed. . . .

"Another characteristic of Jackie—she really was a serious reader. I remember once, as we were packing up to go after one of our meetings, saying, 'Well Jackie, what are you going to read this summer?' She said, 'Gibbon.' Now how many people's summer reading is *The Decline and Fall of the Roman Empire*?"

With Campbell's book, Jackie had to overcome Bill Moyers's initial resistance. Flowers said, "It was always a struggle to get Bill to say 'yes' to a book project. . . . Each time there was a new project he would wonder whether such a book would be at all successful."

The Power of Myth was and is a deeply subversive book, but its subversive message is so sophisticated and seemingly respectful of tradition that its potentially revolutionary nature was not recognized by the legions of readers who consumed it with the enthusiasm of true believers. The parallel PBS television series amplified the dangerous message to the great mass of nonreaders. How could a book about myths and fairy tales pack such a hidden punch? Why does the book, produced almost as an afterthought at Jackie's insistence and against Bill Moyers's initial inclination still resonate more than two decades after its publication?

Joseph Campbell dedicated his life to studying myths and to understanding the cultural tapestry from which they came. The subversive part is that Campbell is so erudite and informed about the creation tales of all human cultures that he can make reasoned, eloquent, cross-cultural comparisons and raise questions sure to offend true believers who are certain that their own myth of creation—say, the Genesis version—has a monopoly on the truth. If Jesus and Buddha and Yoda serve the same spiritual function, who are we to assert the primacy of one over another? Might all religions have been created to answer those questions that linger just outside the current state of our empirical knowledge?

Bill Moyers was not just a former presidential press secretary and outstanding television journalist; he also was once a Southern Baptist minister with a divinity degree from Southwestern Baptist Theological Seminary, so he came intellectually prepared to amicably confront the lifelong learning of Campbell. The interviews that form the core of the book and the PBS series were taped in the last year of Campbell's long life, at the Skywalker Ranch, where filmmaker George Lucas created his *Star Wars* epics. With considerable aid from Flowers, Moyers demonstrated his own prodigious learning, challenging Campbell with far more textured questions than a lesser interviewer could have conceived. Moyers thrusts and Campbell

parries, with the result being a more accessible book than Campbell's earlier tomes.

Moyers himself is reluctant to talk about Jackie, respecting her privacy to
this day, observing in an e-mail response to my queries that she was as guard-
edly discreet about her editing as she was about her personal life. Their long
friendship began in that storied period at the Kennedy White House when
they were thrown together by political circumstance. With Jackie's blessing,
Moyers gave *Publishers Weekly* an interview in April 1993, in which he admitted that Jackie "insisted" that he do several books based on his PBS series
and that "she has an intuitive sense of the author's role." He added, "I'll
never say no again if she thinks there's a book in anything I do."

After the Campbell book, Jackie persuaded Moyers to participate on
three more companion books: two volumes of *A World of Ideas* (1989,
1990) and *Healing and the Mind* (1993). The journalist hosted a series of
in-depth interviews with prominent thinkers of all stripes for his PBS show
A World of Ideas. Many of the interviewees came from academia or the
arts, but they were not the typical glib experts that clog the airwaves. Nor
were they subjected to the censorship of the two-minute sound bite. They
were substantive conversations, centering on issues of American values, or
gateways into the brave new futures that advances in technology promised
the world.

After "Vietnam and Watergate blew volcano-sized holes in the legitimacy of our political discourse," as Moyers put it, he read the national
tea leaves of anxiety and created this series as an antidote by anecdote—a
reclamation of the philosophical basis for American democracy and
a reinvention of the kind of social discourse that Jackie wholeheartedly
favored. Once again, Jackie's judgment proved accurate, and the legacy
of these scholars and visionaries, committed to the perishable medium of
videotape, were transferred to the more permanent medium of the book,
where they can still inform and amuse, inspire and sometimes infuriate.

Covering the transcripts of all the participants is far beyond the scope
of this book, but a few examples can serve as indicators of the quality of
the discourse Moyers teased out of his guests. Where else could one find
Peter Drucker, apostle of management capitalism, and Noam Chomsky,
perhaps one of capitalism's most eloquent critics, in the same series? The
mother-and-daughter team of Barbara Tuchman, historian, and Jessica
Tuchman Mathews, environmental scientist and crusader, are featured.
Onondaga chief Oren Lyons, Hispanic writer Richard Rodriguez, and African American scholar Cornel West all speak to the heritage of American
diversity. Nobel laureates in physics Murray Gell-Mann and Steven Wein-

berg remind us that pure knowledge and technological breakthroughs create the wealth that allows our species to prosper.

Faced with the challenge of running such a formidable intellectual gauntlet, Flowers served as hands-on editor for the book, coaxing the text out of the film record and transcripts. "On the second book I did with Jackie, *A World of Ideas,* she really wanted me to cut it by about half. It was way too long because Bill had in-depth interviews with these folks and then would edit it to a much shorter amount, but the in-depth interviews were really, really good. So I kept most of those in there, and they both thought that it would make a terrible book because it was too long. But in fact that book ended up on the best-seller list because it was in-depth. And I loved it that she allowed me not to cut by half. I mean, I did stay in a little room for two days in New York cutting as much as I could. . . . I just found her very open to work with. She had strong (and good) ideas, but she also was very flexible and energetic."

Bill Moyers's fourth book with Jackie, *Healing and the Mind,* was an exploration of the mind-body connection and its relation to health. It drew on interviews that Moyers conducted for his PBS show with establishment physicians and scientists and various healers committed to alternative or unorthodox medicine. The range of healers in this book was broad, from Ron Anderson, head of Parkland Hospital in Dallas, and neuroscientist Candace Pert, to meditation and stress reduction expert Jon Kabat-Zinn and TV doctor Dean Ornish. Working again with Flowers as editor, Jackie made sure the book's relative passivity on the page, as compared with the video exchanges, would be offset by a great number of stunning illustrations, many of them responses to illness from the creative minds of fine artists.

While working on this Moyers project, Jackie also engaged Naveen Patnaik for his second book, *The Garden of Life: An Introduction to the Healing Plants of India,* a beautifully illustrated survey of India's medicinal plants and herbs, drawing on Indian minimalist art to bring the text to life. Alternative healing fascinated Jackie, and was perhaps to hold out a certain promise for her in terms of her own health during her later years. Before Moyers's book was published, she discussed it briefly with her friend Joe Armstrong, who told me, "The day that Bill turned in the manuscript for *Healing and the Mind,* Jackie and I were having a hamburger at P J. Clarke's, and she said, referring to the book, 'It's wonderful but hopefully I won't need it,' and knocked on the wooden table. Not long after that she became ill."

7

Bon Courage

One cannot help wonder how Jackie, as such an accomplished editor and woman of letters, would have organized her own memoir and recounted her life and her literary endeavors had she been inclined to write an autobiography. She was often encouraged to do so and steadfastly demurred, though of course she probably could have garnered a record advance from any number of publishers. She once told Pierre Salinger, "I want to live my life, not record it."

Investigative journalist-author David Wise discussed the subject of a memoir with Jackie more than once. Better known for his nonfiction, Wise wrote a political thriller, *The Samarkand Dimension*, published in 1987, that was the first spy novel Jackie edited. Dealing with intelligence conspiracies, CIA and KGB intrigues, and psychic phenomena such as telekinesis, it does not seem like the kind of book that would have appealed to Jackie. Several of Jackie's former colleagues expressed their doubts about the extent of the role she played with the book. Wise's fanciful plotline didn't touch on any of the delicate issues of her past, and the story may have held a certain appeal for her in the way that Wise characterized intelligence operatives during the Cold War as bluff-prone poker players in a world where very little was what it seemed.

Interviewed by *Newsweek,* Wise recounted a lunch that he had with Jackie at the '21' Club: "I reminded her that several years before, in her mother's house in Georgetown, I had asked her when she would write her own book. She had laughed and replied. 'Maybe when I'm ninety.' This time, she said more. People change, she said. The person she might have written about thirty years ago is not the same person today. The imagination takes over. When Isak Dinesen wrote *Out of Africa,* she left out how badly her husband had treated her. She created a new past, in effect. And why sit indoors with a yellow pad writing a memoir when you could be outdoors?"

Jackie may at least have been tempted by George Plimpton, who said, "She witnessed so much history, and she was such a marvelous writer. I felt it would be a terrible shame if she didn't get it down on paper." Plimpton was willing to help and made his appeal while Jackie was summering on Martha's Vineyard. "I knew Red Gate Farm [Jackie's summer home] was the kind of place where one could get inspired. I sat down and wrote Jackie a letter—the best letter I ever wrote—offering to come up and work with her on her memoirs. She would tell me whatever she wanted to tell me, we would walk along the beach and talk it through in that marvelous setting, and then I would go away and type it up and give it to her. No one would need to know it ever existed. She could just put it away, and when they needed to, her children could refer to it, and her children's children." When George next visited with Jackie on the Vineyard, she told him, "Well, you know, I don't really want to sit at a window looking out at a field and feel that life is going by."

During a conversation in the late 1980s, even Jackie's mother, Janet, encouraged her, saying, "You are going to work on your memoirs at some point, aren't you?"

Jackie reportedly replied, "Why would I want to do that?"

She may have revealed a deeper reason for her reticence a few years later to her friend and confidant Peter Duchin. The two were having lunch at her apartment, and the bandleader told her in passing that he had just begun writing his own memoir (*Ghost of a Chance*). Jackie warned him, "Peter, you're about to embark on a very difficult journey. I could never do a book like this. It would be too painful."

Obviously, there were many parts of her life that Jackie would not have wanted to relive. As she knew very well, that is necessarily part of the process. She had already made peace with herself and was in no need of further catharsis or drama. A narrative chronicling the anguish she had endured would have been a prolonged emotional ordeal for her to conceptualize and compose, even when balanced by the joys she had experienced. Why would she want to make herself vulnerable in that way? Why take on such a task when editing some of those books that held great personal significance for her was a much safer and more fulfilling way to revisit those earlier chapters of her life?

In 1988, Jackie published *Somerset Homecoming: Recovering a Lost Heritage,* by Dorothy Spruill Redford, with an introduction by Alex Haley. The book reflected Jackie's sense of social conscience and a commitment to racial equality that went back at least as far as her White House days. It also spoke to Jackie because of her belief in family history as an integral component of personal identity and self-knowledge.

The overwhelming success of Alex Haley's *Roots* and the subsequent television series planted a desire in many African Americans to investigate their own family histories. One of these amateur genealogists was a young woman from North Carolina who had split her time growing up between the rural South and the urban melting pot of Queens. Trained as a social worker, Dorothy Spruill Redford began by interviewing all of her older relatives who would talk to her, and then took what slivers of information she could glean and began combing through census records and property tax rolls, slowly adding generations to her ancestral family tree. Of course, she ran into the seemingly impenetrable obstacle of the 1860s, before which slavery was legal, blacks were treated as chattel, and any notion of orderly relatedness was scrambled by the machinations of slave owners who routinely broke up families.

Soon, Redford focused on one particular former plantation in northeastern North Carolina, a place called Somerset. By the 1980s, Somerset had become a sparsely attended state park, the gently decaying colonial mansion serving as a kind of time travel into southern history. The white descendants of Somerset's owners had long moved away, and were not inclined to revive a past that had come to be seen as shameful, but the black and biracial descendants of Somerset would open up to Redford in ways they never would have to white historians. Dorothy Redford slowly came to realize that a reunion at Somerset was in order, and she organized such a gathering. More than two hundred people attended, and there was even a surprise guest, Alex Haley himself, who had been encouraging Redford over the years, and decided to drop by unannounced in 1986.

It is perhaps fitting that Jackie served as editor of the book, in light of a comment Redford makes in its pages: "By the time I began my last year of high school in 1960, the nation was pulsing with change, with a mixture of hope and rage. Rosa Parks had refused to move to the rear of the bus, Martin Luther King had stared them down in Montgomery. And there was a new president in the White House, a man named Kennedy." Jackie knew the civil rights movement figured prominently into JFK's legacy, without which the journeys of familial discovery that Alex Haley, Dorothy Redford, and others would make might have been not only impossible but dangerous even to attempt.

Under Jackie's aegis, Redford worked with writer Michael D'Orso on *Somerset Homecoming*. He explained to me how the book evolved out of a feature story that he wrote about Redford for the *Virginian-Pilot* in Norfolk, where he had been working for several years while also contributing to *Sports Illustrated*. After being contacted by one of Jackie's associates, D'Orso met with Redford and decided he would do the book. He told me, "I got a phone call at the office, at the *Pilot* . . . and the voice said it was Jackie Onassis. And I didn't believe her. I hung up. And then she called right back, and I realized it was her, and I apologized profusely, and she laughed and said, 'It happens all the time.'

"And so we had this wonderful conversation. She told me she was just delighted that I was going to be doing this and really excited about it. . . . She was very good at ushering the writer through the process. . . . When you turned the actual manuscript in she certainly read it, but she had a couple of editors working with her who actually did the line editing."

As described by D'Orso, Jackie was a conceptual editor. But it was the manuscript that enabled Jackie to know what the thinking of the author was, and that sometimes, as with my books, led her into detailed line editing. Her approach on each project depended on the subject and her chemistry with the author. According to Sam Vaughan, the influential publisher and editor Robert Giroux once described the distinction between line editing and book editing: "The truth is that editing lines is not necessarily the same as editing a book. A book is a much more complicated entity and totality than the sum of its lines alone. Its structural integrity, the relation and proportions of its parts, and its total impact could escape even a conscientious editor exclusively intent on vetting the book line by line."

Jackie was always aware of that larger picture and the specific issues in each manuscript. Some authors, like D'Orso, required less guidance than others. D'Orso said, "Dorothy and I worked very hard and very fast. I didn't have a lot of communication with Jackie during the writing of it because they had a deadline that they were already slow on. What they appreciated was . . . that I work with the work ethic of a journalist. A lot of authors out there, as you know, deadlines don't mean much to them. Years pass. But for me, I took a deadline very seriously. . . . We turned that

book around in—gosh!—three or four months. . . . Next I heard from
Jackie was when I turned the manuscript in and I got a wonderful phone
call, and she sent me a wonderful letter as well, which I've kept and kind
of treasure."

The book received favorable reviews, with *The New York Times* suggesting the story was "as much about a remarkable woman as about an
American people." D'Orso was another writer whose talents Jackie appreciated to the point that she invited him to work on another project. His
second book delved into the history of the civil rights movement, and,
again, the subject struck a chord with Jackie. D'Orso recalled, "She wanted
a book to be done on an old former congressman, an eight-term congressman for Alabama named Carl Elliott. Essentially, he was living in the ruins
of his life. He had stood up against the George Wallace machine back in
the sixties; he had campaigned for Kennedy in 1960, which was the next
worst thing to being black in Alabama; and so he'd become a pariah in his
own hometown and home state. It was really a gothic story, a kind of tragedy. And [in 1990] he'd just been awarded the first Profile in Courage
Award that they give annually now."

The Carl Elliott book, *The Cost of Courage: The Journey of an American Congressman,* would be published in January 1992. D'Orso preferred
to keep a respectful distance and never met Jackie in person, but he recalled how their relationship over the years developed by phone and became more personal while he was working with Elliott. "For this particular
book," said D'Orso, "I went to Jasper, Alabama. This is a town up in
North Alabama, in the hills, very, very poor. This was the winter of the
Gulf War, and I was spending it with this congressman who was literally
living in the same house he had launched his first campaign in back in
1948. . . . And his house had holes in the ceiling. He had cashed in his
congressional pension to run against Wallace for governor in sixty-six. It
was kind of like a Don Quixote tilting-at-windmills thing. He lost everything he had . . . a helluva story.

"Anyway, I spent the winter living with Carl. I put pots around the
house. Rain came through. We would eat dinner together . . . and I was
going through a separation and divorce. . . . And Jackie would call me up
about once or twice a month, and she wouldn't even ask me how the book
was going. She would ask me how I was doing, and we would talk about
just relationships and stuff. And I wouldn't even think about the fact that
I'm talking to Jackie Onassis. I'd hang up the phone, and then it would hit
me how surreal this is. I'm here talking about relationships and marriages
with Jackie Onassis, quite personal. She was great. She was a real support
system for me. She really cared.

"After I got home and was working on the Carl Elliott book, the phone rang, and my daughter, Jamie, was six. The phone rang, she answered it, typical little kid. 'Yes, fine, fine.' I could tell somebody's having a little conversation with the kid . . . and then she turns to me and she goes, 'Daddy, it's the dead president's wife.' I had explained to her who Jackie Onassis was at some point. And I don't know if Jackie heard that. I think she did. My daughter loves that story. She didn't quite get how funny it was, until she's grown up now."

Jackie wrote D'Orso a letter, which read, in part, referring to the "beautiful book" prior to publication: "I hope you are pleased with the way it looks. Now DD's publicity machine is grinding away to promote it."

As a curious footnote, Elliott himself, who died in 1999, reminisced in his book that he had met Jackie before she married Jack Kennedy, when she was the young newspaper camera-girl interviewing congressmen.

Early in 1988, Jackie told some of her friends and colleagues, "I'm going to be a grandmother—imagine that!" On June 25, a little more than a month before Jackie's fifty-ninth birthday, Caroline, who had recently graduated from Columbia Law School, gave birth to her first child, Rose, named after the Kennedy family matriarch. Later that same year, while basking in the joys of her family life, Jackie began an intense quest to win over another author, one who would deliver a series of books that were to be counted as some of her greatest commercial victories.

Years later, Jackie would say, "When I read in the papers that this Egyptian [Naguib Mahfouz] had won the Nobel Prize [in October 1988], I thought, We've got to have [The Cairo Trilogy]. I've always loved the cultures of the Mediterranean, and I'd lived in Greece, and it clicked with some other Mediterranean writers I very much admired—Kazantzakis, for instance."

Scott Moyers recounted the story of this acquisition to Carl Sferrazza Anthony, saying, "This is classic Jackie. Naguib Mahfouz had been published in the United States in a very small way for the American University in Cairo Press, and his work was virtually unavailable. She was reading Mahfouz in French. She loved it so much that she successfully lobbied for Doubleday to do The Cairo Trilogy—*Palace Walk, Palace of Desire,* and *Sugar Street*—for which he's probably best known. His novels have a nineteenth-century feel, a huge cast of characters. [They're] about class strife, politics, East meeting West, on a grand canvas."

The acquisition ultimately led to at least twenty books by Mahfouz that are still on Doubleday's backlist of titles, though Jackie edited only the first three. Scott Moyers enthused, "Jackie made it a whole cottage industry, from her vision. This played itself out in a very permanent way, like the Bill Moyers series on healing. She did many wonderful books that made a splash, and delighted people, and books that did well for Doubleday. She also did a high percentage of books that will be around forever."

Alberto Vitale agreed with that assessment, "My most important experience with her was when Naguib Mahfouz got the Nobel Prize, and we wanted to get to him and get his works, and I talked with her and she was instrumental in getting us a contract in Egypt, you know, with the president of the American University in Cairo. . . . Jackie read it in French first because there was no other edition that was readable. . . . We ended up selling those rights everywhere in the world, and it was a success in England. And it made a lot of money, too." Of course, Jackie's personal take on money and commercialism was quite different from that of the executives who ran the company.

The primary translator of The Cairo Trilogy, William Maynard Hutchins, a professor at Appalachian State University of North Carolina, had already been contracted by the American University in Cairo Press when Jackie intervened to secure the rights for Mahfouz's books. She first interviewed him by phone. Hutchins told me, "We agreed to do one volume a year, particularly for the first volume, which was really pretty desperate, but I did just squeak through. Mahfouz wrote the first volume in a rather heavy, long-sentence kind of way, with a lot of back-alley Arabic. And it really wasn't an easy translation. It's this whole thing [over the course of the three books], the family saga from supertraditional to supermodern, and as he progresses his style gets quicker and racier and easier to read, easier to translate, and the vocabulary becomes more normal. . . .

"Mrs. Onassis was saying, 'Well, he's finding his voice'; but that's really not true, because at this point he'd already published something like eight novels; he'd already found his voice, and he was just trying to conjure up this very back-alley kind of existence. . . . There's lots of lots of pencil marks [in the manuscript], and it's very polite, and it's in the margins, and there are question marks, and, 'What do you think about this?' And, 'I don't like this metaphor. . . .' She played just a huge huge role not only in the sort of penciled comment on every sentence, but in acquiring it. And it's very oddly dedicated by her to David Morse, who was some kind of friend in France, or agent, who helped her broker the deal. Only she could have gotten away with quite that. The editor really can't dedicate, but she did.

"She had the French published translation for each of the volumes, and she was going along following that. And the French translation—it's all by the same person, Philippe Vigreux, and it's really quite brilliant; but there are a few things where he didn't bother to do his homework." Jackie never had the opportunity to meet Mahfouz. According to Hutchins, "She sent him love letters. She was a big fan. . . . One of the things about Mahfouz, by the time I was doing this, is that he was already quite old and quite deaf and diabetic. And he had also established a pattern that the translation was not his job. So I was allowed two questions per volume basically. And these were relayed by a nice educated lady who went and screamed in his ear."

Referring again to Jackie's critical notes, Hutchins said, "I mean her penciled comments. . . . I think the worst thing she said was, 'This sounds like a translation from French.' She was very encouraging, and she sent me some little love letters, so to speak. But there was something untoward that happened which cut off the love letters but didn't cut off the editing." The translator explained that he had participated in a symposium that generated some publicity about the Mahfouz project before publication, and Jackie apparently became disgruntled by the timing or the coverage itself. Hutchins lamented, "There was some invisible line, and I had crossed it."

The Cairo Trilogy is a three-part family saga depicting the lives of al-Sayyid Ahmad Abd al-Jawad and his family—his wife, his children, and eventually his grandchildren. It covers the period from 1917 to 1944, as Mahfouz presents the story in distinct chunks rather than one continuous whole. The trilogy is Tolstoyan in its epic sweep as it shows how the family, anchored by a bourgeois shopkeeper, reacts to changing times. First published in Arabic in the late fifties, Mahfouz's trilogy is now regarded as the epic Egyptian novel cycle, and as such stands as a barrier that must be overcome for younger writers aspiring to fill Mahfouz's shoes.

The Abd al-Jawad family is Egypt in microcosm. The Egyptian struggle for independence is reflected within the family by the sons' struggle to free themselves from the dictatorial grip of their father, al-Sayyid Ahmad, who is shown to be a hypocrite, strict and unforgiving at home, only to drop all pretenses when he hangs out with his friends at a local café. The father's strong hand and blind religious belief parallel those of the Egyptian state at a time when it was slowly acquiring its independence from colonial powers.

Female characters take something of a backseat, as Mahfouz explored the patriarchy. Far from authorial misogyny, the depiction of women's lives accurately reflects the status of women in Cairo at the time. The Egypt of Mahfouz is not an open society, so Mahfouz must resort to internal dialogues to demonstrate what his characters are thinking, no matter what they say in public. Much of their public dialogue is stilted and formulaic. What they really mean goes unstated, as a false front must be preserved. Small personal gestures, like a brief wink of the eye, communicate what the speaker intends. *Palace Walk* ends with what appears to be Egypt's successful transition to peaceful independence, but there are upheavals within the family that remain unresolved.

Palace of Desire is an alley near Palace Walk, where one of al-Sayyid Ahmad's sons flees to live in the house once owned by his biological mother. Yasin resembles his father in that he too is an outwardly devout Muslim who lives a life considerably more secular than he would like to admit. Kamal, the youngest son (and the character in the novel cycle most reminiscent of Mahfouz himself), disappoints his father by attending a teachers' training college rather than study law. The disappointment turns into rage when the father discovers that Kamal has written an essay on Darwin. *Palace of Desire* ends with the patriarch suffering a physical crisis just as the Egyptian leader dies and a typhoid epidemic stalks the streets of Cairo.

The concluding novel shifts its focus from al-Sayyid Ahmad's generation to the two generations following him. One son has become a Marxist, another has joined the Muslim Brotherhood, and Kamal seems to be wasting his time writing ethereal prose. Meanwhile, the Abd al-Jawad family has begun its decline. Mahfouz presents this through conversation after conversation, even as the world changes with the onset of the Second World War and the inner vitality of Cairo, well defined in the earlier novels, descends to the ennui of the bored bourgeoisie. Mahfouz's Cairo drew comparisons with Joyce's Dublin and Proust's Paris, parallels not lost on Jackie.

One of Jackie's colleagues, Martha Levin, was assigned to the Mahfouz project after she rejoined the company as publisher of the Anchor Books division in 1988 (having earlier worked in the rights department). Recalling her work with Jackie, Levin said, "I have a very vivid memory of one, to me, hilarious conversation, because she was so insistent on just being one of us. So you had these surreal conversations. She was talking about the patriarch in the trilogy, and how she knew a lot of men like that. And she said, 'You know, I lived in Greece for a while.' I know you lived in Greece! We had completely lovely exchanges. When her mom died [in July 1989], I remember agonizing for a couple of days about whether I should write her a note, or if it was inappropriate for me to write her a note, and my mother said to me, 'If it was any other colleague, would you write a note?' And I said yes. And she said, 'Write a note.' And I did, and I got a lovely acknowledgment."

With the Mahfouz book, Jackie had once again invaded foreign territory overlooked by the other major publishers who were and still are somewhat reluctant to undertake translated works. As Edith Grossman noted in her 2010 book, *Why Translation Matters,* "Our world as dedicated readers depends on the availability of translated works, classical and contemporary, yet in English-speaking nations, major commercial publishers are strangely resistant to publishing them."

A few years later Jackie mounted another venture into Cairo with photographer Robert Lyons's book *Egyptian Time.* The book included a short story by Mahfouz entitled "The Cradle," set in modern Cairo, where the peddlers, donkeys, beggars, and rooftop menageries compete for a young child's attention. Mahfouz had his hero contemplate the vastness of antiquity, thereby posing eternal questions of life, death, friendship, honor, and spiritual belief from a perspective of youthful innocence. The text perfectly complemented Lyons's photographs, many of which juxtaposed the modern squalor of Egypt with ancient ruins and tombs. It is the way that Lyons was able to capture grandeur and decay side by side that distinguished these color portraits of monuments, hovels, and the people who built them.

Robert Lyons shared with me his recollections of how the project came about, with both Jackie and Mahfouz becoming involved. "I was traveling to Egypt and already photographing there, and I had been on a plane reading *Vanity Fair,* and I read this article about Mahfouz at the Ali Baba, which is a café he used to go to every morning. So upon getting to Cairo—I was going on a three-month trip, from Cairo all the way down to the Sudan—at some point I made my way over to the Ali Baba very early in the morning, introduced myself to Mahfouz awkwardly, and asked him if I could do some portraits. He said yes, and we made an arrangement. I made a series of portraits of Mahfouz, and this began my relationship with him.

"I left in October 1989 and got back in January of 1990. . . . And when I got back I had bought all the copies of his books that were available, and they were all by Doubleday. And I noticed that on all the books there was a short paragraph about Mahfouz, but no portrait of Mahfouz. So in my way of hustling, I thought, Well, Jacqueline Onassis is his editor, I'll send her a letter with some promotional photographs of things I did in Egypt. . . . So I sent this package of about six or eight small promotional photographs to Mrs. Onassis, with a note saying, 'You know, I wonder if you'd like me to do some portraits of Mr. Mahfouz,' knowing already that I had them.

"What happened was—this was before e-mail—I guess it was late morning on the East Coast . . . I'd been up late the night before—I was asleep in my loft, and I get this phone call, and this voice on the other end says, 'This is Jacqueline Onassis.' And I think it's some friend of mine making a joke. I said, 'Right, right.' 'This is Jacqueline Onassis,' she said, 'and I'm not very interested in having you do a portrait of Mahfouz, but I'm very interested in your work, and I'd like to speak to you about it.' And by then I was pretty alert from a dead sleep, and I said, 'Oh, I would love to, when would work?'

"Sometime within the next two weeks I flew to New York to meet her with large prints, a box of my Egypt pictures, and to talk to her, because I mentioned in that conversation we had that I'd already spoken to Mr. Mahfouz and that he'd like to somehow work with me, write a preface. That's what I wanted. And when I got there, she really loved the work, and she was very encouraging. She said to me, 'You know, you need to secure the rights. His agents in Egypt'—which was American University in Cairo Press—'are very difficult.' So she was privy to all that, being his editor.

"So I went to see Mahfouz and spent numerous times with him . . . and at one point he kind of laughed and said, 'You know, I don't write prefaces.' And I went, 'Oh my God.' But he, having been a screenwriter, at one point, he found a story that had never been published that would be perfect for my material. . . . And it came to me in Arabic, by the way. Peter Theroux was the translator for the story. I had met him in Egypt, and of course, this delighted [Jackie], because of Paul Theroux's reputation."

The photographer was grateful for the freedom that Jackie granted him in overseeing the design and production of the book. She even sent him to Hong Kong to approve the proofs during the printing process. "She would read through the story," Lyons recalled. "She was involved in the design process. She gave me total control, actually, though, to design the book as I wanted and also to edit the pictures the way I wanted. . . . She was really special because she made things happen. . . . She took risks with people. I was an unknown photographer, and she was used to really well-known people, and she really set me on my way."

To promote the publication, Jackie helped Lyons set up an exhibition of his Egyptian photographs at the International Center of Photography, overcoming the initial resistance of the center's director, Cornell Capa. When told that Capa had been rather crude in offering Lyons a brusque rejection, Jackie told the photographer, "Oh, Robert, he's a hot-blooded Hungarian. Don't pay any attention." Within days, the exhibition was arranged, and Jackie attended the opening as a kind of informal guest of honor, her first appearance at the ICP since the 1970s. Lyons shared the spotlight at the exhibition with two other notable photographers, Yousuf

Karsh and Ernst Haas, but gracefully upstaged them by escorting Jackie through his exhibit.

Lyons also remembered that Jackie had hoped to visit Cairo to meet Mahfouz shortly before her death two years later. "She was going to go with Tempelsman to Egypt; there was a trip planned. . . . She spoke to me and asked me about going, and I was going to try to be there at the same time. . . . It was just at that time when she got ill. . . . It was really sad, because Mahfouz, of course, was very excited. He wanted to meet her, but he hardly ever left Egypt. . . . So at any rate, she didn't make it, but she was planning it."

By the time Jackie began her collaboration at a distance with Mahfouz, she had already laid the groundwork for a number of other projects. She took on a first novel entitled *Up Through the Water,* from a twenty-five-year-old graduate student at the University of Virginia, Darcey Steinke. The impressionable author later described her first meeting with Jackie in an article written for *Vogue.* "We talked about my novel. Like many a young writer, Jackie said, I digressed too often. Flashbacks appeared on almost every page, and I used metaphors like drinking water. *Up Through the Water* takes place over a single summer on Ocracoke Island, on North Carolina's Outer Banks. I had waitressed there summers while I was in college, so I knew the general rhythms of a beach resort, but I didn't know much about narrative structure or motivation. Jackie was most interested in my character, Emily, a promiscuous thirty-five-year-old prep cook. 'She is an undine, who swims with the fish and sleeps with any sailor,' Jackie said. 'How will she deal with aging? Will she be able to be faithful to her boyfriend?' As I listened to her, I thought, How can this most elegant woman in America identify with a profligate prep cook? But Jackie found Emily mesmerizing. 'What is wrenching about her is that one of her loveliest facets, her animal nature, carries with it her doom.'"

With Jackie's blessing and critique, Steinke commenced work on a rewrite, what she described as a lonely endeavor after she moved away from family and friends to San Francisco with a Stegner Fellowship at Stanford. At the time, Steinke's "parents were going through an acrimonious divorce," and she broke up with her boyfriend. With regard to her relationship with Jackie, Steinke insinuated that there may have been some emotional dependency on her part: "Jackie had taken an interest in me above and beyond her role as editor, and I began to crave this attention."

The author also remembered, "Jackie sometimes called me on Sunday afternoons. She told me Truman Capote had told her sister, Lee Radziwill, that he used pink sheets of paper for rewrites, and she wanted me to do the same. . . . Her curiosity for life was boundless; every phone call she recommended books and movies. 'Oh, Darcey, you must go see *Chocolat!*' Included in her letters from her country place in Massachusetts were book reviews she thought might be pertinent to my novel. She often signed these missives, written on light blue paper, 'Bon Courage.' "

After Steinke submitted her rewrite, she received a letter from Jackie saying, "You have tightened up the structure, made it less fragmented, but in doing so you've scraped an awful lot of meat off the bone." In her critique, Jackie included a list of "Thirty-eight Fantasies and Flashbacks that Damage the Flow." Describing her reaction, Steinke confessed, "My heart sank through the floorboards of my San Francisco apartment."

She hastily arranged a meeting and flew to New York, only to receive a rather chilly reception from her editor. After Jackie had taken Steinke to task, the young writer tried to offer some additional rewritten pages from the novel, but she was rebuffed. Steinke recounted their dialogue:

> "You know, Darcey," she said, "you remind me of those little terrier dogs at fox hunts. Have you ever seen them?"
>
> I felt my face flush. "No," I said. I had never been to a fox hunt.
>
> "They're just so nervous and anxious to please."
>
> *Jackie Onassis had compared me to a dog.* I had the uncanny feeling I'd been split in two and was watching myself sitting in her office. She said she wouldn't look at my novel again until I'd done substantial rewriting. I was dismissed.

Despite being upbraided, Steinke went back to work and rewrote the novel a second time. "I sent the new draft off late in the spring of 1988 and got a letter back the next week. '*Up Through the Water* is wonderful, you have done such a good job. It flows—there is a real narrative line. We can really follow each character's thought patterns—one is totally absorbed reading your book.' "

For the most part, when the book was published, in 1989, the critics agreed with Jackie's assessment. Writing in *The New York Times*, Robert Olmstead observed that Steinke's "ability to be inside her characters and nudge them to expanded observation is carried off in a seamless and instinctive prose that often reads more like poetry than fiction."

Steinke concluded her *Vogue* piece with a line about her newfound outlook on life. "I wanted to be like Jackie: a little bit imperious, endlessly enthusiastic, and full of grace." In the years that followed, Steinke went on to enjoy a successful career, and for a time worked for John Jr.'s magazine,

George. She told me that Jackie stayed in touch with her: "I would hear from her now and then. She sent me clippings. . . . A lot of older people will send me clippings. . . . My mother does it. It's just funny to think that Jackie O did it, too."

Jackie and Doubleday passed on Steinke's next novel, *Suicide Blonde*, which made quite a splash for its author. The *Times* called the book "a disturbing, poisonous fable of the dire consequences of derailed passion, a dark primer on how to abuse anyone and anything—from lovers and family members to alcohol and heroin." The tawdry, unrelenting grimness of the tale may have rankled Jackie's more refined sensibility. In a phone conversation with the author, she politely passed on publishing the book.

Also in 1988, Jackie made an acquisition that was even for her a departure, one that surely challenged her more conservative colleagues. She sought out a San Francisco–based comic book artist, Larry Gonick, for two volumes of a work entitled *The Cartoon History of the Universe* (1990, 1994). Gonick told me how Jackie came to be involved: "The series started when it was published by an 'underground' comics publisher, Rip Off Press, in San Francisco, which is best known for *The Fabulous Furry Freak Brothers*. I started the series in 1978 as comic books; they were forty-eight-page comics. These things had a really very underground flavor, and they were something different. They circulated around, and someone approached me from the University of Southern California about doing an animation project . . . and he sent it around. Through him, the comic fell into the hands of a man named Karl Katz, who was the head of the film and TV office at the Metropolitan Museum, and Caroline Kennedy had worked for him at one time. So he's the one who passed the comics to Jackie. He thought if they had overground publishing exposure that there might be a film in it.

"One day I had a call from Karl Katz, and he said, 'I never told you this, but I'm a good friend of Mrs. Onassis.' He said, 'I gave her your comics, and I didn't want to call you until I thought she was actually going to do something with them. The publisher at Doubleday has reviewed them, and I think they want to publish them. Why don't you give her a call?'

"I swallowed hard when I heard that. . . . I called and they relayed the message to Jackie. And she called me when I was at dinner that night, about nine New York time. We had a discussion, and she was very supportive. . . . It took quite a long time to actually finalize the deal. The sales department at Doubleday was very skeptical, and Jackie made them review it again. I don't remember how much time went by. . . . I had lapses in contact for months, and then finally, I was like jumping out of my chair. I took a walk in the neighborhood and ran into a neighbor, who told me,

'Don't get mad. Use humor. You're a humorist.' So I wrote a note, a little handwritten note with a cartoon on it that showed my grave, and on the headstone it said, 'Jackie Onassis called him once.' I basically said, 'Mrs. Onassis, what's going on? I'm dying out here.' And after that, the deal was done within two weeks.

"Once that happened, I booked a ticket to New York. I knew it was real at that point, and I met with her on the twenty-fifth anniversary of the Kennedy assassination, November 22, 1988. I went to Jackie's office at Doubleday. And of course this small, extremely slender person with the famous face and huge, wide-set eyes came out of the office to meet me. She was very friendly and direct, and made me some coffee. It was an entirely positive experience."

Gonick's agent, Vicky Bijur, remembered a meeting that she attended with Jackie, Shaye Areheart, and publicist Ellen Archer. "At the meeting, Jackie mentioned an author photograph. She said, 'Oh, the picture Larry sent was too wimpy.' And she said, 'He has matinee idol looks, and he should have a sexy photograph'—something very specific, something like his hand should be in his pocket, but his thumb should be out. . . . After the meeting, Jackie walked me out, and she stood in the elevator door and held the door with her hand and said, 'Tell Larry we're going to make him a star.' "

"My comic books just went in packaged the way they were," said Gonick. "It was seven comic books bound together, and the whole question was how to market the book, how to promote it. In the course of soliciting promotional blurbs for the book, Jackie sent one to Ann Landers. She actually sent them to a number of people. She sent one to the Dalai Lama. It turned out the Dalai Lama's gatekeeper was Richard Gere, so we got a quote from Richard Gere, but not from the Dalai Lama. The book was limping along at first. It probably sold fifteen or twenty thousand copies. . . . That was pretty good for an underground comic, but it didn't really come close to what my own sense of self-worth demanded.

"Ann Landers eventually wrote back and said, 'I won't just blurb it; I'll do you one better. I'll plug it in my column in early December.' Later, when she plugged the book in her column, it was like an avalanche. She had an enormous readership, and a plug from her guaranteed big sales. So it appeared in Ann Landers's column and literally changed my life forever. It turned me from a struggling cartoonist to an established one within a matter of two or three months. . . . They literally couldn't print books fast enough."

It's not hard to see why Jackie was charmed by this tongue-in-cheek cartoon sprint through thirteen billion years of cosmic history and a few hundred thousand years of human development. She called it a "civilized treat," suggesting it was "very accurate, and a much better account of how civilization developed than many more serious ones I've read."

Larry Gonick is a cartoonist in the same league as R. Crumb and Gilbert Shelton, masters of the underground comic universe that sprang up in San Francisco in the 1960s in reaction to the tired, predictable, flag-waving superheroes who were staples in the D. C. Comics pantheon. With a concision that would leave world historians like H. G. Wells or the Durants with their heads spinning, Gonick's *Cartoon History of the Universe* moves from the primal singularity of the Big Bang to the fall of the Roman Empire in thirteen slim volumes, collected together in this series by his editor, who realized how subversively educational they were. A high school senior who read these volumes attentively would know just about everything required or expected from years of formal history classes.

Gonick told me, "One time I visited Jackie's office with my daughter. When I went to my college twenty-fifth reunion, we went to New York. My daughter was about nine at the time. Jackie said, 'Oh, there's a chocolate place, Serendipity. You should take your daughter.' They served cold truffles and hot chocolate. I said, 'Is this place popular? Do we need a reservation?' She said, 'I'll call one in for you.' She calls them up and says, 'This is Mrs. Onassis. Can you take a reservation for two people? The name is Gonick. That's *G* as in God.'"

The first volume of *Cartoon History* made the *Times* paperback bestseller list, and Doubleday paid a higher advance for the second volume. Before the second volume, there was another regime change at Doubleday. Gonick remembered, "Nancy Evans was let go as the president at Doubleday. I was there for some reason, and Jackie was very downhearted, actually, saying, 'It's all office politics, and I don't like it anymore,' and so on. I came back to San Francisco and suddenly realized that she might quit, that she might go to somebody else, to some other publisher. I would be stuck at Doubleday, and she wouldn't be my editor anymore. So I called her up and said, 'Do you feel bad enough that you might go somewhere else?' She said, 'I don't know.' I told her, 'Well, if you do move to another publishing house, if it's at all possible, I'd like you to take me along with you.' She said, 'Oh, Larry, that's the nicest thing anyone has ever said to me.'"

Harriet Rubin informed me by e-mail that she had the impression Jackie and Nancy Evans regarded each other with mutual respect. "Nancy shook things up at Doubleday, but the company really needed it. It was filled with editors who had retired in place (my editorial assistant had to go upstairs every day to make cocoa for Ken McCormick, a once great editor then in his nineties who shuffled through the hallways like a ghost out of Dickens), and Doubleday books were considered the ugliest and most unsaleable in the industry, which meant that authors and agents didn't consider submitting first-rate projects. Nancy believed that the company needed glamour which she embodied. Nancy modeled herself after Jackie and hoped to make Doubleday a publishing Camelot. Jackie could not have been oblivious to Nancy's adoration."

During her tenure, Evans had dutifully carried out corporate orders from above to fire a number of editors and other pre-Bertelsmann colleagues whom Jackie held in high regard. At one point, editors Marshall De Bruhl, Carolyn Blakemore, and James Bakalar were given their walking papers within twenty minutes of each other in what one former editor described to me as "a bloodbath." When I suggested to Carolyn Blakemore that Evans characterized Jackie and herself as soul mates, she said, "I think Jackie, as far she was able to despise somebody, despised Nancy Evans. . . . I didn't see it directly, although [Jackie] was always writing naughty notes in editorial meetings and usually shooting them at Marshall or me because we'd laugh."

James Bakalar, who now writes for *The New York Times,* added that Nancy "didn't know anything about publishing as far as I could tell. She pretended that she did. It was like the emperor's new clothes."

Jackie's dismay over house politics would eventually cause her to consider making a radical change. I noticed over the years that her complaints became more frequent, even as she managed to increase the number of books she published year after year. Scott Moyers observed that as a result of budgetary constraints under Bertelsmann, "she stopped doing the expensive illustrated photo books." That wasn't really true, as she continued to work with various photographers and artists right up until the end, but there was increasing pressure placed on her to rein in the spending and avoid the higher price tag books.

Despite the commercial success of Gonick's first two books with Doubleday, the powers that be passed on publishing the third volume, despite Jackie's belief in the series. Gonick's agent remembered, "There was to be another volume, and I don't know why they didn't make an offer, because I then had a rather lively auction for it [and sold it elsewhere]. The regime had changed. . . . And the fact is that those two books that she bought at Doubleday still sell, and Larry gets royalties every six months on both books to this day. . . . All of that is a tribute to Jackie. She saw there would be an audience."

Gonick was philosophical about the changes he saw in the industry after the publication of the second volume. "My agent couldn't sell the third one.

Somebody [at Doubleday] added up the numbers and decided they had lost money. . . . And of course the reason they had lost money had nothing to do with me or the sales potential of the books. They lost money because they printed too many copies and they came back. . . . I've done a zillion science books with HarperCollins. So they've done the last two books [in the] *Cartoon History of the Universe* [series]." He added, "To be fair to the industry, there are people who care. But let's not romanticize publishing. There's always been an enormous volume of schlock. It's always been a mix."

During the 1980s, Jackie spent a great deal of time conducting research in the New York Public Library. She developed a close relationship with Vartan Gregorian, who served as president of the library from 1981 to 1989, later becoming the president of Brown University and now heading the philanthropic Carnegie Corporation of New York. A jovial man of obvious refinement and erudition, Gregorian first met Jackie early in the eighties, when she was often accompanied to the library by John Sargent Sr., an NYPL trustee. Jackie spent hours in the stacks, searching for ideas and indulging in the sheer joy of being surrounded by books.

Vartan said of Jackie. "One thing, you see: She was not famous for being famous. After a while you did not treat her as the widow of JFK. You treated her as a cultivated person, perhaps one of the most well-read and cultured. But she did not brag about it or show it. In that connection, let me mention something important about her. As you know, I was born in Iran of Armenian background. I left at age fourteen and a half. But I remember one word: *adab*. *Adab* is savoir faire, in one sense, but also refers to the concept of comportment, of how to behave, etiquette—all of that you're not taught, but you acquire by observing, by doing this. I always felt that Jackie had not only education, but she had *adab*. You felt in her presence that you were talking to somebody who was not lecturing, or talking for the sake of talking, but was very curious in order to acquire answers to certain questions that she was intrigued about." He added, "I was very fond of her. I loved her very much."

Gregorian read a few passages from his memoir, *The Road to Home*, recalling one of Jackie's early visits to the library, when its hours were expanded to include Thursdays. "When we opened the library doors, I was alerted and waiting for the first patron. It was none other than Jackie Kennedy Onassis. She wore blue jeans, a nice jacket, and dark glasses. We celebrated the occasion with a cup of coffee in my office." Vartan added, "And then, at the end of the day, she came to say good-bye. I walked her to the steps, and she gave me a big kiss. A photographer took a picture, and

then said, 'Don't worry, I will never publish this,' which was wonderful."
Jackie later wrote Gregorian a note thanking him for his assistance: "I'm
deeply grateful for the magnificent day you gave us last week. It was the
privilege of a lifetime to be in that beautiful room with all those great stars
and the sun. Everything one cares about most was there. The treasures
revealed to us warrant spending the next five years in the stacks. . . ."

In the editor's acknowledgment page for Jakob Walter's *The Diary of a
Napoleonic Foot Soldier*, published in 1991, Jackie credited Gregorian for
bringing the manuscript to her attention. He sent her a note of gratitude,
saying, "I was overwhelmed that you have dedicated a whole page to me.
My efforts were meager. The credit goes to you for seizing the idea and
actualizing it." The diary consists of letters written by an eighteen-year-old
German stonemason drafted into Napoleon's army as it marched eastward
across Europe in the early nineteenth century. A Columbia University Russian studies scholar, Marc Raeff, a leading specialist in the period, worked
closely with Jackie on editing the book and wrote the introduction.

Walter's letters give an insular point of view, telling what the marching
column looked, felt, and smelled like from inside. The "atrocity exhibitions" that all modern wars came to embody are here described with the
detachment of a paid observer. It is almost as if Walter, at eighteen, did not
yet understand that cruelty and deformity were extraordinary occurrences
in life. He describes them with the same calm that he uses to depict a bivouac
among the people of the Tyrolean Alps. Gregorian had the library provide
Jackie with the original German text, published in 1938 by the University
of Kansas. Of her support for the book, Gregorian quipped, "And who
else would be interested in a Napoleonic foot soldier?"

Recalling Jackie's early days at Doubleday, Gregorian described Jackie's
unique position there and its place in her life. "Jackie gave class in many
ways to Doubleday as being a kind of elite, exquisite publisher. But she
never acted as an employee because she was not working for the money or
for 'the cover.' It was for interest, to have something really interesting to do.
It provided a balance for her, another world in which she could retreat. So
psychologically it was very important for her that she had another home
besides her apartment. She had her work as a *profession*."

Edward Kasinec, who served as Curator of the Slavic and Baltic division, assisted Jackie on five books and was credited by her "for his invaluable guidance" on the Jakob Walter volume. Kasinec also aided her with
the Marquis de Custine's *Empire of the Czar: A Journey Through Eternal
Russia*, published in 1989. Astolphe de Custine was a French aristocrat
whose writings about Russia, based on journeys he made in the 1830s,
contain insights into the Russian people as well as unvarnished and opin-

ionated anticzarist sentiments. He set out for Moscow five years after Alexis de Tocqueville had sailed to America, and produced a journalist's impression of a society in transition. His book reflected the high hopes of the age, a time closer to the French and American revolutions than to any event in the twentieth century. Of course, Jackie had an affinity for material that combined her interests in French and Russian history. Kasinec described the book as "one of her favorites."

Jackie invited historian Daniel J. Boorstin and former American ambassador to the Soviet Union George F. Kennan to write a foreword and introduction, respectively. Recalling their collaboration, Kasinec said, "One day the three of them appeared [in the library] when we were opened to the public, because of course they were on very tight schedules, especially Boorstin . . . I had no place to put them. . . . There was actually no place to put these people, and you can imagine Ambassador Kennan decked out in his watch fobs and three-piece suit—he was always immaculately dressed, George Frost Kennan—and Boorstin, and [Jackie]. And so what I had to do—which was a no-no in those days—was to put them in the stacks and among piles of newspapers and unprocessed books, and they spread all of their stuff out . . . and took it in stride.

"That was a very beautiful book, beautifully designed, based almost exclusively on the visual material held by the Public Library. Even the dust jacket was based on some remarkable watercolors that the Soviets sold us during the nineteen-thirties that are in the Rare Books Division, of some of the sites that the Marquis visited in the eighteen-thirties and -forties. So she was very, very pleased with everything that the library had to offer, because our collections are so incredibly rich in visual and iconographic material, to which she was so sensitive."

Jackie turned again to Russian sources when her Gotham Book Mart friend Andreas Brown brought to her attention another original manuscript by Slavic revivalist illustrator Boris Zvorykin. This led to an illustrated translation of four fairy tales by the beloved Russian writer Aleksandr Pushkin. Pushkin was told similar tales as a child and re-created them in his own inimitable way, thereby memorializing the popular oral poetry of the Russian peasantry. Zvorykin depicted these fables in the style of sixteenth- and seventeenth-century Russian miniatures, complete with elegant calligraphy and complicated interlaced designs, even as he executed these illustrations in the 1920s from his place of exile in Paris, where this book was first published, in French, in 1925.

Published in 1989 under the title *The Golden Cockerel and Other Fairy Tales*, the tales were translated by Jessie Wood, and an introduction was contributed by Rudolf Nureyev. The Russian ballet star relied on his significant other and longtime companion, Robert Tracy, to do the actual writing; both men often socialized with Jackie. She realized that this was one children's book that adults could also treasure as an elegant volume worthy of display on their coffee tables. Jackie deferred to her friends on this work and did not allow her name to appear in its pages.

While the Pushkin book was in the works, a manuscript written by a Polish émigré, Christine Zamoyska-Panek, arrived at Jackie's office. Unbeknownst to Jackie, several years before, a ninety-page outline of the same book had been turned down by another editor at Doubleday. *Have You Forgotten? A Memoir of Poland, 1939–1945,* tells the story of a Polish aristocrat who suffered through the Nazi invasion of her country and joined the resistance. After the German army seized the Zamoyska feudal estate, Christine and her family walked to Krakow with nothing more than they could carry, ending up in a crowded apartment. The Polish aristocracy had long had connections to the Jewish intelligentsia and was sympathetic to their plight. While opposing the Nazi regime meant certain death, Christine Zamoyska-Panek took work as a nurse in a city hospital, and used her position and her relative privilege to shepherd at-risk Jews to secret hiding places, including her own flat.

While this is a moving story, the literature and reportage from postwar Europe is filled with similar tales. Was there something about this particular family's ordeal that attracted Jackie? An interesting clue occurs early in the book, when Zamoyska-Panek mentions that her father's cousin, Isabella Radziwill, offered her country estate to the Zamoyska family. In 1959, Lee Radziwill had become the wife of a Polish prince, Stanislaw Albrecht Radziwill. Caroline Lee Bouvier, better known as Lee Radziwill, was married to the prince until 1974, and if these two Radziwills were related, Jackie may have heard some of these tales long before she became a commissioning editor.

The author confirmed my suspicion about the Radziwill connection. Zamoyska-Panek told me, "I suppose you're right, because the one who married Stanislaw Radziwill was Lee, the sister. Stanislaw is a cousin. She divorced him first, then he died, then she remarried. And she still goes by the name Radziwill. . . . I met him once or twice. [My father's cousin] Isabella was married to Carl Radziwill, and they had a beautiful estate in really the sticks in Poland."

A writer in Maine who helped Zamoyska-Panek with the book, Fred Benton Holmberg, told me, "I'd actually said some very nasty things about the Radziwills in the book, which Jackie left in as a matter of fact. . . . The Radziwills stole the gas from the [Zamoyska] family when they were trying to escape the Russians, and the Radziwills escaped, and the Zamoyskas didn't. The Radziwills were all part of the family. So I'm sure that that's why, when Christine first contacted Jackie, she wanted to look at the manuscript, because of that connection. But when I wrote in the book that they stole the gasoline, she never mentioned it . . . never made any attempt to make me soften it at all."

According to Zamoyska-Panek, who lived in Massachusetts and later in Maine, the manuscript was submitted to Jackie by a friend, and she remembered Jackie calling her about the book six months after it was submitted. Zamoyska-Panek said, "I wrote that book trying to put on paper the way I thought at that time—not today. My whole life philosophy changed. But if you compare what happened to me during the five years of war with other people, you can say that I was on vacation. I was not beaten, I was not arrested. I was very close to trouble and very close to people who were arrested, and we didn't know whether we'd see them or not. The first was my father. He was arrested twice, but survived. But this is all, you know, a little theatrical. Sure it was bad. If you eat three times a day, and then you find yourself where you eat once in three days, it's bad. When you have to put newspapers because that's all you had on your feet. . . . So these are the things. I was hungry, I was cold, I was scared, and I had hope. I was only fourteen when it started. I knew nothing about Germans, and I knew nothing about hate. It didn't exist in my head. . . . Yeah, it wasn't fun, but I never went through torture."

Zamoyska-Panek told me that she communicated with Jackie mostly through letters. "She would send me pages and pages to rewrite or to tell her more, or less, or which photographs to take. I gave all of that work to Holmberg. . . ."

Like others who worked with Jackie at a distance, Holmberg developed a phone relationship with her. They also corresponded but never met in person. He said, "We began talking, but then she discovered in the course of the conversation that I was an ex-minister. And over a period of the next two years we developed really two relationships: One was a very personal relationship talking about our own family situations; and the other was a very professional relationship in terms of the book. And I told Jackie when we first started talking about family tragedies, and we talked about our children.

"She sent me the first letter, I think it was May of eighty-seven, and it was a three-and-a-half-page letter criticizing the manuscript, and she also sent the manuscript back. . . . Every single page had a comment on it. Then I began to be impressed about it, because I thought, Boy, she's really good. . . . She sent a handwritten note on a lined yellow piece of paper. Part of that note said: 'A wonderful book is here, all set to emerge, and I am sure it will in your next draft. Don't be dismayed—I think you will see exactly what needs to be done and it will be SO much easier this time.'

"She sure was a line editor in my case. . . . She never let anything slip. Later she wrote, after much of the rewrite was complete: 'I think what you have rewritten works very well and that you should be congratulated. . . . The only thing I can criticize . . . is that occasionally your vigilance relaxes and you let Christina slip back into broken English.' Jackie and I continually argued about Christina's 'voice'. . . . she continually ended her letters or comments with 'Do call anytime, and if you disagree with any of the suggestions, you must not hesitate to say so.'

"There was one overriding argument that I had with Jackie. Her 'notion' of Christine and my 'reality' of Christine were quite different. Jackie imagined Christine as an elegant, sophisticated, well-trained aristocrat much like herself. I, on the other hand, knew Christine [was] a tough, smart street fighter." Holmberg admitted that there was friction along the way when Jackie tried to enforce a deadline while he was visiting India. "At a certain point she told me I wasn't 'keeping up my part of the contract'! I hate to admit it but she was right. I seldom got rewrites in on time. She really called me to task a number of times, and rightly so, even though I got really pissed."

Zamoyska-Panek said, "People kind of made a goddess out of her in this country, don't they? I don't understand why. She was a completely normal person, but I never could understand why such a reverence. She had a very strong self-discipline, ability to stand up to bad times, which I like personally, because I did the same thing."

The book was published in August 1989, and though it was not widely reviewed, Jackie managed to obtain a promotional blurb for the back cover from Zbigniew Brzezinski, who described it as "A highly personal and very readable insight into the human dimensions of the apocalypse that Poland experienced during World War II . . . romantic, heroic, and even charming."

Both in the office and in her social life, Jackie continued to risk her privacy by striking up friendships with people of interest who crossed her path. Some of them led her to books; others did not, yet offered support in other ways. As she perfected her role as modern-day saloniste, her circle grew remarkably diverse. Certain people gravitated to her on Martha's Vineyard, where she continued to spend her summers. She was befriended there by neighbors such as author William Styron and his wife, Rose, who suggested that in addition to the magnificent seaside splendors her home afforded, part of the appeal for Jackie was that "the Vineyard did not have a history for her."

Jackie tried to develop another book on Indian culture, with a young architect, William La Riche, as its designated writer, but the project fell through. La Riche told me that Jackie also tried but failed to sell a novel of his to Doubleday. His friendship with her thrived over the last eight years of her life. He called her his "great literary encourager." He later told biographer David Spoto (*Jacqueline Bouvier Kennedy Onassis*), "As a trusted friend, Jackie was eager to connect on the deepest level possible, and she had a greater capacity for empathy than anyone else I had ever met. . . . I once asked her how, during the most painful moments of her life, she had the strength to go on, and she replied, 'It never occurred to me not to.'"

La Riche also remembered a car trip that he took with Jackie. "We drove from Manhattan to Princeton in her old 1971 BMW. The windows didn't quite work, but she had a powerful engine put in, and she loved to speed. We were on our way to visit Nina Berberova, a Russian writer. . . . As we passed through the Lincoln Tunnel, Jackie urged me to cross a double line in order to pass a truck—'Just gun it, William!' she urged me."

Jackie was also quite taken by author Jane Hitchcock's book about a troubled mother-daughter relationship, *Trick of the Eye,* and she began a conversation with the writer one evening at a dinner at the Morgan Library. Hitchcock told biographer Christopher Anderson, "She took me under her wing. I wrote two of my books at her house on the Vineyard. . . . She became like a surrogate mother to me and certainly taught me how to behave. . . . I think she had several relationships like this, with women that she guided."

Another member of Jackie's circle, Edna O'Brien, later wrote of her friend, "So many of her qualities—that breathless enthusiasm, a certain giddiness late at night, a passionate love of clothes—revealed the perennial child. But the barriers which she built around herself betray a woman who had espoused self-preservation from the start." O'Brien also surmised, "Distance and distancing were central to her, not only from others but from huge parts of herself. It was what gave her that inexplicable aura. . . . She was caught in the gap between ingénue and empress, between innocence and worldliness."

Romantic tribulations with men and difficult mothers were recurrent themes in Jackie's friendships with the younger women in her life. By all accounts, she was generous with her friends and invested a great deal of her time with them. Joe Armstrong, who had contributed to the meteoric success of *Rolling Stone* during the 1970s, on one occasion had lifted staff morale by playing the song "Dropkick Me, Jesus (Through the Goal Posts of Life)" on a stereo in the magazine's offices, mischievously aiming the speakers out the window over Park Avenue. Armstrong repeated for me the story he told biographer Sarah Bradford: "Jackie was editing a book with a friend of mine, my assistant, Claudia Porges Holland, who told her that story, and and she broke into laughter so hard that she cried and said, 'Get me Joe Armstrong's telephone number.' She called me for lunch and our intense five-year friendship began."

Armstrong added, "When she rang I was so stunned and intimidated really. And I was worried because she asked me to pick the place. I picked a corner at the Four Seasons, because back then people didn't go from table to table to table to visit. I thought if we sat in a corner that she'd be protected there. So we went to lunch and it lasted almost three hours. I had prepared some three-by-five index cards for my lap with subjects, so if conversation stalled then I'd have cue cards. . . . But I never looked down once, because she had so many observations and comments. She made everything easy."

In 1989, about a year after they had their first lunch together, Jackie wrote Armstrong a poignant letter, which he described as "a declaration of friendship." She wrote, in part, "I think it is the greatest treasure in life to find a friend, a new friend, and that is what you are. . . . I want you to know that I would always do as much for you as I feel you would do for me. So if you land in jail and are allowed one call, it should be to me."

Over time, Armstrong came to occupy a special place in Jackie's life. They met regularly, and Joe also became acquainted with Maurice Tempelsman. "She said that Maurice helped her with how to handle business and political situations in the office. And that she looked to him as an adviser. He's charming, and obviously very smart."

Jackie and Armstrong had a mutual friend in Bill Moyers, and both recognized Jackie's efforts to put others at ease in her presence. Like Moyers, Armstrong hailed from Texas, and he recalled, "Bill Moyers and I have been friends for forty-five years. He got me a job with the Peace Corps when I was in law school. He worked with Jackie on all his books, and I once asked Bill, 'Why do you think she intimidates people so much, because she's such a regular, normal person in so many ways?' He said, 'It's because of her place in history. Because she had that dignity for those four days with those two little kids . . . and that image of her husband's brains all over her. She was a unity force in the country, and she didn't ask to be.'"

Armstrong and Jackie had another longtime mutual friend, singer-songwriter Carly Simon, whom Jackie first met on the Vineyard in the mid-eighties. According to an essay Simon posted on her official Web site,

> Jackie Onassis called one day to ask me to write my autobiography. I didn't say "no," but I didn't mean "yes." In fact I tried, because it was Jackie. . . . I wrote some 50 pages and then gave up in a flurry of regret about revelations. I could talk about my own life with all its vicissitudes, long and short

comings, but not those of other people. Jackie understood and also knew that I'd had a rich story-telling past with my own now grown-up children, and so suggested substituting a children's book for an autobiography. In *Amy the Dancing Bear* [1989] there were fragments of my life to be sure. My life as a bear. It was the first book I collaborated on with Jackie and Margot Datz, my illustrator and friend from Martha's Vineyard. Over the years there were to be three others: *The Boy of the Bells* [1990], *The Fisherman's Song* [1991] and *The Nighttime Chauffeur* [1993]. Jackie's role was as a thoughtful editor. She made imaginative suggestions that also made sense.

"Jackie was so proud of Carly," said Armstrong. "She took me to see Carly's opera, *Romulus Hunt,* which a Metropolitan Opera group was performing at John Jay College a few blocks from Lincoln Center. I only saw Jackie cry once, and she did that night when a young boy sang a song—'Everyone wants to dance with my father.'"

I remember Jackie over lunch one day extolling the virtues of Carly's *Amy the Dancing Bear,* and hence the spinoff title for Gelsey Kirkland's *The Little Ballerina and Her Dancing Horse.* Publishing was part of Simon's family background. Her father, Richard L. Simon, was cofounder of Simon & Schuster, and her mother, Andrea, with whom Carly had her issues, sometimes called herself "Mrs. Simon & Schuster." Simon spoke at length about her relationship with Jackie for Marie Brenner's 1994 *Vanity Fair* article "Carly Simon's Mother Load."

Brenner wrote, "I wonder if Carly viewed her as an idealized version of her own mother. Absolutely, she says. And what did Carly imagine she represented for Mrs. Onassis? 'Someone who was so incapable of hiding her feelings that she could be more truly herself around me. Because I was incapable of not being myself around her. . . . I would swear. I would use undignified phrases. It freed her to be the 8th-grader she really was. Jackie loved naughtiness. . . .'"

The two friends sometimes attended movies together in Manhattan. They would meet in the theater restroom in order for Jackie to avoid being spotted by the crowd. She would wait in the bathroom stall for Simon to arrive. Simon told Brenner about the awkward time she had when she and Jackie went to see the opening of Warren Beatty's gangland movie *Bugsy*: "*JFK* was playing at the time. I did my homework. And before choosing a theater, I called around to all the theaters that were playing *Bugsy* to make sure that there was no way *JFK* was at the same theater. I did this perfectly! . . . I picked the Beekman. . . . And we sat down with ten minutes to spare. I was by then so nervous that as we sat down in the darkened theater,

I turned to her and said: 'So, have you seen *JFK*?' And Jackie was horrified. She said: 'No, Carly. Of course not. . . .' I was so nervous about the subject of *JFK* coming up that I brought it up out of sheer perversity."

According to Simon, men were often the subject of her conversations with Jackie, and Jackie offered Simon moral support during her breakup with James Taylor. Jackie confided in Simon about her own past, on at least one occasion making what was a rare admission. "Whenever she told you anything that she considered deeply personal," said Simon, "she would slip into third-person language: 'One felt.' She told me how deeply hurt she had been by Jack's sexual adventures. 'After a while, one does turn off,' she said."

By the 1990s, Jackie had hit her editorial stride and was publishing more books each year than ever before. According to Scott Moyers, Jackie felt that she had fallen short with one of her more ambitious projects. "When she did Marc Riboud's *Capital of Heaven* [1990], it was a stunning visual achievement and best seller in France, but not in America. . . . She was mortified, feeling she had done Riboud a disservice."

Jackie would do several more of her expensive illustrated books over the next three years, though it was more difficult for her to acquire books like Riboud's and sell them to the house. Jackie had visited the photographer in the early eighties when she traveled to China for the opening of the Fragrant Hill Hotel, designed by I. M. Pei. Riboud remembered how the idea for his book was born: "Once, she joined me while I was photographing at the University of Beijing. I introduced her as my assistant. She took notes, I took pictures. For an entire day, among students at the cafeteria and in dormitories, with professors and even the rector, she went completely unrecognized. This greatly delighted her. On that day, I first mentioned my passion for a mist-enshrouded mountain that for centuries inspired Chinese painters. Its name: the Capital of Heaven. Five years later she made a book possible with this very title."

Riboud told me that later, while visiting New York, he presented Jackie with the idea for his book. "I saw her, and I said, 'I have a project I would like to submit to you.' And she said, 'We must make a book.' And she did everything, and all the good things to have . . . the best Swiss printer, and in three different languages, English, French, and German. . . . She pushed for the best, and it was really great. It costs, and publishers are always eager to cover their expenses, you see. So in order to recover, they needed [to sell] thirty thousand books, if I'm not mistaken. And thirty thousand books in the first edition is a lot. And the book was not cheap.

"Anyway, there was a good party at a French cultural center, and she was there. I remember the one thing about the book: Somebody—not me, I would not have asked—mentioned the fact that she could help for the press. She said, 'I want to have nothing to do with the press and nothing to do with the money.'" Riboud added, "I have published twenty-five books, and this book for me remains the best one."

The mountain referred to in the title is in a massif three hundred miles west of Shanghai, near the Yangtze River. The granite peaks of the Huangshan range are perpetually cloaked in mist, and have long been a destination for artists and nature lovers, for whom this is one of the most beautiful landscapes on Earth. Chinese nature painting has expressed this staggering landscape for centuries, lending it what might seem an otherworldly quality indicative of artistic license—until one sees the place itself.

As Jackie observed when she visited Riboud, the Huangshan range is not the highest in the world, and this is part of its charm. The Himalayas have far more altitude, as well as the accompanying permanent snow cover, obscuring the sheer beauty that the granite outcroppings present. The Huangshan range is low enough so that it is infused with rain and mist rather than snow and ice. The unit of travel in the Huangshan is the stair step. Sixty miles of winding trails and stairways crisscross the range, and it takes more than two thousand steps to ascend to the Capital of Heaven or the Lotus Blossom, the two highest peaks. Since the beginning of the seventeenth century and the fall of the Ming dynasty, this range has been a majestic inspiration as iconic in China as Mount Fuji is in Japan.

Some time after the first printing, Jackie told Riboud that a thousand copies of the book were unsold, and informed him that Doubleday wanted to unload them on the remainder market. Riboud said, "And she told me, 'Marc, refuse, turn down this, because it's very bad, a book like this, being sold on the pavement, on the *trattoir* [sidewalk], you know. Very bad.'"

Riboud recalled that Jackie later found a foreign buyer for his remainder books. "I was again in Beijing where Jackie faxed me the good news that a Taiwanese publisher wanted to buy many copies of the book. I replied, 'You take such good care of our *Capital of Heaven* that it will earn you a good place in heaven.'

"We all know of many more deeds which earned Jackie the best place in heaven."

8

When Life Comes First

Jackie set a personal record for the number of books she was responsible for publishing in one year during 1991, with more than a dozen to her credit. Most of these works were published by Doubleday, but she also made it a habit, in the case of books that she was unable to sell to her own house, to act essentially as literary agent for their authors. One of these was the brilliant Russian émigré author Nina Berberova. According to Berberova's translators, Richard Sylvester and Marian Schwartz, writing in their introduction to Berberova's *Moura*, Jackie read Berberova's fiction in French, when it was published in the decade before by Actes Sud, in Arles. Jackie brought Berberova to the attention of Knopf, thus bringing Berberova's six novellas, *The Tattered Cloak and Other Stories*, to American readers for the first time.

Schwartz told me that Berberova "taught at Yale and at Princeton, but as a writer she wasn't well known in the States except for her autobiography [*The Italics Are Mine*]. She became a sensation in France when Actes Sud began publishing her fiction. Mrs. Onassis followed the French book industry—the best seller lists there and whatever was happening there. . . . She had been courting Berberova, but Berberova, while admiring, was not overwhelmed by Onassis's celebrity. Once she told me, 'Oh, she sent me a fruit basket. What do I need with a fruit basket?' What was important to Berberova was that Onassis was trying to find a publisher for her in the States. I had already published some of Berberova's fiction, mostly in England, but we didn't have a good publisher in the States. Onassis felt that Doubleday was not a good fit, but she was instrumental in getting Berberova to Knopf."

That same year, Knopf published another one of Jackie's authors, Jonathan Cott, whose investigative biography *Wandering Ghost: The Odyssey of Lafcadio Hearn* Jackie was unable to bring into Doubleday. Cott told me, "In this case, Jackie said she wanted to publish the Lafcadio Hearn book, but Doubleday wasn't interested in doing so. But she was so encouraging of the project, and so pleased that Knopf was willing to take a chance on it, and she wished it Godspeed."

Hearn was exactly the kind of multicultural historical figure that appealed to Jackie. As chronicled by Cott with his painterly attention to detail, the half-blind late-nineteenth-century Greek expatriate, an early prototype of the bohemian nomad, was an illuminating travel writer and novelist who spent time in Dublin, Cincinnati, New Orleans, and Martinique before finding his final home in Japan, perfecting the craft of self-taught, personal observation journalism before such writing was in vogue. Jackie knew that Cott's book was Doubleday's loss, and it would not be the last time she proved to have better taste and commercial sense than higher-ups in the house.

Steve Rubin, a former journalist and Bantam editor, had been installed as Doubleday president under Bertelsmann, and he would become one of the champions of the profit-oriented publishing paradigm. Over the nineteen years that he was to head the company, one of his major claims to fame in the trade would be the publication of Dan Brown's blockbuster *The Da Vinci Code*. For the remainder of Jackie's tenure at Doubleday, Rubin maintained a tight rein on the purse strings, at a time when a book's bestseller potential became the primary criterion for its acquisition, to the point of editorial and marketing obsession.

Just after Rubin moved into his new office, Jackie wrote to him about one of her pet projects that she had been trying to sell to his predecessor, Nancy Evans. The proposed book involved one of Jackie's longtime friends, the Manhattan socialite and philanthropist Brooke Astor. Dated December 30, 1990, Jackie's typed memo read, in part, "Nancy Evans wanted a book from her, sort of how to live the good life. . . . She is in her eighties. Her first two books, *Patchwork Child* and *Footprints,* are out of print. She has the rights to the former, and Doubleday published the latter. Nancy said possibly we could publish the two together with new photos and a new introduction. I saw a longish introduction stressing the values that have affected her life: love of reading indoctrinated by parents, friendship, work, marriage, civic responsibility, curiosity, seeking out people in all fields, never getting stuck in a rut, gaiety, etc. Of course she is anxious to hear if this fits in with your plans."

Apparently, Brooke Astor's books did not fit into Rubin's plans. Jackie was going to discover that such rejections would occur with more frequency in the years ahead under the Bertelsmann regime. Editors like Shaye Areheart became disenchanted and left Doubleday to find greater freedom and more money elsewhere. Scott Moyers recalled that Jackie "knew that if she really wanted to sign up a book, she could walk in to see Steve Rubin and he'd acquiesce, but she was careful. If nobody felt the book was going to be profitable or believed in it, she wouldn't insist."

After Jackie's death, Rubin portrayed himself as a friend and confidant as well as Jackie's boss. He told Carl Sferrazza Anthony, "Jackie only did books that interested her. She once told me, 'I never think in terms of best sellers. I think in terms of books.' Luckily, so much of what interested her was of interest to a lot of other people. The irony of it is, here's someone who produced a large number of best sellers simply by, in essence, opening up her own sensibility, and in turn, finding that it was somehow a universal among readers. She was a formidable sponsor of projects, representing her books within the process, unselfish and funny when presenting books at editorial meetings. . . . She made herself directly accessible. I called her in the country, at home. She was always available for the publication party of one of our books—the first one there, the last one to leave."

Steve Rubin stayed at the helm until losing his position at Doubleday in 2009, moving on to become president and publisher of Henry Holt and Company. With his departure, the house was downsized and reorganized as a Random House imprint, becoming a mere shadow of what it had been during most of the time that Jackie had been in residence.

All of the books that Jackie published under Rubin in 1991 had been initiated before he became president. Loretta Barrett told me about one book that was published by Doubleday that year that Jackie had decisively encouraged. "I ran Anchor Books for a long time, and at different times Jackie did brilliant reader reports for me. We had some controversial projects. I had a project by Karen Armstrong, who went on to be published by Knopf, and it was on the Crusades [*Holy War: The Crusades and Their Impact on Today's World*], and Herman Gollob was the editor in chief. . . . I signed her up for a book and she was not known in America at that point. She wrote a brilliant book on Christianity, Islamism, and Judaism, and Herman Gollob told me it was anti-Semitic and he wasn't going to publish it. And I said, 'And you're anti-Christian. I mean, Karen Armstrong is not anti-Semitic. That's ridiculous.' And Jackie read the manuscript for me, because she knew the Middle East, because she'd lived in Greece and spent an enormous amount of time in Turkey, and she really knew the history of that area. And she wrote a fabulous report for me. And Herman couldn't argue with it. . . . And then I sent a letter off to Karen, who made the changes, and we moved ahead and published it, and then she left and went to Knopf. It became a best seller."

While describing Steve Rubin as "very savvy," Loretta lamented the fate of Doubleday in later years under its German megaowner. "God knows what Bertelsmann's done to Doubleday. It's tragic, but Americans sold their intellectual life. There isn't a company in New York that isn't far gone. . . . We do not own our intellectual property. Think about that. It was a whole evolution and a movement, and it's just crazy."

One of the limitations under which Jackie operated when she acquired books for the house, like most other editors, was having to win approval from management for the amount of money she could offer to the authors as an advance on future royalties. This sometimes delayed or complicated negotiations with the authors and their agents. Jackie told *Publishers Weekly* editor John F. Baker in 1993, "I don't work with agents as much as some editors, perhaps, though sometimes when something crosses their desk, I hope they think of me and say, 'Oh, she might like that.' "

There was frequently a time lag as Jackie turned to others for approval on budgetary decisions. Like a number of agents who fielded offers from Jackie for their clients, Owen Laster, who represented David Stenn, said, "I did negotiate with her, but it was clear that she was taking down what I said or proposed and then there would always be a subsequent call when she would get back to me. And I definitely had the feeling that somebody else was involved. It wasn't that I'd say something, and then the other party says something, and then I say something. There was always a pause. There was never one phone call. I couldn't say who . . . but definitely I had the feeling that there was someone in the background. She'd often come back and say, 'Oh that's too much.' "

Another one of Jackie's SWAT team assistants who worked on two of my books, Bruce Tracy, was a former actor who would later become an executive editor with the Villard imprint at Random House. He described for Carl Sferrazza Anthony the challenge of evaluating the submissions Jackie received: "When manuscripts came in, you couldn't just drop it right on her. Like any assistant editor, you read it yourself and then passed along your assessment. I hadn't realized that she had already published Jonathan Cott, but he sent in a proposal for two books—one on the priestess Isis, another on the history and mystique of the number 13. I thought they were pretty wacky. I first had made the assumption that the rest of the world had made about Jackie, that she was purely interested in the fussy fine arts and French history. So I wrote that these proposals were not right for us.

"That was the first big lesson I learned about her. I could never second-guess Jackie because—although it sounds like a cliché or exaggeration—she was really interested in everything. . . . For Jackie, more so even than most editors, adventure was a big part of editing. Jackie never categorically dismissed an idea because the subject matter was errant or foreign to her."

As one example of Jackie's ever-widening range of interests, Tracy cited her foray into "the nature of bees, birds, and butterflies," the focus of Miriam Rothschild's *Butterfly Cooing Like a Dove*. Born in 1908, Rothschild was a marvelously unconventional British naturalist, entomologist, and zoologist—a lifelong student of fleas and the daughter of Nathaniel Charles Rothschild, of the famous Rothschild family. The *Times* of London once said of her, "Imagine Beatrix Potter on amphetamines."

Dame Miriam Louisa Rothschild was that most unusual of scientists, one who never had to fill out grant applications to government bureaucracies to fund her work. Born into one of the wealthiest families in Europe, she could underwrite her own studies. She became fascinated with parasitic bugs and was the first to identify the mechanism by which fleas jumped. By the time the idea for *Butterfly Cooing* came to her, she had published more than three hundred scientific papers and a host of other books, and had become a leading conservationist figure in Great Britain, advising Prince Charles on what plants he should encourage at Highgrove.

Rothschild, who died in 2005, created the kind of book that only Vladimir Nabokov, another literary lepidopterist, could have conceived. "Literature and butterflies are the two sweetest passions known to man," intoned Nabokov in a radio interview cited approvingly by Rothschild.

Books like this do more to prove the essential unity of science and art than a hundred C. P. Snow lectures. For one thing, artistic depictions of nature, in the age before the invention of photography, were the only way scholars had of knowing what something looked like and, in many cases, how it fit in to the warp and weave of everyday life and human culture. From a silkscreen of Japanese butterflies to a detail of Goya's *Adoration of the Trinity* featuring a luminescent dove, from a fourteenth-century folio by Guyart des Moulins of Noah releasing the dove to a search for land for an overcrowded ark, or an evocative Balthus painting showing a moth flittering around an oil lamp in the presence of a naked girl, Rothschild found museum pieces that illustrated her scientific aesthetic. She even drew a subtle comparison between Nabokov and Balthus, both famous for their fascination with nymphets.

Marianne Velmans handled the Rothschild book in London and remembered it and the author with great affection. "It was so beautiful and so eccentric and so off-the-wall. I'm so glad we did it then because if I came up with this project now, everybody would just hoot with laughter. I don't remember how it evolved, but I got involved because I published it over here, and I did go and visit Miriam Rothschild at her house. It was wonderful. It was like going into *le grand monde,* or something, or a hidden estate—a garden gone wild. . . . And she only wore rubber Wellington boots because she didn't believe in leather. . . . But that was the amazing thing about Jackie. She knew . . . such a wonderful variety of people to work on these projects which were really quite artistic."

In her foreword, Rothschild credited Jackie's friend at the Met, Karl Katz, with passing the manuscript on to Jackie and serving as "for one brief moment almost a joint author." Simon Rendall, a London-based designer, worked with Rothschild on the book, which was another ultralavish, glossy production featuring numerous photographs and art reproductions. He had previously worked with Rothschild on a book entitled *Dear Lord Rothschild: Birds, Butterflies, and History.* In a phone call from London, Rendall told me, "Miriam worked on her own terms. She wouldn't tolerate editors really. She knew what she wanted to do, and all she wanted really was someone who could do it for her. And she was therefore not very good with conventional publishers on the whole.

"*Dear Lord Rothschild* was done with a friend of hers, because she liked working with friends. . . . And her chauffeur would scoop me up in London and drive me down to where she lived, and she would say, 'You're to stay here until you've finished.' I would be locked in, and she wouldn't take no for an answer. Or she wouldn't understand that one had other things to do. . . . I mean, I should say that Miriam was one of my very best, dearest friends.

"I don't really know quite how she got to Mrs. Onassis, but I think she was quite excited about the idea. They were two very strong-willed women, I think, who weren't going to give way. But anyway, Miriam managed to persuade Mrs. Onassis, and [*Butterfly Cooing Like a Dove*] was the title Miriam chose. No one was going to persuade her that it wasn't a very convincing or selling title. That was what she wanted, and that was what she was going to have. . . .

"She liked to be accurate, of course, and that was important to her as far as fleas and other things; but as far as literature was concerned, I think imagination played a big role in her interpretation of things. Somehow we produced a book. But it was quite hard work, and at times it was not, we felt, with the support of New York. . . . During that time I think Mrs. Onassis had three assistants. The files were lost twice, and I don't think the original files were ever found.

"Also I suspect that if the hands were already on, as Miriam's hands were already on, that it was probably quite difficult for [Mrs. Onassis] to be involved. . . . I mean there was an elaborate dance around the two of them. I suspect they both enjoyed slightly being involved in a project to-gether, but also not being closely involved in it, if you see what I mean. It was a very daring concept and it was an interesting idea, but like all those ideas, Miriam desperately needed an editor who could pull her into shape. And no one did that. If it had an editor who would have knocked out a quarter of it perhaps . . . sort of tightened things up . . . then I think the book would have been wonderful. Miriam wanted it her way, that was it. It was a mad book and it needed a mad editor. I think they were well suited. . . . I think Miriam right from the very beginning felt that it was going to be a match, with Mrs. Onassis, of titans."

Shifting mental gears again, Jackie published two more books that year on dance, Martha Graham's memoir, *Blood Memory,* and Francis Mason's, *I Remember Balanchine.* While she was working on these books, Jackie ex-plained over one of our lunches, that one of her goals was "to make a seri-ous contribution to dance literature." When one of Doubleday's editors retired, Jackie "inherited" Francis Mason as one of her authors. He was de-scribed by James Wolcott as a character who "might have stepped out of a Louis Auchincloss novel, only without the stiff rectitude and plaster dust"— which is exactly how I remember him.

Before he passed away in 2009, Mason, the elegant balletomane and longtime editor of *Ballet Review,* recollected that he was also peripherally involved in the Martha Graham book, though it was a project he pre-ferred not to remember. "I, at that time, was chairman of the Martha Gra-ham Company and close to Martha. I'm a very lucky man, really. I got to know very well Graham and Balanchine. And Martha was a treasure, a joy in my life. That book indeed Jackie worked on hard. Martha's col-league at her dance company, Ron Protas, a jackass, manipulated and did everything but sleep with her. Protas was in the middle between Jackie and Martha. It was her last months, last year of her life, and she got that book

done. Protas was always manipulating her. It got nasty in one way or another, and Jackie had a hard time, getting that done the way she wanted it
done."

The first question Martha Graham addresses in her memoir is why she
became a dancer. Her answer invokes Greek mythology, the Zen masters,
quotations from Emily Dickinson and William Goyen, the studio of El
Greco, the French poet Saint-John Perse, T. S. Eliot, and the composer
Edgard Varèse, among others. Wide-ranging as these cultural references
might be, their invocation on the first few pages suggests the contribution
of a ghostwriter—in this case, Howard Kaplan. Kaplan would later serve
in a similar capacity when Jackie published a memoir by longtime Alvin
Ailey dancer Judith Jamison, who served as the company's artistic director
until 2010.

Graham's book recounts the rise to fame of a young girl from Santa
Barbara High School to the Manhattan showplaces for ballet and modern
dance, and in the process, chronicles the rise of an arts culture in America
(one that Tom Wolfe termed the "statusphere") from the 1920s to the
1980s. Graham's life story is an endless list of places in which she performed, dancers with whom she worked, choreography created, and celebrities accommodated. The book was far shorter than its listed 280 pages, as
more than one hundred photographs were interspersed throughout, providing a marvelous slide show more entertaining than the text.

Martha Graham is the very icon of modern dance, but her aesthetic
insights and operational philosophy are nowhere in sight in this memoir.
Any reader expecting to understand the differences or separation points
between ballet and modern dance will be seriously disappointed. Any reader
expecting a manifesto of the kind that Dalí provided for the surrealists or
Balanchine and Lincoln Kirstein for classical ballet—what likely Jackie was
hoping for—had best look elsewhere.

Bruce Tracy was quoted by Carl Sferrazza Anthony in 1997 saying,
"Martha Graham died before her autobiography was scheduled for publication, and we had to rush it into print." Describing Jackie's approach as
editor, Tracy added, "Although many editors no longer do this, she always
put pen to paper in her particular process of editing, with a sense of what
the elements meant to the whole. Jackie could be sitting here with you and
me, and if a specific turn of phrase struck her, she would whip out her
book and write it down. She enjoyed language. If you see her edited manuscripts, you realize she was like a conductor. . . . If anything nice was said
about her projects, Jackie would say who did what, always giving credit
where credit was due—to assistants, designers, whoever."

Francis Mason's lengthy interview book devoted to the Russian émigré

choreographer George Balanchine was a potentially provocative exploration. The idea for the book came to him when he attended Balanchine's
funeral in 1983 and wondered how the many mourners might contribute
to the choreographer's legacy. Was he a genius touched by the angels or a
demonic taskmaster obdurately insensitive to the dangerous physical demands he was imposing on the dancers in his company? Or was he a little
bit of both? In promoting his brand of the world-class phenomenon that
American ballet became, Balanchine touched off a massive talent emigra-
tion from the studios of Moscow and Leningrad to the stages and rehearsal rooms of Manhattan. He remains to this day, years after his death,
the controversial seminal figure in twentieth-century balletic expression in
America.

Mason's book was not interpretive. It did not attempt to answer the
paradox posed by the opening questions. Instead, it was a series of in-
depth transcribed interviews, compiled by Mason, with dancers who
flourished under Balanchine's system. Mason had previously coauthored,
with Balanchine, the book *101 Stories of the Great Ballets*. In *I Remember Balanchine* there were reminiscences of many of the greats—Alexandra
Danilova, Lincoln Kirstein, Maria Tallchief, Moira Shearer, Rudolph
Nureyev, Peter Martins, Edward Villella and Ray Bolger. But there were
giant omissions as well—Margot Fonteyn and Gelsey Kirkland, Mikhail
Baryshnikov and Natalia Makarova, Suzanne Farrell and Jerome Robbins.

Jackie had once invited Balanchine to the White House, and he used
the occasion to encourage her to increase support for ballet and the arts.
Apparently charmed by Jackie, he later told a TV journalist, "I would only
want to be president if I could have Jacqueline Onassis as my First Lady,
and then, with her help, do what should be done to bring beauty into
people's lives."

Mason penned a tribute essay about Jackie, in which he described her
demand that he shorten his 650,000-word manuscript by "200,000 words
in 60 days." Jackie told him, "You have a new form of biography here but
you have to focus on the recollections that fill out Balanchine's portrait.
Cut their autobiographical reminiscences and repetitious adorations and
concentrate on what each has to say on what Balanchine was really like as
a man and artist."

The author took his editor's advice only so far. The voices present in
the book are all important, but they are largely uncritical, more willing to
laud Mr. B.'s genius than to analyze dispassionately his methods and the
fief-building yet arbitrary nature of the steel-vise grip he had on what is
today an increasingly marginalized art form. Mason excused Farrell and
Robbins; they were both working on books of their own. He did not ex-

plain why Baryshnikov refused him or why he chose not to approach Kirkland or Makarova. The reluctance of Balanchine's last wife, the polio-stricken Tanaquil LeClercq, to participate was another glaring omission from this book.

Mason did interview eighty-four former associates of Balanchine, mostly dancers, but also a couple of orthopedists and arts administrators. The great majority of them relate charming tales of artistic commitment and the benefits of hard work. Under Jackie's editorial guidance, this book was and is a valuable resource about a titan of the ballet universe, but it is not the last word. The definitive critique of Balanchine's genius and wide-ranging influence has yet to be published.

In October 1991, Jackie published two more books that could not have been less similar to each other in terms of subject matter: *No Minor Chords: My Days in Hollywood,* by the German-born pianist, conductor, and composer André Previn, and another pictorial tome, *The French Woman's Bedroom,* by Mary-Sargent Ladd, who was a friend of Jackie's and a contributing editor at *Vogue* (now married to a Frenchman, Baron Bernard d'Anglejan). Though neither of these books was likely to be very successful commercially, both offered the kind of offbeat charm that held a special appeal for Jackie.

In his dedication to this slim volume of memoirs from the fifteen years he worked on film scores in Hollywood, Previn thanked Jackie, "whose unerring judgment was probably tempered by her enjoyment of slightly wicked stories." Previn grew up in Los Angeles, a refugee from his native Germany, from whence his entire family had departed after Hitler gained power. As a child prodigy, he found himself scoring his first films while still a teenager, and he worked his way from copyist to composer within the tightly defined studio system that operated during all the years he labored in Hollywood. But Previn was classically trained and also had an ear for jazz, so was able to escape the Hollywood ghetto after he had attained some recognition. Sick of shoehorning his music to fit in between actors' lines and special sound effects, Previn left the studio system in 1964, just when it was about to crumble before the onslaught of independent pro-ducers and outside auteurs.

Suggesting that Previn's book would make enjoyable vacation reading, *The New York Times* called it an "amiable, intelligent memoir." In a tribute essay written after Jackie's death, Previn recalled that after submitting fifty pages of the book to Jackie, "She called and asked me to come by her of-fice, where she proceeded to reduce me to helplessness by suggesting that I might be the logical successor to Mark Twain and S. J. Perelman. This was the first of many meetings, sometimes in her office, other times over lunch or dinner, and encouraging flattery began to be tempered with extremely shrewd and invaluable criticism. . . . Her faith in the project, and indeed in all her projects, was absolute, and I cannot imagine anyone not being the better for having worked with her."

Previn was one to whom Jackie confessed the secret motive behind her dark glasses. The conductor said, "Once, over lunch, I asked her whether it ever bothered her that every pair of eyes was trained upon her. 'That's why I always wear my dark glasses,' she said. 'It may be that they're looking at me, but none of them can ever tell which ones I'm looking back at. That way I can have fun with it.' A smile of almost pure glee illuminated her face."

Jackie also kept an eye on her Upper East Side neighbors. Repeating a story that I heard from several of her authors, designer Michael Flanagan recalled, "I don't know how Jackie defended her own life from prying eyes. But I remember what a friend of mine told me years ago. One night he was among a handful of people invited to Jackie's apartment for dinner. Somehow everyone got to talking about their secrets, and Jackie, in a giggly mood, said she sometimes spied on her [neighbors] with binoculars. Her neighbors wore 'weird pajamas,' she said, and they did 'strange things like you wouldn't believe.' My friend was impressed. It's like the whole world has its eyes on her, he said. Then she goes home and she turns the whole game around, and the joke's on them!"

Also on the receiving end of Jackie's editorial blandishments was Mary-Sargent Ladd, a cousin of John Sargent Sr. Both are members of the Brahmin family that included the famous portraitist John Singer Sargent. In her youth, Ladd was photographed by Richard Avedon for a *Junior Bazaar* layout arranged by Diana Vreeland, and she was also well acquainted with Jackie's good friend Jessie Wood and her mother, Louise de Vilmorin.

Ladd related how her book came about. "Jackie, whose wedding I went to in Newport, was an old friend. Jackie's question during one of our lunches, which would happen whenever I was in NYC, was the following: 'You have had such an interesting life, you have worked for *Vogue* and *House and Garden*,' etc. etc. 'Wouldn't you like to do a book for me?' I was naturally amazed she would ask and flattered, but also apprehensive."

As the author observes in her introductory essay on bedroom art and design in France, some of life's most important events take place in the bedroom. She also notes that it was only with modernity that the bedroom became a safe haven from the rest of the world. The book characterizes an earlier era in France when *les années de gloire pour la France,* the bedroom was a place for receiving visitors, and was where honored guests were entertained and even sumptuous meals consumed. The bed was not merely a functional object. It was the most important and expensive piece of furniture in a haute bourgeois house, and the room in which it sat was not a private sanctuary but a gathering place for kith and kin. With Jackie's blessing and oversight, Ladd assembled an exquisite sampling of modern boudoirs that honored the tradition.

The reader is treated to the private salons of princesses and countesses, baronesses and marquises, women with names like Rothschild, Castaing, and Ravenel. These are the privileged who can indulge their every sensual fantasy and their every eclectic design whim. Or they are arbiters of French taste, like Charlotte Aillaud, the European editor at large for *Architectural Digest*, and Jeanne Lanvin, whose bedroom was reconstructed at the Musée des arts décoratifs in Paris. It is a book in which one woman, Jacqueline Delubac, goes to bed with an original Roualt staring her in the face. In accord with the shared vision of author and editor, it is a book in which the concept of elegance is given visual expression, even if, for most of us, these Frenchwomen's bedrooms are merely a curiosity never to be experienced firsthand.

Drawing once again in 1991 on her art world connections, Jackie added another feather to her publishing cap when she shepherded an autobiographical work by one of the twentieth century's leading art historians, Sir John Pope-Hennessy, whose dazzling career Jackie had followed for years. According to the author, the idea for his memoir, *Learning to Look: My Life in Art,* originated with an article he wrote in 1986 for *The New York Times*, "Portrait of an Art Historian as Young Man." Pope-Hennessy was also a skilled museum acquisitions expert and administrator, and the author of a score of books on the art and sculpture of the Italian Renaissance.

Jackie's old friend Thomas Hoving had given Pope-Hennessy a position at the Met after he lost the directorship of the British Museum. Hoving later wrote about him in his memoir, *Making the Mummies Dance*: "The 'Pope' was a brilliant, intense man, who often seemed snobbish and arbitrary. . . . To many the man was insufferable, yet as a professional, I always found the man matchless. He might seem to look down on everyone from the tip of his nose, but I knew that to be an affectation. His voice— high-pitched, a parody of upper class English—was not a reflection of his character. His odd image always tainted him . . ."

Some of those qualities are apparent in Pope-Hennessy's weighty tome, and Jackie may have tried to soften some of the less palatable edges. A self-taught historian, Pope-Hennessy was not terribly interested in being forthcoming or confessional about the events of his life in the book, but rather was intent on presenting his impressive curriculum vitae and an exegetic catalogue of artworks. His emphasis was on the Italian Renaissance, about which he had already written a score of books by the age of seventy-seven, and on the forty consecutive summers he was able to spend among the wonders of Florence and hill towns of Tuscany, along the way lamenting the metamorphosis that museums have undergone from temples of the privileged elite to Disneylands for the masses.

While the *New York Times* review of the book displayed little enthusiasm, the *Times* art critic, John Russell, provided a quote for the back cover, suggesting that Pope-Hennessy exhibited "a delight in human exchange, a sense of high drama and a sense of irresistible fun which make him a much-prized companion." Russell, like his wife, Rosamond Bernier, was also a longtime friend of Jackie's. In a reminiscence he contributed to *Time* magazine, "Portrait of a Friendship," he described some of Jackie's endearing quirks: "It was a fantasy of hers that everybody else's life was much more interesting than her own. 'Think of the plots that are being hatched down there!' she would say, looking down from the balcony of the Four Seasons restaurant, with her Schlumberger bracelets dangling over the edge. At lunchtime at Les Pleiades, the much missed art-world restaurant, she would say, 'What do you suppose they're buying and selling over their cold sea bass?'

"When it came to a book project, she was one of the all-time great bubble blowers. Never did those bubbles burst, either. Scheme after scheme was launched and christened." Russell also observed, "Above all, she brought a minute attention to the affectionate reassurances that keep friendship alive. Though capable of a holy rage when it was called for—for instance, when a famous figure of the day weaseled out of a book he had promised her for Doubleday—it gave her enormous pleasure to keep friendships in repair."

Rosamond Bernier revealed the identity of that "famous figure" her late husband was referring to when she told me, "I was very close to Philip [Johnson]. In fact Philip gave the wedding when John Russell and I married. We were married at his place, at the Glass House. And we were very friendly, and I did a number of programs about him for CBS. In other words, I knew him extremely well. And after doing all these interviews I had so much material about him. . . . Jackie wanted me to do a book about him because I had very precise ideas of how to illustrate it. . . .

"We had actually started working on the design of the book, and Jackie, Doubleday was to publish it, you see. And I had a great deal of material. And suddenly somebody came in I think to Doubleday to suggest another book on Philip, a couple, two people, and Philip had behind our backs agreed to these two other people—for them to write the book about him. And I had probably had lunch with him the day before, and he'd never mentioned it. He acted in the most shabby, shameful way. . . . Well, after all, there was a question of moral ambiguity—his attitude towards the Nazis, as you know, was not everything one would have hoped for. There must have been some strange defect in his character, because it was such a strange thing to do. So she and I were both absolutely furious, and we had lunch on our own, and Jackie said to me very, very seriously, 'I want you to swear and promise that you will never speak to Philip again.' And I promised, and I never did. Nor did she."

Jackie's family, of course, remained the center of her life even as she continued to dedicate herself to her career. John Jr. had finally passed the New York State bar exam, and Caroline's first two children, Rose and Tatiana, were a constant source of pride and delight for Jackie. Caroline's first book, *In Our Defense: The Bill of Rights in Action*, was also published in 1991 (by William Morrow, not Doubleday). Two years later, Caroline gave birth to a son, John. Her grandchildren called her "Grand Jackie." With her authors, Jackie spoke fervently of her two lawyer children who were now making their marks in the world, and of her beloved grandchildren. "She had the most peace in her life those last four or five years," said Joe Armstrong. "She had that balance, and I think it was a really happy time for her."

With the children in her life in mind, she had commissioned another children's book in 1990 that would be published the following year. The author is a well-known American percussionist based in England, Jody Linscott, who has performed with countless rock-and-roll luminaries such as Elton John, The Who, Paul McCartney, Eric Clapton, and James Taylor. She credits her two children for inspiring her two books that Jackie edited: *Once Upon A to Z: An Alphabet Odyssey* and *The Worthy Wonders Lost at Sea: A Whimsical Word Search Adventure*. Linscott also composed a series of songs, to accompany the first book, though her music was not released at the time. Both books were illustrated with collages created with layers of color paper by Joe Armstrong's former *Rolling Stone* assistant Claudia Porges Holland, now an artist.

I met Linscott in Manhattan in 2009 while she was touring. She related the fortuitous circumstance that brought her first book to Jackie's attention. "It began with the lack of alphabet books in the bookstores that I thought had any kind of intelligence for kids, and I had two small kids. So I bought some little book that for the *A* page it said, 'American, Ants,' and then for the *B* page it said, 'Bird and Bite.' It was all really so stupid. So I added my bit on the American ants, and then did the same with the *B*s and *C*s. And . . . I thought, Oh, maybe I can write my own. . . . Claudia, the illustrator, saw it and she loved it. . . . So she did three pictures, and suddenly it looked like a book, and then we were kind of daydreaming about that."

According to Linscott, ten years before, while Holland was working at *Rolling Stone,* publisher Jann Wenner had recommended that she act as a tour guide for Jackie on a trip to St. Martin. "For two weeks Claudia showed Jackie all around the island, and I think Jackie was charmed by her artwork and said, 'Oh, you must do something with this one day.' Well, ten years went [by] . . . and I said, 'Well, come on. What the hell. Call her up. She might remember you.' Claudia called her one afternoon . . . and left a message, and Jackie called her back that same afternoon and said, 'Bring your project in.' "

Linscott continued, "I didn't know what to expect, having never been published. But I come from a publishing family. My grandfather was a senior editor at Random House, and he used to edit Robert Frost, William Faulkner; he gave Capote his break. . . . His name was Robert Newton Linscott. . . . I didn't have much of an education myself, but I knew what it was to be a good editor, I knew what it meant for an artist in an old-fashioned sense to have somebody . . . nurturing . . . somebody who would develop an artist, stick with them. . . . I remember my father used to say that my grandfather used to treat his authors like his brood and really look after them. . . . That's how she was. She gave us a party at the launch of the first book published. It was a lovely party in a gallery on Madison. . . . And all Claudia's artwork was framed beautifully and hung up on the walls, and there were loads of guests who came, and Jackie came."

Linscott and Holland published their next book with Jackie two years later, and a third book was in the planning stage; but, like many of Jackie's authors, they were "orphaned" after Jackie passed away, and their series discontinued without support from the house. "The second book was . . . about a band, the Worthy Wonders. They travel the world, they get mixed up in the local culture, the language, the food, the dress; so it would be kind of an educational slant with music as a nice way to educate kids about different countries around the world. . . . There's another book, where they do a gig in India, but she died before we could get it published." Linscott added that after Jackie was gone, Doubleday "dropped everybody like a stone."

While working with Linscott and Holland on their first book, Jackie took on a young Texas novelist, Elizabeth Crook, whose book *The Raven's Bride: A Novel of Eliza, Sam Houston's First Wife* had been submitted by Bill Moyers, a family friend of Elizabeth and her father. This book, too, would be published in 1991 by Doubleday. The title alluded to a gift John Kennedy gave his wife early in their relationship, a biography of Sam Houston, *The Raven,* by Marquis James.

The embarkation point for Elizabeth Crook's novel was the mystery of what happened to the 1829 marriage of Sam Houston and Eliza Allen. Houston was then the thirty-six-year-old governor of Tennessee and a close ally of Old Hickory, the incoming President Andrew Jackson. Eliza Allen had just turned twenty and was the daughter of one of the well-off Tennessee Democrats who supported Houston and Jackson. Their marriage lasted eleven weeks. The scandal of its dissolution led to the governor's abrupt resignation and eventually led him to forge westward to Texas, where he would become the first head of the Republic of Texas; after Texas joined the union, Houston served as the state's first senator and later its governor. He was one of those historical figures whom JFK celebrated in *Profiles in Courage,* though Eliza Allen is not mentioned in that book.

Crook's novel had previously been scheduled for publication the year before by Texas Monthly Press, and was in bound galleys ready to be printed. But when the press was bought out by Gulf Publishing of Houston, their fiction titles were abruptly canceled. Crook related the fortunate turn of events that led her to a two-book deal with Jackie. "It wasn't an agent that took *The Raven's Bride* to Mrs. Onassis; it was Bill Moyers, and he was real sweet about it. He asked me how the book was coming along, and I told him it had just basically been canned. He asked if I had a copy, and I said I had one bound galley but it was wrinkled and looked bad. . . . He said to send it to him; he wanted to take it to Jackie Onassis at Doubleday. I told him Doubleday had already rejected the manuscript—twice, actually. . . . But he said he thought she might like it. So I sent him the wrinkled galley, and he sent it to Jackie.

"I was completely dumbfounded that she called directly. I was in London with my parents, pretty depressed about the book, standing in a little kitchen eating pork and beans out of a can. My dad answered the phone. I'll never forget the look on his face when he heard her voice. I have no memory of what I said to her, but I remember she told me she had read the book in two days, that she loved it, and that Doubleday would like to acquire it. In the end, she bought *The Raven's Bride* along with a second book I was writing, which we eventually named *Promised Lands. Raven's Bride* was ready to go to print; she suggested a few minor changes but basically used what Texas Monthly had already produced, including the artwork for the cover."

Crook wrote, in an essay for the *Austin American-Statesman,* "It seemed, in the beginning, that she trusted me before I had earned it. I became skittish. Not knowing what, if anything, I had done to deserve her trust, I feared what I might do by accident to lose it. Not that she confided private thoughts to me. Rather, she trusted me not to ask about them. I never did. I felt that in a small, implicit way I had been enlisted as another guardian of Camelot."

Crook remembered a book party that Bill Moyers and his wife, Judith, gave for her at their home, and a thank-you note that Jackie sent to Judith afterward. "It's one of the most glowing, warm letters I've ever seen, and shows how kind she was to her writers. She says, 'What a joyous, unforgettable party it was. I don't think you will ever make anyone except your family as happy as you made Elizabeth tonight. It would not have been the same in any house but yours and Bill's. . . . All that you have and care about creates a warmth that makes everyone who steps into it so happy, feeling so much better about life, the world, their colleagues, themselves. People go to California and roll on the grass for days to get that feeling (I hear).' "

During one of our phone conversations, Crook told me, "I was always worried to talk to her because I was afraid the conversation might take some turn that would reveal my general ignorance. I grew up in a small town in Texas where we didn't have museums or theater. My family was into books and politics, but not so much into art. I had never been to an opera or professional ballet. So the first time I met Jackie I was concerned. But she talked about horses. I guess she took stock of me and landed on that subject. I had written a lot about horses in my books. I remember feeling immediately comfortable once I was with her."

Crook also speculated about Jackie's interest in her first novel's characterization of Sam Houston's wife. "A couple of people suggested—I can't even remember who, but a couple of people who knew her—suggested that she probably felt some sense of identification with Eliza Allen because Eliza was an extremely private person. Just before she died Eliza asked that all of her papers be destroyed . . . all likenesses, portraits, everything. She made a very strong bid for anonymity right at the end, so there was virtually nothing left of her to go on when I was trying to put this story together. And I think that Jackie was intrigued by that, and respected it."

Jackie later informed booksellers with a promotional letter that *The Raven's Bride* had won critical raves and become a national bestseller. Crook's second novel, *Promised Lands,* published three years later, was also historical fiction, telling the story of the Texas revolution of the 1830s and the events surrounding the infamous Goliad massacre. Texas was then a Mexican colony, but it was experiencing waves of immigration from the east as land-seeking Americans journeyed west in search of their homestead. Slaveholders from southern states streamed into Texas, hoping it would become a proslavery state, while northerners moved there hoping just the opposite. Tennesseans such as Sam Houston and Davy Crockett plotted to bring armies composed of Cherokees and other Native Americans into Texas, where they would expel the Mexicans and grant free land to all who had assisted—thus setting the stage for this imaginative re-creation of history.

If the Alamo massacre was the nineteenth-century equivalent of 9/11 or Pearl Harbor, then this novel depicts the much larger social context during which that infamous act took place. By creating fictional characters with resonance, Crook personalized this chapter of history, well known to Texans but understood much less completely by Americans in other regions. In so doing, she produced a historical novel that continues to live up to that genre's implicit promise—to describe an epoch more accurately by fabulation and storytelling than by massive accumulation of facts and their supporting documentation.

Crook noted that "*Promised Lands* was the one that Jackie really edited for me," and explained that the editorial task involved cutting the manuscript by 178 pages. "There were a lot of subtle things that she did in terms of clarifying characters and scenes and the history and so forth, but I would say that her greatest contribution was in knowing, down to the sentence, what had to go. And that was—that is a gift that she had."

Crook continued, "She was incredibly smart, and yet people are always surprised by the fact that she was a working editor. Maybe it was her demeanor—that she had that soft voice and didn't project herself as a powerhouse. Somehow people seemed to think that she was not a real editor. But I saw her knowledge when she would find minute historical anachronisms or mistakes, and I would think, How could she know that? Then I began to realize, Wow, this woman is brilliant. . . ."

Composing her own affectionate reminiscence, Crook had Jackie's critical notes and letters in front of her, and wrote, "Looking through them now I see the ways she shaped my stories. She knew where the drama was, and where it wasn't. I see the words 'CUT' and 'DELETE' many times, written in capitals and underlined for emphasis. Page 334: 'Cut baby crying.' Page 345: 'Cut chickens.' Page 364: 'Overkill. Can you delete?' On page 101 of one rough draft she has written, 'Much of Kate and William's relationship is cloying. You must eliminate some of her angst, their coy dialogues, her hemming and hawing, etc.' And pages later, 'Too much Coon Dog. Too much Crucita. Don't let yourself go overboard with Coon Dog. There is too much about the stump of his tail.' She was always as attuned to what should be left out as to what should be put in. 'De la Rosa—one could fall in love with him. But when you overdo describing him, it undercuts his power, makes him sound out of Central Casting.' And 'Baby Samuel is so overdescribed it could turn one off babies.'

"It is the affirmations, not the strictures, though, that I remember best. 'You must be glowing,' she wrote in reference to a particularly good review. 'I have never seen anything so superlative in my life.' In one handwritten letter I will always treasure, she wrote, 'I am so impressed by what you have done, I just can't tell you. You have pared down and tightened a sprawling overwritten first draft into an immensely moving novel.'

"Yet with all her kindness, she had no tolerance for sap. 'Don't allow yourself to be repetitious or sentimental,' she wrote in reference to an early draft. 'It back-fires.' Page 56: 'Melodrama; I'd eliminate.' Page 308: 'This is pretty trite. Can you recast?' Page 600: 'Overwritten, overwrought.' She cared that every sentence be correct in language, in emotion, and in detail."

Crook also remembered, "In the beginning, I asked if she would prefer to see each chapter as I wrote it, or several at a time. She chose the latter. 'But if you need some hand holding through the forest,' she wrote, 'you must do whatever makes you feel best.'

"She sent me the first copy of my second novel at about the time she was diagnosed. Right up to the month before she died she continued to champion the book at Doubleday, pressing the editor in chief for more promotion funds. In my last communication from her, in the midst of all the turmoil that goes with the publication of a book, she wrote, 'Stay calm! You have a winner.'

"There were times I disagreed with her suggestions. . . . But she sustained my effort and her editing improved my books in ways impossible to measure. To use a childish image, which she likely would have labeled maudlin and affected, and which in fact is, but to use it anyway because it keeps returning to me in a vivid way, I see her as a fairy godmother. She appeared at a difficult time and gave me what I wanted most—to see my books in print. Then she disappeared."

Crook offered one more telling observation, saying, "When she died, I remember just thinking, I have no one at Doubleday that I feel is going to in any way look after this book or anything." Such concerns were shared by many of Jackie's authors at the time, and they were well founded, especially in terms of the quality of the production and design elements that she demanded as editor.

There were times, of course, when Jackie had no choice but to compromise on those production and design issues; however, when she was no longer on the scene to ensure quality control with her books, constraints would be enforced by management.

Jackie's powers of persuasion again came into play when she pursued the Russian author and playwright Edvard Radzinsky for the translation of his book *The Last Tsar,* about the death of Nicholas II. Thanks to the tolerance marked by the onset of perestroika, Radzinsky was able to draw upon archival and eyewitness accounts heretofore unavailable under the Soviet regime. Scott Moyers said, "She did take on some books nobody believed in that turned out to be phenomenally successful, like *The Last Tsar*. She convinced everyone, they began to see her viewpoint, and went with it."

Before Jackie acquired the book, the author had to convince her that the book was worthy of publication. Radzinsky and his agent met with Jackie in her office in 1991, along with a starstruck translator. Radzinsky told me, "That was a very funny story because we had discussed what to do with book and my literary agent showed it to Jackie before discussion. I just come. At that time I had no English absolutely. And we wait for a translator from our embassy. But unfortunately instead of translating, she saw Jacqueline and was in great shock. I understood that I had to talk myself with no help from her."

Somehow, with his limited English, the author managed to convey his concept of the book to his prospective editor, explaining with a few English phrases that he saw the story in biblical terms. In his view, the czar and his family, with their Russian Orthodox faith, forgave their Bolshevik killers before the firing squad claimed their lives. Of that meeting with Jackie, Radzinsky said, "When I saw her first time, her faith and her life were on her face, I could see. And for me, it was maybe most important moment in my life, because it was not only book for me, it was my mission. . . . I didn't write book about terrible Bolsheviks who execute czar's family, I wrote a book about forgiveness, about people before their deaths who were able to forgive. When I explained to her, she understood. It's this idea, I think, she felt it, like religious moment. And when I told that the book would be not about the execution of the Romanovs, but about forgiveness of the Romanovs before their deaths, I think in this moment she decided to be editor and to publish this book. She told my agent, 'I like this idea about forgiveness.'"

Radzinsky also appreciated the fact that the story of the Romanovs and their tragic end must have called to mind Jackie's own history, though out of consideration for her feelings, he never brought up the subject of the JFK assassination. He told PBS writer Karen Kelleher in 1999, "When my literary agent told me she was interested in the book, I understood immediately. I understood because assassination of Kennedy was one of the top mysteries of this century. And assassination of the czar's family continued to be top mystery of the century too."

Radzinsky told PBS that he appreciated Jackie's insistence on the selection of a cover photograph of the czar, sitting dejectedly on a tree stump in the country with armed guards over his shoulder. "The book was printed in twenty countries, I saw endless covers, but she did the best. Why? You see this last czar, this unhappy Nicholas who sits with such sad face, but in his face, I read, what to do? We have today the same collapse of former empire, and we have today the same question, what to do?"

Radzinsky worked with translator Marian Schwartz, whose work Jackie was already familiar with since Schwartz had translated Berberova's books, though they had never met. Schwartz said, "One of the things that really amazed me about her was she was doing line editing. After I turned in the manuscript and was visiting family in New York she called me on Saturday night. Wasn't she supposed to be out gallivanting? No, she was calling about very specific details. She had sent the author to Texas about two months into the project—he spent ten days with me—to recast the book for the American audience, and she had a very close eye on the text.

"She made major investments in this book: editorially, with her own line editing; investing in sending him to Texas; and also the tremendous thought she put into the timing of publication. With respect to the work I did with Radzinsky, the English edition is so different from the Russian original that other translations are done from my translation. To start with, the first long section in Russian was a mind-numbing pilgrimage through Russian history till you get to the last Romanovs. When Radzinsky came down here he said, 'Well, what do you think of the introduction?' I said, 'Well, actually, I don't think it works at all.' Radzinsky is a playwright and so is used to revising for different audiences. His immediate reply was to start with something completely different. And before I knew it, the first forty pages were gone."

Schwartz also shared her memory of meeting Jackie in person. "I was invited for tea at her apartment. I hadn't know her that long, just since the project began. We had worked over the phone intensively for all those months, though. Of course, my mother wanted to know what I was going to wear, but I didn't care what I wore. I had no idea what I was going to wear. Obviously nothing unusual. Whatever translators wear. I didn't think Onassis cared what I wore either, to be honest. It was tea in the afternoon. I wasn't going in a ball gown just to meet Jackie Onassis.

"I arrived wearing flannel slacks and a sweater. I was led into the library to wait for her. . . . There was a big square coffee table covered with books—in fact there were books everywhere, not just on top of shelves and tables, but under the tables. The way books are when people really like books. They're not stashing them; they actually can't bear to put them away. And when she came in, I was looking at a book, and she proceeded to tell me all about that book. When the tea tray was brought out, she had to even out the stacks of books so the tray wouldn't fall over. That was charming."

When Jackie undertook *The Last Tsar*, the life and death of Nicholas II was already an oft-told story from which Robert K. Massie created a bestseller in 1969 with his *Nicholas and Alexandra*. Speculation about the possible survival of one of the czar's daughters, Anastasia, and the grisly details of the family's execution, kept the story alive, with Ingrid Bergman playing Anastasia in a full-blown Hollywood spectacle. How could this subject sustain yet another examination by Edvard Radzinsky, an author who was little known in America except for a few translated plays?

The answer lies in the chaos that the Soviet Union underwent during the decade of its slow collapse. Radzinsky, a czarist sympathizer, began getting mysterious calls and letters from old men and women who claimed to have been on the scene in Ekaterinburg in the summer of 1917, when the Romanov family was finally put to death. After unearthing a report by the commander of the firing squad, he later told *The New York Times*, "The report was so terrible, so chilling, so horrible, that at first I didn't want to publish it."

This sprawling subject required deft handling by both Schwartz as translator and Jackie as editor. They had to devise a format that would most clearly present not only the author's complicated feelings about these moments of history but also the reminiscences of the welter of witnesses who had sprung forth. The latter task was especially challenging, because there were numerous reasons to embellish or downplay the gruesome details of the Romanovs' last days. These were witnesses who had allegedly experienced something at the onset of adulthood that they were now trying to recall as they approached senescence.

Since there were many anecdotes in the book, and since all involved difficult Russian names for the average American reader to absorb, clarity and order of presentation were critical. And under Jackie's direction, the book clarifies the murky details of the Russian Revolution and the subsequent cataclysm of civil war, making them more comprehensible and accessible to the English-speaking world.

Looking back five years after the book was published, Bruce Tracy, who as Jackie's assistant had a desk in the hallway outside her office, recalled, "In the summer of 1992, *The Last Tsar* was about to come out, and suddenly, I had this great opportunity to go to London for a week, basically for the cost of airfare. If I went, however, I would miss this big book party at the Russian Tea Room. I had been working with Jackie on this book, and I didn't want to seem cavalier. So I went in to talk to her, apologetically saying, 'I just got this chance to go to Europe, and I've never been.' She looked at me like I had two heads. 'Of course, you go,' she said. 'Life comes first.' "

The Last Tsar spent more than three months on the *New York Times* bestseller list, and Jackie had plans to follow up with Radzinsky's biography of Stalin, though she was to be interrupted by her illness. The author again had a concept that appealed to his editor: He intended to place his investigative emphasis on the psychology of the Russian leader rather than dwelling on Stalin's crimes and crafting a political portrait.

"When I told her I will write about Stalin, she thought it's impossible because there is no poetry in the subject," Radzinsky told me. "I explained that unfortunately this devil Stalin was poet in his views. Bad poetry, but it was poetry. He had poetry in his life—very black poetry. And I told Jackie that the story, it's not about monster. It's the story about how the man became monster. The man who was real revolutionary and how all dreams . . . changed for the only dream of dictatorship. But she absolutely understood my idea to write about Stalin . . . like a human being . . . not only about nonstop monster. . . . She told me it's really very important because it's big lesson of future, his life."

Radzinsky told Jackie that Stalin kept books in his library written by former comrades like Leon Trotsky and various artists and writers whom he had murdered over the years. The author salvaged the remains of Stalin's library and later informed Jackie that he had made an astonishing discovery—that Stalin "continued to have conversations with his victims, with his notes in their books." The book would be entitled *Stalin: The First In-depth Biography Based on Explosive New Documents from Russia's Secret Archives.* The hype of the subtitle doesn't sound like Jackie, and the book's original title was more elegantly posed as *The Three Stalins.* But there were a number of other changes that would be imposed on the book by Doubleday in Jackie's absence.

Jackie had intended to carry out this project by duplicating the editorial and production process that had made *The Last Tsar* such a success, again employing Marian Schwartz as translator. According to Schwartz, "Jackie had always said, 'When we do the next book, I'll get you a better contract.'

Working with her, she would make these promises, and I would think and then I would call Scott Moyers, and I would say, 'Can I get this in writing?' And he'd say, 'There's no need. She'll do it.' And of course she always did. Whatever she promised, she always did it. Except that she died and her promises were not in writing."

Schwartz also lamented the fate of *Stalin* as the book played out under the changed circumstances. "I think as far as her ability as a text editor, she showed me how to make things pop, how to bring things out. A lot of people have shown me different ways to do that, but she really made things shine. One testimony to that is that none of Radzinsky's subsequent books did as well as the first. In fact the review for the next one, on Stalin, said something to the effect of, 'What happened?' Because nobody edited the book. They translated it. Nobody did what she did. Nobody gave it that sheen."

The Last Tsar reads and is carefully paced like a well-plotted murder mystery. *Stalin,* on the other hand, lacked the organizing intelligence that marked Radzinsky's earlier investigation, leaving the reader adrift in a Sargasso Sea of details, many of questionable relevance. Jackie sensed the potential of *Stalin,* and for an author like Radzinsky, the access to previously taboo files was the opportunity of a lifetime. So it is disappointing that this biography is slowed down by the weight of its own sources. It is as large as the Stalin biographies by Robert Service and Simon Sebag Montefiore, but lacks the novelist's touch that both those books possess; nor did it convey the incandescent moral probity of Orlando Figes's *The Whisperers* or Martin Amis's *Koba the Dread.*

Without Jackie to follow through with the editing and without Schwartz as translator, *Stalin* was one of those strange cases where more proved less. Radzinsky remembered discussing his work at a final meeting with Jackie, when she told him, "That's great! That image." He heard the news of her death months later when he was visiting Poland, where *The Last Tsar* was being published. He later expressed his sense of loss, saying cryptically, "For me, she did not die. She went out of the room, and then very soon she came back [in spirit]."

9

All Will Be Well

Even in her last years, there was no letup from the crazies who tried to penetrate Jackie's office sanctum at Doubleday, whether in person, by mail, or by phone. Scott Moyers remembered, "Her real direct phone line was 9747, and 9728 was the line to which the switchboard would transfer all incoming calls asking for Mrs. Onassis. I called that the kook line. You had to steel yourself for anything when it rang—UFO reports, conspiracy theorists, troubled people spewing out surrealism. And you'd get weird things in the mail—adult videos, women from Brazil proposing marriage to her son. It wasn't always funny. Someone once sent a gun. But she never had to take those calls, or open those letters."

I remember the gun incident, because Gelsey Kirkland and I had lunch with Jackie that same week and we had read about it in the press. The weapon, a Smith & Wesson .38, arrived in a package with forty rounds of ammunition and a letter asking Jackie to support the sender's upcoming presidential campaign. FBI agents later apprehended the culprit in California and described him as mentally unbalanced. At our lunch, I asked Jackie if such incidents didn't give her second thoughts about running around the city without protection. She told us, "Oh no, I couldn't live that way. I'd be paralyzed."

The invasions of Jackie's privacy by mercenary photographers continued during her final years, but she handled them with a sense of humor. Once, while she was swimming with Carly Simon during a Vineyard getaway, helicopters circled over their heads, and Jackie quipped impishly to Carly, "They must know you're here!"

Meanwhile, except for pictures snapped in front of her building, the sanctity of Jackie's Fifth Avenue apartment was for the most part respected. Tour bus guides sometimes deliberately pointed out the wrong building to their ogling passengers. The apartment itself had been decorated and redecorated over the years. Mark Hampton, one of the designers who also worked on her Vineyard home, was widely acknowledged as a scholar and historian of interior design, as well as a renowned designer. His other clients included Pamela Harriman, Brooke Astor, Henry Kravis, Mike Wallace, Lauder, the Henry Kissingers, and the Carter Burdens. Hampton was a friend of Jackie's, and knowing of his interest in the evolution of the field, she enlisted him for a book. In an obituary that appeared in *The Washington Post* on July 30, 1998, Jura Koncius wrote, "Mark Hampton, the interior designer who died last week in New York, left a chapter unwritten in his 1992 book, *Legendary Decorators of the Twentieth Century*. It was the one on Hampton himself."

Hampton's widow, Duane, an author, editor, and former trustee of the Municipal Art Society, told me that she and her husband had become friends of Jackie's through her sister, Lee. "In the whirlwind years of the seventies and eighties in New York, I think it was often the case that you weren't able to pinpoint precisely when you met people—so many were in the mix. I don't know exactly when we met Jackie, maybe through Brendan Gill at the Municipal Art Society? Maybe through Louis Auchincloss? But we got to know her well because of Lee Radziwill, who had been a good friend since the mid-nineteen-seventies. . . .

"When Lee was thinking of marrying someone her sister had never met, Jackie asked her to bring him to dinner at her apartment. Mark and I got a quick SOS from Lee to please join the party, she needed some friends to round out the company (Mark, a chatterbox, could be counted on to keep the conversation flowing). So there were five of us around Jackie's table. Perhaps the prospective suitor didn't pass muster since the marriage never happened, but as an unforeseen circumstance of the evening, Mark and Jackie began a friendship."

While they had previously had discussions about working together on a book, Mark Hampton formally proposed *Legendary Decorators of the Twentieth Century* to Jackie almost five years before it was published. In a letter to the decorator dated December 16, 1987, Jackie wrote, "I am delighted by your letter and its beautiful calligraphy. *Of course*—the book you suggest would be absolutely wonderful to do with you—only you could do it." Hampton later credited Jackie for suggesting the title. "It was her idea. She said 'legendary' was a word that always catches people's eyes on shelves in bookstores."

Between his decorating schedule and personal life, Hampton had some difficulty meeting chapter deadlines, and Duane recalled Jackie phoning to check on his progress. Duane told me, "I would get calls, usually early in the morning, too early, but not rudely early, and this little whispery voice would say, 'Duane, could you tell Mark to please hurry on that chapter?' Or just, 'Remind him it's due.' That sort of thing . . . gentle prodding."

Hampton gave an interview about the experience of working with Jackie to *The Washington Post* after her death. He recalled that they decided together which decorators would be included in the book. He said, "She knew so many of them personally. Her favorites were Billy Baldwin and John Fowler. And she adored Stéphane Boudin in Paris. She shared so many stories about them with me." The insular world of these decorators and the upper-crust families toward whom they tailored their services is one that Jackie had known since she was a child.

In this book of twenty-two decorator profiles, Hampton included his own mentors: David Hicks of London; Mrs. Henry Parish II, and Eleanor McMillen Brown. He illuminated their styles with his own eye-pleasing watercolors, often illustrating work done in one particular room, most frequently a den or gathering room. This book collects an important area of artistic history that is easy to overlook, because interior decorating is a most personal kind of art, and the people living in these opulent homes are not always eager to show off their private spaces. Most of Hampton's profiles were devoted to decorators from the first half of the century. He concentrated on traditionalists, not the paradigm-breaking moderns.

Hampton was one of those for whom Jackie sometimes included sketches with her letters. Needling her author about a June 1991 deadline, she sent a letter at the beginning of May with a sketched flower and the caption, "No lilies of the valley for you unless you deliver!" She provided him with copious notes on each chapter and each decorator. In one of her letters, she noted after reviewing the manuscript, "Albert Hadley is fascinating—and the way you present his contribution most illuminating. But I found it a bit wordy and repetitious in spots. The extra phrases are underbrush which prevents one from seeing the trees. So I pruned here, there. Change what you don't like." She tacked on a postscript on Boudin, who, at her invitation, had played a leading role in the renovation of the White House: "No one who knew or worked with Boudin didn't love him . . ."

On the back jacket of the published book is a portrait of Hampton rendered by Henry Koehler, an artist whom Jackie and Hampton had known for years, and who was a Yale classmate and friend of Tom Guinzburg's. Based in Southampton, Koehler was and still is known as a master of sport and equestrian subjects. Jackie had acquired a number of his paintings over the years. Her social interconnections were so numerous that one is frequently struck by the uncanny truth of the six degrees of separation phenomenon. Koehler told me, "My late wife [Audrey Carey Koehler] was a decorator, and Mark was a great pal of both of us, as was Jackie. Nancy Tuckerman, who was her roommate in school and lifelong friend and official secretary, was my wife's cousin, so that was another attachment. Jackie had a painting of mine very early of a horse show, and three pictures of sailing, which is another subject I used to do. One of them was a present long, long ago from the three Kennedy sisters to the three Kennedy brothers, and it was the little boat that they grew up on in Hyannis Port. And in each of the paintings was the Kennedy brother with his wife on the boat."

In September 1992, the same month that Mark Hampton's book came out, Jackie published a political novel, *Protect and Defend,* written by another old friend, Jack Valenti, the longtime head of the Motion Picture Association of America. Back in 1963, his advertizing agency, Weekley and Valenti, handled some of the press relations during JFK's visit to Dallas. As a result, Valenti was in the famous photograph with Jackie as witness to Lyndon Johnson's swearing in ceremony aboard *Air Force One.* Valenti subsequently served as special assistant to President Johnson.

In his memoir, *This Time, This Place,* Valenti explained that the premise of his book involved a vice president who entered the primaries to run against an incumbent president. The title of the novel derived from the presidential oath of office. According to Valenti, after he started writing the book, a friend of his daughter's, Helen Bartlett, suggested that he allow her to submit part of the manuscript to Jackie. Bartlett was the goddaughter of JFK, and her parents, Charles and Martha Barlett, had first introduced Jackie to Jack at a dinner at their home after Kennedy was elected to Congress.

Valenti recollected in his memoir that two months after his manuscript was submitted, he had given up hope of ever hearing from Jackie, until one day his phone rang. "In an instant, I recognized the soft feathery voice. 'Jack, this is Jackie. I read the chapters of your new book, and I want to publish it.' I damn near fainted." Valenti's son, John, remembered hearing his father tell that story. "My father," said John, "he and many of his friends and colleagues were all famous people either in the arts, in the movie business, or in the corporate world. But I think that as long as I knew him, he was just enraptured by Ms. Onassis. I can recall him telling me one time, 'John, you're not going to believe what happened to me to-day.' I said, 'What, Daddy? What went on?' And he said, 'Well, I got a call from Jackie Onassis today.' He said, 'My office gets calls from world-famous people, and they just patch them through, but when Jackie Onassis called, my secretary, I thought she was just going to fall all over herself.' I can remember my dad imitating her [Jackie], and he said she would talk in this lovely voice. "Jaaaack? It's Jackie calling, how are you?' Then she goes, 'I love your book.' My father said, 'John, I thought I just had died and gone to heaven right there.' "

Describing his work with Jackie, Valenti wrote, "We talked numerous times on the phone and in person in her office as she outlined ideas for improving the text. As we grew to know each other better, I felt increasingly comfortable in her presence. She wrote me frequently, as I did her. . . . Oddly, or maybe not so oddly, her words on paper sounded exactly like she talked, in softly expressed exclamatory sentences. She was precise in her editing suggestions, and she understood with clarity the insecurity of first novelists (or at least this one)."

Valenti also recounted a lunch that he had with Jackie in 1992 at Manhattan's Raphael. At one point, Jackie brought up her past, saying, "Jack, you mentioned Mrs. Johnson. . . . She and Lyndon were so dear to me. They allowed me to stay in the White House for eleven days without a single word of discontent. Such a long time, too long. I read recently that Mrs. Roosevelt was gone from her private quarters within forty-eight hours of the death of her husband."

Shaye Areheart was also at that lunch with Jackie and Valenti, and it was she who would later publish Valenti's memoir at her Random House imprint, Harmony Books. (Areheart also had an imprint in her name, until it was dissolved in 2010.) Valenti recalled running into Areheart in Washington, D.C., in 2004: "As Shaye and I chatted, I mentioned the lunch at Raphael. 'Oh yes,' she said, 'I remember it very well. It was the first and only time I ever heard Mrs. Onassis speak about the time of the assassination. . . . She was so fond of you, Jack. The fact that she wanted to edit your book ought to tell you that.' "

Valenti's book is somewhat dated now and seems rather tame in light of more recent potboilers both in fiction and in real life. The president in the novel is reminiscent of LBJ, saddled with reelection woes because of an unpopular foreign policy and constantly rising inflation. A centrist Democrat, the president appears to be the sure loser to a rising Republican governor, a result that the vice president deems unacceptable, leading him to hatch a plan to challenge his boss in the upcoming Democratic primaries. All this is realistic and plausible, but Valenti's point is both familiar and simplistic, that political ambition can be a deadly virus. The vice president strikes a deal with foreign intelligence operatives to "expose" his boss's secret plan to achieve a rapprochement with the military junta that has just taken over the leadership of China. Of course, events spiral out of control and the nation's political establishment becomes caught up in a national security crisis of epic proportions.

This might have made for a cracking good read, except for the fact that the storyline became overly complicated. However, since all the action takes place either in the halls of government or the salons of Georgetown, Valenti used some of his insider knowledge to offer compelling descriptions of the physical layout and history of the White House, and the effect that elite social gatherings may have on policy.

Looking back after Jackie's death, Valenti would lament the fact that he had never expressed to Jackie his great affection for her. While hoping that she knew how he felt about her, he wrote, "Most of all, I still have my memories of a woman who while she lived truly owned the heart of the world. She still does mine."

While working on Valenti's novel, Jackie again turned to one of her allies in the preservation moment, David Garrard Lowe, an activist with the Municipal Art Society and later president of the Beaux Arts Alliance, a not-for-profit organization that celebrates the cultural links between the United States and France. Lowe's book, *Stanford White's New York*, would be published in the summer of 1992. Lowe was founder and director of the gallery of the New York School of Interior Design, where, in 1987, he had mounted a highly praised exhibit on Stanford White that had caught Jackie's attention.

At his Beaux Arts office, located in the parish house of a little church on New York's Upper East Side, Lowe told me, "She knew my writing, particularly *Lost Chicago,* which had been selling well for years. . . . Of course, there had been other books done on Stanford White, but mine was unique because it focused exclusively on New York. She was the ideal editor for the project because she was so New York and knew so much about the city. When I talked to her or asked her questions, she understood what I was talking about, whether it was Augustus Saint-Gaudens's *Diana* atop White's Madison Square Garden or the history of the Colony Club. . . .

"We first met fighting to save St. Bartholomew's Church on Park Avenue. . . . I vividly remember a bitterly cold night when those protesting the threat to the church and its community house, led by Mrs. O.'s close friend, Brendan Gill, the distinguished theater critic of *The New Yorker*, gathered with our candles before the church's matchless portal, designed by White. It was a kind of preservationist prayer meeting and it became a bond between Mrs. O. and me. . . .

"I had heard in the weirdest way that she liked my manuscript. I had a leak in the ceiling of my top-floor apartment on East Seventy-ninth Street, and I was waiting for the plumber to return my telephone call. The telephone rang, and I quickly blurted out, 'It's about time!' A soft, almost girlish voice asked, 'David?' There was a pause during which I was speechless. 'I love the book,' [she said.] I knew she had been reading it because she had just flown back from Martha's Vineyard and a friend of mine who was on the plane spotted her with the manuscript and had telephoned me. I never expected that Mrs. O. would be in touch with me so quickly. So there I was shouting, 'It's about time!' to one of the most famous people in the world. We set up a meeting in September [1991], but before she hung up, Mrs. O. whispered, 'David.' 'Yes.' 'I hope the next time you'll use your nice voice.'

"We always got along well, except if something went wrong when we were working on layouts at the Doubleday offices. . . . There was an art director with whom I did not always see eye to eye. I had been an editor at *American Heritage* for a long time, so I had a quite lot of experience in dealing with illustrations, as had [my assistant,] Sally Forbes. . . . One day I was quite unhappy about the relationship of some of the pictures to the text, and Sally agreed with me. So I regret to say that I lost my cool: 'I don't know whether or not I want this book to be published by Doubleday!' I announced, and stalked out of the conference room. Not long after I got home, the phone rang. 'David?' It was Mrs. O.'s beguiling voice. 'Don't shoot yourself in the foot.'

"Treasuring historic photographs as I did, it was wonderful to work with someone who appreciated them. She chose the cover of the book, a stunning photograph of the spectacular domed ceiling of the reading room of White's Gould Library on the old campus of New York University in the Bronx. . . . Mrs. O. had a great eye. . . .

"Our relationship was intricately layered. She said one time: 'This is our dirty little secret.' This secret had nothing to do with the making of books. I'm a traditionalist. I almost always wear a coat and tie and I am a member of this singular little Episcopal Church on the Upper East Side which she knew about, very high-culture, with incense and bells and lots of Latin. She approved of this historic ritual, this, as it were, old-fashioned Catholicism. . . . Thus, we had this secret bond of cultural conservatism. I always called her Mrs. Onassis, and later, when I got to know her better, Mrs. O. One day she said, 'I really appreciate that. You know, there are secretaries at Doubleday who call me Jackie.'

"Another element of 'our dirty little secret' was our fathers. Both loved horses—my father owned and trained Thoroughbreds . . . lived rather grandly, and had a minimum of practicality when it came to financial things. In their peculiar ways they were good fathers. Both Mrs. O. and I had gone away to boarding school—I to a somewhat eccentric Southern military academy and Mrs. O. to Farmington. Sometimes we would talk about our youth. . . . [She said], 'David, did you ever wonder if your father was paying the tuition?' I said, 'Yes!' She said, 'So did I.' "

Lowe continued, "For both Mrs. O. and for me, Paris was, in the words of Hemingway, 'a moveable feast.' . . . One August when I was writing the book, I rented a small but charming apartment on the rue Cassette in Paris. It faced the sublime towers of Saint Sulpice and was near the Luxembourg Gardens. . . . 'Show me the pictures that you found in Paris,' she queried excitedly when I returned to New York. We did an entire chapter on Paris in 1879, the first time White was there. She loved to bring the Parisian world into the book."

Before Frank Lloyd Wright, Stanford White was America's premier celebrity architect, born before the Civil War in the slums of New York's East Village, and immortalized by E. L. Doctorow in *Ragtime* (played with gusto by Norman Mailer in the film version). When not acting the bon vivant, Stanford White was busy creating buildings that enthralled his Manhattan patrons. He designed Judson Memorial Church, the Washington Square Arch, the Metropolitan and Players clubs, and a series of mansions that were owned by the Whitneys, the Vanderbilts, the Pulitzers, and the Stuyvesant Fishs. White's creations were heavily influenced by his trips to Europe, and in his book, Lowe shows readers period photographs of the Luxembourg Gardens, the Trocadero Palace, and the cathedrals at Notre-Dame and Saint-Sulpice, facilitating comparison with White's later work. Jackie, fully cognizant of Europe's architectural history and the relentless growth of Manhattan, saw this book as a tribute to a bygone era, one that valued design and appearance more than mere function.

The author remembered a book party that brought a chilling reminder of Jackie's past. "We had a rather grand publishing party at the Municipal Art Society in the old Villard Houses on Madison Avenue. Of course, Jackie was there. I had invited two grandsons of Stanford White, Peter and Robert. When I told her who Robert was, she immediately asked him,

'How did your father turn out?' She was referring to Lawrence Grant White, the son of Stanford White, who had been murdered in 1906. She was obviously thinking of John-John [and his father]. Until that moment I had never had a glimmer of awareness of the parallels. And thank God I hadn't. Their deaths, in a way, so similar, so unexpected, you know, Stanford White, shot three times by the obsessed Harry K. Thaw, while he watched a performance on the roof garden of Madison Square Garden. It was as unexpected, as unlikely as Dallas was unexpected, unlikely.

"In conjunction with the party, we mounted a really splendid exhibit of images from *Stanford White's New York* in the galleries of the Municipal Art Society. Shortly before the party, Mrs. O. said to me, 'I'd like to read from our book. You write so beautifully.' I was flattered and pleased. She was not the sort of person who often read in public. In fact, I believe this was the only time she did read from a book that she had edited. I can see her now, in the corner of the big exhibition room, exquisitely dressed as always, surrounded by those striking images of New York. . . . There was a small platform and a microphone and it is not too much to say that everyone was breathless. And, of course, she read beautifully."

Jackie was painfully aware that the design and production quality of her books were in jeopardy, with the budgetary ax at Doubleday wielded by in-house marketing and managerial CYA bureaucrats rather than book lovers, much less those publishers of yore who used to be called "gentlemen." The Stanford White book was one of those that took a hit in terms of budget. Lowe explained, "They had to, for financial reasons, cut down the trim size of the book about an inch all around, and I was, naturally, very unhappy about it. Such a reduction at the last minute is fairly unusual. I sense that Doubleday was going through a funny period."

Lowe knew what some of Jackie's other authors also knew. "Someone had offered Jackie her own imprint in another house. She said something to me—she didn't go into detail, but she said, 'Do you think if I get an imprint, would it be just for my name?' And I said, 'There are two answers: one, your name; but two, you have a record now in publishing quality books, and particularly illustrated books.' She didn't want her name just to be used. And I know that she was thinking of it seriously, and I know she wasn't one hundred percent happy. She didn't go into that, but I could tell because she called me about the trim size and was very embarrassed. It's the only time I ever heard that in her voice.

"After her death, Louis Auchincloss, who was an old dear friend of mine, and I used to talk about that. I said, 'When she'd been offered this imprint, she had a little doubt. I understand that.' But, he said, 'She shouldn't have.' And she talked to him about it, I think. They were quite close."

In 1993, Jackie told John F. Baker of *Publishers Weekly,* "I love my colleagues, I love Doubleday," and Steve Rubin chimed in, "I don't know what we'd do without her." But Alberto Vitale, who was then running Random House for Bertelsmann, told me, "She wanted to come to Random House, and I wanted her to come to Random House, but for many reasons that were not clear to me at the time but became clearer later on, obviously relating to her health, a change was not something she wanted to do at that time."

I suggested to Vitale another reason Jackie may have chosen not to change houses: I had heard, from one of Doubleday's former editors who had moved over to Random House, that Jackie had been misled into thinking that there would be the kind of scandalous publicity she had experienced when she left Viking. Of course, the prospect of publicity and seeing her name in the press again would have given Jackie pause. Vitale said, "There would have been no scandal whatsoever if she had come to Random House. Actually, there would have been tremendous positive community for her, you know. I think her decision was personal."

In an e-mail, Vitale later added, "Also, I am sure that Doubleday did all they HAD to do to retain her. She was very good and a major asset. She actually never turned me down, as we did not make her a formal offer. But our conversations were very cordial, and she implied that at that time she did not want to make a change. You realize that any such change would have required a tremendous amount of work and stress. We continued to stay in touch until she left Doubleday probably to take care of her health. I do not think that Steve Rubin misled her, as he is a very honest straight shooter! I, however, still think that she should have come to RH, and I am glad to hear that so many people that I highly regard thought so, too. By the way, I do not believe that her own imprint would have been necessarily in her name, for obvious reasons."

Vitale meant that she would not use her name to sell books and promote an imprint. There would be no Jacqueline Onassis Books. Apparently, the possibility of changing houses was not something that Jackie discussed with her colleagues in-house, if only as a matter of discretion. Neither Bruce Tracy nor Scott Moyers ever heard that Jackie had considered such a move. And Steve Rubin informed me by e-mail, "There is no doubt in my mind that my very good friend Alberto Vitale approached her, but my guess is that she never considered it seriously enough for her to broach it with me." Of course, such a house change would have been an enormous disruption for Jackie, however tempting it might have been.

During her last year, Jackie continued to develop new projects, including an idea for another book by David Garrard Lowe. "When she first became ill we were talking of another book. . . . I talked to her, and I had to be very straightforward. I said, 'Are you going to be around?' I meant, are you going to be at Doubleday? She said, 'Of course!' The idea of her dying didn't even enter my mind, because you don't want to have an editor sign a book contract with you and then leave, because it's an orphan."

After Jackie was gone, Lowe wasn't given the opportunity to publish any more books with Doubleday, but went elsewhere with an idea that Jackie had encouraged. He said, "We kept in communication, and my agent Carl [Brandt] talked to her, and we had a good book idea, which later became *Art Deco New York,* which was published by Watson-Guptill. . . . [That book] came out fine, but it would have been wonderful to work with her on it."

Jackie managed to publish three more books in 1993, including another excursion into the dance world: Judith Jamison's memoir, *Dancing Spirit.* Jamison had been a principal dancer with the Alvin Ailey American Dance Theater and became its artistic director after Ailey passed away in 1989. She was arguably the most celebrated African-American dancer of all time, mastering ballet, modern dance, and the Broadway stage.

Jackie had followed Jamison's career, and I interviewed Jamison during her twentieth anniversary season as artistic director, in 2009. She told me that Jackie used to watch classes. "I remember her coming to the old school on Sixty-first Street. And she used to just come in unannounced. We knew she was going to come. I used to say, 'Oh, does she need an escort from the front door?' And she would float right through. No one would bother her. We were all with our mouths hanging open. She'd come to the office and sit down and just be as relaxed as everyone else."

In *Dancing Spirit,* Jamison, who hails from Philadelphia, described her training, crediting all of her teachers and coaches in meticulous detail, her interpretive approaches to particular roles, and her tours around the world with the Ailey troupe. She told me she dictated much of the story by phone to writer Howard Kaplan while she was traveling with the company. In the book, she proudly related how she discovered the roots of dance in the indigenous performances she witnessed in Ghana and Kenya, South Africa and Senegal. She was more reticent about revealing her personal life in the book.

Jamison also told me that Jackie had not asked her for a tell-all book, and that she would not have agreed to write that kind of book. "I had no intention of going through a catharsis. It was not a cathartic experience for me. Maybe now that I'm older I can have a cathartic experience. This for me was nobody's business but my own, and that's what she agreed with. So the kind of book that I wanted to write was inspiring for young people."

That same year, with *Taming the Storm,* Jackie published a biography of Frank Johnson, the federal judge who, according to Bill Moyers, "altered forever the face of the South" with his rulings during the civil rights struggle. The author of the book was was a young journalist, Jack Bass, who had previously written *Unlikely Heroes,* a book about southern judges and their role in the implementation of the historic *Brown v. Board of Education* decision. Bass had interviewed Johnson for that book and knew that he had been a law school buddy of the controversial Alabama governor George Wallace, and that the two had even double-dated on occasion before becoming adversaries later in life. Bass informed me that he had proposed the Johnson book to his previous editor, Alice Mayhew at Simon & Schuster, who "expressed interest in the book, but saw it sort of as a regional book."

Jackie had a grander vision of this biography, as well as a personal interest in the story that again traced back to her White House years. The author told me that he was intrigued by Jackie's interest in Judge Johnson, who had been the subject of a two-part *Bill Moyers Journal* broadcast that aired in 1980. Bass said, "When the book was finished and getting ready to go into print—I'd met her once at the beginning of the process—I wanted to come up and talk about promotion. She said, 'Well, you're welcome to come, but we can't pay for it'—I believe that was probably the way it was expressed. When I went up there on my own to discuss the promotion, my reward was she was going to take me to "21" for lunch. And I was curious a little bit about how she got interested in Johnson. I think I asked my agent, who was a lawyer who had worked for Robert Kennedy in the Justice Department. He said, 'Well, why don't you just ask her?' So I did. I asked her, 'How did you get interested in Judge Johnson?' And she looked as though no one's ever asked her that question before. And she paused, reflected just a moment, and said, 'I guess it goes back to hearing Jack and Bobby talk about him.'"

The author, who is now writing a book on the Supreme Court's role in ending Reconstruction, was particularly grateful that Jackie had not cut a lengthy exposition about Robert Kennedy's actions when Martin Luther King Jr. was arrested in Decatur, Georgia, in October 1960. "The story that's found in all the Kennedy assistants books, Schlesinger and all the rest of them, is about how Bobby Kennedy got King out of jail. What set everything in motion was Jack Kennedy's early morning call to Georgia's Democratic governor Ernest Vandiver. Campaign manager Bobby Kennedy's put-up story was a tactical political ploy simultaneously aimed at protecting his brother from the wrath of contemporary southern white voters and energizing black voters." Jackie did not have any objections to

Bass reporting that aspect of Kennedy history, and the book won the 1994 Robert Kennedy Book Award, with Schlesinger one of the judges.

Also in 1993, Jackie published *Poet and Dancer,* a novel by Ruth Prawer Jhabvala, who, at the time, was best known as an Oscar-winning screenwriter on Merchant-Ivory film productions, mostly British period pieces like *A Room with a View* (1985), *Howards End* (1992), and *The Remains of the Day* (1993), and for her previous novels, which connect the otherworldliness of modern India with the experience of Indians when they travel or settle in the urban Western world. *Three Continents* and *Heat and Dust* are books that might make one believe that Jhabvala is Indian, a precursor of Salman Rushdie and Arundhati Roy. But she is not. Her background is German-Jewish; her family fled the Nazis in 1939 and immigrated to England. She later married a Parsi Indian and moved to New Delhi as a young bride. After two and a half decades, she moved again, to New York City.

Poet and Dancer was the first of her novels that was not intimately concerned with the issues that immigrants in a strange country often face. It described a different kind of pathology—the pathology of family. The novel is bleak in a way that the author's other works are not, but it is a bleakness that seems to rise from her vision of a detached and alienated city like New York. She writes as if to suggest in India among poor people, there is humor, warmth, and dignity; in Manhattan among the strivers, there are only family secrets and the intemperate behaviors caused by the material gods that seem to possess those who inhabit the Upper East Side. Jackie might have recognized some of her neighbors in this book.

In May 2009 Jhabvala wrote me a letter about her collaboration with Jackie, saying: "Unfortunately, I was with her for only one book, and by the time my next novel was ready, she had left us. My experience with her really was a dream. There was the fact of her *standing*. Since she personally, and tirelessly, approached everyone who could be useful in promoting her chosen book, everyone was of course happy to oblige her. But that was only the extraneous aspect of her work as an editor. I'm sure she wouldn't have taken on anything that she herself didn't deeply care for, and consequently her commitment was total: it was *her* book and *her* author. I always felt that for her the two were indissolubly entwined, and that her love and care for the book also embraced its author.

"There were so many dazzling personal touches. On the morning of publication day, a wonderful bouquet of flowers arrived to greet you; and later that day a *leather-bound* edition of the book itself. And everything accompanied by a handwritten note, full of affection. She herself had chosen every detail of the publication, including of course the jacket art—in my case, it was one of my husband's watercolors, which she had gone downtown with him to choose in his gallery. The result was the most beautiful cover I've ever had, and [it] has remained so.

"Also, what I appreciate very much was that for her the book's worth was intrinsic, essential, and completely unrelated to sales figures. Whatever its fate in the literary and commercial marketplace, her faith in it and in its author—and as I said, for her they were one entity—remained as steady and pure as on that first day when she had chosen us."

In May 1994, just after Jackie passed away, Jhabvala told *The New Yorker,* "She seemed to know exactly the right thing to do and to say. And yet you did get this feeling of shyness with her—all the social graces you could ever have, but with this shyness. I have the same thing, and I think we understood each other very well. In one of her last notes I had from her, she wrote, 'Isn't it wonderful the way our friendship is growing and growing.'

"I just finished my most recent manuscript, and she knew that I was going on a trip, and she called me to say, 'Can I have it before you go?' I'd like to think that she had it—the most precious part of me—by her at the end."

Unlike the fate experienced by some of Jackie's other writers, Jhabvala saw her next novel, a complex family mystery entitled *Shards of Memory,* published by Doubleday during the year after Jackie's death, as the contract for the book had already been signed. Other authors Jackie left behind would not fare as well with the publishing house. She left an editorial vacuum that was understandably impossible to fill. In a sense, Jackie and a number of her authors were to be posthumously "plutoed" by the publisher.

During her last year, Jackie had at least a dozen books in various stages of development, and of those that were published, most would not appear until after her death. Jackie had Jonathan Cott provide text for a book of Emily Dickinson nature poems. When Jackie said that she thought the book should contain illustrations, Cott introduced her to a friend of his, the artist Mary Frank, who was the first wife of the photographer Robert Frank and a remarkable sculptor and painter in her own right.

As Cott told me, "Jackie must have been quite ill at that time—though I didn't have an inkling of that—but one afternoon she met me at Mary Frank's downtown New York City studio to look at her wood and clay sculptures and her paintings. After the visit, Jackie wrote me a letter that said, 'I *loved* going to Mary Frank's with you. She is someone so extraordinary to have brought into one's life.' Mary did scissor-cut shadow paper illustrations for the book, and we of course were going to dedicate the book to Jackie in any case. But she died before it came out, so we chose as a dedication a beautiful Emily Dickinson quote that expressed how we both felt about her."

The poem on the dedication page read:

> *Unable are the loved—to die—*
> *For love is immortality—*
> *Nay—it is Deity.*

Frank remembered Jackie visiting her at her Manhattan studio. "First of all, she really looked at work, which, as you can probably imagine, everybody doesn't do. . . . And she talked quite a bit about poetry, obviously not only knowledgeable, but, more interesting, with a real love and, I felt, a very real understanding."

Not published until 1995, *Skies in Blossom: The Nature Poetry of Emily Dickinson* was to be a personal collection of "the simple News that Nature told" by the woman who was better known as a gardener than as a poet during her lifetime. The book opens with an appreciation by editor Cott, after which it reproduces forty-three of the nearly 1,800 poems that were discovered after Dickinson died at the early age of fifty-five. Interspersed are delicate paper cuttings done by the artist Mary Frank, austere renderings of things in their natural order that complement the poetic selections.

Cott finds parallels between Dickinson's poems and Zen haikus and Japanese Buddhist aesthetics. He compares the simplicity of her minimalist poems with the clearing of the mind advocated by the late Zen master Shunryu Suzuki. He locates the traditional meter of Congregational hymns in her spare verse, and tentatively speculates that Dickinson, a well-known recluse, might be reductively diagnosed today as a borderline or bipolar personality. He speaks of "many Emilys, each of them in awe of the ineffable wonder and mystery of existence, each of them silently holding up a flower."

Mary Frank told me, "Jackie really was very attentive with the shadow papers, the pieces for the book. The process could not be simpler. It's cutting with the scissors and holding them up in the air so light comes through as I cut. I never draw and then cut; I just have to use the scissor like it would be both my eye and a pen. And I did hundreds, hundreds, in order to get quite a number for the book. The real ones, the actual ones, the paper is just off-white; it's not that color in the book at all. And they weren't really supposed to be that color. Initially, I was very upset because of course after she died nobody cared about the book—it was only she who cared about the book . . . but then she was so sick, and then she died. They would have just dumped it, I think, not bothered to publish—but they were, I guess, committed to do it. That's my feeling. Because when I complained about the color, I knew that if she wasn't there, nobody was going to care. And then I just made my peace with it and now I love the book for what it is. . . .

"I went into the hospital—I can't figure the timing—with osteomyelitis, I don't know, some horrible thing, and she must have known. I wasn't in touch with her so I suppose Jonathan told her, and she sent me this very particularly exquisite bouquet of flowers, I mean—I'm a gardener—very unusual flowers, very touching. And I was in tremendous pain, and they were very, very special. And then she sent me a wonderful postcard, and I did not know then that she had cancer. But she must have been referring to that, that she knew how sick she was then. It had some reference to how strange or wonderful or something to meet you at this point. . . . It was really a very lovely card, and it was obviously a moving card, but I couldn't know what she was referring to. And then when I came out of the hospital, I think she died very soon after. We were supposed to have a date and talk about the book. . . . But I was very happily struck, in meeting her for that short period, how intensely she seemed devoted to being an editor, and that's what was very compelling for me."

During that same year, Michael Flanagan approached Jackie with an idea for a book based on a gallery show of his artwork. He had in mind an art book based on his paintings that centered around two old railroads, the Powhatan and the Buffalo & Shenandoah, running through Virginia, West Virginia, and Maryland. After seeing these sterling color images of Americana, Jackie encouraged him to write text, to create a story and put together a different kind of book. He told me, "She suggested what kind of narrative it should be, and then I saw a novel that I hadn't envisioned before. She knew what this book should be before I did."

A literary agent eventually submitted Flanagan's book to various publishers, and Doubleday was outbid by Pantheon, which offered an advance twice as high as what Jackie's higher-ups were willing to allow her to offer. His book, *Stations: An Imagined Journey,* was published in 1994. Flanagan summed up the paradigm shift that had taken place in the trade. "It wasn't just about Jackie, it was about that whole world. I don't think we realized it at the time, but it was giving way to a much more corporate-driven mentality, which is where we are now." Jackie never voiced any chagrin that she had lost out to another publisher. Flanagan said, "She was thrilled for me."

Jackie would become gravely ill before Flanagan could show her the galleys of the book, and he remembered, "She didn't get to see it, unfortunately, but she knew it was in the works. I called her at home and spoke to John briefly, and he told me things were really bad. I think it was the night before she died, and he was only able to give her my best wishes. I just wanted to share my happiness with her about the book. I didn't realize how far gone she was because they were really trying to be very discreet about it. It was heartbreaking."

Another ambitious book that Jackie was working on during 1993 would also not quite fulfill her original vision when it was published in her absence the following year. *Toni Frissell, Photographs: 1933–1967* is a photobiography that drew on a treasure trove of more than 23,000 photographic negatives, transparencies, and contact sheets archived at the Library of Congress. Toni Frissell, who passed away in 1988, was a photographer and journalist who worked for publications as diverse as *Vogue* and *Sports Illustrated,* and had photographed Jackie's wedding reception in 1953 in Newport, Rhode Island. She covered global events like World War II and private spreads like the enormous King Ranch in Texas. Toni Frissell revolutionized fashion photography by seeking out natural settings for her models. This prefigured the famous *Sports Illustrated* swimsuit edition, which extended the idea by arranging shoots in the most far-flung locales on the planet. Frissell has taken her rightful place among artists like Steichen, Avedon, and Capa as mid-twentieth-century icons.

Frissell worked occasionally in color, but the majority of her most unforgettable images are black-and-white. Her portraits provide glimpses of humanity often absent in the more formal portraits of Karsh or Avedon. Winston Churchill, dressed in his Order of the Garter on Queen Elizabeth's 1953 coronation day, flashes a quizzical grin. Earlier, his seated portrait at Blenheim was used as his official photograph. Frissell excelled at humanizing British and American nobility. At the wedding of Jacqueline Bouvier and JFK, the sheer number of Kennedy family members threatened to block her view, until Jackie said, "Toni is a friend of mine. Let's give her a chance to get a good picture before the guests arrive." Frissell documented the occasion with a series of celebrated shots of the bride and groom and their wedding party.

George Plimpton provided an introduction to the book, and Toni Frissell's photographer daughter, Sydney Frissell Stafford, contributed a foreword and spent many hours carrying out research at the Library of Congress to organize the photographs. Plimpton suggested that with this book Frissell's life and photographs had been "plucked from oblivion." He told *The New York Times,* "Jackie always admired Toni Frissell's work, the quality and versatility of her enormously prolific career. She was very excited about this book. She asked me to write a very long introduction." The dedication page of the book reads, in part, "Jacqueline Kennedy Onassis made an impossible dream a reality in this extraordinarily beautiful book."

But to some extent, that dream proved impossible without Jackie's discerning eye and editorial presence to follow through on the project, initially much to the chagrin of Sydney Frissell Stafford. If one compares the printed photographs in the books with the source images from the Library of Congress, one can see that quite a few of the photos have blurred backgrounds due to altered contrast and loss of detail—Rex Harrison's face is somewhat washed out in a shot with Lilli Palmer; the background clarity is lost in a 1952 Mike Todd shot; and the image of the seated Winston Churchill is slightly distorted. I asked J. C. Suarès to explain the loss of detail in the images, and he told me, "Simple explanation: the production department switched printers to save money. Happens all the time."

In the spring of 1994, Doubleday published yet another of Jackie's books, *Lost in the Taiga: One Russian Family's Fifty-Year Struggle for Survival and Religious Freedom in the Siberian Wilderness,* authored by Moscow journalist Valery Peskov. The designer of that book, an in-house veteran, Terry Karydes, recalled that Marysarah Quinn assigned the book to her, and that Jackie insisted that a photograph be changed at the last minute. "I had just come back from traveling, and I'd been in Istanbul and traveled down Asia Minor. . . . So when I took this Russian book, I had all this Byzantine art in my mind. And *Lost in the Taiga* is about the church and Russia. I'm an interior designer. I didn't do the cover. So I had this piece of art on the title page that I thought was a church window. It came to a point like those Russian domes, and I thought it was perfect, a window from a Russian church. She made me change it [to a cross]. . . .

"She was really appreciative of the layouts. I remember when she looked at the layouts, she really looked at them. Then she did something that people don't usually do. She took her hand and she ran her fingers up and down the paper, like a tactile response. Usually people just take a visual response. She said, 'Ooooh! These are lovely!' . . . And then she immediately started telling me what was wrong with them in such a nice way. To her it looked sort of Asian. I said, 'Well, it is actually a Russian Byzantine church.' She said, 'Yeah, but it comes across on first impression that it could be anything, like Balinese.' That's not exactly what she said, but something non-Russian, more Asian. So I had to try and do it over. And by the time I was doing it over and came to show it again with the cross, she had already started to work from home because she was ill.

"The thing that was really interesting to me was that I told her—I was so psyched because I had just come back from this trip to where my grandparents came from, which is Asia Minor. . . . And she said, 'Oh, Ari's parents are from there.' . . . And we had like a twenty-minute conversation about Asia Minor. . . . It was just very interesting because I never expected her to bother to talk to me. I was floored. And she said, 'Did you go to Halicarnassus?' And I had to think because she used all the ancient names. . . . Oh, she means Bodrum. And then she said, 'Well, you should read this poem by Cavafy.' Within that year she had passed away, and it turned out to be the poem that Tempelsman read at her funeral. I thought, Oh my God, she wasn't kidding—that was her favorite poem."

Lost in the Taiga is a journalistic account of the Lykov family, whose members were Old Believers, schismatics from the Russian Orthodox Church dating to the mid-seventeenth century. The family lived alone in the Siberian taiga wilderness, so isolated from the world that only in 1978 were they discovered by a group of geologists. Their self-imposed exile dated back to 1932 and the early days of Stalinism. By the time the author, Peskov, met them in 1982, only thirty-seven-year-old Agafia and her eighty-one-year-old father, Karp, were still alive.

The book, which became a bestseller in France, was translated from the Russian by Marian Schwartz, who remembered, "Jackie died before it was published, but the contract was with her, and the beginning of the project was with her. This was not fiction; it was about a family of Old Believers who had lived alone in the taiga for sixty years without seeing any human beings except each other. The book is a megadose of human interest and got good reviews, but it's an odd duck in terms of audience. Today it's very popular among survivalists, who are fascinated by how the Lykovs survived. The book is still in demand but is hard to find. . . . I believe about eighteen thousand copies were printed, and those are gone. I still get letters from people saying, 'What happened to Agafia? Is she alive?' "

This book is the modern equivalent of the tales of first contact that South American, African, and Australasian explorers wrote in centuries past. While there may be some still-to-be contacted tribes in the upper reaches of the Amazon Basin, it's a pretty good bet that the Lykovs were the last remaining Christian isolationists. *Lost in the Taiga* included a photo section for which Jackie made selections, presenting both aerial shots of the Lykovs' garden and shack and the rugged terrain surrounding them, as well as ground portraits of the individual Lykovs. Since photography was a sin for these Old Believers, the photos were taken surreptitiously.

Jackie continued to make occasional public appearances during 1993. Before heading off to her Martha's Vineyard home on Memorial Day for her annual summer vacation, she attended a gala for American Ballet Theatre and served as honorary chairperson for the evening. In June, Jackie and Tempelsman returned to France for what was to be the last time. They enjoyed a voyage on the Rhône River, visiting the Provence region where Jackie's Bouvier ancestors had originated, and the Camargue, which Tempelsman called "Jackie's France." They also spent time wining and dining in Paris, and by chance that same month Jackie published another book on French history, *Paris After the Liberation: 1944–1949,* written by the London-based married couple Antony Beevor and Artemis Cooper.

At the time much had been written about the Nazi occupation of France and the efforts of the underground Resistance. Less well known were the chaotic postwar years during which France conducted its *Épuration légale,* the "legal purge" of French officials who participated in or cooperated with the detested Vichy government. This period, which Jackie had studied extensively, also saw a three-way struggle for power in France, with the communists on the left, the Gaullists on the right, and the social democrats defending the fragile center.

Paris After the Liberation reads like a novel, with the familiar names of de Gaulle and Malraux, Sartre and Camus, Picasso and Cocteau, Koestler and Céline popping up in the most unlikely of combinations. Of course, this was another historical sojourn for the book's dyed-in-the-wool Francophile editor, who had known many of the major figures who were a part of this era. Beevor and Cooper not only tell this complicated story in fascinating detail but also paint a portrait of a devastated Europe struggling for subsistence after five years of aerial terror, and they describe the intellectual machinations that the intelligentsia put themselves through in order to remain allies with the devious communists and the naive but gung-ho Americans.

Beevor pointed out a family connection he shared with Jackie. "Curiously, my brother at one point was engaged to [Jackie's half-sister] Janet Auchincloss. I think it was in 1965. They were about to get married, and then she was ill and went back to the States. So I saw quite a lot of Janet then and also occasionally her mother, 'big Janet,' and her brother Jamie, who used to come down to stay with us in Kent. Funnily enough, although we communicated a lot with Jackie while writing the book, I never actually met her. We just spoke on the telephone."

In their book, Beevor and his wife made use of diaries left by her grandfather, Alfred Duff Cooper, 1st Viscount Norwich, who served as British ambassador to France from 1944 to 1947. Beevor told me that the book was already set to be published in England when Jackie acquired it. "That was all fixed up with Hamish Hamilton here. I think Jackie got to hear about it—I'm not sure how that came about—and she grabbed the book when at Doubleday, which obviously for us was absolutely wonderful. She turned out to be a superb editor with excellent judgment. Her comments were extremely subtle and elegant, but also clear at the same time.

"One little story quite amused me: I remember getting terribly excited in a French archive—it's part of the Ville de Paris archive—where I found what I thought was the absolutely perfect jacket photograph. I sent this with huge excitement to Jackie. And back came the most elegant putdown I've heard in my life. On one of her pale blue cards decorated with a white cockleshell, she simply wrote: 'Dear Antony, I think you should understand that over here choosing a jacket is rather akin to a Japanese tea ceremony.' It was a very, very elegant way of saying: 'Stay out of it, because designers here do not like authors messing around with jacket selection.'"

I reminded Beevor that a professor of modern French at the University of Leeds, David Coward, had reviewed the book favorably for *The New York Times,* but suggested with his opening line, "In the 1940's, France went to war with herself yet again, and the tale, told with relish by Antony Beevor and Artemis Cooper in this fascinating book, is calculated to stir mixed feelings in the devoutest Francophile." The author told me, "Yes, interestingly the French didn't like it. Well, let me put it this way: Some French liked it. It was very much French left-wingers who didn't like it. That was certainly true. What they didn't like particularly I suppose was the mixture of the serious and the frivolous which was the reality in Paris at the time. Paris was living on the edge, because nobody knew whether there was going to be a Communist coup d'état or a right-wing coup d'état at almost any moment. That was reflected in the diaries of people at the time. . . .

"But what many French disliked so intensely about the book was the way it showed how they basically had no control over their own fate at that particular stage. They were part of the world game between the Soviet Union and the United States, and it was a question of which side you chose. And also the fact that we could not resist taking a little bit of fun at the vanities of the Aragons and the other intellectuals, which was something the French do not appreciate.

"The other thing they didn't like, of course, was that we mixed social, political, and intellectual history. Their academics believe strongly that all of these are separate disciplines and must be kept completely apart. . . .

But in fact, the whole point particularly during that tortuous postwar period is the importance of all the interreactions between all these different areas. And I think that's also what Jackie liked so much."

Beevor continued, "By the time we'd more or less finished the book, we were really under very heavy pressure because the fiftieth anniversary was looming and we had to get the book finished in time. I showed the last chapter to my wife, Artemis, and she had to come back, saying that it did not work. I was exasperated, but I knew she was right. Then, our English editor, who was highly admired, also could not see what was wrong. So we sent it over to Jackie—this was literally about three weeks before she died, and she must have been already very ill by then. Yet she put her finger on the problem in a second. . . . And as soon as she said it, everything was clear and we were able to finish. And then to our horror we heard . . . that she had died."

Beevor also remembered that Jackie had wanted to acquire a book by his mother, Kinta Beevor. "The other book she also was very keen on, and wanted to publish, but was stopped by Doubleday, was my mother's memoir, called *A Tuscan Childhood*. It described her childhood in this extraordinary castle in Tuscany, which my grandparents rebuilt and [for which they] created a garden on the roof. Jackie was obviously very taken by the book. She wrote to me saying that the most important thing that anybody can do, which I think is something she very much felt herself, is to create a home and a center for a family, which has a sort of mystical element to it. I am sure that that is what intrigued her about the book. . . . But when Jackie was interested in the book Tuscany seemed to mean very little in the States. Finally, after *Under the Tuscan Sun* was published, everybody wanted a Tuscan book. So eventually it was published in the States, but this, sadly, was quite a number of years after Jackie had died."

I asked the author if his own book was treated differently by the publisher after Jackie was no longer on the scene. "I had a sense that there were certain issues, with a loss of direction in that particular way. It's always terribly important for a book to have its interests protected by an editor. And, of course, if you have a powerful and charismatic one, that makes a huge difference. . . . And, you know, it's always difficult to judge, particularly in a foreign country. It all depends on how much coverage a book has had, how much you can actually do with it; but I didn't think very much was done in the way of a paperback or anything like that. . . . But I am not really in a position to judge. . . . I'm afraid that in publishing, whenever you have a change of editor, or an editor leaves the publishing house and responsibility for a book is handed over to someone else, you'll never get the same sort of attention that you had before. Editors by definition are not interested really in looking after other people's babies. They're very bad foster parents."

Like many of Jackie's books published by Doubleday, *Paris After the Liberation* was allowed to go out of print. However, Beevor and Cooper were fortunate: Penguin would reissue the book ten years later in a revised edition.

In the summer of 1993, Jackie made frequent visits to Oak Bluffs, a section of Martha's Vineyard that had been the home of generations of affluent African Americans. There she met with Dorothy West, a writer who had been well known for her work during the Harlem Renaissance. More recently, Dorothy, who was born in 1908, had published some of her short stories in the weekly newspaper the *Vineyard Gazette,* and Jackie had read them. Later, Dorothy submitted her unfinished second novel to Jackie.

Scott Moyers explained to biographer Sarah Bradford how Dorothy West came to Jackie's attention: "So, simply because Jackie was famous and lived on Martha's Vineyard and was the only editor she's ever heard of, she sent her the first sixty pages of this novel with the outline and a copy of the Virago edition of her previous book. Stuck it in the mail and sent it to Doubleday. I opened it up and there it was, clearly a classic by this historic figure, a second novel after forty years. . . . Dorothy was having problems writing it, so in the summer when Jackie was in Chilmark, she would drive over to Oak Bluffs every week to see how she was doing. If Jackie hadn't paid those weekly visits the book would never have been finished, and that book, *The Wedding,* is hailed as a real classic."

Dorothy West, who would outlive Jackie by four years, wrote about her editor in a tribute essay before her book was finished, saying, "In a brief time we became friends, sharing the same sense of honesty and respect. She, this elegant and gracious woman, and this writer of considerably more years would bond in a miraculous way. I think I was as unique to her as she was unique to me. I was without self-consciousness and so was she. Neither of us felt we had to apologize to the other for being . . . different from the other and indeed were enchanted by the difference. . . . She came to see me every Monday to assess my progress, driving herself in her blue Jeep, losing her way fairly regularly. . . . Though there was never such a mismatched pair in appearance, we were perfect partners."

Jackie's work with West might have been beyond the call of duty for some editors. Mary Helen Washington is a University of Maryland professor and author who contributed a preface to a book of short stories by

Dorothy West, *The Richer, the Poorer,* which was published in 1995 by Doubleday, as was *The Wedding.* Washington knew West and appreciated the challenge that Jackie must have encountered during her visits with the writer. Washington told me, "I met Dorothy several times. I had quite a relationship with Dorothy. She [Jackie] was an angel then because Dorothy was a very difficult person to interview. I mean, when I say difficult— she was a very sweet person, absolutely lovely and gracious and very, very much a Bostonian. You know, she talked with the broad 'a,' like to-MAH-to, and very kind of proper. But she would ramble and ramble and ramble. None of her sentences that I can remember ever had a period."

In her preface to *The Richer, the Poorer,* Washington wrote, "After 1945, Dorothy West made her home permanently on Martha's Vineyard, where she wrote *The Living Is Easy* in 1948 and her second novel, *The Wedding,* in 1994. Spanning almost seventy years, West's writing career links the Harlem Renaissance with the social realism of the thirties and forties and popular fiction of the eighties and nineties. In her most recent fiction she continues to observe the tensions and triumphs in the lives of middle- and upper-class blacks, at times critiquing the false values in their lives, yet always representing these lives in vivid detail."

While Toni Morrison's depictions of slave life and black degradation are suffused with phantasmagorical dreams and appearances by watchful spirits and ancestors, West chose a more realistic style to weave her tale. By so doing, she created an epic as real as *Beloved* or *Roots,* but one in an understated, minor key, a key more in keeping with the subtle grace that her characters learned to adopt over the generations.

In her *New York Times* review, novelist and short story writer Susan Kenney wrote, "Difficult as it may seem at first to separate Dorothy West the survivor and the legend from the author who has finally delivered a long-awaited book, you have only to read the first page to know that you are in the hands of a writer, pure and simple." Jackie surely would have been pleased.

In 1993 Jackie acquired the Russian historian W. Bruce Lincoln's *Between Heaven and Hell: The Story of a Thousand Years of Artistic Life in Russia.* It was to be another of her works left to die on the vine at the troubled house, and in 1998 it was published by Viking Penguin. Reviewing the book for *The New York Times,* Richard Lourie noted, "Lincoln has chosen to use the standard scholarly transcription of Russian names, a decision that a savvy editor would have vetoed from the get-go; it results in such eyesores as Chaikovskii." Judging by the care that Jackie took to make her past Russian works accessible, she would never have allowed such awkward spelling if she had been able to follow through with Lincoln on the editing.

Jackie celebrated her sixty-fourth birthday on Martha's Vineyard on July 28, 1993. She was in good cheer when Joe Armstrong visited her the following month and was her houseguest for a week. He said, "I took her a cassette of the Beatles' 'When I'm Sixty-Four,' and I played it on her stereo and her knees just buckled she started laughing so hard. I said, 'You never heard this?' And she said, 'Never!' The Beatles made that thirty-five years ago, when sixty-four seemed like ninety. All of the sudden sixty-four is no longer old, so she thought that was hysterical."

Some years before, at a dinner arranged by John Russell and Rosamond Bernier, the poet Stephen Spender asked Jackie what she thought of as her greatest achievement. She said, "I think that my biggest achievement is that after going through a rather difficult time, I consider myself comparatively sane." Earlier, after her second husband died, Jackie was able to voice her philosophy most eloquently: "I have been through life and suffered a great deal, but I have had happy moments, as well. Every moment one lives is different from the other. The good, the bad, hardship, the joy, the tragedy, love and happiness are all interwoven into one single, indescribable whole that is called life. You cannot separate the good and the bad, and perhaps there is no need to do so." She also expressed the humility that had grounded her through the years of fame. "Even though people may be well known, they hold in their hearts the emotions of a simple person for the moments that are the most important of those we know on earth: birth, marriage and death."

Back in New York City in the fall, Jackie appeared at the Brooklyn Academy of Music for a children's dance performance celebration of the 500th anniversary of Columbus's discovery of America. In October, with President Bill Clinton and her children at her side, she took part in the rededication of the John F. Kennedy Library. During this period, she showed no sign of curtailing her activities or slowing down on the job. Bruce Tracy later observed, "Even though she was in her midsixties, there was never any inkling of her workload lessening. I had no notion of Jackie thinking about retiring. She carried on as if she was going to go on for twenty years."

Jackie was quietly immersed in a project for which she would fight a private war to see realized on her own terms. This was to be an unusual illustrated children's book carried out under the authorship of an artist and animation filmmaker, Peter Sís. Scott Moyers explained, in *As We Remember Her,* "Peter Sís is a Czech artist, a well-known children's book illustrator who grew up in Prague and defected in the 1980s. He had always wanted to do a book about his childhood for his daughter Madeleine, who was growing up in the new world, so she could know about her father's old world past. *The Three Golden Keys* is about a balloonist who comes into this ancient city of his childhood and goes home. It's dark. All the city is dark. No one is in the streets. He follows a cat from a locked door, and is led to these three landmarks, and at each one, something comes to life and tells a Czech fairy tale, and gives him a golden key. It's an allegory for the reclamation of a Czech identity after communism."

A former vice president at Doubleday under Steve Rubin, Marly Rusoff told PBS writer and author Karen Kelleher that Peter Sís "came to Jackie's attention in the May/June 1991 edition of *Print* magazine. He designed the cover with one of his painted eggs." But there was more to that story, which led to an invitation from Jackie for Sís to show her his portfolio. He explained that fortunate turn of events to me one afternoon over coffee at the Met, saying, "I did a painted egg for the cover, which was to show what is the creative spirit, and she loved those painted eggs. But what happened really was that she somehow knew Michael Patrick Hearn, who's a great expert in children's books. And he had a story about a little girl who was born inside of the egg, and comes out of the egg. Michael suggested I would illustrate the book, so this is how I brought my portfolio including the pictures of the painted eggs. Jackie and I met and started to talk. Gradually, we were talking about other stories . . ."

Jackie and Sís discussed several books that he might illustrate, including Jules Verne, Italo Calvino's *The Baron in the Trees,* and Alain-Fournier's *Le Grand Meaulnes.* Sís said, "She was more like people I was used to talking to in Europe, like my father—great storytellers with knowledge of many different cultures. I had the same feeling with Mrs. Onassis. She would know all the legends, all the references."

Later in 1991, before Jackie and Sís had settled on the idea for his book, she and Tempelsman traveled to Europe. Sís recalled, "And then she surprised me because she went to Prague, incognito, as the guest of President Havel and stayed for four or five days. And she was really into Prague architecture and she surprised me by knowing the names of the houses she was interested in and she was into this whole history and the mixing of the cultures, like the German and Czech culture and the Jewish culture and the Italian architects coming from up north. Prague was like a melting pot of Europe, which I think she was very much aware of that. She loved it, and she said, 'Why don't you think about doing a book about Prague?'

"She said, 'Just try to be as free as you want. Do whatever you want.

Whatever you want, you put in that book. If it's going to be dark, and if it's going to be scary, and if it's going to be strange, you do it. . . .' I also remember she was amazing in defending that book. Lots of people said, 'This is dark, and this is strange,' and she would go to all these meetings—I remember the meetings when I was waiting for her, when she was sitting with some board of people. Most people don't realize. They would think she could do what she wanted, that she had a carte blanche; but she really did work like any other editor and go and defend the book, defend the size, the numbers, the printing, why is she doing it. And I remember those meetings, and that she was saying, like, 'How are we going to push it through?' "

Recalling Sís's book, Scott Moyers said, "Jackie specifically insisted that she must do this children's book. The typical children's book is thirty-two pages long. Sís said he had done sixty-four illustrations. Jackie said, 'Let's use them all because this is your life's book.' "

Sís credited Jackie with rescuing him from an emotional impasse while he was doing the artwork at his studio. "At the same time I was undergoing a real change in my life. We had a newborn baby, and she wants me to do book about Prague. After seven years I can go to Prague because the Wall came down. So if I didn't have American wife, if I didn't have a little baby, I could have gone. But also it was a dilemma, how do you do book about Prague? Do you go in the streets and paint it as it is, or do you do it as a book of memories? I thought I will never go back. You try to remember what each street looked like, and you realize you have lots of gaps. So I like the idea that I will do it in New York as a dream about the place.

"But what happened was that she made this project much bigger than it was supposed to be. She said, 'Let's do it as a big book.' Instead of thirty-two pages, I was doing sixty-four. And I told her, 'Look, this can take much longer time. This is like a big project.' And she said, 'I know. But don't worry about it. We want something special.' . . . And my wife had this little baby, and we were on Lafayette Street, and I got a studio across the street, which was a big professional building. . . . I had a little room, and I put all these pictures which would be inspiring of angels in Prague and everything on the walls. And it was very hot, and twice a day I would go see the baby. The project was taking much longer than we agreed to do it, and time was passing on. It was like three months, and she started to be worried. And instead of calling and saying, How far are you, because she [had] said, 'You can take all the time you want,' she decided she would come and see how far I was.

"And that was a funny story in a way because she drove in some little car absolutely alone downtown. She didn't have the address of the studio, but she had address of where we lived. So we had this intercom, and my wife, who's with the baby, and somebody buzzes. She says, 'Hi, this is Mrs. Onassis.' So my wife says on the intercom, 'He's across the street in the studio.' So Mrs. Onassis comes to the studio. It's a big building with twelve floors, and each floor has got twenty-five offices with Mark Morris Dance Company, with film editors, writers, graphic artists. So she goes to a number of these offices looking for me. People don't know me really but they know her.

"Then she finds me. We had a wonderful afternoon. I thought it was so sweet that she would come, no Secret Service or anything. . . . Why doesn't it happen with more editors, that just when I was in that moment, as every creator is—How am I going to move this? It's going nowhere—she came, and she said, 'Oh, this is so wonderful.' And she caught in that moment to give me great hope and inspiration to go another ten miles."

During a trip Jackie made to Sweden, she sent Sís postcards with artworks that directly related to Prague and illustrations he was rendering for the book. Sís said, "She once sent me a postcard from Stockholm of *The Librarian,* a painting by Giuseppe Arcimboldo belonging to Prague from the sixteenth century. . . . It was amazing that she would remember that, because it was taken by the Swedish army, which we might have talked about, but I wouldn't remember that George Washington slept under a tree in White Plains, necessarily. Jackie's card read, 'Look what I saw in Skokloster Castle, taken as booty from Prague. . . . I thought it was a good omen.'"

Once again, Jackie took control of the production of the book. Sís said, "At that time everything was printed in Asia because it was cheaper. Not with her. She wanted the best possible. She said, 'It's going to be done in Italy.' And it was printed in Italy. . . . And then of course I was finishing the book till like February, so I was so busy with that that I didn't pay attention, wouldn't know how she was. And then it was done, and we met. I still had a chance to show it to her and was told about her condition."

Sís remembered meeting with Jackie to review his illustrations. "If anyone wants to know what is the fulfillment of my life in New York, it was when I brought in the pictures for our book. We put them all over the conference table at Doubleday, and on the floor. While she looked at the pictures, I could see Times Square behind her. I felt this is wonderful. This is the American dream come true."

Jackie wrote Sís a note in April 1994, a month before she died, telling him, "Your book is so magnificent. Each drawing looks into the well of an artist's mind and creativity, like nothing I have ever seen before." Scott Moyers pointed out that Jackie "did not like books dedicated to her, but Peter just insisted on getting this in: 'Thank you for a dream, JO.' She saw the original illustrations, and she edited the text, but she never saw the finished book." Sís explained that he added the dream line expressing his gratitude to his editor in May, "when she so unexpectedly, for me at least, was gone."

Most of Jackie's authors were unaware of the chain of events that began in November 1993 and led to her death six months later. Like the rest of the world, most of her friends and authors heard of her illness only when it was announced by Nancy Tuckerman in February of the following year. Joe Armstrong said, "All this just came out of the blue. She had flu off and on that fall and looking back, it must have been the cancer. And then over Thanksgiving she fell off that horse. . . . I remember calling her after her accident, and she didn't even want to blame the horse." Jackie was in Middleburg, Virginia, participating in a fox hunt on November 21, when she fell from her horse on a jump.

After the fall, she was unconscious for a half hour. Her friend Bunny Mellon's physician examined her, and a swollen lymph node was discovered in her groin. The doctor thought it was probably an infection and prescribed an antibiotic. Jackie flew back to Manhattan the following day and, with her children, attended a requiem mass for their father, as she had on this day for the past thirty years. The mass was held at St. Thomas More, a small Catholic church in the Upper East Side not far from her home. Police were present that night because there was fear that Jackie or one of her children was being stalked by a suspicious man who had inquired about the mass the day before.

Jackie continued to ache intermittently with flulike symptoms that fall but rarely missed a day of work. She spent Christmas that year with her children, grandchildren, and Tempelsman in her Peapack, New Jersey, home, which she described as "my sanctuary away from Manhattan." She had driven her BMW, laden with gifts, to meet her family, along the way listening to the album *Duets* that Carly Simon had recorded with Frank Sinatra. The source of her greatest stress was John Jr., who was then thirty-three years old and had recently been named the "Sexiest Man Alive" by *People* magazine. He had left his job at the Manhattan district attorney's office and was considering starting a magazine with his friend Michael Berman, a plan that would eventually be realized in 1995 when John founded his glossy monthly, *George*.

Concerned about her son's future, Jackie had him speak with Joe Armstrong, who remembered, "When John knew he was ready to leave the DA's office, Jackie asked me to meet with him, to talk to him about what he might do next. Jackie admired the fact that he was so open to new and unusual ideas, so curious, that he loved adventures. She identified with

John—he was so full of life and good humor, a constant spark—but she worried about him, too."

In January, hoping a vacation would provide the cure for Jackie's ills, Tempelsman took her sailing in the Caribbean, but their trip had to be cut short when she experienced severe pain in her groin and neck. After returning to New York, they consulted Dr. Carolyn Agresti, at New York Hospital-Cornell Medical Center. Tests of Jackie's enlarged lymph nodes revealed non-Hodgkin's lymphoma, and she soon embarked on what was to be four futile courses of chemotherapy. Her visits to the hospital were carried out in secret, with her wearing a hooded cape and checking in under an assumed name.

Tempelsman, who was the first person Jackie informed of her diagnosis, was a constant companion, as were John and Caroline, and she remained upbeat with friends and colleagues. She joked that the turban she wore to cover her hair loss during the chemo would "start a new fashion trend." She told Arthur Schlesinger, "I have always been proud of keeping so fit. I swim, I jog, and I do my push-ups, and walk around the reservoir—and now this suddenly happens." Schlesinger noted that Jackie was laughing at herself, and he recalled, "She seemed cheery and hopeful, perhaps to keep up the spirits of her friends, and her own. Chemotherapy, she added, was not too bad; she could read a book while it was administered. The doctors said that in fifty percent of cases lymphoma could be stabilized. Maybe she knew it was fatal. Maybe she didn't know at all, but even if she did, she still had hope for some other future."

After visiting Rose Kennedy early that year at the old Kennedy compound in Hyannis Port—the ailing matriarch was then 103 and would outlive her—Jackie returned to work. She had informed her colleagues about her condition shortly after she was diagnosed. "She never once complained of any pain," said Scott Moyers. "She never once let anything show. She kept coming in. She was so indomitable. She was so upbeat. Sometimes, she had Band-Aids on, and bruises from the therapy, but she carried on with her projects until the end. And then there was the day that she was rushed to the hospital the first time. When she came to consciousness in the hospital, she realized she had an appointment with Peter Sís, over whose work she had so lovingly labored, and the first thing she thought about and said was, 'Please call Peter Sís and tell him I won't be able to make it.'"

In the months before her death, Jackie and Sís had been planning a book based in part on his father's experiences teaching documentary filmmaking in Tibet during the 1950s. Sís's book, *Tibet Through the Red Box,* was eventually published in 1998 by editor Frances Foster at Farrar,

Straus and Giroux to great acclaim (and in 2003, Sís became a MacArthur fellow). During 1994, the editors at Doubleday continued to string him along. Sís said, "There was Scott and there was Bruce, but you could tell it's unfolding. . . . You could see the department was slowly sort of coming apart. And they made me believe they will do the books for quite some time. . . . It was like almost a year they were like, 'Yes, we will do this.' "

But Doubleday never acquired another book from Sís, who said, "I think that whole division got dismantled. . . . I think Bruce Tracy and Scott Moyers stayed, but not for long. It was the end of an era for sure. And it was a very strange thing because later I had a meeting with Doubleday-Random House, because Doubleday became part of Random House. And I had a meeting with the head of the children's division, and it was the same floor, same office where Jackie was. And that was so creepy. It was terrible."

Gelsey Kirkland and I received similar treatment on another book we had been discussing with Jackie unaware of her illness. In February, I submitted an offbeat mystery novel, *The Theatricals,* written by an old friend, John Leone, who was a veteran Hollywood screenwriter. Jackie wrote a letter later that month, saying, "Your friend can certainly write! He had my heart thumping—I've given it to the powers above at Doubleday and will let you know the minute I hear." It was only after Jackie was gone that I heard from Bruce Tracy, who informed me without explanation that the novel had been rejected.

On the same day that Jackie's illness was announced in the press, she had a meeting with Elizabeth Smith Brownstein, who was then director of research for the Smithsonian World television series. After seeing a National Gallery exhibition, "Treasure Houses of Britain," Brownstein came up with an idea for a film. She told me, "I created the idea of a television series that would cover many different kinds of houses, and I raised money and traveled around the country for two years really. . . . I came up with a huge proposal for a television series. And of course thinking that Jackie Onassis had limitless pockets, I sent the proposal . . . thinking that she would take out her checkbook.

"Well, I mailed the proposal to her at Doubleday on a Monday, and on Thursday the same week, the telephone rang. I was in my bedroom, and I was getting ready to go to work, and I said, 'Hello.' And this voice, this inimitable voice, said, 'This is Jacqueline Onassis. I found your idea thrilling and inspiring and would like to talk to you about it.'

"Well, of course I was about to say, 'Look, lady, whoever you are, get the . . .' Then I thought, God, I sent her the proposal on Monday and here she is, calling me back. So I composed myself with difficulty, and we talked at some length, and she said, 'I would like to meet with you.' And I'm a little bit fuzzy on when she said—'I want to do a book as well as the television series'—but her idea was based on previous experience, particularly with Bill Moyers.

"I went up to see her the following week. . . . And we were scheduled for a forty-five-minute interview. I was there, she was there, my producer . . . her assistant editor, Scott Moyers, and several other people. . . . But we talked for two hours, and we had an absolutely marvelous time discussing the kinds of people [who might become involved]. She said, 'Oh, I know Bunny Mellon. Perhaps we could get to her . . .'

"Obviously I was very interested to see what she was wearing and what she looked like. And so I started at the shoes and worked my way up. And then I got to her hair. And it was this billowing, beautiful mane, and I thought, Oh, this woman has everything, how unfair. And then I looked again and realized this is a wig, not her hair. . . . So I didn't know what on earth could possibly have been the reason for that.

"But anyway, the interview concluded with great handshakes. I'd asked her if I could call her Jackie, and she said, 'Oh yes, of course.' And we left. I got home that night, and the next day friends began to call and say, 'Did you see? Did you see?' I said, 'What?' And they said, 'Her illness was announced publicly for the first time.' And then of course I realized that she must have been going through chemo before our meeting for some time.

"But really we were able to talk for I think a month or more on the phone about her vision for the book. . . . It was fascinating because she was so literate. She knew film, she knew literature, of course, and on top of all that, she shared—'Well, when Jack and I were in Wisconsin, you know, for the primary. . . .' This was February, and of course she died in May. And so after a month or so obviously she was in no shape to talk any further. . . . Certainly I don't know what would have happened if she had lived. . . . But several months after that . . . Scott Moyers called me. He had moved over to Simon & Shuster, and he said, 'We would like the book. We think that it can stand alone with or without a television series.' So that is how it became a book." *If This House Could Talk: Historic Homes, Extraordinary Americans* was published in 1998, thanks to Moyers, who has since become a literary agent.

Not everyone fared poorly at Doubleday in the wake of Jackie's passing. Robert Lyons had a book under way with Jackie and managed to find support from editor Martha Levin. Lyons told me, "That book is called *Another Africa,* and that book is with Chinua Achebe. And what happened— I finished the Egypt work, and by the time the book was out, I was working in other parts of Africa. And I have in fact this original very poor maquette dummy that I brought to Mrs. Onassis, and we were discussing it, because by then she started to take a harder hand in the editorial process with me, and in the picture sequence, and in what this could be about. And she was really instrumental in discussing that with me. This was just before she had the riding accident. And then, of course, as you know, things changed drastically and dramatically. . . .

"I went back to Martha Levin, who said to me, 'Well, you know, I'd love to do this.' Chinua's poems had never been published in the U.S.A. at that time, only in England. And I had a very good relationship with Chinua, and he offered me material that had never been published as well. So Jackie was actually there at the beginning of that project, and giving me counsel."

A few other authors left Doubleday for other houses simply because they couldn't bear the idea of working there without Jackie. One of them was John Loring, who had collaborated with Jackie on all of the Tiffany books. He told me, "She and I had a huge list of books we wanted to do. She would jokingly say, 'Oh, I suppose when we're both eighty, we'll be writing *Tiffany Mushrooms*.' And once she wasn't there I just couldn't continue there. I did [a Christmas] book, and then afterwards I moved to Abrams because Jackie was not there anymore. . . . I was terribly spoiled by the experience of having her work with me. Of course it's never been the same without her."

In April 2003 David Stenn published an article in *Vanity Fair* about a documentary film, *Girl 27*, which he was making. Released in 2007, the film was nominated for the Grand Jury Prize at the Sundance Film Festival, but the project began as a story idea that Jackie had encouraged Stenn to pursue a decade earlier. As he recalled in *Vanity Fair*, "'What,' asked Jacqueline Onassis, 'are we going to do next?' It was September 1993. She had just edited *Bombshell: The Life and Death of Jean Harlow*. . . . Now, over lunch at the Peninsula Hotel in Manhattan, I told Jackie of an intriguing topic I'd stumbled onto in my Harlow research. A month before the star's death, in 1937, a dancer named Patricia Douglas had been raped at a wild MGM party thrown by Louis B. Mayer. Instead of bartering her silence for a studio contract or cash, Douglas went public with her story and filed a landmark lawsuit. One person I interviewed told me, 'They had her killed.'

"I didn't believe that, I told Jackie, because, though MGM was then the world's most powerful movie studio, with its own railroad and in-house police force, it would never have gone to such an extreme. Jackie smiled and said, 'Well, why don't you find out what *did* happen? You're the only person who can, David.'"

This was certainly the kind of sensational tale that Jackie might have published, but without her as editor, Stenn decided to pursue only the film. He was one of those authors who appreciated Jackie's old-school approach as the kind of editor who shepherded her writers and gave them the opportunity to develop their talents. He said, "She cultivated authors, not subjects. In today's publishing market, it's all about what you're writing about, not that *you're* writing—and unless you've got an author who sells, you don't keep publishing someone simply because you believe in them. Jackie *nurtured,* and thought long-haul. To me, it was akin to the Hollywood studio system: You sign someone, hone their talent, and think long-term. It's a big investment financially, time-wise, and resource-wise, but that's why they call it the Golden Age of Hollywood: That system understood talent needs to be nurtured. It was like the Renaissance guilds— and Jackie was very much of a Renaissance woman. She felt an editor invests in an authorial voice. You may not relate to their subject, but you respect their talent—which is a deeper form of respect."

According to Carl Sferrazza Anthony, referring to her illness, Jackie told one of her friends at the time, "I'm almost glad it happened because it's given me a second life. I laugh and enjoy things so much more." Even during that winter, she continued to walk in Central Park with Tempelsman, and one day with her granddaughters she took part in a playful snowball fight. *Schindler's List* was the last movie she attended.

Her assistant during her first years at Doubleday, Hope Marinetti, wrote to Jackie during this period. Marinetti remembered, "The years went by and I kept in touch a little bit, but then I thought, Oh my God, she doesn't need to be hearing from me. But then when I found out she was sick, I sent her a letter, just saying I'm thinking about you, don't know if you remember me, and sent her a picture of me and my dog. And it must have been just about a month before she passed, I go to my mailbox and there was that blue stationery, and a handwritten note from her, saying, 'Of course, I remember you,' and just the sweetest, nicest things. She didn't have to take the time to write back to me. I mean I'm not anybody important in terms of the course of history. But that was so typical, that she would write this beautiful handwritten note."

Jackie kept up with her correspondence and sent letters to a number of her friends and authors. To John Loring, she wrote, "Everything is fine. Soon we can have another festive lunch." Louis Auchincloss said, "John Kenneth Galbraith told me that she was ill, and I said, 'Will she get better?' And he said, 'No, she will not.' And that was the first that I knew. And it was only a very short time after that. So I wrote her a letter at that time and I got this answer just a few days before she died. 'Dear Louis I do thank you for your beautiful letter. I was touched by your writing it. All will be well, I promise.' "

Jackie used that phrase, "all will be well," in quite a few of the notes she penned during this agonizing time, to express her own faith and to alleviate the concerns that others felt about her health. Biographer David Spoto speculated that she may have been making a reference to the medieval English mystic Julian of Norwich. Jackie was familiar with her writings and the often quoted line, "All shall be well, and all shall be well, and all manner of thing shall be well." While Jackie remained rooted in Roman Catholicism, she had her own highly personal interpretation of the faith that she fell back on, having seen her mother excommunicated for marrying Auchincloss, and having been threatened with excommunication herself after she married Onassis.

Scott Moyers told Carl Sferrazza Anthony his feelings when Nancy Tuckerman informed him that Jackie was not going to recover. "All I could think was that this was a true tragedy because I got a strong sense that this woman, at this point, had life figured out. And that she had surrounded herself with this constellation of cultured, wonderful people, that she had interests that she cared deeply about, she was constantly immersed in new and stimulating ideas, that she had strong family ties, that her personal life was absolutely solid, that she had places she loved—Virginia, the Vineyard, Manhattan. God, this woman had finally figured it out, and then it was snatched away."

Jackie was not in denial about her condition. On March 22, after several lengthy discussions with her children, Tempelsman, and her attorneys, she signed her will, which was a long, complex document. While leaving most of her estate to John and Caroline, she provided for a number of cash bequests to various friends, relatives, and servants. As previously planned, Jackie also arranged to be buried in Arlington National Cemetery, beside John F. Kennedy and their children: Arabella, who was stillborn, and Patrick, who died shortly after birth.

During this period of making preparations, according to Edward Klein (*Farewell, Jackie*), who cited an unnamed eyewitness who claimed to have been in the room, Jackie and Nancy Tuckerman went through all of the love letters that Jackie had received over the years and burned them in the fireplace. That story may be apocryphal, though Jackie did stipulate in her will that none of her papers should be published until after the deaths of her two surviving children. At one point, surveying the Fifth Avenue apartment, Jackie told Caroline and John, "Sell everything. You'll make a lot of money." Following their mother's advice, two years later they arranged to auction many of her books, artworks, and personal effects at Sotheby's—an event that became something of a spectacle. Among the books sold were some that Jackie had edited, inscribed by her authors.

Jackie would soldier on into April and welcomed the new season: "Isn't it something? One of the most glorious springs I can remember. And after such a terrible winter." Joe Armstrong and Carly Simon, who had recently lost her mother, had Jackie and several other friends join them for lunch at Simon's rambling Central Park West apartment. The guests included Peter Duchin, Brooke Hayward, and filmmaker Ken Burns. "She kept saying," said Armstrong, "'Just four more weeks and I'll be myself again, and I'll get my life back.'" She was still hoping that further chemotherapy might cure her.

Duchin said, "We didn't have a conversation about her battle with cancer. We all knew she was ill. She was very brave about it. Of course, we didn't go into any detail. I remember her saying she got tired a lot quicker. But she was very chipper. And she said, 'I am going to beat it.'" That afternoon before they parted, Simon gave Jackie the sheet music to a song she had written for her, "Touched by the Sun." The next day Jackie called Simon and Armstrong to recap the lunch and to say she was overwhelmed by the lyrics Carly had written for her.

On April 14, Jackie had to be hospitalized when she developed an ulcer as a result of steroid treatments. There were still other, more radical therapies that were suggested to her, but Jackie decided against trying to prolong her life that way, wishing to preserve her dignity. She remained composed and put on a brave face. She was still able to hide her illness from friends. Cary and Edith Welch saw Jackie briefly on Wednesday, May 11, on their way to Europe, without realizing how serious her condition was. Cary told Sarah Bradford, "One of the things I find difficult to understand . . . when we came back from Europe following her death, I was handed by our son Thomas a heap of newspaper accounts of her last days, and according to those, on the day that we saw her she would have been so absolutely undone by disease that it would have been impossible to have the kind of conversation that we had—and I find that quite at odds with our experience."

On Sunday, May 15, Jackie, looking quite frail, took a last walk into Central Park with Tempelsman and her grandchildren. The next day she was feeling poorly and had chills. She was taken to the hospital, where it was discovered that the cancer had spread to her liver. On Wednesday, in great anguish and knowing the end was near, Jackie went home to Fifth Avenue. One of her last visitors was her stepbrother, Hugh D. (Yusha)

Auchincloss Jr., who had served as an usher at her wedding to JFK. He later wrote of his visit, "I knew that she knew it was time to go on, and she would not like to keep her maker waiting. She left without self-pity . . ."

One of the most poignant commentaries was given to me by Louis Auchincloss: "In February 1991, I had the grave misfortune to lose my darling wife, Adele, in a battle with cancer. Jackie dropped this wonderful letter at my apartment house the following morning. 'I just heard this afternoon. I still can't believe it. My heart goes out to you and your wonderful sons. . . . All I can think of is the gallantry of her long and final battle—and yours who accompanied her through it. You will know the beautiful words, they must be Shakespeare's: "Nothing became her life so as her manner of leaving it." The cards that life will deal you, you never know or imagine them. . . . It seems to me that all Adele did in her life was to give—to her family, to things that mattered to the community, to the world. She should not have had to suffer so. There are not many people who are obviously so profoundly good as she was. Everyone whose life her spirit touched will remember, will acknowledge, will miss her forever.' I could have written the same of Jackie, alas, only three years later."

Jackie died at ten fifteen on the night of Thursday, May 19. The following day John Jr. made the announcement to the press, saying that she passed away "surrounded by her friends and her family and her books and the people and the things that she loved. And she did it in her own way and in her own terms, and we all feel lucky for that, and now she is in God's hands."

On Monday, May 23, there was a private wake at her Fifth Avenue home attended by more than one hundred guests. In the drawing room was a burnished mahogany casket draped by her antique satin bedspread. Carly Simon described the scene to Edward Klein, saying, "It was a traditional Irish wake, and it turned me off. It was like walking into a cocktail party." Simon was later devastated and left in tears after she tried to leave a parting gift on Jackie's coffin, only to be asked to leave by Caroline's husband, as only family members were allowed such an intimate final gesture. Monsignor George Bardes of St. Thomas More Church had been asked to speak and later recalled, "The apartment was filled with people, senators, celebrities. Caroline received everyone. It was so hot and crowded that someone fainted, and a doctor had to bring them around."

Jackie's funeral was held the following day at St. Ignatius, the same church in which she had been baptized and confirmed. By all accounts, the service was one of solemn pageantry. In attendance were her family, friends, colleagues, and some of her authors, including Louis Auchincloss, George Plimpton, Bill Moyers, David Garrard Lowe, Deborah Turbeville, and Judith

Jamison. Jamison later said, "For me, it seemed absolutely reflective of her, and her tastes. As soon as I heard [the] Fauré *Requiem* [*in D minor*], that was it. I was no good after that."

David Garrard Lowe told me, "I sat with Senator [Daniel Patrick] Moynihan, an old acquaintance and a wonderful man. Of course, it was profoundly sad, because it was a funeral, not a memorial service, and she had just died and she was not old. At the recessional, I remember the coffin coming down the aisle, and behind it the children, Caroline and John-John, then Teddy and Ethel, Bobby's widow, and Lady Bird Johnson. It was a veritable *This Is Your Life*. The organ was playing 'America the Beautiful.' As the coffin came nearer, I turned away. I couldn't look, fearing that I would start to cry. The atmosphere was heaving with an overwhelming sense of finality. As I turned, Senator Moynihan murmured, 'I can't look, either.' . . . When I rose to leave, I was struck by the fact that the enormous sanctuary was not full. Only people who had been invited were there. But outside, Park Avenue was thronged with a silent crowd watching the coffin being put into the hearse as it began its journey to Arlington."

Television cameras were not allowed, but a sound system was provided for those who had gathered outside. John Jr. opened the service by telling the congregation how difficult it had been to decide on the readings: "We struggled to find ones that captured my mother's essence." He explained, "Three things come to mind over and over again and ultimately dictated our selections. They were her love of words, the bonds of home and family, and her spirit of adventure."

There were Bible readings and prayers, and a moving eulogy delivered by Ted Kennedy. Jessye Norman sang Franz Schubert's "Ave Maria" and César Franck's "Panis Angelicus." Caroline and Templesman read two of Jackie's favorite poems, "Memory of Cape Cod," by Edna St. Vincent Millay, and "Ithaka," by C. P. Cavafy. Caroline read the Millay poem from a book that Jackie won as a literary prize at Miss Porter's School in 1947. At the podium, Maurice recited Cavafy's poem, which Jackie knew by heart. It invoked the adventures of Ulysses, the pilgrim's arrival at the Homeric destination of Ithaka marking the journey's end.

> *When you start on your journey to Ithaka,*
> *then pray that the road is long,*
> *full of adventure, full of knowledge . . .*
>
> *Then pray that the road is long.*
> *That the summer mornings are many,*

> *that you will enter ports seen for the first time*
> *with such pleasure, with such joy!*

After finishing his reading of the poem, Maurice paused, and then added a short stanza of his own, allowing his listeners to appreciate some of what he shared with Jackie during their long companionship:

> *And now the journey is over.*
> *Too short, alas, too short.*
> *It was filled with adventure and wisdom*
> *Laughter and love, gallantry and grace.*
> *So farewell, farewell.*

With her office sanctuary, Jackie had shielded herself so effectively from the public during those last nineteen years that the four-day media orgy of hagiography marking her death revealed virtually nothing beyond the celebrity persona, although it was noted in passing that Jackie's career as editress had lasted longer than either of her marriages. Frank Rich writing in *The New York Times* lamented that the woman Jackie was remained a mystery, inadequately eulogized by the mantralike repetition of four words: "grace, dignity, style, class." The image of Jackie crouching on the floor surrounded by manuscript pages never appeared in the media coverage, which ultimately yielded to a dazzling kaleidoscope drawn from other chapters of her life.

A year later, fourteen of Jackie's authors said their farewells by composing tribute essays for a slender blue hardcover book that her publisher distributed as a private, limited edition for family and friends. Such a modest volume was a fitting, elegant gesture, even while it omitted reference to many of the works that comprise her legacy. The vision Jackie brought into editing embraced the recognition that every life has its own riches and meaning, waiting to be revealed by what she called "the hard work of writing." Over the years Doubleday and Viking allowed many of Jackie's books to go out of print. They were no longer deemed commercial, though perhaps in this Google age of wonders, we can hope they will somehow survive, as will the wisdom she imparted by the example of her own beautiful voyage.

Books Published by Jacqueline Kennedy Onassis

Viking Press

Chase-Riboud, Barbara. *Sally Hemings.* 1979.

De Pauw, Linda Grant, and Conover Hunt, with Miriam Schneir. *Remember the Ladies: Women in America, 1750–1815.* 1976.

Kennedy, Eugene. *Himself! The Life and Times of Mayor Richard J. Daley.* 1978.

Mellon, James. *The Face of Lincoln.* 1979.

Onassis, Jacqueline, ed. *In the Russian Style.* 1976.

Onassis, Jacqueline Kennedy, ed. *The Firebird and Other Russian Fairy Tales.* 1978.

Penn, Irving, and Diana Vreeland. *Inventive Paris Clothes, 1909–1939: A Photographic Essay.* 1977.

Doubleday

Adams, William Howard. *Atget's Gardens: A Selection of Eugène Atget's Garden Photographs*. Introduction by Jacqueline Kennedy Onassis. 1979.

Appelbaum, Stephen A. *Out in Inner Space: A Psychoanalyst Explores Alternate Therapies*. 1979.

Auchincloss, Louis. *False Dawn: Women in the Age of the Sun King*. 1984.

Bass, Jack. *Taming the Storm: The Life and Times of Judge Frank M. Johnson, Jr.* 1993.

Beevor, Antony, and Artemis Cooper. *Paris After the Liberation, 1944–1949*. 1994.

Bernier, Olivier. *At the Court of Napoleon*. 1989.

———. *The Eighteenth-Century Woman*. 1982.

———. *Louis XIV: A Royal Life*. 1987.

———. *Pleasure and Privilege*. Foreword by Louis Auchincloss. 1981.

———. *Secrets of Marie Antoinette*. 1985.

Campbell, Joseph, with Bill Moyers. *The Power of Myth*. 1988.

Catlin, George. *Drawings of the North American Indians*. 1984.

Cook, Don. *Ten Men and History*. 1981.

Cott, Jonathan. *Isis and Osiris*. 1994.

———. *The Search for Omm Sety*. 1987.

Cott, Jonathan, ed. *Skies in Blossom: The Nature Poetry of Emily Dickinson*. Illustrated by Mary Frank. 1995.

Cott, Jonathan, and Christine Doudna, eds., with Rolling Stone Press. *The Ballad of John and Yoko*. 1982.

De Combray, Richard. *Goodbye, Europe*. 1983.

Crook, Elizabeth. *The Raven's Bride*. 1991.

———. *Promised Lands*. 1994.

Custine, the Marquis de. *Empire of the Czar*. 1989.

Eggleston, William. *The Democratic Forest*. 1989.

Elliott, Carl. *The Cost of Courage: The Journey of an American Congressman*. 1992.

Farber, Robert. *By the Sea* (acquired by Doubleday, published by Melrose Square). 1987.

Frissell, Toni. *Toni Frissell: Photographs, 1939–1967*. Introduction by George Plimpton. 1994.

Giles, Sarah. *Fred Astaire: His Friends Talk*. 1988.

Gonick, Larry. *The Cartoon History of the Universe*, Volume 1. 1990.

———. *The Cartoon History of the Universe*, Volume 2. 1992.

Graham, Martha. *Blood Memory*. 1993.

Hampton, Mark. *Legendary Decorators of the Twentieth Century*. 1992.

Jackson, Michael. *Moonwalk*. 1988.

Jamison, Judith. *Dancing Spirit*. 1993.

Jhabvala, Ruth Prawer. *Poet and Dancer*. 1993.

———. *Shards of Memory*. 1995.

Kennedy, Eugene. *Father's Day*. 1981.

———. *Queen Bee*. 1982.

Kirkland, Gelsey, with Greg Lawrence. *Dancing on My Grave*. 1986.

———. *The Little Ballerina and Her Dancing Horse*. 1993.

———. *The Shape of Love*. 1990.

Ladd, Mary-Sargent. *The French Woman's Bedroom*. 1991.

Lincoln, W. Bruce. *Between Heaven and Hell: The Story of a Thousand Years of Artistic Life in Russia* (acquired by Doubleday, published by Viking Penguin). 1998.

Linscott, Jodi. *Once Upon A to Z: An Alphabet Odyssey*. Illustrations by Claudia Porges Holland. 1991.

———. *The Worthy Wonders Lost at Sea: A Whimsical World Search Adventure*. 1993.

Loring, John. *The New Tiffany Table Settings*. 1981.

———. *The Tiffany Gourmet Cookbook*. 1992.

———. *Tiffany Parties*. 1989.

———. *Tiffany's 150 Years*. 1992.

———. *Tiffany Taste*. 1986.

———. *The Tiffany Wedding*. 1988.

Lowe, David Garrard. *Stanford White's New York*. 1992.

Lyons, Robert. *Egyptian Time*. 1992.

Mahfouz, Naguib. The *Cairo Trilogy: Palace Walk, Palace of Desire*, and *Sugar Street*. 1990, 1991, and 1992.

Mason, Frances. *I Remember Balanchine*. 1991.

Moyers, Bill. *Healing and the Mind*. 1993.

———. *A World of Ideas: Conversations with Thoughtful Men and Women About American Life Today and the Ideas Shaping Our Future*. 1989.

———. *A World of Ideas II*. 1990.

Patnaik, Naveen. *The Garden of Life: An Introduction to the Healing Plants of India*. 1993.

———. *A Second Paradise: Indian Courtly Life, 1590–1947*. 1985.

Peskov, Vasily. *Lost in the Taiga: One Russian Family's Fifty-Year Struggle for Survival and Religious Freedom in the Siberian Wilderness*. 1994.

Plimpton, George. *Fireworks: A History and Celebration*. 1984.

Pope-Hennessy, John. *Learning to Look: My Life in Art*. 1991.

Previn, André. *No Minor Chords: My Days in Hollywood.* 1991.

Pushkin, Aleksandr. *The Golden Cockerel and Other Fairy Tales.* Introduction by Rudolf Nureyev. 1990.

Radzinsky, Edvard. *The Last Tsar: The Life and Death of Nicholas II.* 1992.

————. *Stalin: The First In-depth Biography Based on Explosive New Documents from Russia's Secret Archives.* 1996.

Ramati, Raquel. *How to Save Your Own Street.* 1981.

Redford, Dorothy. *Somerset Homecoming: Recovering a Lost Heritage.* 1988.

Riboud, Marc. *The Capital of Heaven.* 1990.

Rothschild, Miriam. *Butterfly Cooing Like a Dove.* 1991

Simon, Carly. *Amy the Dancing Bear.* 1989.

————. *The Boy of the Bells.* 1990.

————. *The Fisherman's Song.* 1991.

————. *The Nighttime Chauffeur.* 1993.

Sís, Peter. *The Three Golden Keys.* 1994.

Sloane, Florence Adele. *Maverick in Mauve.* Edited by Louis Auchincloss. 1983.

Steinke, Darcey. *Up Through the Water.* 1989.

Steinkraus, William C., ed. *The De Nemethy Method: Modern Techniques for Training the Show Jumper and the Rider.* 1988.

Stenn, David. *Bombshell: The Life and Death of Jean Harlow.* 1993.

————. *Clara Bow: Runnin' Wild.* 1988.

Turbeville, Deborah. *Unseen Versailles.* Introduction by Louis Auchincloss. 1982.

Udall, Stuart. *To the Inland Empire: Coronado and Our Spanish Legacy.* 1987.

Valenti, Jack. *Protect and Defend.* 1992.

Vreeland, Diana. *Allure.* 1980.

Walter, Jakob. *Diary of a Napoleonic Foot Soldier.* 1991.

Walton, William, ed. *A Civil War Courtship: The Letters of Edwin Weller from Antietam to Atlanta.* 1980.

Wenner, Jann, ed. *The Best of Rolling Stone: 25 Years of Journalism on the Edge.* 1993.

West, Dorothy. *The Wedding.* 1995.

Wise, David. *The Samarkand Dimension.* 1987.

Zamoyska-Panek, Christine. *Have You Forgotten? A Memoir of Poland, 1939–1945.* 1989.

Zaroulis, Nancy. *Call the Darkness Light.* 1979.

Sources

Introduction

Interviews

Joe Armstrong, Louis Auchincloss, Liz Smith (interview and e-mail correspondence), Gloria Steinem (via e-mail correspondence), J. C. Suarès (interview and e-mail correspondence).

Books and Periodicals

Adler, Bill, ed. *The Eloquent Jacqueline Onassis*. New York: William Morrow, 2004.

Berg, A. Scott. *Max Perkins: Editor of Genius*. New York: E. P. Dutton, 1978.

Dunne, Dominick. "Forever Jackie." *Vanity Fair,* July 1994 (Naveen Patnaik quote: "If you produce one book . . .").

"First Lady Jacqueline Kennedy Onassis, 1929–1994." Reprint of Senator Edward Kennedy's memorial eulogy delivered at St. Ignatius Loyola Church, New York City, May 23, 1994. Memorial Tributes in the One Hundred Third Congress of the United States. Washington, D.C.: U.S. Government Printing Office, 1995.

Hamilton, Edith. *The Greek Way*. New York: W.W. Norton, 1993.

Jackie: Behind the Myth. PBS broadcast, November 29, 1999 (Katell Le Bourhis).

"Jackie on Her Own." *Newsweek,* September 29, 1975.

Mailer, Norman. "The Prisoner of Celebrity." *Esquire,* December 1983.

Rubin, Harriet. *The Princessa: Machiavelli for Women: The Art of Women, Age, and Power*. New York: Doubleday Business, 1997.

Silverman, Al. *The Time of Their Lives: The Golden Age of Publishers, Their Editors and Authors*. New York: St. Martin's Press, 2008.

Steinem, Gloria. "Gloria Steinem on Jacqueline Onassis," and "Jacqueline Onassis on Working." *Ms.,* March 1979.

1. A Special Destiny

Interviews

Louis Auchincloss, Rich Barber, Peter Beard, Stephen Birmingham, Jimmy Breslin, Barbara Burn, Linda Grant De Pauw, Thomas Guinzburg, Christopher Holme, Conover Hunt, David Garrard Lowe, Deborah Nevins, Daniel Okrent, Marc Riboud, Harriet Rubin (e-mail correspondence), Miriam Schneir, Elisabeth Sifton, Becky Singleton (e-mail correspondence), Theodore Sorensen, Gloria Steinem (e-mail correspondence), Gael Towey, David Zinsser.

Books and Periodicals

Adler, Bill, ed. *The Eloquent Jacqueline Onassis*. New York: William Morrow, 2004.

Anderson, Christopher. *Jackie After Jack: Portrait of the Lady*. New York: William Morrow, 1998 (Marc Riboud and Jackie in Central Park quote).

Anthony, Carl Sferrazza. *As We Remember Her: Jacqueline Kennedy Onassis in the Words of her Friends and Family*. New York: HarperCollins, 1997.

Beard, Peter. *Longing for Darkness: Kamante's Tales from Out of Africa.* New York: Harcourt Brace Jovanovich, 1975.

Birmingham, Stephen. *Jacqueline Bouvier Kennedy Onassis.* New York: Grosset & Dunlap, 1978.

———. "The Public Event Named Jackie." *New York Times,* June 20, 1976.

Bradford, Sarah. *America's Queen: The Life of Jacqueline Kennedy Onassis.* New York: Viking Penguin, 2000 (Karen Lerner).

Capote, Truman. *Answered Prayers: The Unfinished Novel.* New York: Random House, 1987.

Churcher, Sharon, and Ellen Hawkes. "The Mother of the Bride." *Ladies' Home Journal,* August 1986.

De Pauw, Linda Grant, and Conover Hunt, with the assistance of Miriam Schneir. *Remember the Ladies: Women in America, 1750–1815.* New York: Viking, 1976.

Dunne, Dominick. "Forever Jackie." *Vanity Fair,* July 1994.

Epstein, Jason. *Eating: A Memoir.* New York: Alfred A. Knopf, 2009.

Fay, Paul. *The Pleasure of His Company: John F. Kennedy,* New York: Harper and Row, 1966.

Gibson, Barbara, and Harriet LaBarre. "The Rose Days: My Years as Rose Kennedy's Secretary." *Ladies' Home Journal,* April 1978.

Heymann, C. David. "The Very Private Life of Jacqueline Kennedy Onassis." *Cosmopolitan,* June 1986.

Jackie: Behind the Myth, PBS broadcast, November 29, 1999.

"Jackie's World." *People,* April 18, 1977.

"Jacqueline Kennedy Onassis, 1929–1994." *Newsweek,* May 30, 1994.

Jovanovich, William. *The Temper of the West: A Memoir.* Columbia, SC: University of South Carolina Press, 2003.

Kashner, Sam. "A Clash of Camelots." *Vanity Fair,* October 2009.

Kelleher, K. L. *Jackie: Behind the Myth of Camelot.* Bloomington, IN: Xlibris Corporation, 2000.

Kennedy, Jacqueline Bouvier, and Lee Bouvier. *One Special Summer.* New York: Delacorte Press, 1974.

Kennedy, John F. *Profiles in Courage.* New York: Harper & Brothers, 1955.

Krebs, Albin. "Jacqueline Onassis Is Editor at Viking." *New York Times,* September 17, 1975.

Manchester, William. *The Death of a President.* New York: Harper & Row, 1967.

Martin, Douglas. "Paul B. Fay Jr., 91, Buddy of President Kennedy, Dies." *New York Times,* September 30, 2009.

McLendon, Winzola. "The New Jackie." *Ladies' Home Journal,* January 1976.

"Miss Onassis Denies Her Father Planned Divorce." *New York Times,* April 18, 1975.

Nevins, Deborah. *Grand Central Terminal.* New York: Municipal Art Society, 1982.

Onassis, Jacqueline Kennedy (uncredited). "Being Present," The Talk of the Town. *New Yorker,* January 13, 1975.

Peer, Elizabeth. "Jackie on Her Own." *Newsweek,* September 29, 1975.

"Remembering Jackie." The Talk of the Town. *New Yorker,* May 30, 1994.

Sidey, Hugh. *John F. Kennedy: President.* New York: Atheneum, 1963.

Silverman, Al. *The Time of Their Lives: The Golden Age of Publishers, Their Editors and Authors.* New York: St. Martin's Press, 2008.

Sorensen, Theodore. *Counselor: A Life at the Edge of History.* New York: Harper, 2008.

Steinem, Gloria. "Gloria Steinem on Jacqueline Onassis," and "Jacqueline Onassis on Working." *Ms.,* March 1979 ("I remember a taxi driver . . ." and other references).

2. In the Russian Style, by Way of Paris

Interviews

William Howard Adams (interview and e-mail correspondence), Joe Armstrong, Rosamond Bernier, Ferle Bramson, Jimmy Breslin, Barbara Burn, Barbara Chase-Riboud, Thomas Guinzburg, Christopher Holme, Eugene Kennedy, Suzanne Massie, Delfina Rattazzi (e-mail correspondence), Jeannette Seaver, Elisabeth Sifton, Becky Singleton (e-mail correspondence), Judith Straeten, Gael Towey, Frederick Vreeland (e-mail correspondence and interview), Nicholas Vreeland, David Zinsser

Books and Periodicals

Adler, Bill, ed. *The Eloquent Jacqueline Onassis.* New York: William Morrow, 2004.

Anthony, Carl Sferrazza. *As We Remember Her: Jacqueline Kennedy Onassis in the Words of Her Friends and Family.* New York: HarperCollins, 1997.

Baker, John F. "Star Behind the Scenes." *Publishers Weekly,* April 19, 1993.

Brady, Mathew. See http://memory.loc.gov/ammem/cwphtml/cwbrady.html.

Breslin, Jimmy. "The Hierarchy of Decency." *Chicago Tribune,* May 19, 2002.

Chase-Riboud, Barbara. *Sally Hemings.* New York: Viking, 1979; Chicago Review Press, 2009.

Dwight, Eleanor. *Diana Vreeland.* New York: William Morrow, 2002.

Eller, Claudia. "DreamWorks Suggests Writer 'Cribbed' from Earlier Work," *Los Angeles Times,* December 3, 1997.

Hoving, Thomas. *Making the Mummies Dance: Inside the Metropolitan Museum of Art.* New York: Simon & Schuster, 1993.

"Jacqueline Kennedy Onassis, 1929–1994." *Newsweek,* May 30, 1994.

Kennedy, Eugene. *Himself! The Life and Times of Mayor Richard J. Daley.* New York: Viking, 1978.

Kennedy, Eugene. "As an Editor, She Was a Total Professional. *New York Newsday,* May 24, 1994.

Kennedy, John F. "Remarks at a Dinner Honoring Nobel Prize Winners of the Western Hemisphere," April 29, 1962. *Public Papers of the Presidents of the United States,* excerpt link: http://www.presidency.ucsb.edu/ws/index.php?pid=8623&st=&st1=.

Krebs, Albin. "Notes on People." *New York Times,* September 17, 1975, November 2, 1976, April 5, 1977.

Loke, Margarett. "Writer Who Cried Plagiarism Used Passages She Didn't Write." *New York Times,* December 19, 1997.

Maynard, Joyce. "Heiress, Working Girl." *New York Times,* March 6, 1977.

———. "Jacqueline Onassis Makes a New Debut," *New York Times,* January 14, 1977.

Mellon, James. *The Face of Lincoln.* New York: Studio Books, 1979.

Morris, Bernadine. "Metropolitan Toasts a Dazzling Russia of Old." *New York Times,* December 7, 1976.

Onassis, Jacqueline, ed. *In the Russian Style.* New York: Viking and the Metropolitan Museum of Art, 1976.

———. *The Firebird and Other Russian Fairy Tales.* Introduction by Jacqueline Kennedy Onassis. New York: Viking, 1978.

Onassis, Jacqueline. Letter to Vava Adelberg, July 17, 1979, located on History-For-Sale Web site, December 1, 2009, http://www.historyforsale.com.

Penn, Irving, and Diana Vreeland. *Inventive Paris Clothes, 1909–1939: A Photographic Essay.* New York: Viking, 1977.

"Remembering Jackie." The Talk of the Town. *New Yorker,* May 30, 1994.

Rich, Frank. "Who Stole History?" *New York Times,* December 13, 1997.

Talley, André Leon. *A.L.T.: A Memoir,* New York: Villard, 2003.

Todd, Olivier. *Malraux.* New York: Alfred A. Knopf, 2005.

Vanity Fair: Four Centuries of Fashion from the Costume Institute of the Metropolitan Museum of Art. New York: Metropolitan Museum of Art, 1977.

Warhol, Andy, and Pat Hackett. *The Andy Warhol Diaries.* New York: Warner, 1989.

Weinraub, Bernard. "Filmmakers Of 'Amistad' Rebut Claim by Novelist." *New York Times,* December 4, 1997.

———. "Plagiarism Suit Over 'Amistad' Is Withdrawn." *New York Times,* February 10, 1998.

3. A Tale of Two Houses

Interviews

William Howard Adams, Ann Appelbaum, Jeffrey Archer, Joe Armstrong, Rich Barber, Loretta Barrett, Carolyn Blakemore, Barbara Burn, Peter Duchin, Patrick Filley (e-mail correspondence), James Fitzgerald, Thomas Guinzburg, Eugene Kennedy, Eric Nicholas, Deborah Owen, Kenneth Pitchford, Les Pockell, Raquel Ramati, Sally Richardson, Glenn Rounds, Harriet Rubin (e-mail correspondence), Elisabeth Sifton, Al Silverman, Becky Singleton (e-mail correspondence), Nancy Stauffer, Deborah Turbeville, Amanda Vaill, Samuel Vaughan, Nicholas Vreeland, Nancy Zaroulis (correspondence).

Books and Periodicals

Adams, William Howard. *Atget's Gardens.* Garden City NY: Doubleday, 1979.

"Americana: Situation Wanted, References Available" *Time,* October 24, 1977.

Anderson, Christopher. *Jackie After Jack: Portrait of the Lady.* New York: William Morrow, 1998.

Anderson, Jack, and Les Whitten, *Washington Post,* December 14, 1977.

Anthony, Carl Sferrazza. *As We Remember Her: Jacqueline Kennedy Onassis in the Words of Her Friends and Family.* New York: HarperCollins, 1997.

Appelbaum, Stephen A. *Out in Inner Space: A Psychoanalyst Explores the Alternative Therapies.* Garden City, NY: Anchor Press/Doubleday, 1979.

Archer, Jeffrey. *Shall We Tell the President?* New York: Viking, 1977.

Baker, John F. "Star Behind the Scenes." *Publishers Weekly,* April 19, 1993.

Beevor, Antony, and Artemis Cooper. *Independent,* May 21, 1994.

Behrens, David. "A Long Way from Camelot." *Newsday,* July 26, 1979.

Birmingham, Stephen. "The Public Event Named Jackie," *New York Times,* June 20, 1976.

Boston Globe, October 12, 1977.

Bradford, Sarah. *America's Queen: The Life of Jacqueline Kennedy Onassis.* New York: Viking Penguin, 2000.

Breslin, Jimmy. "It Was a Life Well Spent." *Newsday,* May 20, 1994.

Carmody, Deirdre. "Mrs. Onassis Resigns Editing Post," *New York Times,* October 15, 1977.

Crick, Michael. *Jeffrey Archer: Stranger Than Fiction.* London: Hamish Hamilton, 1995.

Diliberto, Gioia. "A Working Woman." *People,* June 18, 1984.

Guinzburg, Thomas. Columbia University, Butler Library, oral history, February 1980.

Hoenig, Gary, "Mrs. Kennedy Quits." *New York Times,* October 16, 1977.

"An Illustrated Benefit for Books." *New York Times,* November 3, 1977.

"Jackie's World." *People,* April 18, 1977.

Kaufman, Joanne. "Polite Answers to Rude Questions." The Talk of the Town. *New Yorker,* January 16, 1995.

Klein, Edward. *Just Jackie: Her Private Years.* New York: Ballantine, 1998 (author interview with Dr. Stephen Appelbaum).

Leonard, John. "Presidents in Trouble." *New York Times,* October 10, 1977.

McGrath, Charles. "Corlies Smith, Editor of All-Star Authors, Dies at 75." *New York Times,* November 24, 2004.

Menaker, Daniel. "Redactor Agonistes." Barnes & Noble review, September 14, 2009, http://bnreview.barnesandnoble.com/t5/Reviews-Essays/Redactor-Agonistes/ba-p/1367.

Onassis, Jacqueline. Correspondence with Ray Roberts. University of Texas, Harry Ransom Center archive.

Ramati, Raquel. *How to Save Your Own Street.* Garden City, NY: Dolphin Books, 1981.

Schlesinger Jr., Arthur M. Letter to Jacqueline Kennedy Onassis, William Walton Papers, JFK Library. *Journals: 1952–2000.* New York: Penguin, 2007.

Silverman, Al. *The Time of Their Lives: The Golden Age of Great American*

Publishers, Their Editors and Authors. New York: St. Martin's Press, 2008.

Spoto, Donald. *Jacqueline Bouvier Kennedy Onassis: A Life.* New York: St. Martin's Press, 2000.

Steinem, Gloria. "Gloria Steinem on Jacqueline Onassis" and "Jacqueline Onassis on Working." *Ms.,* March 1979.

Thayer, Mary Van Rensselaer. "First Lady Will Be 'Found Laughing with Tucky,'" *Washington Post,* February 23, 1963.

Tuckerman, Nancy. Letter to Dr. Stephen Appelbaum, November 7, 1977, online auction of Jacqueline Onassis memorabilia, www.historyforsale .com, 2009.

Vreeland, Diana, with Christopher Hemphill. *Allure.* Garden City, NY: Doubleday, 1980.

Walton, William. *A Civil War Courtship: The Letters of Edwin Weller from Antietam to Atlanta.* City: Doubleday, 1980.

———. Correspondence. John F. Kennedy Library archives.

Zaroulis, Nancy. *Call the Darkness Light.* Garden City, NY: Doubleday, 1979.

4. An Office with a Window

Interviews

Joe Armstrong, Louis Auchincloss, Peter Beard, Olivier Bernier, Paul Bresnick, Jonathan Cott, Christine Doudna, Eugene Kennedy, John Loring, Hope Marinetti (interview and e-mail correspondence), John Sargent Jr., J. C. Suarès.

Books and Periodicals

Anderson, Christopher. *Jackie After Jack: Portrait of the Lady.* New York: William Morrow, 1998.

Auchincloss, Louis. "Belles Lettres." *Quest,* May 1997.

Baker, John F. "Star Behind the Scenes." *Publishers Weekly,* April 19, 1993.

Bernier, Olivier. *At the Court of Napoleon.* New York: Doubleday, 1989.

———. *The Eighteenth-Century Woman.* Garden City, NY: Doubleday, 1982.

———. *Louis XIV: A Royal Life*. Garden City, NY: Doubleday, 1987.

———. *Pleasure and Privilege*. Foreword by Louis Auchincloss. Garden City, NY: Doubleday, 1981.

———. *Secrets of Marie Antoinette*. New York: Doubleday, 1985.

Cook, Dan. *Ten Men and History*. Garden City, NY: Doubleday, 1981.

Cott, Jonathan and Christine Doudna, eds. *The Ballad of John and Yoko*. Garden City, NY: Rolling Stone Press and Doubleday, 1982.

Diliberto, Gioia. "A Working Woman." *People*, June 18, 1984 (Dan Cook, Jann Wenner, and Sarah Lazin).

"Facing Clink, Ron Vows No Jackie Clicks." *New York Post*, March 24, 1982.

Jackie: Behind the Myth. PBS broadcast, November 29, 1999.

Kachka, Boris. "Old School." *New York Magazine*, January 3, 2005 (Louis Auchincloss).

Kennedy, Eugene. "As an Editor, She Was a Total Professional." *Newsday*, May 24, 1994.

———. *Father's Day*. Garden City, NY: Doubleday, 1981.

———. *Queen Bee*. Garden City, NY: Doubleday, 1982.

Klein, Edward. *Farewell, Jackie: A Portrait of Her Final Days*. New York: Viking, 2004.

———. *Just Jackie: Her Private Years*. New York: Ballantine, 1998.

Loring, John, *The New Tiffany Table Settings*. Garden City, NY: Doubleday, 1981.

———. *The Tiffany Gourmet Cookbook*. New York: Doubleday, 1992.

———. *Tiffany Parties*. New York: Doubleday, 1989.

———. *Tiffany's 150 Years*. New York: Doubleday, 1992.

———. *Tiffany Taste*. Garden City, NY: Doubleday, 1986.

———. *The Tiffany Wedding*. New York: Doubleday, 1988.

Steinem, Gloria. "Gloria Steinem on Jacqueline Onassis" and "Jacqueline Onassis on Working." *Ms.*, March 1979.

5. Unseen Vistas and Avant-Gardens

Interviews

Louis Auchincloss, Shammi Bannu, Richard de Combray, Robert Farber, Michael Flanagan, Sarah Giles, Marcia Jacobs, Kenneth Pitchford, Deborah Turbeville, Samuel Vaughan, Nicholas Vreeland, Albert Yokum.

Books and Periodicals

Auchincloss, Louis. "Belles Lettres." *Quest,* May 1997.

———. *False Dawn: Women in the Age of the Sun King.* New York: Double-day, 1984.

Anthony, Carl Sferrazza. *As We Remember Her: Jacqueline Kennedy Onassis in the Words of Her Friends and Family.* New York: HarperCollins, 1997.

Bradford, Sarah. *America's Queen: The Life of Jacqueline Kennedy Onassis.* New York: Viking Penguin, 2000.

Brenner, Marie. *Great Dames: What I Learned from Older Women.* New York: Three Rivers Press, 2001.

———. "Jackie Tops at Shunning the Limelight." *Los Angeles Times,* October 23, 1983.

"The Dashing Writer in Jackie O's Life." Headliners. *New York Post,* March 31, 1983.

De Combray, Richard. *Goodbye Europe: A Novel in Six Parts.* Garden City, NY: Doubleday, 1983.

Dunne, Dominick. "Forever Jackie." *Vanity Fair,* July 1994.

Farber, Robert. *By the Sea.* Los Angeles, CA: Melrose Square, 1987.

Fee, Gayle, and Laura Raposa. "Jackie's Private Letter to Joan Up for Bid." *Boston Herald,* February 23, 2007.

Flanagan, Michael. "Famous." Unpublished manuscript.

Jackie: Behind the Myth. PBS broadcast, November 29, 1999.

"Jackie Onassis Finds Handsome New Love, Writer Richard de Combray." *Star,* April 19, 1983.

Keillor, Garrison. "Remembering Plimpton." *A Prairie Home Companion,* October 1, 2003, http://prairiehome.publicradio.org/features.

Kelleher, K. L. *Jackie: Behind the Myth of Camelot.* Bloomington, IN: Xlibris, 2000.

McNamara, Katherine. "A Conversation About Publishing with Samuel S. Vaughan," http://www.archipelago.org/vol3-2/vaughan1.htm, accessed February 21, 2010.

Paris Review, Twenty-fifth Anniversary issue, *Spring 1981.*

Patnaik, Naveen. *A Second Paradise: Indian Courtly Life, 1590–1947.* Garden City, NY: Doubleday, 1985.

Pitchford, Kenneth. *The Beholding.* Bloomington, IN: Xlibris, 2005.

Plimpton, George. *Fireworks: A History and Celebration.* Garden City, NY: Doubleday, 1984.

Sloane, Florence Adele. *Maverick in Mauve.* Garden City, NY: Doubleday, 1983.

A Tribute to Jacqueline Kennedy Onassis. New York: Doubleday, 1995.

Turbeville, Deborah. *Newport Remembered: A Photographic Portrait of a Gilded Past.* New York: Abrams, 1994.

————. *Unseen Versailles.* Garden City, NY: Doubleday, 1982.

6. *Moonwalk* and the Power of Myth

Interviews

Joe Armstrong, Loretta Barrett, Gelsey Kirkland Chernov, Jonathan Cott, Stephen Davis, Stuart P. Feld, James Fitzgerald, Betty Sue Flowers, Thomas Guinzburg, Peter H. Hassrick, Robert Hilburn, Jerry Jacka, Jan Legnitto, Les Pockell, Harriet Rubin (e-mail correspondence), John Sargent David Stenn, Jr., J. C. Suarès (interviews and e-mail correspondence), Samuel Vaughan, Alberto Vitale (interview and e-mail exchange), Karen Van Westering, Albert Yokum.

Books and Periodicals

Anthony, Carl Sferrazza. *As We Remember Her: Jacqueline Kennedy Onassis in the Words of Her Friends and Family.* New York: HarperCollins, 1997.

Baker, John F. "Star Behind the Scenes." *Publishers Weekly,* April 19, 1993.

Bradford, Sarah. *America's Queen: The Life of Jacqueline Kennedy Onassis.* New York: Viking Penguin, 2000.

Campbell, Joseph, with Bill Moyers. *The Power of Myth.* New York: Doubleday, 1988.

Cott, Jonathan. *Iris and Osiris.* New York: Doubleday, 1994.

————. *The Search for Omm Sety.* Garden City, NY: Doubleday, 1987.

De Nemethy, Bertalan. *Modern Techniques for Training the Show Jumper and the Rider.* New York: Doubleday, 1988.

Dunne, Dominick. "Forever Jackie." *Vanity Fair,* July 1994.

Eggleston, William. *The Democratic Forest.* New York: Doubleday, 1989.

Gross, John. "An 'It' Girl's Progress to Hollywood." *New York Times,* September 6, 1988.

Jackie: Behind the Myth. PBS broadcast, November 29, 1999.

Jackson, Michael. *Moonwalk.* New York: Harmony, 2009.

————. *Moonwalk,* New York: Doubleday, 1988.

Jowitt, Deborah. "Through the Flames on Thin Soles." *New York Times,* October 19, 1986.

Kirkland, Gelsey, and Greg Lawrence. *Dancing on My Grave*. Garden City, NY: Doubleday, 1986.

———. *The Little Ballerina and her Dancing Horse*. New York: Doubleday, 1993.

———. *The Shape of Love*. New York: Doubleday, 1990.

Larson, Stephen, and Robin Larson. *A Fire in the Mind: The Life of Joseph Campbell,* New York: Doubleday, 1991.

McDowell, Edwin, "At Doubleday, the New Boss's Ideas Start to Take Hold," *New York Times,* August 8, 1987.

Moyers, Bill. *Healing and The Mind*. New York: Doubleday, 1993.

———. *A World of Ideas: Conversations with Thoughtful Men and Women About American Life Today and the Ideas Shaping Our Future*. New York: Doubleday, 1989.

———. *A World of Ideas II*. New York: Doubleday, 1990.

Patnaik, Naveen. *The Garden of Life: An Introduction to the Healing Plants of India*. New York: Doubleday, 1993.

"Shaye Areheart of Harmony Books on Conversations LIVE! Radio," October 13, 2009, www.blogtalkradio.com.

"Singer Michael Jackson Hurt When His Hair Catches Fire." *New York Times,* January 28, 1984.

Spoto, Donald. *Jacqueline Bouvier Kennedy Onassis: A Life*. New York: St. Martin's Press, 2000.

Stenn, David. *Bombshell: The Life and Death of Jean Harlow*. New York: Doubleday, 1993.

———. *Clara Bow: Runnin' Wild*. New York: Doubleday, 1988.

Suarès, Jean-Claude, and J. Spencer Beck. *Uncommon Grace: Reminiscences and Photographs of Jacqueline Bouvier Kennedy Onassis*. Charlottesville, VA: Thomasson-Grant, 1994.

Tucker, Ken. "Summer Reading; Firing Your Father Isn't Easy." *New York Times,* June 5, 1988.

Udall, Stewart. *To the Inland Empire: Coronado and Our Spanish Legacy*. Garden City, NY: Doubleday, 1987.

Wolcott, James. "Sex and Drugs and Folderol." *Vanity Fair,* November 1986.

Young, James L. *A Field of Horses: The World of Marshall P. Hawkins*. Foreword by Jacqueline Kennedy Onassis. Dallas, TX: Taylor Publishing Co., 1988.

7. Bon Courage

Interviews

Joe Armstrong, Louis Auchincloss, James Bakalar, Vicky Bijur, Carolyn Blakemore, Michael D'Orso, Sarah Giles, Larry Gonick, Vartan Gregorian, Fred Benton Holmberg (interview and e-mail correspondence), William Maynard Hutchins, Edward Kasinec, William La Riche, Martha Levin, Robert Lyons, Dorothy Spruill Redford (correspondence), Marc Riboud, Darcey Steinke, Derek Ungless, Samuel Vaughan, Alberto Vitale, Christine Zamoyska-Panek.

Books and Periodicals

Anderson, Christopher. *Jackie After Jack: Portrait of the Lady.* New York: William Morrow, 1998.

Anthony, Carl Sferrazza. *As We Remember Her: Jacqueline Kennedy Onassis in the Words of Her Friends and Family.* New York: HarperCollins, 1997.

Baker, John F. "Star Behind the Scenes." *Publishers Weekly,* April 19, 1993.

Bradford, Sarah. *America's Queen: The Life of Jacqueline Kennedy Onassis.* New York: Viking Penguin, 2000.

Brenner, Marie. "Carly Simon's Mother Load." *Vanity Fair,* August 1995.

Custine, the Marquis de, with Daniel Boorstin. *Empire of the Tsar: A Journey Through Eternal Russia.* New York: Doubleday, 1989.

Duchin, Peter, with Charles Michener. *Ghost of a Chance: A Memoir.* New York: Random House, 1996.

Dunne, Dominick. "Forever Jackie." *Vanity Fair,* July 1994.

Elliott, Carl Sr., and Michael D'Orso. *The Cost of Courage: The Journey of an American Congressman.* New York: Doubleday, 1992.

Ferguson, Sarah. "In Short Fiction." *New York Times,* October 11, 1992.

Giles, Sarah. *Fred Astaire: His Friends Talk.* New York: Doubleday, 1988.

Gregorian, Vartan. *The Road to Home: My Life and Times.* New York: Simon & Schuster, 2003.

Grossman, Edith. *Why Translation Matters.* New Haven, CT: Yale University Press, 2010.

"Jacqueline Kennedy Onassis, 1929–1994." *Newsweek,* May 30, 1994.

Johnson, George. "New & Noteworthy." *New York Times Book Review,* August 11, 1991.

———. "New & Noteworthy." *New York Times Book Review,* September 3, 1989.

Klein, Edward. *Farewell, Jackie: A Portrait of Her Final Days.* New York: Viking, 2004.

Lyons, Robert. *Egyptian Time.* New York: Doubleday, 1992.

Mahfouz, Naguib. The Cairo Trilogy: *Palace Walk, Palace of Desire,* and *Sugar Street.* New York: Anchor, 1989, 1991, 1992.

McNamara, Katherine. "A Conversation About Publishing with Samuel S. Vaughan," http://www.archipelago.org/vol3-2/vaughan1.htm, accessed February 21, 2010.

O'Brien, Edna. *Independent* on Sunday. May 22, 1994.

Pushkin, Aleksandr. *The Golden Cockerel and Other Fairy Tales.* Introduction by Rudolf Nureyev. New York: Doubleday, 1990.

Redford, Dorothy Spruill, with Michael D'Orso. *Somerset Homecoming: Recovering a Lost Heritage,* New York: Doubleday, 1988.

Riboud, Marc. *Capital of Heaven.* New York: Doubleday, 1990.

Salinger, Pierre. *P.S.: A Memoir.* New York: St. Martin's Press, 1995.

Simon, Carly. *Amy and the Dancing Bear.* New York: Doubleday, 1989.

———. *The Boy of the Bells.* New York: Doubleday, 1990.

———. *The Fisherman's Song.* New York: Doubleday, 1991.

———. *The Nighttime Chauffeur.* New York: Doubleday, 1993.

Spoto, Donald. *Jacqueline Bouvier Kennedy Onassis: A Life.* New York: St. Martin's Press, 2000.

Steinke, Darcey. "The First Lady of Letters," *Vogue,* February, 2005.

———. *Up Through the Water.* New York: Doubleday, 1989.

A Tribute to Jacqueline Kennedy Onassis. New York: Doubleday, 1995.

Walter, Jakob. *The Diary of a Napoleonic Foot Soldier.* New York: Doubleday, 1991.

Wise, David. *The Samarkand Dimension.* New York: Doubleday, 1987.

Zamoyska-Panek, Christine, and Fred Benton Holmberg. *Have You Forgotten? A Memoir of Poland, 1939–1945.* New York: Doubleday, 1989.

8. When Life Comes First

Interviews

Gretchen Achilles, Joe Armstrong, Barbara Bachman, Loretta Barrett, Rosamond Bernier, Elizabeth Crook, Baroness Mary-Sargent d'Anglejan, Owen Laster, Jody Linscott, Francis Mason, Simon Rendall, Harriet Rubin (e-mail correspondence), Marian Schwartz, Marianne Velmans, Alberto Vitale

Books and Periodicals

Anthony, Carl Sferrazza. *As We Remember Her: Jacqueline Kennedy Onassis in the Words of Her Friends and Family.* New York: HarperCollins, 1997.

Armstrong, Karen. *Holy War: The Crusades and Their Impact on Today's World.* New York: Doubleday, 1991.

Baker, John F. "Star Behind the Scenes." *Publishers Weekly,* April 19, 1993.

Berberova, Nina. *Moura: The Dangerous Life of the Baroness Budberg.* New York: New York Review Books Classics, 2005.

"Books for Vacation Reading." *New York Times Book Review,* May 31, 1992.

Cott, Jonathan. *Wandering Ghost: The Odyssey of Lafcadio Hearn.* New York: Alfred A. Knopf, 1991.

Crook, Elizabeth. *The Raven's Bride: A Novel of Eliza, Sam Houston's First Wife.* New York: Doubleday, 1991.

———. *Promised Lands.* New York: Doubleday, 1994.

Flanagan, Michael. "Famous." Unpublished manuscript.

Graham, Martha. *Blood Memory.* New York: Doubleday, 1991.

Honan, William H. "A Playwright Applies His Craft to Czar Nicholas II's Last Days." *New York Times,* August 12, 1992.

Hoving, Thomas. *Making the Mummies Dance: Inside the Metropolitan Museum of Art.* New York: Simon & Schuster, 1993.

Jackie: Behind the Myth. PBS broadcast, November 29, 1999.

Kelleher, K. L. *Jackie: Behind the Myth of Camelot.* Bloomington, IN: Xlibris, 2000.

Linscott, Jody. *Once Upon A to Z: An Alphabet Odyssey.* New York: Doubleday, 1991.

———. *The Worthy Wonders Lost at Sea: A Whimsical Word Search Adventure.* New York: Doubleday, 1993.

Martin, Douglas. "Miriam Rothschild, High-Spirited Naturalist, Dies at 96." *New York Times,* January 25, 2005.

Mason, Francis. *I Remember Balanchine:* New York: Doubleday, 1991.

Onassis, Jacqueline. Memorandum to Stephen Rubin. December 30, 1990, http://www.historyforsale.com, accessed April 1, 2010.

Pope-Hennessy, John. *Learning to Look: My Life in Art.* New York: Doubleday, 1991.

Previn, André. *No Minor Chords: My Days in Hollywood.* New York: Doubleday, 1991.

Radzinsky, Edvard. *The Last Tsar: The Life and Death of Nicholas II.* New York: Doubleday, 1992.

———. *Stalin: The First In-depth Biography Based on Explosive New Documents from Russia's Secret Archives.* New York: Doubleday, 1996.

Rothschild, Miriam. *Butterfly Cooing Like a Dove.* New York: Doubleday, 1991.

Russell, John. "Portrait of a Friendship." *Time,* May 30, 1994.

Sargent-Ladd, Mary. *The French Woman's Bedroom.* New York: Doubleday, 1991.

A Tribute to Jacqueline Kennedy Onassis. New York: Doubleday, 1995.

Wolcott, James. "James Wolcott's Blog." *Vanity Fair,* September 27, 2009, http://www.vanityfair.com/online/wolcott/.

9. All Will Be Well

Interviews

Joe Armstrong, Louis Auchincloss, Loretta Barrett, Jack Bass, Antony Beevor, Elizabeth Smith Brownstein, Jonathan Cott (interview and e-mail correspondence), Mary Frank, Duane Hampton, Judith Jamison, Ruth Prawer Jhabvala (correspondence), Terry Karydes, Henry Koehler, Peter Kruzan, Martha Levin, John Loring, David Garrard Lowe, Robert Lyons, Hope Marinetti, Francis Mason, Scott Moyers (e-mail correspondence), Harriet Rubin (e-mail correspondence), Stephen Rubin (e-mail correspondence), Marian Schwartz, Peter Sís (interview and e-mail correspondence), David Stenn, J. C. Suarès, Bruce Tracy (e-mail correspondence), John Valenti, Alberto Vitale (interview and e-mail correspondence), Mary Helen Washington, Albert Yokum.

Books and Periodicals

Anthony, Carl Sferrazza. *As We Remember Her: Jacqueline Kennedy Onassis in the Words of Her Friends and Family.* New York: HarperCollins, 1997.

Auchincloss, Hugh D. "Growing Up with Jackie." *Groton School Quarterly,* May 1998.

Auchincloss, Louis. "Belles Lettres." *Quest,* May 1997.

Baker, John F. "Star Behind the Scenes." *Publishers Weekly,* April 19, 1993.

Bass, Jack. *Taming the Storm: The Life and Times of Judge Frank M. John-*

son, Jr., and the South's Fight over Civil Rights. New York: Doubleday, 1993.

Beevor, Antony, and Artemis Cooper. *Paris After the Liberation, 1944–1949.* New York: Doubleday, 1994.

Bradford, Sarah, *America's Queen: The Life of Jacqueline Kennedy Onassis.* New York: Viking Penguin, 2000.

Brownstein, Elizabeth Smith. *If This House Could Talk: Historic Homes, Extraordinary Americans.* New York: Simon & Schuster, 1998.

Cott, Jonathan, and Mary Frank. *Skies in Blossom: The Nature Poetry of Emily Dickinson.* New York: Doubleday, 1995.

Coward, David. "France at War with Herself." *New York Times,* September 11, 1994.

Frissell, Toni. Foreword by Sydney Frissell Stafford. Introduction by George Plimpton. *Toni Frissell, Photographs: 1933–1967.* New York: Doubleday, 1994.

Hampton, Mark. *Legendary Decorators of the Twentieth Century.* New York: Doubleday, 1992.

Hearn, Michael Patrick. Letter to the Editor. *New York,* June 20, 1994.

Jackie: Behind the Myth. PBS broadcast, November 29, 1999.

Jamison, Judith. *Dancing Spirit.* New York: Doubleday, 1993.

Jhabvala, Ruth Prawer. *Poet and Dancer.* New York: Doubleday, 1993.

———. *Shards of Memory.* New York: Doubleday, 1995.

Kaufman, Marjorie. "Photographer 'Plucked from Oblivion.'" *New York Times,* August 28, 1994.

Kelleher, K. L. *Jackie: Behind the Myth of Camelot.* Bloomington, IN: Xlibris, 2000.

Kenney, Susan. "Shades of Difference." *New York Times,* February 12, 1995.

Klein, Edward. *Farewell, Jackie: A Portrait of Her Final Days.* New York: Viking, 2004.

Koncius, Jura. *Washington Post,* July 30, 1998.

Lincoln, W. Bruce. *Between Heaven and Hell: The Story of a Thousand Years of Artistic Life in Russia.* New York: Viking Penguin, 1998.

Lowe, David Garrard. *Stanford White's New York.* New York: Doubleday, 1992.

Lyons, Robert. *Another Africa.* Text by Chinua Achebe. New York: Anchor, 1998.

Mason, Francis. *I Remember Balanchine.* New York: Doubleday, 1993.

Peskov, Valery. *Lost in the Taiga: One Russian Family's Fifty-Year Struggle for Survival and Religious Freedom in the Siberian Wilderness.* New York: Doubleday, 1994.

"Remembering Jackie." Talk of the Town. *New Yorker,* May 30, 1994.

Rich, Frank, "The Jackie Mystery," *New York Times,* May 26, 1994.

Russell, John. "Portrait of a Friendship." *Time,* May 30, 1994.

Sís, Peter. *The Three Golden Keys.* New York: Doubleday, 1994.

———. *Tibet Through the Red Box.* New York: Farrar, Straus & Giroux, 1998.

Spoto, Donald. *Jacqueline Bouvier Kennedy Onassis: A Life.* New York: St. Martin's Press, 2000.

Stenn, David. "It Happened One Night . . . at MGM." *Vanity Fair,* April, 2003.

Valenti, Jack. *Protect and Defend.* New York: Doubleday, 1992.

———. *This Time, This Place: My Life in War, the White House, and Hollywood.* New York: Harmony, 2007.

West, Dorothy. *The Wedding.* New York: Doubleday, 1995.

———. *The Richer, the Poorer.* New York: Doubleday, 1995.

Bibliography and Archives

Selected Bibliography

The books listed below were utilized in the research for this book. Some are also cited in the chapter-by-chapter sources referenced in the narrative.

Adler, Bill, ed. *The Eloquent Jacqueline Onassis*. New York: William Morrow, 2004.

Alderman, Ellen, and Caroline Kennedy. *In Our Defense: The Bill of Rights in Action*. New York: William Morrow, 1991.

———. *The Right to Privacy*. New York: Alfred A. Knopf, 1995.

Anderson, Christopher P. *Jackie After Jack: Portrait of the Lady*. New York: William Morrow, 1998.

Anthony, Carl Sferrazza. *As We Remember Her: Jacqueline Kennedy Onassis in the Words of Her Family and Friends*. New York: HarperCollins, 1997.

————. *First Ladies, Volume II: The Saga of the Presidents' Wives and Their Power, 1961–1990,* New York: William Morrow, 1991.

Archer, Jeffrey. *Shall We Tell the President?* New York: Viking Press, 1977.

Armstrong, Karen. *Holy War: The Crusades and Their Impact on Today's World.* New York, Doubleday, 1991.

Astor, Brooke. *Footprints: An Autobiography.* New York: Doubleday, 1980.

Beard, Peter. *Longing for Darkness: Kamante's Tales from Out of Africa.* New York: Harcourt Brace Jovanovich, 1975.

Berg, A. Scott. *Max Perkins: Editor of Genius.* New York: E. P. Dutton, 1978.

Birmingham, Stephen. *Jacqueline Bouvier Kennedy Onassis.* New York: Grosset & Dunlap, 1978.

Bowles, Hamish, Arthur M. Schlesinger, and Rachel Lambert Mellon, eds., and the Metropolitan Museum of Art. *Jacqueline Kennedy: The White House Years: Selections from the John F. Kennedy Library and Museum.* New York: Bulfinch, 2001.

Bradford, Sarah. *America's Queen: A Life of Jacqueline Kennedy Onassis.* New York: Viking Penguin, 2000.

Brenner, Marie. *Great Dames: What I Learned from Older Women.* New York: Three Rivers Press, 2001.

Brownstein, Elizabeth Smith. *If This House Could Talk: Historic Homes, Extraordinary Americans.* New York: Simon & Schuster, 1998.

Capote, Truman. *Answered Prayers: The Unfinished Novel.* New York: Random House, 1987.

Clinton, Bill. *My Life.* New York: Alfred A. Knopf, 2004.

Clinton, Hillary Rodham. *Living History.* New York: Simon & Schuster, 2003.

Crick, Michael. *Jeffrey Archer: Stranger Than Fiction.* London: Hamish Hamilton, 1995.

David, Lester. *Jacqueline Kennedy Onassis: A Portrait of Her Private Years.* New York: Citadel Press, 1994.

Davis, John H. *The Bouviers.* New York: Farrar, Straus & Giroux, 1969.

————. *Jacqueline Bouvier: An Intimate Memoir.* New York: John Wiley and Sons, 1996.

Davis, Margaret Leslie, *Mona Lisa in Camelot: How Jacqueline Kennedy and Da Vinci's Masterpiece Charmed and Captivated a Nation,* Cambridge, MA: Da Capo Press, 2008.

Duchin, Peter, with Charles Michener. *Ghost of a Chance: A Memoir.* New York: Random House, 1996.

Dwight, Eleanor. *Diana Vreeland.* New York: William Morrow, 2002.

The Estate of Jacqueline Kennedy Onassis: April 23–26, 1996. New York: Sotheby's, 1996.

Evans, Peter. *Ari: The Life and Times of Aristotle Socrates Onassis*. New York: Summit Books, 1986.

Fay, Paul. *The Pleasure of His Company: John F. Kennedy*. New York: Harper & Row, 1966.

Goodman, Jon, Hugh Sidey, Letitia Baldrige, Robert Dallek, and Barbara Baker Burrows. *The Kennedy Mystique: Creating Camelot*. Washington, D.C.: National Geographic, 2006.

Graham, Katharine. *Personal History*. New York: Alfred A. Knopf, 1997.

Gregorian, Vartan. *The Road to Home: My Life and Times*. New York: Simon & Schuster, 2003.

Gross, Michael. *Rogues' Gallery: The Secret Story of the Moguls and the Money That Made the Metropolitan Museum of Art*. New York: Broadway Books, 2009.

Grossman, Edith. *Why Translation Matters*. New Haven, CT: Yale University Press, 2010.

Hamilton, Edith. *The Greek Way*. New York: W. W. Norton, 1993.

Hampton, Duane. *Mark Hampton: An American Decorator*. New York: Rizzoli, 2010.

Heymann, C. David. *Bobby and Jackie: A Love Story*. New York: Atria Books, 2009.

———. *A Woman Named Jackie: An Intimate Biography of Jacqueline Bouvier Kennedy Onassis*. New York: Lyle Stuart, 1989.

Hoving, Thomas. *Making the Mummies Dance: Inside the Metropolitan Museum of Art*. New York: Simon & Schuster, 1993.

Jovanovich, William. *The Temper of the West: A Memoir*, Columbia, SC: University of South Carolina Press, 2003.

Kaplan, Fred. *Gore Vidal: A Biography*. New York: Doubleday, 1999.

Kelleher, K. L. *Jackie: Beyond the Myth of Camelot*. Bloomington, IN: Xlibris Corporation, 2000.

Kennedy, Caroline, ed. *The Best-Loved Poems of Jacqueline Kennedy Onassis*. New York: Hyperion, 2001.

Kennedy, Jacqueline Bouvier, and Lee Bouvier. *One Special Summer*. New York: Delacorte Press, 1974.

Kennedy, Joan. *The Joy of Classical Music: A Guide for You and Your Family*. New York: Nan A. Talese, 1992.

Kennedy, John F. *Profiles in Courage*. New York: Harper & Brothers, 1955.

Keogh, Pamela Clarke. *Jackie Style*. New York: It Books, 2001.

Klein, Edward. *All Too Human: The Love Story of Jack and Jackie Kennedy*. New York: Pocket Books, 1996.

———. *Farewell, Jackie: A Portrait of Her Final Days*. New York: Viking, 2004.

———. *Just Jackie: Her Private Years*. New York: Ballantine Books, 1998.

Koestenbaum, Wayne. *Jackie Under My Skin: Interpreting an Icon*. London: Fourth Estate, 1996.

Larsen, Stephen, and Robin Larsen. *A Fire in the Mind: The Life of Joseph Campbell*. New York: Doubleday, 1991.

Leamer, Laurence. *The Kennedy Women*. New York: Villard Books, 1994.

Leaming, Barbara. *Marilyn Monroe*. New York: Crown, 1998.

———. *Mrs. Kennedy: The Missing History of the Kennedy Years*. New York: Free Press, 2001.

Lester, David. *Jacqueline Kennedy Onassis*. New York: Birch Lane Press, 1994.

Lincoln, W. Bruce. *Between Heaven and Hell: The Story of a Thousand Years of Artistic Life in Russia*. New York: Viking Penguin, 1998.

Lowe, Jacques. *Camelot: The Kennedy Years*. Kansas City, MO: Andrews McMeel, 1996.

Manchester, William. *The Death of a President*. New York: Harper & Row, 1967.

Mars, Julie. *Jackie*. Kansas City, MO: Andrews McMeel, 1996.

Massie, Suzanne. *Land of the Firebird: The Beauty of Old Russia*. New York: Simon & Schuster, 1981.

Moutsatsos, Kiki Feroudi, with Phyllis Kara. *The Onassis Women: An Eyewitness Account*. New York: G. P. Putnam's Sons, 1998.

Mulvaney, Jay, and Dominick Dunne. *Jackie: The Clothes of Camelot*. New York: St. Martin's Press, 2001.

Nevins, Deborah. *Grand Central Terminal*. New York: Municipal Art Society, 1982.

Pottker, Jan. *Janet and Jackie: The Story of a Mother and Her Daughter, Jacqueline Kennedy Onassis*. New York: St. Martin's Press, 2001.

Radziwill, Lee. *Happy Times*. New York: Assouline, 2001.

Rubin, Harriet. *The Mona Lisa Stratagem: The Art of Women, Age, and Power*. New York: Warner Books, 2007.

———. *The Princessa: Machiavelli for Women*. New York: Doubleday Business, 1997.

Sidey, Hugh. *John F. Kennedy: President*. New York: Atheneum, 1963.

Silverman, Al. *The Time of Their Lives: The Golden Age of Great American Publishers, Their Editors and Authors*. New York: St. Martin's Press, 2008.

Schlesinger, Arthur M. Jr. *Journals: 1952–2000.* Edited by Andrew Schlesinger and Stephen Schlesinger. New York: Penguin, 2007.

Sís, Peter. *Tibet Through the Red Box.* New York: Farrar, Straus & Giroux, 1998.

Smith, Liz. *Natural Blonde.* New York: Hyperion, 2000.

Sorensen, Theodore. *Counselor: A Life at the Edge of History.* New York: Harper, 2008.

Spoto, Donald. *Jacqueline Bouvier Kennedy Onassis: A Life.* New York: St. Martin's Press, 2000.

Suarès, Jean-Claude, and J. Spencer Beck. *Uncommon Grace: Reminiscences and Photographs of Jacqueline Bouvier Kennedy Onassis.* Charlottesville, VA: Thomasson-Grant, 1994.

Talley, André Leon. *A.L.T.: A Memoir.* New York: Villard Books, 2003.

Taraborrelli, J. Randy. *Jackie, Ethel, Joan: Women of Camelot.* New York: Grand Central Publishing, 2000.

Thayer, Mary Van Rensselaer. *Jacqueline Bouvier Kennedy.* New York: Doubleday, 1961.

———. *Jacqueline Kennedy: The White House Years.* Boston: Little, Brown, 1971.

Todd, Olivier. *Malraux,* New York: Alfred A. Knopf, 2005.

A Tribute to Jacqueline Kennedy Onassis. New York: Doubleday, 1995.

Truman, Margaret. *First Ladies: An Intimate Group Portrait of White House Wives.* New York: Random House, 1995.

Turbeville, Deborah. *Newport Remembered: A Photographic Portrait of a Gilded Past.* New York: Harry N. Abrams, 1994.

Valenti, Jack. *This Time, This Place: My Life in War, the White House, and Hollywood.* New York: Harmony Books, 2007.

Walters, Barbara. *Audition: A Memoir.* New York: Alfred A. Knopf, 2008.

Warhol, Andy. *The Andy Warhol Diaries.* Edited by Pat Hackett. New York: Warner, 1989.

West, Dorothy. *The Richer, the Poorer,* New York: Doubleday, 1995.

Wiseman, Carter. *I. M. Pei: A Profile in American Architecture.* New York: Harry N. Abrams, 1990.

Young, James L. *A Field of Horses: The World of Marshall P. Hawkins.* Foreword by Jacqueline Kennedy Onassis. Dallas: Taylor Publishing, 1988.

Archives and Periodicals

Columbia University, Butler Library: Oral History, Thomas Guinzburg
Harry Ransom Center, University of Texas: Ray Roberts Papers
John Fitzgerald Kennedy Library: William Walton Papers
New York Public Library: Rare Book Collection and Diana Vreeland Papers
Beinecke Rare Book and Manuscript Library, Yale University: Nina Ber-
    berova Papers
Library of Congress: Digital Collections, Toni Frissell
The Museum of Television and Radio Library
Municipal Art Society Library Archives, Newsletters, 1984–1994

A number of individuals allowed me access to their correspondence with Jacqueline Kennedy Onassis. Their letters provided additional insight into her work as an editor.

Most of the attributed quotes throughout the book are taken from author interviews. Other quotations appeared in publications cited under the chapter-by-chapter sources. Publications used for research include *Vanity Fair, Time, Newsweek, The New Yorker, New York, Quest, Publishers Weekly, Ms., The Paris Review, U.S. News & World Report, People, McCall's, Town & Country, Ladies' Home Journal, The New York Times, The Washington Post, Los Angeles Times, The Boston Globe, Boston Herald, New York Post, New York Daily News,* and *New York Newsday.*

Permission to quote from previously published articles was given to me by Louis Auchincloss ("Belles Lettres," *Quest,* May 1997), Elizabeth Crook ("Remembering Jackie Onassis," *Austin American-Statesman,* May 27, 1994), David Stenn ("It Happened One Night . . . at MGM," *Vanity Fair,* April 2003), and Eugene Kennedy ("As an Editor, She Was a Total Professional," *New York Newsday,* May 24, 1994). Michael Flanagan kindly permitted me to quote from his unpublished manuscript, "Famous." To all of those who contributed to the research process, both individuals and institutions, I am deeply grateful.

Acknowledgments

The genesis of this book is buried in the hundreds of critical notes given to me by Jacqueline Kennedy Onassis and in our many exchanges while working on three books over a period of nearly ten years. That was my learning curve as a nonfiction author, and Jackie emphasized from the start that my role, like hers as editor, was "to be invisible." She meant by that not to unduly impose my own style or point of view on my subject, but rather to rely on anecdotes and documentation to create the narrative. That was just one of many lessons she put across to the slow learner I was. To this day and with this work in particular, I remain in her debt.

While noting that biography is ultimately based on facts, Virginia Woolf once observed that this literary form is "made with the help of friends," referring to the friends of the subject. In this case, Jackie's friends included many of her authors and colleagues. Without their assistance at every turn, this book could not have been written. Most of the contributors with whom I had exchanges are listed in the sources for each chapter, while a few preferred not to be named. Among those to whom I am indebted for their kind assistance and insights are the late Thomas Guinzburg, Joe Armstrong, David Stenn, Harriet Rubin, Gloria Steinem, Albert Yokum (for his design wisdom), Becky Singleton, Richard Malina, John Loring, Olivier Bernier, Eugene Kennedy, Elizabeth Crook, Elisabeth Sifton, Barbara Burn, Rich Barber, J. C. Suarès, Loretta Barrett, Peter Sís, Jimmy Breslin, Liz Smith, Peter Duchin, Peter Beard, William Howard Adams, David Garrard Lowe, Jonathan Cott, Betty Sue Flowers, Amanda Vaill, Duane Hampton, Rosamond Bernier, Antony Beevor, Jody Linscott, Darcey Steinke, Jack Bass, Raquel Ramati, Robert Lyons, Martha Levin, Vartan Gregorian, Edward Kasinec, Edvard Radzinsky, Alberto Vitale, Samuel Vaughan, Daniel Okrent, Deborah Turbeville, Theodore Sorensen, and the late Louis Auchincloss.

In addition, I want to gratefully acknowledge the contributions that were made by Ruth Prawer Jhabvala, Marian Schwartz, Delfina Rattazzi, Sally Forbes, Marianne Velmans, Deborah Owen, Jeffrey Archer, Mary Frank, Karen Van Westering, William La Riche, James Fitzgerald, Les Pockell, Jan Legnitto, James Raimes, Jeannette Seaver, Henry Koehler, Glenn Rounds, Nancy Stauffer, Mary Helen Washington, Nicholas Vreeland, Frederick Vreeland, Hope Marinetti, Marcia Jacobs, Judith Jamison, Terry Karydes, Jacqueline Rogers, Jerry Jacka, William Hutchins, Conover Hunt, Linda Grant De Pauw, Christine Zamoyska-Panek, James Bakalar, Carolyn Blakemore, Marc Riboud, Barbara Chase-Riboud, Peter Kruzan, Mary-Sargent D'Anglejan, Michael D'Orso, Larry Gonick, Vicky Bijur, Michael Flanagan, Sarah Giles, Derek Ungless, Beverly Gallegos, Gretchen Achilles, Gael Towey, Peter Hassrick, Stuart Feld, Barbara Bachman, Robert Farber, Richard de Combray, Christine Doudna, Shammi Bannu, Owen Laster, Fred Holmberg, Suzanne Massie, David Zinsser, Deborah Nevins, Ann Appelbaum, Eric Nicholas, Elizabeth Brownstein, Jane "Kit" Caplan, Judith Straeten, John Valenti, Heidi Waleson, Stephen Davis, Robert Hilburn, Ferle Bramson, Christopher Holme, Dorothy Spruill Redford, Paul Bresnick, Stephen Rubin, Bruce Tracy, Scott Moyers, and the late Francis Mason.

To all who shared their memories and insights, including those whom space does not allow me to name, I am extremely appreciative and hope that I have represented them in full measure in the narrative.

At Thomas Dunne Books, I want to thank Tom Dunne for his perspicacity and faith in the project, editor Margaret Smith for her discerning guidance, production editor David Stanford Burr, and copy editor Janet Byrne for their assiduous attention to detail. I am also grateful for the support of Sally Richardson at St. Martin's Press, and John Sargent Jr. at Macmillan, both of whom contributed interviews. I was also fortunate to receive astute feedback from M.K.C.

My ever resourceful literary agent, Peter Sawyer, at the Fifi Oscard Agency, and his associates Kevin McShane and Carmen La Via, offered me their wise counsel throughout the project. My research assistant and editorial consultant, Deane Rink, was unstinting and thorough in his efforts. Susan Ray accomplished the monumental task of transcription and provided additional research and editorial assistance. I offer my heartfelt thanks to Gelsey Kirkland Chernov, Misha Chernov, editorial consultants Bonnie Egan and Judith Katz, David Fallon, Rudolph Wurlitzer, Tamie Lynn, Wayne Jackson, Nancy Salisbury, Peter Stelzer, Susan Sharaga Swadener, Dean Willis, Mark Scheerer, John McKinley, Dave Rutkin, Susan Aasen, Rosalie O'Connor, Cynthia David, Garry Bale, Julie Cencebaugh, Wayne Lawson, Anne Correa, Adleta Kneiflova, Nikita Parikh, Steve Kurland of Shakespeare & Co. Booksellers, and Evan Lai, of ECL Landscape Design. And a special note of thanks to Dr. Michael J. Dattoli, Jennifer Cash, Ginya Carnahan, and Meg Brockett of the Dattoli Cancer Center of Sarasota for their encouragement of my writing in another field.

Finally, I want to express my endless gratitude to my sister, Paula Lawrence Jackson, and to Karen Chase of the dedication, my beloved companion whose support sustained me throughout the two years I devoted to researching and writing this book.

Index